# Accessing and Browsing Information and Communication

# Accessing and Browsing Information and Communication

Ronald E. Rice, Maureen McCreadie, and Shan-Ju L. Chang

The MIT Press
Cambridge, Massachusetts
London, England

This book was set in Sabon in QuarkXPress by Asco Typesetters, Hong Kong.

Library of Congress Cataloging-in-Publication Data

Rice, Ronald E.
Accessing and browsing information and communication / Ronald E. Rice, Maureen McCreadie, and Shan-Ju L. Chang.
p. cm.
Includes bibliographical references and index.
ISBN 978-0-262-18214-0 (hc.: alk. paper), 978-0-262-53648-6 (pb.: alk. paper)
1. Information retrieval. 2. Research. 3. Communication in information science. 4. Human information processing. I. McCreadie, Maureen. II. Chang, Shan-Ju L. III. Title.
ZA3075 .R53 2001
025.5′24—dc21 00-054898

# Contents

# Tables and Figures

# Preface

The basic argument of this book is twofold. First, accessing and browsing resources are fundamental human activities, considered in a variety of ways and under a variety of terminologies across a variety of research areas. Second, they are insufficiently understood or identified in any particular research area or service situation, so that unidentified aspects or uninspected biases prevent people from providing and obtaining the desired or necessary resources. This book reviews literature from a wide range of research areas on these two fundamental human activities—accessing and browsing resources. Further, it considers two fundamental human resources—information and communication. These reviews are used to identify common and unique perspectives of each of the research literatures. These perspectives are integrated to develop preliminary frameworks that are both more general and more comprehensive than any particular research area's treatment of the concepts. Then, using multiple sources of evidence, these preliminary frameworks are evaluated, refined, and validated.

Some notable features of this book include

- Extensive and comprehensive review of related theory, research, practice, and implications from a wide range of disciplines
- Analysis of converging contexts such as mass media, online information services, libraries, public spaces, grocery stores, the Internet and World Wide Web, store windows, architectural design, advertisements, organizational communication, and information system evaluation
- Comparison of common and unique conceptualizations across multiple disciplines
- Development and refinement of general, interdisciplinary frameworks
- Explicit operationalization of concepts within a broad array of dimensions
- Clear explanation of methodological procedures
- In-depth qualitative and quantitative analysis of case studies, intentionally chosen to increase theoretical variance

- Extensive use of tables and figures to summarize and illustrate the concepts and analysis
- Comprehensive bibliography

This book is primarily intended for researchers, teachers, graduate students, and service providers interested in issues of accessing and browsing resources (here, information and communication). We would hope that the reviews, operationalized concepts, and refined frameworks could be of use to reference librarians, organizational managers, system designers, message designers, consumer researchers, policymakers, social psychologists, and others. Its scope, coverage, and detail make this a rigorous academic book, but there is very little statistical analysis, and all theoretical materials are fully described with case-based examples.

The development of the concepts from a wide variety of research literatures and the detailed case studies should make the material broadly applicable and understandable. As the fundamental conceptual and empirical bases of the book come from a wide variety of related research literatures, it would seem that by definition this book would be relevant to the over half-dozen areas represented here. We would hope that this book could become a foundation for a new approach to information seeking and could serve as part of an established curriculum that wishes to extend its boundaries to factors earlier in the traditional information-seeking process, to communication processes as well as to information, and across disciplines and practice areas.

We thank editor Doug Sery for his encouragement and comments, two anonymous reviewers for their helpful suggestions, and Deborah Cantor-Adams and Alice Cheyer for their exquisite copyediting. We thank Jim Snow of Princeton, New Jersey, a graduate of the Rutgers University M.L.S. program, for the fine indexing.

We also thank Gary Marchionini, Barbara Kwasnik, Marcia Bates, Christine Borgman, and Donald Case for their thoughtful research and discussions on browsing.

Ron Rice particularly thanks William Paisley for his ground breaking interdisciplinary work in communication and information and his wise advising during my days at Stanford University and beyond.

## Acknowledgments

Portions of this material are adapted or reprinted, with permission from Elsevier Science, from:

McCreadie, M., and R. E. Rice. 1999. Trends in analyzing access to information. Part I: Cross-disciplinary conceptualizations. *Information Processing and Management* 35 (1): 45–76.

McCreadie, M., and R. E. Rice. 1999. Trends in analyzing access to information. Part II: Unique and integrating conceptualizations. *Information Processing and Management* 35 (1): 77–99.

Although very little of the following is directly reprinted (almost all of the material on browsing is considerably different), we would like to acknowledge the following source:

Chang, S.-J., and R. E. Rice. 1993. Browsing: A multidimensional framework. *Annual Review of Information Science and Technology* 28: 231–271.

# Accessing and Browsing Information and Communication

# 1

# The Importance of Accessing and Browsing Information and Communication

It is well understood that in the last generation the United States and other developed countries have become information societies, where most of the economy, and the central nature of work, is involved in creating, processing, communicating, using, and evaluating information. Major social changes emphasizing the importance of information seeking include rapidly increasing knowledge work and cognitive demands from digitized symbols, interconnectedness of and interaction with information technologies and networks, and forms, sources, and amounts of information (Marchionini 1995, 3–4).

Information seeking is an enduring topic of theoretical, practical, and economic relevance, treated in many textbooks, research studies, commercial products, and university courses that consider the processes and outcomes of people's attempts to acquire and use information. Further, with the development of the Internet, online databases, CD-ROMS, interactive retrieval interfaces, and digital libraries comes the promise of nearly unlimited retrieval of information.

At the same time, however, a new focus on the user and the user's context has developed to challenge many of the traditional approaches to the design of information systems and the study of information seeking. Further, there are many concerns about increasing information inequity and the "digital divide," whereby many people and groups may be excluded from this growth in information services and opportunities. Many people complain of overload, confusion, frustration, becoming lost, not knowing where to go to find what they need, or not being able to interpret and evaluate information after obtaining it.

This book argues that many of these tensions, contradictions, and challenges arise from an incomplete conceptualization of what has been traditionally (but less so recently) called the information-seeking process. This traditional approach conceives of information seeking as an intentional process whereby a user, with a more or less known problem, uses some kind of information resource (usually a print or computer medium, such as a library's card catalog or online catalog or the Internet) to find some specific facts or data that would resolve the problem. Typically, this process takes the form of matching a user's search query with terms from a database of indexed key words or even full text.

However, this traditional, narrow conceptualization of information seeking may in fact be the last, most easily observable, perhaps not even primary stage of a complex set of activities—ongoing, conscious as well as unconscious, intentional as well as serendipitous, and social as well as political and cognitive. Borgman (2000, 7) argues that tasks are becoming more interdependent and their boundaries blurring. There are also many more information types and formats, sources, access points (virtual, temporal, and physical), and strategies. So it is increasingly difficult to identify and distinguish the components of information seeking, and less justifiable to define information seeking in a traditional way as consisting of the activities between the recognition of an information need and the acquisition of relevant information. Marchionini (1995) also sees "information seeking as a broader process rather than the more limited notion of information retrieval" (ix) and argues that "a variety of disciplinary perspectives are needed to advance our state of knowledge and to develop better systems" (x). Information seeking is "a process in which humans purposefully engage in order to change their state of knowledge" (5). It is much more general and dynamic than "information retrieval"; it overlaps with learning and problem solving in that its results may be stored for later use, but differs somewhat because the results may also be discarded after immediate use.

Further, this process not only involves "information" in the form of useful symbols stored and represented in some medium, but also "communication," the exchange and creation of meaning through interaction among social actors via a variety of media ranging from face-to-face to hypermedia World Wide Web sites. As Buckland (1991b, 8) concurs, "Interpersonal communications and mass communications clearly ought to be within our scope"; he also notes that Mooers (1951) referred to information retrieval as "communication through time" (61). Because "organizations are societies of minds," "information use for interpretation involves the social construction of reality, and information representation and delivery should support the multilevel interaction of social discourse" (Choo 1995, 1, 25). In line with cybernetic theory, information does not "flow through a system" but is the basis for "mutually constitutive interactions" (Hayles 1999, 11). Even the more formal manifestation of information—documents—"is embedded in ... communities and relationships" (Borgman 2000, 99), such as opinion leadership, invisible colleges, citation and co-author relationships, journal and disciplinary norms, and so on.

Rather, accessing and browsing information and communication are highly consequential and multidimensional aspects of the information user's entire experience —often even including barriers to that experience. Indeed, we argue that general issues and processes of accessing and browsing information and communication are fundamental and very general human behaviors, not limited solely to the arena of seeking print or computer information. This book reviews literature from a wide range of disciplines on these two fundamental human activities to develop preliminary integrated frameworks for understanding accessing and browsing. Then, using multiple sources of evidence, these preliminary frameworks are evaluated, refined, and validated. The final result is an interdisciplinary approach to understanding two basic human behaviors, accessing and browsing, with respect to two basic human resources, information and communication. In line with recent developments in conceptualizing information seeking, we propose that the process of seeking information is a broad, pervasive aspect of human behavior and that a user-centered, interdisciplinary approach is required to fully understand it.

Studies of human information-seeking behavior in the fields of library studies and information science have long suffered from a lack of coherent theories because of narrow assumptions about information environments and information needs and uses (Chang 1993; Dervin 1980; Dervin and Nilan 1986; Durrance 1989; Johnson 1996; Katzer and Fletcher 1992; Roberts 1982; Wersig and Windel 1985; Wilson 1981). Roberts (1982) challenges the implicit assumptions of most user studies that information behavior is rationally motivated and organized, and that information activities only take place within recognizably artificial information environments such as the formal information system of a single organization. In the same vein, Katzer (1987) argues that in a world of information overload, limited time, and interpersonal pressures, it is difficult for us to achieve optimal rationality. This concept of bounded rationality corresponds to Simon's (1976) satisficing theory, which states that people tend to look for a course of action that is satisfactory, or good enough, rather than optimal. Thus, research in the area of user studies has become more focused on discovering the motivations, obstacles, contexts, and dimensions of people's information-seeking behavior and what uses they make of information in various settings.

This book extends these approaches by developing interdisciplinary frameworks for *accessing information and communication* (part I) and *browsing information and communication* (part II), thus extending the scope of the information-seeking process.

## Accessing Information and Communication

### Defining the Parameters of Access

Access can be understood from the perspective of privileged, as well as excluded, access. In many cases, gaining access to information requires gaining access to relevant interpretations of a society, group, or organization (Geertz 1973). Membership in a community is recognized in different ways by different "tribes" (Taylor 1968). For example, insider stock trading cannot occur without "insiders" (and by implication, "outsiders"). In the context of technological systems, there are those with the necessary skills and access to the technologies, those with some skills and partial access, and those without. At a more basic level, there are those with the knowledge that such systems exist and those lacking that knowledge. Such divisions or distinctions have existed historically in the academic research tradition. For example, across academic disciplines, women have generally been treated as "other," as deviant, as outside the norm (Simone de Beauvoir 1989, xxi). It has been in accordance with such standards that evaluation has been carried out.

In the context of information science, the "standard" human type might more saliently be described as elite. Historically, the development of information science as a field of research is rooted in the need to control and gain access to scientific information (Sparck Jones 1981), information that plays a role in a nation's relative position of power in the world. In developing our field based on this perspective, we have focused on elites, on their needs, applications, and uses of information. In so doing, we have risked making access to pertinent information more difficult and less likely for nonelites, for a vast and perhaps majority population of "others."

This unintentional limiting of access illustrates what Stuart Hall (1982) refers to as hegemonic power. A critical reading leads to an understanding that the power in this context lies not only in conscious decisions to control access. It lies primarily in the power to set and follow the terms of the debate, to define the parameters for form and content, to establish the framework for the very notion of what information can mean. Hall describes two groups of participants in the "struggle over access to the very means of signification":

> those accredited witnesses and spokesmen who had a privileged access, as of right, to the world of public discourse and whose statements carried the representativeness and authority which permitted them to establish the primary framework or terms of an argument;... and

> those who had to struggle to gain access to the world of public discourse at all; whose "definitions" were always more partial, fragmentary and delegitimated; and who, when they did gain access, had to *perform with the established terms of the problematic in play.* (81; emphasis in original)

In the example of information science, the scientists, researchers, and corporate players are those with privileged access, those who determine the language in use, the questions asked. Others are left outside the arena of public discourse.

**Barriers in Libraries and Information Science**

In a library setting we encounter hegemonic structures, barriers, and power systems. Insiders such as reference librarians or frequent system users, at the very least, understand the "rules of the game" (Taylor 1968) and have realistic expectations about what needs they might address through information. Others, outsiders, may never become users because the barriers to the inside—such as the necessary belief that access to a periodical article might be applicable to situations in their particular lives, or issues and situations that fall within the existing framework of citations and documents, or the required knowledge of a variety of formats and functions of computer technologies in order to retrieve the information—experiential barriers that inevitably leave a potential user feeling "stupid" and like an "outsider," are too great to overcome. When "others" do gain access, they must perform within the established terms of the problematic in play (Hall 1982).

In particular, the boundaries around what constitutes the population of interest (concerning issues of access as well as users) to library and information science researchers have been drawn very narrowly. It is rare for user studies to account for those who never enter the inside, who never use a library or information system. Although Belkin (1978) points out difficulties in studying information in its most general sense, definitions of the discipline (Belkin and Robertson 1976; Wersig and Neveling 1975) do not necessarily rule out a broader theoretical understanding of what information means, nor do they rule out a consideration of "others" in addition to elites.

Given arguments that purchasing power will increasingly be the price of entry to the inside circle of participating citizens (Murdock and Golding 1989), that a complex of social and economic disadvantages becomes compounded over time, making entry into the world of elites less and less likely for the majority of the population (Gandy 1988), or that technology has increased tremendously the power of bureaucratic insiders relative to that of individual outsiders (Gandy 1989; Singer 1980), it is clear that the information-rich have *privileged* access to information. The struggle to gain access for "others" requires that they learn and adapt to the framework of those with privileged access to the world of public discourse (Hall 1982).

An alternative perspective might view information systems as designed with the potential to address issues of access for those outsiders who, thus far, have carried out their lives beyond the scope of interest of research on information science. Given the potential implications of widely differential levels and types of access to information, from diverse research perspectives, it is time to expand our focus, to include "others" in our research, and to consider access issues and dimensions outside narrowly drawn boundaries of specific disciplines or professions.

**Importance of Access as Focus of Research**

Historically, evaluation in information retrieval has focused on the effectiveness of a system (Robertson 1981), and "system" has traditionally implied a computer-based set of technology and software. Generally, this has meant how well a given system retrieves representations of documents (descriptors, citations, abstracts, text) in response to requests for information as represented by a query statement—usually referred to as relevance judgments (for example, Swanson 1965). Most such studies say nothing about the role of access in system evaluation. However, if a user is in a position to make a relevance judgment (Saracevic 1975), evaluate the utility of information (Cleverdon 1974; Cooper 1973a; 1973b), measure satisfaction (Auster and Lawton 1984; Tessier, Crouch, and Atherton 1977), or put information to use (Dervin 1983; Wilson and Streatfield 1977), several dimensions of access necessarily are already involved and have already been achieved. Implicit in the information-seeking process are dimensions of access, many of which occur or are addressed long before a user formulates (or finds herself unable to formulate) a query statement.

For several decades researchers have been aware that the quantity or quality of information available from a system is frequently less important to users than is the degree of ease with which they gain access to the information (Taylor 1968). Although researchers have begun to look at access to information systems (Culnan 1983; 1984; 1985; Gerstberger and Allen 1968; Hart and Rice 1991; Hiltz and Johnson 1989; O'Reilly 1982; Rice and Shook 1986; 1988), these studies have focused primarily on physical access to systems or access to other individuals through communication media. Other dimensions of access—for example, cognitive, affective, political, economic, and cultural—are also worthy of exploration.

We know very little about the potential dimensions of access or about users' awareness or perceptions of such dimensions of access to information. Yet access to information and communication affects many aspects of our lives, from economic well-being to privacy rights, from workplace management and monitoring to policy and decision making, and transnational business operations. With access underlying many different areas of everyday life, and implicit in much research, we need to understand its dimensions in order to consider seriously its implications. As we consider system design and evaluation, it is necessary to ask what the objectives are when these systems are employed in the individual's communication process (Budd 1987). Do we expect information systems to meet the needs only of those who already have access to such systems, or do we expect access to be open also to potential (currently non-) users? Is physical access sufficient, or are many other dimensions of access necessary, sufficient, or facilitative? In considering potential implications of increased access to information (for example privacy issues, or protection from corporate espionage or computer viruses), what are the pertinent dimensions? Such questions carry important implications for theory and method as well as for policy issues and freedom of information.

An explicit understanding of the dimensions of access, and of the access issues a user must address in the information-seeking process in any given situation, is likely to contribute to improved design, development, implementation, and evaluation of future information systems and services. Further, it may help inform policy debates about access to information and information systems in society by explicitly identifying previously implicit aspects of access and by describing interrelations among what are often seen as separate aspects of access.

Access is covered, or at least mentioned, in a variety of communication- and information-related literatures. Each vantage point illuminates access issues from a unique perspective. Every research literature, then, stands to be informed from new perspectives of other bodies of literature. Rice (1988) has noted the difficulty of integrating growing research on computer-mediated communication systems. The same difficulty lies in other areas of research that are by nature interdisciplinary. Certainly, the notion of access to information is interdisciplinary. An understanding of how the concept is treated in different research areas will contribute to a fuller understanding of access and its underlying dimensions. This, in turn, may contribute to integration of research across situations, disciplines, systems, and research processes.

### Research Questions

To develop a framework identifying the underlying dimensions of accessing information and communication, part I considers the following research questions:

1. What are the common issues and concerns implied by discussions of access-related issues in several relevant research areas (see chapter 3)?
2. What are the influences and constraints on access to information (see chapter 3)?
3. What are the assumptions and primary issues or foci of each research area that lead to the differences among them (see chapter 4)?

To test the framework, this study raises the following research questions:

4. How well does the framework capture/organize participants' perceptions of access to information across situations, individuals, and settings (see chapter 6)?
5. Do the study results suggest additional components or dimensions for the framework (see chapters 6 and 7)?

## Browsing Information and Communication

The ultimate goal of information systems and services has been to serve human needs for information and facilitate information-seeking and retrieval processes. To this end, much recent research has addressed the concern for better understanding of information seeking and application from the user's point of view (Dervin and Nilan 1986; Durrance 1989; Hewins 1990; Taylor 1991).

A commonly observed form of information seeking is browsing. Browsing has been observed and investigated in the context of information seeking in the library in general (Ayris 1986; Bates 1989; Ellis 1989; Hancock-Beaulieu 1990; Hyman 1972) and has increasingly assumed greater importance in human-machine interaction in particular (Belkin et al. 1987; Croft and Thompson 1987; Oddy 1977). Browsing as a concept and an activity appears to be a fundamental part of human behavior, which takes place in diverse contexts in daily life. People tend to follow "the principle of least effort" and may be constantly gathering, monitoring, and screening information around them as they go through daily life. Indeed, browsing has been conceived as a way to overcome information overload and is routinely employed as a screening and monitoring technique by many information system users (Baker 1986b; Hiltz and Turoff 1985).

The concept of browsing has both scientific and popular meanings, and appears in a wide variety of literatures, including library studies, consumer research, mass media studies, organizational communication, and information science. However, the concept appears rather infrequently, and is considered differently, in each literature. Previous browsing-related research has mostly focused on browsing as a search strategy rather than browsing per se, and has been limited to a specific context (e.g., libraries) or information source (e.g., books or databases). A deeper appreciation of browsing as a fundamental behavior across various resources, situations, and contexts is needed. To the extent that browsing is a fundamental human information-seeking behavior, it appears to have scientific significance, though research about it seems still in a primitive stage. The concepts and nature of browsing have not been systematically studied and are thus not well understood. Because of this, there are at least five important issues or problems associated with research on browsing.

### A Common but Not Well Understood Phenomenon

We all experience browsing to different degrees in various contexts in order to make sense of the world around us, such as when we read newspapers or go window shopping. We also browse to resolve an anomalous state of knowledge when we seek information in libraries or through computers. In its common use, *browsing* means to look through or glance at reading materials or goods for sale casually or randomly (Random House Dictionary 1987). The word *browsing* has been used by different groups of researchers often without a clear description or definition, or with specific but different meanings assigned to it. It has been construed as a search strategy in library studies and information science, a viewing pattern in media research, a screening technique in organization literature, and an entertaining activity in consumer research. All these different conceptualizations of browsing lead to the questions: What is the nature of browsing? and What are the underlying dimensions of browsing that allow us to understand those different yet related conceptualizations?

### Confusion between Browsing and Searching

Because what constitutes browsing behavior and what characteristics are associated with it are not well understood, considerable confusion between the concepts of searching and browsing arises. For example, as Bates (1989) points out, in online databases, the term *browsing* is used in a very specific and limited sense, usually referring to reading short lists of alphabetically arranged subject terms or reading citations and their associated abstracts. On the other hand, in the library setting, there has been a tendency to see browsing as a casual, don't-know-what-to-do behavior, in contrast to directed searching. Herner (1970, 414) states that "much of what we call 'searching' is, upon dissection, primarily browsing. However, traditionally we tend to separate out searching when we think about browsing, placing the search on a more rigorous plane. In doing so, we are probably deluding ourselves, and mean levels of browsing rather than searching versus browsing." It has been suggested that a better conceptualization of information seeking or searching is the level of browsing involved. Yet we do not have good vocabularies to describe and discuss various forms or levels of browsing.

**A Bias toward Specific, Direct Searching**

Although browsing is a prevalent form of human behavior, usually associated with library users as a means of searching for information, a tendency to emphasize and more highly value direct, precise searching as opposed to iterative, exploratory searching, such as browsing, has been common in library and information science literature (Greene 1977; Hancock-Beaulieu 1989; Hyman 1972). This bias is due partly to the fact that we do not know very well what motivates people to browse and partly to some unrealistic assumptions from researchers and librarians about users, their information needs, and the nature of information seeking. Until recently, these assumptions have been that users have static information needs, know exactly what they are looking for, and are output-oriented. Although some information-seeking situations are specific (e.g., item-searching behavior), in many cases users are in an anomalous state of knowledge (Belkin, Oddy, and Brooks 1982a; 1982b) and their needs for information are difficult to articulate in a verbal form (Taylor 1968) or they do not have predefined search criteria (Hildreth 1982). Their expression and interest in an information situation may change dynamically during the searching and browsing activities (Hildreth 1987a). Hildreth (1987a) notes that most end-users are not going after a specific known item, and that the process of searching (involving browsing) and discovery is more central to end-users' searching objectives and satisfaction. Further, Stone (1982) supports that (at least for humanities scholars) the assumptions used in delegating searching to intermediaries —what is required is known and can be communicated—are not realistic. She suggests the importance of the humanist's need to browse on the basis of the view that the search process itself is as important as the results.

As Bawden (1986) points out, "Although the importance of browsing is generally recognized, its nature appears to be little understood.... Little is known of the success rate of this sort of information seeking and still less of those factors which are likely to encourage it and make it more productive" (211). As browsing becomes a valid alternative search strategy (that is, it is no longer undervalued or associated with unskilled users), two important questions arise: What motivates people to browse? and What is the relationship of browsing to other types of information-seeking behavior? Without a better understanding of browsing behavior, conceptualization of information-seeking behavior cannot be complete.

**New Issues Raised by Information Technology**

Along with the proliferation of microcomputers, the emergence of diverse forms and contents of databases (including audiovisual materials), and continuing development of technology (e.g., hypermedia, the World Wide Web), browsing as an information search strategy has assumed a greater importance as end-user searching has become commonplace. Research has shown that there are significant differences in end-users' and intermediaries' information-seeking behaviors. Among others, they differ in their knowledge of mechanical (e.g., syntax) and conceptual (e.g., search logic) aspects of searching. Borgman (1986b) addressed this issue when she discussed the nature of the searching problem associated with most existing information systems that have been designed for direct searching that has been well-expressed in advance. This has made many end-user systems difficult to use because those systems demand previous training and a high cognitive load from users (Marchionini 1987). Browsing (in the sense of recognizing as opposed to specifying) is increasingly seen to be a valid alternative search strategy to keyword searching (Fox and Palay 1979; Oddy 1977). Moreover, perceived as a natural means of information seeking that requires no training and demands less cognitive load, browsing has been put forward as the most important form of searching for casual use (Tuori 1987) and for certain types of information (e.g., pictorial or audio databases) (Batley 1989).

As in many other aspects in life that are influenced by technology, these important differences and relations between browsing and other types of information-seeking behavior such as direct searching suggest different implications for system design. Indeed, many information systems have not succeeded because their designers failed to take into account various users' information requirements and behavior patterns (Antonoff 1989; Buckley and Long 1990; Shim and Mahoney 1991). Interactive systems of all sorts will need to support various search strategies, including browsing (Bates 1989; Ellis 1989). A prerequisite to such design is a better understanding of the influences on browsing, what functions browsing serves, and what the consequences of browsing may be.

Such understanding will also have implications for system evaluation. Traditional relevance-based evaluation criteria in information retrieval assumes that finding information is the goal of using an information system. As more applications and more diverse contents of databases become available to users for direct access, databases are not only searched to find information but also browsed to learn about information or to gain general technology skills or even for intrinsic entertainment (such as "surfing the Web"). Thus, relevance judgments based on the final output may not be adequate. Research on browsing may have useful suggestions for such critical issues as how to account for such learning effects and how to devise appropriate criteria in evaluating a system's support for browsing activities, or its "browsability."

### Research Questions

Part II sets out to explore the phenomenon of browsing in an attempt to develop a coherent conceptual framework within which various interpretations and conceptualizations of browsing can be related. The purpose of this study is to provide a better analytical language for understanding important aspects of browsing as human information-seeking behavior. To develop a framework identifying the underlying dimensions of browsing for information and communication, part II considers the following research questions:

1. What is the nature of browsing?
2. Why do people engage in browsing?
3. What are the underlying dimensions of the browsing process?
4. What types of browsing exist?
5. What influences browsing?
6. What are the consequences of browsing?

### General Approach

Parts I and II are based upon two related research projects (Chang 1995 and Chang and Rice 1993; McCreadie 1997 and McCreadie and Rice 1999a and 1999b). Both were motivated and structured by a similar general method. Specifics of the methods are provided in their respective parts.

The general research method guiding both projects includes three basic steps: (1) developing—analyzing and synthesizing the research literatures of related areas to propose a preliminary framework; (2) testing—conducting a main case study to check the framework and content coding, revising the framework and content coding accordingly, and for the access framework only, conducting a follow-up case study to ensure theoretical variance; and (3) refining—evaluating and assessing the revised framework to arrive at a refined framework. Figure 1.1 summarizes this process.

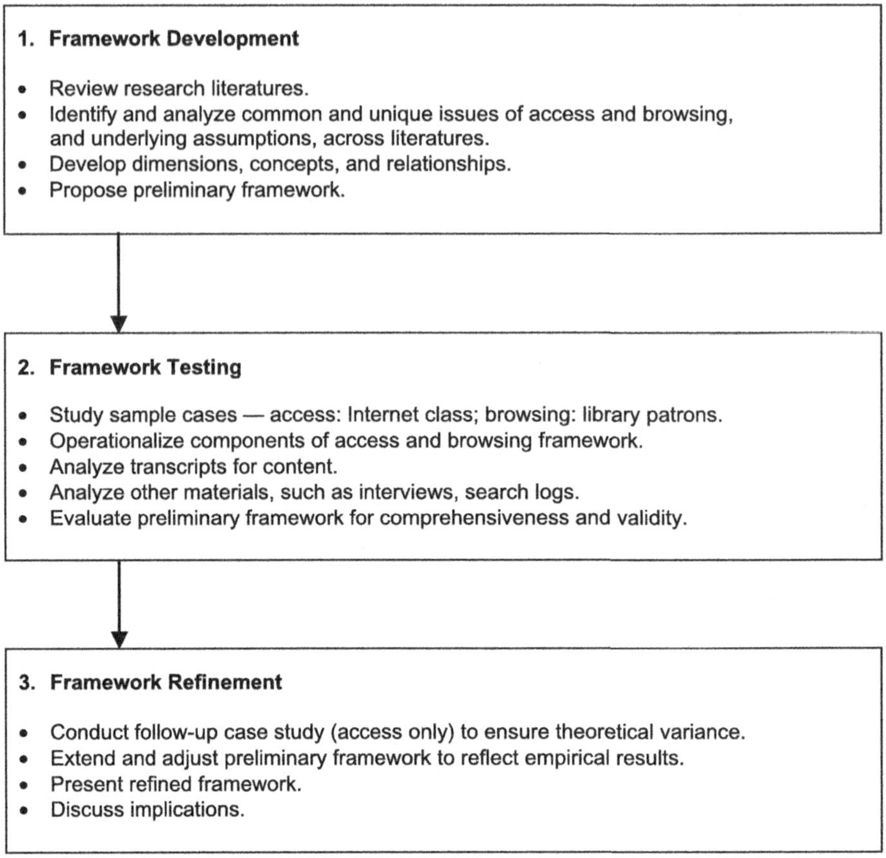


**Figure 1.1**
Framework Development Process

## Framework Development

The first step was an extensive review and analysis of the literatures of several research areas. Allen's (1996) advocacy of a user-centered approach to designing information systems, Borgman's (2000) development of the global information infrastructure concept, and Choo's book (1995) on organizational scanning all take such an interdisciplinary approach. Literatures of the selected research areas represent a broad range of perspectives, increasing the likelihood of the developing theory's accounting for a wider range of characteristics. Concerning *access*, six literatures were reviewed: library studies, information science, "information society," mass communication, organizational communication, and economics of information. Concerning *browsing*, six literatures were reviewed: library user studies, end-user computing and information science, consumer research, audience research, organizational research, and environmental planning and architectural design.

Divergent views were represented, including potentially conflicting perspectives, in order to account for as full an explanation as possible of the phenomenon under consideration and to expand the frame of thinking. Reconciliation of divergent views raises the theoretical level and generalizability of the results (Eisenhardt 1989). We identified candidate research areas most likely to cover the spectrum of related concerns and shed light on issues of access or browsing. For each research area, the focus on issues of access or browsing guided and limited the selection of which publications and books to include in the review process.

We note here that the particular designation of each research literature, and the materials that are reviewed as part of each literature, may well be questioned. For example, it might be more current to group library studies and information science into one category, or group them with "information society" and information economics, and even end-user computing and information systems, all in the recently labeled "social informatics." Further, distinctions among some literatures are difficult to make, especially for those fields that are interdisciplinary in nature. For instance, there is an overlap between the library literature and information science literature in the treatment of computer applications such as online public access catalogs (OPACs). However, while the various common and unique perspectives and assumptions of each literature are interesting in themselves, that analysis is only a by-product of our general intention to survey as much relevant literature as possible in order to generate a comprehensive, interdisciplinary framework. Thus, particular regroupings of some of these research literatures would not change the essential framework. Still, we accept that some may disagree with our general groupings and labelings of the literatures and with what we list as unique perspectives in specific literatures.

While we tried to be comprehensive, it may well be that we missed some key publications, although we have tried to update our prior work to include the most recent relevant books. However, the reviews here are more complete within the traditional literatures of information science, library studies, and information society than any prior study of access or browsing, and we also apply concepts and results from literatures that are typically well outside these traditional areas, such as mass communication, consumer research, audience research, and environmental planning and architectural design. It may well be, though, that some other research literatures could provide additional concepts, dimensions, and results that would slightly alter or expand our proposed frameworks. We invite the reader to explore these possibilities, and adapt and improve our initial attempts.

The next step was to create outlines of and notes on the publications, highlighting perspectives or comments on, and explanations or questions about, access or browsing. We then generated databases (one for access, one for browsing) of references and abstracts, capturing from the notes and outlines key treatments of access or browsing. The databases served as an organizing and analytical tool, allowing multiple runs at identifying and grouping categories, and seeking a balance between comprehensiveness and parsimony in working toward identifying theoretical propositions on which to build frameworks for understanding access and browsing information and communication.

**Framework Testing and Refinement**

The purpose of the framework testing stage was to compare the preliminary frameworks against the behavior and perceptions of real users addressing situations arising in their everyday lives. These were evaluated through in-depth case studies (involving observations, computer search logs, interviews, and surveys) to test the validity and scope of the particular framework and its theoretical propositions.

Testing the initial theoretical propositions (identified through the literature review) through case studies generates data that can either confirm the emergent propositions of the frameworks or provide the opportunity to revise or expand the frameworks, thus refining and extending the theory under development. According to Yin (1989), a case study approach is the preferred strategy when designing a study that aims to be explanatory, exploratory, or descriptive. He defines a case study as "an empirical enquiry that investigates a contemporary phenomenon within its real-life context; when the boundaries between phenomenon and context are not clearly evident; and in which multiple sources of evidence are used" (23). The case study approach can provide description, test theory, or generate theory (Eisenhardt 1989).

This method allows testing of the theoretical framework and relies on replication logic (Yin 1989). First, the main case study may have revealed inadequacies in the preliminary framework, providing an opportunity for the investigator to refine both the theoretical framework and data collection plans. Cases may yield evidence confirming the theoretical propositions of the framework, thereby lending support for the validity of the framework. Cases may also yield evidence contradicting the propositions of the framework, thereby offering insight for refinement or extension of the theoretical framework.

**Discussion of Implications**

Finally, each part presents its extended and refined interdisciplinary framework and discusses the implications and potential applications of the framework as well as limitations for future research. The results have the potential to contribute to the development of theories about communication and information, the choice of research and evaluation methods in studying information seeking and use, and the design and use of communication media and information systems. In addition, such a framework has the potential to inform policy issues and practice by clarifying dimensions of access or browsing that, from some perspectives and thus in various practices, have been omitted from consideration altogether, or by emphasizing aspects that have received attention from multiple research literatures.

# I

# Accessing Information and Communication

# 2

# Perspectives on Access in Six Research Literatures

Accessing information and communication may occur over a wide range of conditions and phases, as noted in many research literatures, such as those in library studies (including information seeking), information science (including information retrieval, system design, and end-user computing), "information society" (including new technologies), mass communication (including cultural analyses), organizational communication (including surveillance, management of information systems, and knowledge management), and economics of information (including political economy of information).

## Library Studies

Libraries function to provide access to information. Although access issues were only implicit for many years, the very point of cataloging or public service or reference, aside from preserving information (documents), has been to facilitate access to information. Over time, the ease with which a library patron could gain access to information and the range of accessible information have changed and expanded. Over the last two decades in particular, the American Library Association has increasingly focused on redefining the mission of libraries with attention to broader access to information (Galvin 1991). Recent recommendations from the Lacy Commission (American Library Association 1986), a national symposium on Information Literacy and Education for the 21st Century (U.S. National Commission on Libraries and Information Science 1991), the White House Conference on Library and Information Studies (U.S. National Commission on Libraries and Information Science 1992), and a symposium sponsored by the Research Libraries Group on Electronic Access to Information (Chiang and Elkington 1993) identify access to information as their current highest priority. Borgman (2000) summarizes the extensive and worldwide efforts to develop greater and more integrated global access. The current focus on access to information highlights the need to investigate more fully the processes of gaining access to information and the influences and constraints on access.

**Traditional Library Approach: Access to Information in Print**

The various uses of access "refer to one or more aspects of providing means of access to information, of enabling users to accede either to a source of information or, in a fuller sense, to knowledge, to understanding.... All of the provision and use of retrieval-based information services is concerned with access to information" (Buckland 1991b, 77–78). Traditionally, libraries have provided access to books, periodicals (D. Schiller 1989), and citations (Hildreth 1987a), in other words, to information in print format or to information in print about information in print (citations). Cataloging and reference services assist the library user in gaining access to books, periodicals, or citations. Investigation of reference services led to an interest in question negotiation (Taylor 1968), which implicitly indicates an understanding that the information to which one seeks access may not be accurately or exhaustively represented by a query statement. It implies also that the reference interview is part of a communicative process of information seeking (Dervin and Dewdney 1986). Borgman (2000, 53) notes that dictionary definitions of access emphasize concepts of freedom, ability, permission, liberty to obtain, make use of, enter, communicate with, enter, pass, and exit. She defines access to information, in the context of digital libraries, as "connectivity to a computer network and to available content, such that the technology is usable, the user has the requisite skills and knowledge, and the content itself is in a usable and useful form" (57).

Buckland (1991b) identified six general dimensions of access: (1) identification (including both the general location as well as the specific resource), (2) availability (allowing inspection, either through object or representation), (3) user's price (time, effort, discomfort, social capital), (4) provider's cost, affected by allocators' resources and social values, (5) understanding/cognitive access (sufficient expertise to understand resource), and (6) acceptability (credibility, counternormative). He noted that information systems as simple suppliers of information-as-thing require only the first four; information systems as providers of information-as-knowledge require all six. He extended the understanding of access to information beyond the traditional printed books, periodicals, and citations by adding "access to evidence." Buckland's inclusion of access to evidence moves library studies beyond the limitations of access to information in print, and both underscores and accounts for the essential role libraries have played in preserving, building upon, and providing access to knowledge or representations of knowledge.

Other conceptualizations of access, particularly to computer networks, include pervasiveness, affordable cost, usability, subsidization, successful retrieval of desired information, and the ability of users to also be producers (Borgman 2000; Keller 1995). These aspects of access to information illustrate that in library studies (in general), access has meant access to information that is already available in some tangible or usable form, though it is expanding to include vehicles for the production or distribution of information or representations of information.

### Access to Knowledge: Information Literacy

For academic libraries in particular, access issues have long been linked with scholarly practice, tracking evidence, and documentation of knowledge. In recent years, academic librarians have identified the need to focus on teaching information literacy (Breivik and Gee 1989; U.S. National Commission on Libraries and Information Science 1991)—the skills that enable people to find, evaluate, and use information effectively to solve a problem or make a decision.

At the secondary school level, Kuhlthau's (1985; 1991) work investigates the process of gaining access to information and adds a rarely considered but pervasive aspect of access: affect. Kuhlthau lays out seven stages of the library research process, each of which includes task, thoughts, feelings, actions, and strategies. Her work assumes that individuals continually reshape their thinking through experience.

The user's experience can influence the expectations for access to information. Those whose experience is congruent with the organization and content of information systems are likely to experience greater success in gaining access than those whose experience leads them to expectations inconsistent with what is available or to expectations of failure to gain access, either of which serves to influence the access process (Agada 1999; Chatman 1991). As a user's experience grows to involve use of new information and communication technologies, his expectations change with regard to access. The social and procedural transitions that accompany technological advances in providing access to information raise significant challenges for library service providers.

### Transition from Ownership to Access

Traditional library studies thinking assumes that access to information means access to published books and periodicals as well as to citations. Technological advances and networking capabilities have raised the expectations of users such that access to a citation is frequently no longer satisfactory. Users' expectations have shifted increasingly to demand full-text documents and links to information in electronic format. These transitions have implications for the role of libraries, as they shift from collection warehouses to points of access to information regardless of location (McCombs 1991), and for librarians, as they redefine their professional role from citation database intermediary to full-text document provider (Pfaffenberger 1990) or from performing searches to aiding users in carrying out their own online searches (Via 1991).

Tyckoson (1991) reviews the implications for three categories of librarian in this transition from ownership to access to information without geographic boundary. Public service librarians are increasing emphasis on document delivery, even when the source can reside anywhere in the world. The current selection methods of collection development librarians, tied to the assumption that materials are housed in a local collection, must shift to an access paradigm that allows for selection among several levels of access to information. Ownership becomes a subset of access, applicable only to those materials in highest demand. Tyckoson predicts that materials in moderate demand will require purchase of right of access, while those in low demand will be ordered as needed, perhaps through cooperative collection development. Libraries can afford neither to own nor to access materials not in demand. For technical services librarians, transition to a paradigm of access means a reevaluation of their functions. Their greatest challenge is to integrate large amounts of information into a local catalog representing an array of materials from remote sources.

This transition in the library world carries with it implications for education in general and for education for librarianship in particular. Intner (1991) argues that access librarians require computer expertise, communication skills (with attention to listening), research and problem-solving skills, the ability to take risks, and the ability to train others. All five new skills are required in addition to the continued need for knowledge of information and how to find it, familiarity with one's institution and its people, and an understanding of library systems and services. In addition, she argues, access librarians have a new responsibility to take on leadership roles, including organizational goal setting. These skills are based on the assumption that access to information is a right, based in a constitutional right to participate as a citizen. This assumption is indicative of a view of the library as an integral part of a democratic society.

## Information Democracy

Libraries have historically been viewed as democratizing agencies. Free and equal access to information is a major concern of the profession of librarianship (Froehlich 1992). "Information seeking is becoming more fundamental and strategic for intelligent citizenship" (Marchionini 1995, 4). One quarter of the recommendations and petitions adopted by the White House Conference on Library and Information Science concern access to information. "The common thread of recommendations in this section is the strong belief of Conference delegates that all public information must be freely and easily accessible to all Americans" (U.S. National Commission on Libraries and Information Science 1992, App., 33). Some assume that general public access to information will reduce social and political inequities (Pfaffenberger 1990). An inherent conflict lies between the library ethos of free public access and the reality of the cost of online searching. This conflict raises fears of contributing to an information elite and the possibility that access to information and reference service will be based on ability to pay.

In 1983, Carol Nemeyer, then Associate Librarian of Congress, created the Commission on Freedom and Equality of Access to Information. Its report and recommendations, published in 1986, sparked controversy, in part because the commission proposed imposing user fees as a method for achieving equitable access to information in electronic formats. American Library Association policy specifically identifies charging for information services as discriminatory in publicly supported institutions. According to Galvin (1991), the controversy exemplifies the amorphous state of the library world's concept of information access as a social and professional goal. He argues that "additional criteria for adequate and effective access remain to be specified" (139) in order to understand what access means and should mean in an electronic information age.

Universal service, a concept developed by the early AT&T corporation, and institutionalized in the Communications Act of 1934, explicitly stated that access to telephone service (dial tone) by all U.S. households was a social necessity. This principle emphasizes the importance of reducing economic and technical barriers to access to the national communication network (Borgman 2000, 54). This basic philosophy is maintained in current policy statements and debates about the national information infrastructure, emphasizing access by providers and users to information, services, and other users. However, the specific forms and boundaries are hotly debated—for example, should the basic criterion be expanded to include the Internet, e-mail, and broadband/video dial tone? Yet Borgman (2000) emphasizes that even if a "global digital library" becomes a reality, many people will still not have access to the required technology and systems, and many materials will never be in electronic format.

The tensions that come to the fore in considering libraries as democratizing agents raise the issue of barriers to access, including physical and language barriers, economic barriers, and confidentiality concerns. For example, economic costs to users and to institutions that provide information can function as barriers to access. Government cutbacks in support for libraries as well as for investigative and reporting agencies limit what is publicly available. As more information becomes available exclusively through electronic data sources, those without access to the requisite equipment and software and the skills to make use of them will be barred from access. Some barriers simply add challenges. Some preclude access altogether.

## Information Science

Allen (1996, ch. 11) argues that information science research has been dominated by post hoc evaluative methods and results, leading to unintended consequences because, if the base system is not carefully crafted on the basis of user needs and resources before design begins, incremental improvements will not make a usable system. Analysis of the information science literature on evaluation of information systems reveals a progressive shift in focus from a system-centered perspective to a management perspective to a user perspective (Dervin and Nilan 1986; Su 1987).

### Issues Related to Relevance

Central to this shift in the development of theory and evaluation is the notion of relevance. Relevance, according to Saracevic (1971; 1975) is a primitive concept intuitively having to do with the success of the communication process. It is a notion of the measure of the effectiveness of the contact between a source and a destination in a communication process.

At least three different understandings of relevance have been applied in information retrieval evaluation (Belkin 1981; Belkin and Vickery 1985; Saracevic 1975; Swanson 1977): (1) logical relevance (judgment is based on the propositions of the request being included in, or logically deducible from, the text), (2) destination's relevance (judgment is based on the relationship between the topics of the formal question and the retrieved documents), and (3) situational relevance (judgment is based on the user's entire desire and need state at the time of receiving the text).

A difference in one's understanding of relevance can easily lead to a difference in relevance judgment (Belkin and Vickery 1985; Saracevic 1975; Swanson 1977). In addition, if the information retrieved is not of significance in the everyday world of the user (Chatman 1991; Schutz and Luckmann 1973), what does it matter if query and document match?

In practice, the user makes the relevance judgment based solely on evaluation of the output of the information retrieval interaction—usually bibliographic data and perhaps an abstract. The potential value of the information remains unknown until the information is consumed—read, understood, applied, used in some way. Thus, relevance judgments focus evaluation on only one part of the search and use process. To evaluate information primarily on the basis of relevance is to fail to address "ineffable concepts" (Belkin 1981) such as need and motivation, or background and context, which are present prior to the user's interaction with a system. Also, it fails to account for access to the value of the information or to ways of evaluating the information, for concepts such as satisfaction, or for the uses to which information is put, all of which follow the point of interaction between user and information system.

### User Focus

There has been a general trend (Belkin 1980; Dervin 1989; Dervin and Nilan 1986; Dervin and Shields 1990; Paisley and Parker 1965; Saracevic 1971; 1990; Taylor 1968; Wersig 1979) toward focusing on the role of the user in the information retrieval process and toward an understanding of information use as socially situated (see, for example, Allen 1996; Berger and Luckmann 1966; Boulding 1961; Budd 1974; Schutz and Luckmann 1973). Human-centered models conceptualize "information seeking as a problem-solving activity that depends on communication acts" (Marchionini 1995, 29). These include (1) sense-making (Dervin 1992), whereby people attempt to make sense of their current situation as they try to overcome gaps or obstacles; (2) anomalous states of knowledge (Belkin, Oddy and Brooks 1982a), involving iterative and interactive dialogues between users and systems; (3) Taylor's (1962) multiple levels of information needs (visceral, conscious, formalized, compromised); (4) Kuhlthau's research (1993), which argues that cognitive and affective perspectives develop and change through seven stages: task initiation, topic selection, prefocus exploration, focus formulation, information collection, search closure, and initiation of writing; and (5) Allen's (1996) user-centered model of system design. From this perspective information is seen as a tool to help the user in addressing an anomaly, discomfort, problem, or gap in her life. Information systems can provide one avenue of access to ways of reducing this gap, provided a variety of conditions of access have been met. Allen's (1996) general design principles emphasize the resources users apply in expressing their needs, which form the basis for designing for usability. If designers know the resources needed for the task, and the resources held by user, they can create system features that augment and ensure user access to resources to complete their information task. Simultaneously, the same information systems can present barriers to access to information and can contribute to the widening of the knowledge gap between those who have access and those who do not.

For example, being able to even express one's information needs is influenced/constrained by one's individual or collective knowledge structures, which in turn are influenced/constrained by one's knowledge of the world, knowledge of a language, knowledge of what relevant informants know (shared cognition), and knowledge of the social situation and conventions. There are also many constraints on how designers access those users. For example, social constraints and authorizations influence system designers to select particular informants, phrase questions in particular ways, and even choose the time and place for eliciting statements of need (Allen 1996, ch. 5). Thus there are many constraints on system designers' access to understanding users' information needs, and thus the nature of the systems they create.

As another example, Cramton (1997) analyzed 13 dispersed teams of six business and information systems graduate students, each working together to develop a business plan for six weeks using only asynchronous electronic communication: a group decision support system, telephone, and fax. She found that problems of information distribution and interpretations were "rampant," influencing the interpersonal and collaborative relationships. She categorized the problems into five types: (1) failure to communicate contextual information, (2) difficulty in communicating the salience of information, (3) unevenly distributed information, (4) differences in speed of access to information, and (5) difficulty interpreting the meaning of silence (such as nonconfirmation of e-mails or faxes, sometimes because the recipient was ill or did not have access to the system).

Access lurks implicitly in our definitions of request or query, in a user's ability to identify a need, in the very awareness that information systems are available, and in trusting that information useful in addressing that need exists and is retrievable through an information system. It lurks in our assumptions that a scientific document presents form, content, and cognitive level that provide the user with access to the *value* of information.

Access lurks in the social and cultural contexts of information seeking (Durrance 1989), which are tied to the degree to which an individual is an insider to a given information system's culture (Kiesler, Siegel, and McGuire 1984; Sproull, Kiesler, and Zubrow 1984) and therefore to the rules required to gain access to the information potentially available through it. Users in different contexts may not always experience the same degree of access. An expert (insider) in one setting may be a novice or casual user (nonmember) in another (Brown 1986; Cuff 1980). This is one reason gatekeepers are so important (and will be discussed in more detail later): they can serve as intermediaries between a subculture and more general societal information resources (Agada 1999).

## Information Society

Research on the "information society" (for example, Bell 1973; Bellin 1993; Beniger 1986; Doctor 1991; 1992; Dordick 1987; Paisley 1980; Porat 1977; Ruben 1985; Schement 1989; Schement and Lievrouw 1987; Siefert, Gerbner and Fisher 1989) indicates, from various perspectives and with differing explanations, a common understanding that developing societies are increasingly reliant on information and information services for the functioning of their supporting structures. More and more, information is directly or indirectly the source of income, of decision making in everyday life situations, and, in turn, an important determinant of the quality of life. Lievrouw (1994) argues that this is associated with a shift from an "informing" environment emphasizing mass media, to an "involving" environment emphasizing new interactive media. Access to both information and understanding—often through communication—of the source, then, becomes crucial.

Access becomes the intersection or the gap between what we are able to know about potential benefits of information and what we are able to know about resources available to gain access. Given ability, access becomes the intersection between trust that information appropriate to a need exists and lack of awareness of that possibility. Given trust and awareness, access becomes the intersection between privilege and struggle to gain procedural knowledge. Given procedural knowledge, access becomes the intersection between evaluating potential benefits of the information and weighing them against available resources. Public access to information and communication are considered the necessary foundation for a democratic, civil society.

Agada (1999) applied Dervin's (1976) Information Needs Analysis Scheme and Taylor's (1986; 1991) Information Use Environment concept (a "set of elements which affect the availability, access to, and use of information by a group ... [and] determine the criteria by which information is deemed relevant and useful" [74]) to study the information needs of 20 informal gatekeepers in an African-American community. As did Chatman (1991), Agada found that they emphasized shorter-term and pragmatic needs, coping information rather than infrastructural or transformative information. The gatekeepers experienced considerable bureaucratic run-arounds and referrals, and believed "that the information or resources they need do exist but are made inaccessible to them by 'outsiders' who control the 'system.' Such perception may explain why they are unaware of many services that could benefit them" (80). Some of the information may in fact have been physically accessible but not accessible cognitively or practically, because of jargon or unreachable criteria. Nearly one quarter of their preferred information sources were interpersonal—neighbor, friend, or acquaintance—mostly because of context, relevance, orientation, shared perspectives, trusthworthiness, and credibility. Thus, as Taylor argued, and others have found (Chatman 1991; Chen and Hernon 1982; Ettema and Kline 1977; Fortner 1995; Genova and Greenberg 1979; Savolainen 1995), the contextual factors of one's Information Use Environments are highly influential and include communication skills, media preferences, motivation levels, interest, social norms, boundaries between "insiders" and "outsiders," and familiarity with sources.

Harris and Dewdney's (1994) study of battered women trying to use formal help systems is a comprehensive and rigorous analysis of institutional and social barriers to information. Barriers may include not knowing what information is needed, not knowing where to locate it, delays in requesting or obtaining information, not knowing that relevant information is available, receiving inaccurate or inappropriate information, and the information not existing (see also Doctor 1992; Durrance 1984). Julien's (1999) study of adolescents' seeking information about career decision making found similar barriers and lack of awareness: 40 percent of the 400 twelfth graders didn't know where to go for help, and felt they had to go to too many different sources. Kerwin (1993) clearly distinguishes, however, between ignorance (not aware of, don't have) and ignoring (choosing not to confront a problem or seek relevant information). Chatman (1991) and Harris and Dewdney (1994) argue that these two situations are highly interrelated. Not everyone wants to engage in total information access and communication participation (Fortner 1995). Allen's (1996) conceptualization of information seeking also recognizes information avoiding as well as information seeking.

Microlevel barriers include troublesome exchanges between clients and information providers because of misunderstandings, language problems or differences, social isolation, distrust of service providers, finding information that disqualifies the seeker from further information, lack of initiative, vague use of language, inattentiveness, causing confusion for the helper, inconsistency of request with helper's mandate, helpers prematurely close exchange because they think they know what the client needs, or the seeker's expectations are mismatched (Harris and Dewdney 1994; Julien 1999). Such experiences increase the frustration, confusion, and risk for the seeker, accumulating over interactions. Based on their structured interviews with 500 randomly selected households, and telephone interviews with

160 community professionals and help agency representatives, Harris and Dewdney proposed a set of information- or help-seeking principles: (1) information needs arise from the help seeker's situation; (2) the decision to seek help or not is affected by many factors; (3) people tend to seek information that is most accessible; (4) people tend first to seek help or information from interpersonal sources, especially from people like themselves; (5) information seekers expect emotional support; and (6) people follow habitual patterns in seeking information.

Claims for new technologies include that they can bridge gaps between rich and poor, powerful and powerless, haves and have-nots (for example, Downing 1989; Freire 1969; Furlong 1989; Greenberger and Puffer 1989; Pfaffenberger 1990), or that they widen existing gaps, blocking access to those already without access (Gillespie and Robins 1989; Hudson 1988; Jansen 1989; Rubinyi 1989). Another perspective holds that new technologies may enhance or hinder access to information in a democracy (Deetz 1989a; 1989b; Dervin 1980; 1989; Lievrouw 1994; Murdock and Golding 1989), in the workplace (Deetz 1990; Garson 1988; Kraut 1989; U.S. Congress 1987; Zuboff 1988), or in a broader social or cultural context (Bourque and Warren 1987; Dervin and Shields 1990; Krendl, Broihier, and Fleetwood 1989; Larose and Mettler 1989; Mulgan 1991; Pool 1983; U.S. Congress 1990; Weinberg 1987). Increased concentration of media ownership, selling and packaging information as entertainment, the growing shift from access-based fees to usage-sensitive pricing, and high entry costs for global information/media systems all indicate that the information society may be limiting, rather than increasing, democratic and civil participation (Lievrouw 1994). "Americans will have to begin to make active decisions about what information they want, from whom, and for how much, and whether the political empowerment that comes with active information seeking is worth the personal effort" (356).

### Mass Communication

The research perspectives considered thus far look at access to information primarily from the viewpoint of an information seeker or user, or an information provider or intermediary. Mass communication research adds another viewpoint—that of the producer or distributor of information. Access to information production and distribution, and to the individuals and institutions that produce and distribute information, emerges as a significant factor in understanding access to information.

Those who determine coverage for the nightly network television news programs set the agenda of interest for millions of viewers. The images we watch, the events we learn about, the details we attend to are all reliant on what is available. Given that the major source of news for the U.S. public is television, those who determine news coverage also determine what is available to find out about. In other words, they set the agenda for public concern and discourse. Research shows that media agenda setting is unidirectional and that lead stories shape the public agenda far more powerfully than ordinary stories (Behr and Iyengar 1984). In other words, television news sets the agenda for public concern, but public concerns do not reciprocally influence what information television news makes available. Selection of news coverage and degree of detail, background, and coverage over time tend to reflect social, political, and economic biases (Adams 1986).

How can this occur? After all, journalists are taught a commitment to impartiality. Herman and Chomsky (1988) propose a propaganda model of the performance of the mass media in the United States to explain how the authors view the media as managing public opinion. They posit a set of news filters as influencing attention given an item, placement, tone, repetitions, and framework of analysis. The news filters include size, concentrated ownership, owner wealth, and profit orientation of mass media firms; advertising as the primary income source of mass media; reliance of media on information provided by government, business, and "experts" funded and approved by agents of power; flak (negative responses to a media statement or program) as a means of disciplining the media; and anticommunism as a national religion and control mechanism. These filters, they argue, allow the process to occur so naturally that media news staff see themselves as objective. Also, free-market principles are at work; therefore, they suggest, "Most biased choices in the media arise from the preselection of right-thinking people, internalized preconceptions, and the adaptation of personnel to the constraints of ownership, organization, market, and political power" (xii).

This propaganda model is not inconsistent with arguments put forward by Bagdikian (1990) and H. I. Schiller (1981) that an increasingly smaller number of major corporations now own and control virtually all major sources of published and broadcast information, including books, magazines, films, television, radio, and audio recordings. In short, a few massive corporations produce our culture (H. I. Schiller 1989). It is also consistent with Hall's (1982) explanation of the role of the media in consensus building, in the context of hegemonic power constructs, with those in power having access to establish the agenda and define the terms of the dialectic in play, and those not in power struggling to gain access. In operating outside the framework of those in power, many also struggle to gain access to interpretation and debate, and thereby are limited in their opportunities to gain access to political choices (Murdock and Golding 1989).

## Organizational Communication

Organizations receive stimuli, interpret them, store, retrieve, and transmit information, generate judgments, and solve problems, through individuals as information processors, and through organizational systems and structures. Choo (1996) summarizes the significant models of organizations from an information use perspective. He integrates these perspectives in his "information model of the organization," which emphasizes six basic issues: (1) the information-processing requirements of organizations, specifically reducing uncertainty and equivocality; (2) the acquisition of information by organizations, through decisions to act or to seek information; (3) the satisficing and symbolic information-processing behaviors of organizational members because of cognitive and social limits; (4) the nature of information in organizations, affected by use, predictability, and location; (5) the use of information in organizations, ranging from objective signal to highly political and "irrational" symbol; and (6) the role of information technology in organizational information processing—to reinforce and shape the decision premises, change the perception of information sources, augment the information-processing capacity of organizations, or alter the organizational structures to coordinate economic activity. Choo's (1995) model of organizational information management includes (1) information needs influence information acquisition; (2) information acquisition influences information products/services (which add value); and (3) information distribution. (4) These both influence information use, (5) which influences adaptive behavior, (6) which in turn influences information needs and information acquisition. Finally, (7) information organization and storage interacts with information products and services (2) and distribution (3).

In considering the literature on organizational communication, three research areas stand out in their concern with issues of access to information.

### Electronic Surveillance in the Workplace

Braverman (1974) argues that modern technologies contribute to the de-skilling of the labor force. With the de-skilling of collar positions of all colors (blue, pink, and white), the occasional role played by access to information in defining job category and rank (Braman 1989), and the possibility of constant surveillance of workers (Botan and McCreadie 1993), access to information gathered through surveillance is one form of access to power (Doctor 1991).

In 1789, Jeremy Bentham (1969) advanced a design for what he thought was the ideal form for organizing human endeavors. The panopticon, as the model is called, is designed to allow an observer (guard, manager, medical personnel) in a central tower the capability of viewing at any time the activity of occupants (prisoners, workers, patients) of the cells in the multisided building surrounding the tower. This annular building is only one cell deep at any point, and each cell is constructed such that light passes through from the outward face to the inner wall, which faces the tower. Thus, the activities of the occupants are illuminated to view from the tower. The tower is shaded so that the observer is not also observed. As a result, cell occupants are at all times exposed to observation from the tower, without knowledge of when or whether they are being observed.

The panopticon has since been used to illustrate the power relationship between observed and observer, the major effect of which is that the one observed internalizes the constraints of the relationship, monitors his own behavior as if observation were continuous, and thus becomes the bearer of his own discipline (Foucault 1977). Some analysts (Botan and McCreadie 1993; Gandy 1989; Zuboff 1988) have pursued study of the power relationship played out in the workplace, where new technologies make possible the functioning of an electronic panopticon. With the capability of gathering data any time an electronic communication system is in operation (Rice and Borgman 1983), any time truck drivers operate their vehicles (U.S. Congress 1987), or any time a job applicant submits to pre-employment screening (U.S. Congress 1987), serious questions are raised regarding access and privacy (Linowes 1989; Rule 1974) and the tension inherent between them.

This tension between issues of access and privacy can similarly be considered in a spatial context as the tension between access and exposure (Archea 1977). The individual with access is able to monitor the behavior of others, while exposure refers to the extent to which others can monitor or view the individual. Simultaneously, managerial access to organizational members, especially through walking around and exposing oneself to spontaneous information and work activities, is a recommended procedure for fostering greater understanding and openness (Katzer and Fletcher 1992). Similar tensions are evident between access and security, or access and control, issues that arise in the design and management of information systems. Access to technology and influences and constraints on access emerge as subsidiary issues. Information sharing in organizations is inherently political, influenced by domains, leaders, culture, language, and information resources, via controlling access to and use of the variability and flow of information (Choo 1995).

### Management of Information Systems and Media Choice

In general, information systems in the workplace are designed to provide authorized personnel with access to various kinds of information, which the users may provide or which may be provided through other sources. Usually, the focus in the literature on management of information systems is not on the employee and the potential infringement on her privacy, but rather on the function of an information system from a management perspective. From that vantage point, the access issues lean more toward influences on and outcomes of media choice, how to control who has access and to what they can gain access, and on the organizational consequences of obtaining or not obtaining information. Information in this context can be in electronic format (computer data files, for example), in written form (reports or paper files), face-to-face (conversations or group meetings), or in a range of other formats, including new media such voicemail or telefacsimile transmissions (Berlo 1960; Daft and Lengel 1986; Randolph 1978; Reinsch and Beswick 1990; Rice 1987).

In the literature on management of information systems, concerns with access to information are frequently more specifically concerns of access to equipment or media (Culnan 1984; 1985; Hiltz and Johnson 1989; Rice and Shook 1988). Research in this area indicates that perception of access to information systems is an important factor in whether or not an employee uses a system. Greater perceived accessibility leads to greater likelihood of use (Culnan 1983; 1985; O'Reilly 1982) and increased accessibility also leads to increased system usage, which in turn tends to increase perceived accessibility, leading to more use (Culnan 1983) and to reported increases in effectiveness (Rice and Shook 1988). Although system use alone is not sufficient to lead to more use, *successful* system use does tend to lead to more use (Hiltz and Johnson 1989).

Christensen and Bailey (1997) combined the managerial media selection research with information source research. "The source refers to the person or place in which desired information is stored, and as such is a necessary component in the communicative act of information acquisition" (377). Their research showed that source attributes (here, accessibility of a manager or of a library, though they review the constraints of hierarchical level, social influences, function, resource availability, etc., on accessibility of sources) and media characteristics (level of media richness) have both direct effects and interaction effects on information acquisition behavior. The participants selected the richer medium in the less routine conditions, and the appropriate medium when the source was accessible; but these interacted, such that for routine tasks, when library access was restricted, they chose a richer medium, and for nonroutine tasks, when manager access was restricted, they chose a leaner medium. One implication of these results is that "organizational factors leave junior managers to contend with source restrictions that may result in suboptimal media selection for task demands, leading to information acquisition failures stemming from unnecessary complication of routine tasks and oversimplification of novel tasks" (385).

This area of study identifies several potential influences and constraints on access to information that have not been as fully explored elsewhere. Marchand and Horton (1986) note that as much as one quarter of a knowledge worker's time can be spent in inefficient information-seeking activities. Choo (1995, 57–67) summarizes relevant research to propose a model whereby (1) managerial information needs stimulate information seeking, (2) which generates information use, (3) which in turn creates new information needs. This cycle is in turn influenced by (4) problem situation (both internal and external), (5) organizational roles (informational, decision, interpersonal), and (6) managerial traits. However, most influences and constraints in the literature are related to using technology in the process of gaining access to information. These include access to a system's command language (Culnan 1985) or appropriate query language (Culnan 1984), both of which are related to competence in using a system to gain information (Rubinyi 1989). Response time (Culnan 1984), access to interaction through computer-mediated systems (Rice 1984), and access to online databases (Hart and Rice 1991) are additional factors.

Access to accurate information becomes an issue in an organizational context in which individuals might intentionally withhold or distort information (O'Reilly 1978). Access to networking, both interpersonal and technological, can make the difference between gaining access to information or not (Albrecht and Adelman 1987). Improved access to information and communication by a multiactor system also may mean increased span of control and quickness of control by central actors and decreased control of decision making by local actors (such as by military leaders in the field). "It follows that information-handling capability should be seen as a defining variable in organizational structure and in the distribution of power within that structure" (Buckland 1991b, 186). Solomon's (1997a) ethnographic study of three annual iterations of a work-planning process in a public agency showed that personal communication, both from within and outside the agency, provided important cues as to the timing and meaning of information, as the actual processes of seeking and using information were chaotic, interrupted, and nonlinear. Even among resource-poor groups, those better connected to communication networks have been shown to be better able to take advantage of technological aids to access (Rubinyi 1989).

Cognitive factors are implicitly considered in connection with judging the quality of information potentially retrieved (O'Reilly 1982) or evaluating whether information is useful in the workplace (Kanter 1977). Affective and interpersonal factors are touched upon implicitly insofar as they are part of trusting colleagues as information sources (O'Reilly 1978), the extent to which one's feelings influence acceptance of an information system (Rice 1984), the degree to which they are related to the frustration of dealing with information overload (O'Reilly 1980), or the relative costs and benefits of using a system (Hart and Rice 1991).

**Knowledge Management**

Much of the knowledge management literature presumes that knowledge represents a given world, is universal and objective, results from information processing, is transferable, and enables problem solving (von Krogh and Roos 1996). However, as Dervin (1976) distinguished between conceptualizations of information as objective, subjective, and sense-making, various authors in the interdisciplinary field of knowledge management distinguish between knowledge as an objective "thing" that can be stored, manipulated, and transmitted, and knowledge as a human resource created and sustained through interaction (Pemberton 1998). Cues used in sense making in the agency studied by Solomon (1997b) were extracted through scanning, browsing, use of information systems, and interactions with others, enacting adaptations to the work projects that led to further extractions and enactments. Hayles (1999) suggests that "a historically specific construction called the human is giving way to a different construction called the posthuman" (2) based on the conceptualization of information as disembodied and separable from, and privileged over, its material carrier/marker. This development identifies the potential of distributed (social) cognition and knowledge management but also complicates the conceptualization and practice of individual agency (4).

The knowledge management literature distinguishes between individual and organizational knowledge. Knowledge may only exist through social cognition, and organizations and individuals may both influence the development and maintenance of knowledge at each level (Corner, Kinicki, and Keats 1994; Walsh and Ungson 1991). Further, knowledge may be tacit, cultural, or not sayable for a variety of reasons (Boisot 1998; Choo 1995; 1998; Polanyi 1997), or may be articulatable or explicit (Davenport and Prusak 1998), such as know-how, know-why, and know-what (Sanchez 1997). Knowledge may facilitate exploitation of current resources and competencies, or exploration, innovation, and experimentation (March 1999). Ways to convert tacit knowledge to shared explicit knowledge include socialization, externalization, combination, and internalization (Choo 1998).

In our terms, knowledge may both facilitate retrieval of stored information and facilitate access to new information. An overreliance on exploitation, while seemingly highly efficient and effective, forecloses exposure to new information and may result in organizational failure in dynamic environments. Finally, knowledge can be conceptualized as an asset that flows through production or as an asset stored until it needs to be brought to bear on decision-making processes (Boisot 1998). Choo (1998) analyzes three ways that organizations use information: (1) sense making (managing ambiguity), (2) knowledge creating (managing learning), and (3) decision making (managing uncertainty). Choo argues that while all three information uses are crucial for organizational survival, the literature typically emphasizes information for decision making. Choo's overall model emphasizes both formal and informal channels, and personal and impersonal sources, for how organizations store, retrieve, share, and use information.

Spender (1998) distinguished four types of organizational knowledge (or uncertainty) derived from an individual/social dimension and an explicit/implicit dimension: (1) individual/explicit is "conscious," (2) individual/implicit is "automatic," (3) social/explicit is "objectified," and (4) social/implicit is "collective." Of particular significance is objectified knowledge, as it represents a "single, rigorously structured and coherent discourse" (240), but it is also the most difficult to manage and foster because it is derived from, and requires, collective knowledge. One of the prime values of collective knowledge is that it is inherently a public good—that is, is not diminished by distribution—can be reapplied within the organizational system, and allows access to greater diversity of interpretations as responses to uncertainties. Paradoxically, collective knowledge usually has no value when controlled solely by individuals, that is, it is then no longer a public good. Further, this information-based public good can be destroyed by mismanagement and overconsumption, especially by free riders, particularly when collective knowledge is scarce.

Pervasive, though often implicit, throughout the discussion of knowledge management are considerations of gaining, providing or controlling access to information or knowledge, from individuals to other individuals, to the organization, within the organization, and across organizations. Information seeking and acquisition moderate relations between threats and action (Thomas, Clark, Gioia 1993), such as by increasing awareness of a problem or openness to change (Armenikas, Harris, and Mossholder 1993), or social support, which reduces uncertainty, supports interpretation, and reduces dependencies (Albrecht and Adelman 1987; Johnson 1996).

## Economics of Information

Information differs from material goods in several highly consequential ways, such as requiring few material resources; being expandable, substitutable, transmittable, diffusable, shareable; and having a value highly dependent on the user and the context (Buckland 1991a; Cleveland 1985; Johnson 1996). The evaluation of information depends on the individual's "information field," composed of familiar and accessible sources, directly or indirectly mediated and unmediated (Johnson 1996), or similarly, by one's "information use environment" (Taylor 1986; 1991).

In discussions of information as an economic good (for example, Arrow 1979; Bates 1988; Hall 1981; McCain 1988), questions arise regarding assessing the future value of information as well as its present assessment, e.g., pricing, market processes, and allocation of investments and benefits. The value of information is not fixed as it is for most commodities; it is contextually determined. Its full value is not known until it is used (Arrow 1979); this implies that assessment of information requires "upfront" costs and other information. Again, access lies at the intersection between knowledge of potential benefits and knowledge of potential costs (Hardy 1982). In addition, there is the possibility of ancillary value (for example, public dissemination of information of educational or social value) to the individual user, to others through another individual's use of information, and to society (Bates 1988).

**Information as Public or Private Good**

Another critical issue is the extent to which specific types of information are a public or a private good. Other costs, for example, time spent reading reviews, effort expended in seeking a particular document, discomfort experienced navigating an unfamiliar information system, or inconvenience in being placed on hold waiting to consult with a lawyer or contractor are all considerations in gaining access. Access to the information, to the value of the information, and to ways of assessing the value of that information are of interest.

**Buying Citizenship Rights**

Implicit in the notion of democracy lies the assumption of informed participation of its citizens (Gandy 1988). It is also assumed that citizens have equitable access to information, advice, and analysis to enable them to know their rights and to pursue them (Murdock and Golding 1989). Several analysts have argued that privatization of information (Murdock and Golding 1989; H. I. Schiller 1981; 1989), ownership of information production and dissemination operations by powerful financial conglomerates (Bagdikian 1990; Compaine 1985; Dreier and Weinberg 1979), and government actions to selectively disseminate information (Braman 1989; Murdock and Golding 1989; H. I. Schiller 1988) have tied information access, and therefore the ability to exercise political rights, to economic market forces.

## Summary

Understanding the many factors involved in information access requires accounting for a variety of perspectives. Indeed, even the same user in different situations is likely to view and be viewed differently.

Dervin (1989) has warned that categories of users are inventions of researchers and not necessarily the users' own constructions, though they may be for some. Traditional categories, she argues, lead to reification of existing gaps between haves and have-nots, perpetuating patterns of use and exposure. They move us toward neither new theoretical understandings nor new research questions. As has been demonstrated in other, not unrelated, fields of study, a reexamination of research from a new perspective (for example, Gilligan's (1982) criticism of Kolhberg's studies of moral development, or the replication of Perry's (1981) studies by Belenky et al. (1986) to reveal differences in perspectives of men and women in the process of epistemological development) can result in a reinterpretation of findings that alters the identification of some groups from outsiders or deviants to simply different from the dominant (Dervin 1980; Ettema and Kline 1977). Feminist analyses of technology in the lives of women (for example, Jansen 1989; Kramarae 1988a; Lewis 1987; Treichler and Wartella 1986; Turkle 1988; Weinberg 1987) serve as an example of one perspective that has proven to differ from traditional "malestream" (Kramarae 1988b) analyses. Other perspectives (Deetz 1989a; 1992; Hall 1982; 1989; Slack 1984) view the issues from new analytical vantage points and thus have shed light on how technologies and society are related.

In other words, the perspective from which we carry out research defines the questions we ask, the interpretation of the findings, and therefore the conclusions we draw and the impact of our research (Harding 1991; Jansen 1989). If gaining access to information and communication relies on the perspective from which one views an issue or on the questions one asks, then any study of issues related to access to information must make explicit what one can see from a given perspective and, correlatively, what is invisible from that same perspective. That is one of the aims of this part of the book.

Within each of the research literatures that address issues of access to information, a range of perspectives and points of focus emerge. For example, within the frame of information science, evaluation of information systems and their use has been carried out from a limited perspective, one that focuses on a narrowly circumscribed group with privileged access. Consideration of access issues in research on library studies, information science, the "information society," mass communication, organizational communication, and economics of information raises awareness about the nature of information as an economic and social good, new technologies and the potential they bring for barriers or bridges to access, democratic principles and the assumption of informed participation of citizens and their equal access to information, power relationships and privacy issues and their implications for management and policy decisions, and the perspectives from which access is viewed. All are important in understanding access to information. In addition, such consideration makes clear both the pervasiveness of issues of access and their complexity.

We need, therefore, a framework to guide an integration of research across literatures and processes that is applicable across situations and across technologies and systems. This framework can serve to inform further research with sensitivity to issues of access with implications for those with privileged access as well as for those struggling to gain access to information. The remainder of part I presents the formative development and evaluation of such a framework.

# 3

# Common Concepts Across Research Liferatures

This chapter addresses five questions, based on the prior reviews of the six research literatures:

1. What are the underlying conceptualizations of information?
2. What are common concerns about access-related issues?
3. What are common facets of the information-seeking process?
4. What are the roles of mediation and technology in accessing information?
5. What are the common influences and constraints on access to information?

## Conceptualizations of Information

Information is a concept that is used in multiple ways in everyday language as well as in the research literature (see Belkin 1978; Belkin and Robertson 1976; Buckland 1991a; Case 2000; Fox 1983; Hayes 1993; Levitan 1980; Machlup and Mansfield 1983; Schement 1993; Wellisch 1972; Wersig and Neveling 1975). Buckland (1991b) provides perhaps the most extensive and philosophical discussion of the components and dimensions of information, including how information can be limited, reduced, transformed, or varied over time. He identifies three major conceptualizations of information: (1) process (change of what someone knows, an intangible process), (2) knowledge (an imparted intangible or its representation; change in beliefs, level of uncertainty; an intangible entity), and (3) thing (objects with the attribute of being informative; an expression, description, or representation; a tangible entity). Buckland does not present these as opposing definitions of information; rather, they are three forms, states, or elements. The extent to which information-as-thing becomes information-as-process and then information-as-knowledge depends on the situation, which involves access, cognitive skills, and prior knowledge (Buckland 1991b). Thus becoming informed varies greatly by person, information system, identified attributes of the object, and object. Case (2001)

**Table 3.1**
Conceptualizations of Information

| Conceptualization | Description | Assumptions |
|---|---|---|
| Thing (commodity/ resource) | A message, a commodity, something that can be produced, purchased, replicated, distributed, sold, traded, manipulated, passed along, controlled | Assumes sender to receiver<br>Assumes receiver makes of message what sender intends |
| Data in environment | Objects, artifacts, sounds, smells, events, visual and tactile phenomena, activities, phenomena of nature | Accounts for unintentional communication |
| Representation of knowledge | Documents, books, periodicals, some visual and auditory representations<br>Abstractions of information (e.g., citations, indexes) | Assumes printed document is primary representation of knowledge<br>Assumes primacy of scientific/technical knowledge |
| Part of process of communication | Part of human behavior in process of moving through time/space to make sense of world | Assumes meanings are in people, not in words<br>Assumes human behavior is basis of understanding of the process |

suggests that significant differences in definitions of information are derived from different assumptions about (1) intentionality of the user or communicator, (2) utility of the information, (3) physicality of the information (material, conceptual, observable), and (4) truth or accuracy. Here, we identify and illustrate the range of what is meant by information through four common dimensions across the six research literatures, hoping to shed light on assumptions about information that have implications for notions of information access. Table 3.1 summarizes the following broad conceptualizations and underlying assumptions derived from the literatures.

### Information as Thing (Commodity/Resource)

Some literatures emphasize information as a thing (see reviews by Bates 1988; Buckland 1991a), a commodity that can be produced, purchased, replicated, distributed, manipulated, passed along, controlled, traded, and sold. This conceptualization is consistent with a model of sending information as a message (encoded into some material form) from sender to receiver. It may include an assumption that the receiver will interpret and understand the message as intended by the sender. It may also allow for value to be added as the information is disseminated or exchanged.

### Information as Data in the Environment

Other literatures tend to view information more broadly, to include data in the environment, available for interaction with human information-processing capabilities. This category includes objects, artifacts, sounds, smells, visual and tactile phenomena, activities, events, or the phenomena of nature. As Buckland (1990) points out, it is easy to assume that all communication is intentional. In practice, however, one is informed also by perceptions of things that are communicated unintentionally. The discoveries one makes in the process of browsing (see part II), or the inferences another makes about an individual's character or performance based on observation of the individual (Archea 1977), particularly when the individual is unaware of being observed, serve as additional examples of unintentional communication available in the environment.

Choo (1995, 3) argues that the environment should not be considered as providing organizations with access to information, but rather as a potential field of information that the organization must proactively seek, access, and search. So, as Weick (1979) argues, the environment is enacted by the organization rather than existing as an easily identifiable and bounded set of fixed information. Indeed, modern environments are complex, turbulent, and constantly changing. Thus, information development and management becomes a much more significant organizational factor than physical and fiscal assets. The three primary components of this information management are (1) connecting (ability to access knowledge and information), (2) sharing (exchanging and integrating information and understanding core processes), and (3) structuring (creating meaning from organizing, associating, and interpreting data), both within and across organizational boundaries (Haeckel and Nolan 1993). Choo (1995, 13) emphasizes, then, that successful organizations do not merely process objective information but also manage insights, intuitions, images, and symbols, and foster knowledge creation throughout the organization.

### Information as Representation of Knowledge

Some researchers view information as a representation of, or pointer to, knowledge (Buckland 1991b). The tradition of scientific method and scholarly publication is a clear example of this conceptualization (Lievrouw 1988). Card catalogs or databases of citations to scientific documents illustrate an abstraction of a representation of knowledge, providing information about where or how to pursue a representation of information, such as in documents, books, and periodicals. Traditionally, this view of information has been based on the assumption that the printed document is the primary representation of knowledge. Recent years have seen a proliferation of alternatives to print, such as representations of knowledge available on video- or audiotape, videodisc, CD-ROM, Internet, or other electronic and computer media.

Representations include, or often have associated with them, "metadata," or data about data (Borgman 2000, 69; Dempsey and Heery 1998). Access to information requires access to metadata, which may be grouped into intrinsic data (about the content, form, genre, title, author, what resources exist) and extrinsic data (about external information such as where the resources are located, in what form they are encoded or displayed, their history, ownership, required techniques and tools, genre, evaluation, cost, access rights) as manifested in the "Dublin Core" metadata criteria. Borgman (2000, 73–79) groups metadata into the categories of (1) description (annotations, hyperlinks, indexes), (2) administration (acquisition, rights, versions, location, storage and removal, usage data), (3) intellectual access ("aboutness," classification codes and descriptors, automatic abstracting, patterns of access by groups of users), (4) intellectual organization (grouping or organizing materials, association, authority control), (5) technical specifications (hardware and software requirements, formats, compression and scaling, security and privacy, usable network standards, display resolution), and (6) preservation management (condition, life cycle, restoration actions). These metadata categories need to be both formalized in some way, and allowed to be expanded and customized for particular user communities, so that providers can create materials with universal access points, users can access systems knowing there are both common and specific conceptualizations of the resources and they are potentially able to discover relevant resources, and institutions can organize the materials and support the association and retrieval of materials.

### Information as Part of Communication Process

Usually, informing occurs through communication; thus information systems are communication systems. Information interaction is a dialogue in which informants and users communicate with each other (Allen 1996). An information device may bring together a set of interpreters, guides, and intermediaries who add their own understanding to the cognitive content. Some literatures conceptualize as part of human behavior in the communication process of moving through space/time to make sense of one's world (Atwood and Dervin 1982). From this view, meanings are in people rather than in words or data (Berlo 1960), and knowledge is what users do with data rather than what data do to users (Budd 1987). For example, participants in the agency studied by Solomon (1997c) did not conceive of separate stages of information, information search, or information seeking. Information use was just all of a piece, embedded in sense making while trying to accomplish their work. They captured and processed meaning through cognitive, affective, and action styles, which were somewhat related to the person's role and work task, and somewhat related to personal strategies. An assumption of this conceptualization of information is that understanding must be based on observation of human behavior in the information-seeking and sense-making processes, and on the meanings intended and interpreted by the participants (Agada 1999; Chatman 1991).

## Conceptualizations of Access to Information

Table 3.2 summarizes how the reseach literatures conceptualize access to information in six broad categories.

### Access to Knowledge

The most common categorization is access to knowledge and its representations (Budd 1987; Davenport and Prusak 1998; Gandy 1993). Information, through use and application, becomes a linked network of knowledge (Allen 1996), so specific information represents a larger, holistic network. O'Reilly (1978) discusses access to information in an organizational context. This usually assumes that a message can be sent and received as intended by the sender and that the message, or the knowledge derived from it, might influence decisions made within the organization. He argues that employees might intentionally manipulate information (including withholding it) to serve the ends of the sender, particularly when directed from a subordinate to a superior within the organization. "Psychopathic manipulation" can occur as a function of a social or technological system, imposed through rules and procedures, subsystem structures, or membership selection methods (Singer 1980). The result is that the individual is unable to correct errors, adding an additional barrier to gaining access to knowledge.

In the contexts of libraries and information science, the most familiar examples of access to knowledge include printed documents such as books and periodicals (Chen and Hernon 1982; D. Schiller 1989), citations to documents (Bates 1986b; Blair and Maron 1985; Borgman 1989), databases of citations (Hart and Rice 1991), and data (Borgman 1989). These are representations of knowledge and, when put to use, potential building blocks for new knowledge. Access to evidence in support of facts (Buckland 1990) can be gained either through observation and experience, or through use of print and other representations of knowledge.

**Table 3.2**
Conceptualizations of Access to Information

| Category | Examples | Implications |
|---|---|---|
| Knowledge | Message sent, information flow<br>Observation, visual sources, evidence<br>Documents, books, periodicals, numerical or digital data, databases, citations<br>Analysis, advice, interpretation, debate, answers, education | Can lead to decision making, control over information flow, to quality of life, quality of work life<br>Can lead to power, influence, to socioeconomic opportunities: equity, funds, legal advantage, participation in democratic society and citizenship activities |
| Technology and media | Range of technologies and media: computer, telephone, movies, books, newspapers, magazines, music, TV<br>Information delivery systems, systems that generate, store, create information<br>Interface or command language, software, programming<br>Use of system<br>Linking technologies: interactive, communication, networking technologies | Assumes that access to technologies leads to access to information<br>Assumes an infrastructure of support<br>Assumes knowledge of how to use<br>Can lead to access to multiple data sources, automatic methods of surveillance, increased control, creativity<br>Compounding effect: access to one technology can increase future access, experience, advantage |
| Communication | Making sense of things: content, comprehension, retention, explanation<br>Making use of information: accuracy, relevance, format, level, decision making<br>Connectivity<br>Communication competence | Assumes communication competence<br>Requires broader meaning of relevance<br>Can lead to social, political participation with implications for democracy, equity, power relations<br>Compounding effect: access likely to lead to greater competence, access |

**Table 3.2** (continued)

| Category | Examples | Implications |
|---|---|---|
| Control | Over who has access to what to whose advantage<br>Over the agenda, terms of debate, content, organization, design, program<br>Over processes and flows of information<br>Over production of culture | Assumes power and control are associated with information and knowledge<br>Compounding effect: those who control access more likely to decide, design in favor of others most like them |
| Goods/ commodities | Information as social, economic good with value, costs, benefits<br>Distribution of control capacities, availability of resources<br>New markets for information industry | Assumes potential for public good, social value<br>Value not known until used<br>Compounding effect: potential for economic barriers and paths to be reinforced by social dynamics |
| (Knowledge of and ability to exercise) rights | Services: governmental, communication, information<br>Advocacy<br>Privacy | Can influence right to participate as citizen<br>Compounding effect: those most in need often least likely to obtain services |

Typically, the literature presents accessibility as a greater influence on information use than on amount or quality of the information, because of access costs and unpredictable potential value of retrieved information (Rice and Shook 1988). However, Choo's research (1995) shows that environment turbulence, strategic use of scanned information, and ambiguity of situation all interact to influence whether accessibility or quality of information is the greater influence.

The pursuit of knowledge as part of the communication process carries implications for the well-being of the individual or a society, such as access to education (Hiltz 1986) or access to answers to questions (Doctor 1992; Paris 1988; Pfaffenberger 1990). Access to advice on, or analysis of, political or economic issues may influence the degree to which an individual can participate as a citizen (Murdock and Golding 1989). Access to knowledge can also be understood as access to creating or distributing information, such as through the mass media (Bagdikian 1990), through interactive media or bulletin boards, or through publication in the scholarly or popular press or on the Internet.

Access to information as knowledge can lead to political power (Doctor 1992; Gandy 1993), decision-making power (Braman 1989; Gandy 1988), and citizenship activities (Gandy 1988; Palmquist 1992). It can also influence socioeconomic opportunities (Braman 1989; Doctor 1992), including funds, legal advantage, and equity. Such access can determine the sustainability, innovativeness, and cooperativeness of organizations in their attempt to manage knowledge (Davenport and Prusak 1998). Further, such access can influence the quality of work life (Palmquist 1992; U.S. Congress 1987; Zuboff 1988) and, indeed, the quality of life in general. Information is the organizational "meta-resource that coordinates the mobilization of the other assets in order for the organization to perform" (Choo 1995, xi).

### Access to Technology and Media

For some, access to information necessarily implies or requires access to technology, or may not extend before or beyond the point of interaction with the technological system. For others, technology is, at the very least, an issue of major concern in gaining access to information (Bourque and Warren 1987; Culnan 1985; Gandy 1988; 1993; Hiltz and Johnson 1989; Rice 1988; D. Schiller 1989; Weinberg 1987). What might seem to be easily accessible to the majority of the Internet user population may be contributing to the digital divide by preventing access to those with different physical abilities (sight, hearing, use of hands, etc.—see http://www.digitaldividenetwork.org).

The technology may be as commonplace as the telephone (Pool 1983; Rakow 1988) or as specialized as the combination of computers, telescopes, and communication technologies that allow us to gather information about explosions on the far side of Jupiter. Information technology, in general, includes any means of information processing, handling information-as-thing, including pen and paper, photocopying, computer systems, and library. Access to technology sometimes means access to a range of media such as movies, newspapers, books, magazines, music, academic performance, or television (Dorr 1980; Greenberger and Puffer 1989; Innis 1951; McLuhan and Fiore 1967). Ordinarily, in these examples, someone else has created or produced what is available and technology serves as an information delivery system. Therefore, some refer more explicitly to access to information as access to information systems for generating, storing, distributing information or representations of information in offices, libraries, government agencies, and so on (Bates 1986b; Borgman 1989; Budd 1987; O'Reilly 1982; Sparck Jones 1988). More generally, information systems/technology include (1) communication (conveying information, intentionally and more or less directly), (2) retrieval-based information services (user retrieves information-as-thing through a system), and (3) observation (not otherwise communicated or retrieved) (Buckland 1991b). Buckland clearly distinguishes information from information technology.

Marchionini (1995) devotes a chapter to discussing how computer-mediated information technologies have altered information seeking. Physical changes include greater amount of information, easier access across time and space, varying and user-adaptable formats, and a different range of user actions (more abstract, less physical). Conceptual changes include different ways of organizing, representing, and accessing information, more powerful and focused interfaces and intellectual tools, higher levels of interactivity, more diverse information and communication resources, and greater support for and expectations about information seeking. Access to technology can lead to an increased likelihood of monitoring or surveillance, isolation and standardization, but also to increased opportunities for interaction, flexibility, and creativity (Kramarae 1988).

It is a common, but mistaken, assumption that access to technology is necessarily equivalent to access to information (Gillespie and Robins 1989; Murdock and Golding 1989). It is true that technological developments have the potential to improve access. For example, digitizing new and old materials can improve access in a variety of ways: (1) creates multiple copies, including ability to make copies on demand, (2) increases access points, so that people who would not otherwise be able to visit a physical site (a museum or library) can experience the materials, (3) increases manipulability (such as recovering recording tracks, zooming, changing features), and (4) the related digital metadata (indexes, keywords) can be associated with other documents for retrieval and interpretation. However, there are disadvantages as well, involving issues of (1) legal evidence and signatures, (2) small hues and shadings lost, (3) short life span, increasing incompatibility, (4) required technological interface, unlike paper and eyesight, (5) cost (e.g., scanning is expensive), (6) copyright, and (7) required sophisticated indexing and descriptive metadata. Thus a digital library will maintain digital documents, digitized documents, and pointers to nondigital documents (Borgman 2000, 67).

Since television programming is under the user's control only to the extent that the user has the option of selecting from among existing programs, television is more likely to establish an agenda of interest for a viewer rather than to address a specific preexisting need or question. When using a more interactive information delivery system, such as an online database, the user must first have user privileges for, and select, a database that matches both the content and the comprehension level of her search, then be able to navigate the interface or the command language of the system, and understand the nature of the results (such as abstracts or bibliometric descriptors) (Culnan 1985). On the Internet, the interaction can be even more complex. The user must have access to technology (a computer, modem, and phone line or network connection), to communication software, to an account on the Internet, and to knowledge of how to navigate the Net. In addition, access to information is enhanced when the user also knows of appropriate electronic lists or bulletin boards with a critical mass of members (Williams, Rice, and Rogers 1989) and is sufficiently experienced in use of both the technology and the Net to be able to search, upload, download, and interact effectively. Cataloging and indexing terms both increase and narrow access, often in invisible ways, by both providing and excluding terms and other metadata to search on (Borgman 2000, 108). Institutional, material, and technological choices related to preservation, licensing, distribution, and compatibility have significant implications for access to content over time (Borgman 2000, 200–205.)

Use of a system is not equivalent to accessing information (Baroudi, Olson, and Ives 1986; Dervin 1989; Gerstberger and Allen 1968; Hiltz and Johnson 1989; Singer 1980). Certainly, access to information relevant to the context and situation of a particular user at a particular point in time cannot be assumed (Chatman 1991; Dervin 1980). A library patron might successfully use an online catalog to identify materials in the collection relevant to a particular situation, but the actual materials may be in use elsewhere or otherwise unavailable. Thus access to and use of information/communication technologies does not automatically mean having access to information.

**Access to Communication**

Access to information is sometimes viewed as access to communication, particularly if communication is understood as sense making, or moving through time/space to make sense of one's world (Dervin 1976; Dervin and Nilan 1986). Access to information thus includes access to content, to comprehension, to retention, or even to appropriate timing of interaction (Bates 1993; Dorr 1980; Hill 1984; Rice 1988; Solomon 1997a). Gaining access to such comprehension or understanding occurs only when communication is relevant to the individual information seeker, user, or audience member (Harris and Dewdney 1994). Thus, information may remain "tacit" because no one else completely understands something (Spender 1998) or even because, as everyone in the situation already understands something, it does not need to be said (Boisot 1998).

Such access relies on a view of relevance that is determined not by matching query statements with bibliographic references, but by matching the applicability of what is ascertained to the everyday life of the individual (Agada 1999; Bodker 1989; Chatman 1991; Dervin 1980; Freire 1969). For example, the format in which communication occurs is likely to influence the ability of the interactants to understand or make sense of information. If one is unable to see, a printed document is not very useful. Also, different individuals learn or understand better from different perspectives than others (Belenky et al. 1986; Kolb 1984) or using different kinds of intelligence than those generally valued and encouraged in schools (Gardner 1983).

Access to information can also imply access to connectivity or interpersonal networks (Crane 1969; Dervin 1980; Doctor 1992; Granovetter 1973; Hiltz 1986; Rice and Borgman 1983; Rice and Love 1987). Marchionini (1995, 18) argues that human-computer interaction research analyzes interactions, interactivity, and interfaces between computers and humans. Indeed, he refers to the "interface" as a communication channel, the design of which requires a deep understanding of humans and systems, and an appropriate balance between the two.

Communication competence is required for participation in the social, economic, and political spheres of society (Gandy 1988; Murdock and Golding 1989). Those who gain access and who participate regularly are likely also to gain experience with such systems and processes, thereby improving further their communication competence and increasing opportunities and skills for access in the future. The converse is also true, and the impact of such deficiencies tends to compound over time, leading to a growing knowledge gap or digital divide.

### Access to Control

Access to information can be understood as access to control of participation and of content (Bates 1993; Doctor 1992; Johnson 1996; Mulgan 1991). The holder of a TV remote control, for example, gets to decide which channel to watch, how long to stay with that channel, the volume level, or whether to browse through the channels at a leisurely pace, stopping to evaluate the offerings of a channel, or to whiz through the channels until something eyecatching stops the process, sometimes also controlling what is available for others.

Of course, the perspective from which one views the issues influences expectations for those implications. For example, Doctor (1991) identified polar positions as to how political and economic systems are likely to change in relation to control. A Luddite analysis (Webster and Robins 1986) foresees the centralization of the tools of control and a widening gap between the advantaged and disadvantaged. Other analyses (for example, Cherry 1985) posit the decentralization of control of information and subsequent decentralization of power.

Access to control can imply control over who gains access to what information to whose advantage (Braman 1989). In the workplace, control over information flows is an ongoing concern, including who has access to what types of information, through work monitoring, whether overt or not (Gandy 1989; Garson 1988; U.S. Congress 1987). This control is sometimes directly useful to, and controlled by, the user. The work environment and its arrangement also leaves the individual exposed to view by others and, at the same time, provides to access to observe the environment and activities within it (Archea 1977) as well as to obtain and contribute to the public good of collective knowledge (Spender 1998). Some are concerned that monitored information could lead to the exclusion of certain individuals or classes of individuals from potential employment (Doctor 1992; Gandy 1993).

Corporations often go to great lengths to gain advantage in a particular market by gathering and protecting information about the potential buyers of their products, and by gathering information about competing corporations and protecting against such information's becoming available to the competition. When the institution is in the business of creating information, such as the entertainment or publishing businesses, then access to control can mean control of culture (H. I. Schiller 1981; 1989) and of what information is available for others. As the number of such institutions grows smaller with takeovers and consolidations, fewer and fewer sources of information or perspectives on any particular issue may be available (Bagdikian 1990; H. I. Schiller 1989). Media systems thereby contribute to building consensus in support of dominant or hegemonic constructs (Hall 1982), or, by determining what to cover on the nightly news, they set the agenda of interest among viewers (Protess and McCombs 1991).

In political terms, access to control can also mean access to influencing policy with regard to information. Braman (1989) has documented that legal decisions are likely to favor institutions over the individual. In social services, the provider may intentionally or unconsciously attempt to maintain control over the interview process, criteria for acceptance, and provision of information, depending on the social status and approach of the help seeker (Agada 1999; Harris and Dewdney 1994). Gandy (1993) argues that access to multiple data sources can lead to the creation of new data sets that can be applied to control future access to insurance or employment, for example. In gathering information about the individual that would not otherwise be available, and of which the individual may not have knowledge, access to information by institutions that gives them control over individuals compounds what is already an imbalanced relationship.

National regulations, laws, and philosophies impose different political constraints on access to information and communication. For example, Borgman (2000, 239) reports that Kedzie (1997) found a strong relationship between Internet diffusion and indicators of democracy within different countries. But she concludes, after noting the centralized control of traditional media as well as computer networks in various countries, that "the availability of a global information infrastructure does not guarantee freedom of speech or access to information" (240). She also notes that individuals' dependence on institutions (that control, authorize, and monitor user privileges, identity, and accounts, content, networks, specific resources, and media), whether national or corporate, is increasing rather than decreasing.

**Access to Goods, Commodities**

Access to information can be understood to imply access to economic or social goods or commodities. From this perspective, access can carry with it costs, benefits, and value (Bates 1988; Chatman 1991; Culnan 1984; Hart and Rice 1991; McCain 1988). According to Mulgan (1991), control is never acquired without cost. In fact, Bates (1993) argues that social, economic, and political costs serve to control or constrain access to information.

Information behaves uniquely compared with other commodities in the marketplace. For example, the general principles of supply and demand as they relate to cost or value do not hold when applied to information. The value of information remains unknown until it is "consumed" (Arrow 1979). Information goods violate characteristics necessary to achieve social efficiency in that ownership cannot be enforced, and public good externalities stem from characteristics unique to information use, in particular, lack of rivalry (information is not necessarily depleted for some as it is used by others) and lack of exclusivity (additional consumers can be served at potentially zero cost) in consumption (Hall 1981). Although copyright laws provide legal avenues for corporations to control and benefit from their information products, information remains infinitely reproducible (Bates 1988). However, while the value of information typically depreciates as it becomes obsolete (Hall 1981), it does not necessarily depreciate over time: consider the rise in the social acceptance and value of Mozart's music after his death.

Access to information can influence or redistribute income, wealth, or status. Because of its potential as a public good, information production is frequently subsidized by the government, such as through libraries, especially government depository libraries, and schools. However, more such research has been contracted to private agencies, curtailing free public access because many libraries have not been able to afford the purchase price now imposed as a result of privatization (Schiller and Schiller 1988). However, privatization of information production can also be viewed as having led to new markets for the information industry.

Yet a move toward privatization of information sources may limit consideration of ancillary social value, the additional value to society of use of information, in assessing value overall (Bates 1988). Ordinarily in the marketplace, those commodities that have the greatest likelihood of being consumed are those that are produced, so "Markets for information goods which are both costly and infrequently purchased ... will suffer the greatest distortion from asymmetrical information" (Hall 1981, 157). Those with limited resources stand to gain more from access to information in terms of potential economic, social, and political improvement than do others who start from a position of greater advantage (Gandy 1988). Yet because they are also less likely to possess resources such as awareness of sources of information or the ability to express their needs clearly, they are less likely to gain access. As Chatman (1991) points out, the reasons for this are complex but include factors such as ability to anticipate benefits, which is partially reliant on a belief that access to information truly of value to the life of the individual is likely.

Other potential costs of seeking or gaining access to information include the time spent weighing the costs and potential benefits of a search, the time it takes to carry out the process, or the uncertainty or discomfort inherent in carrying out an unfamiliar process. Other potential costs fall in the category of risk: risk of losing time, money, or face. A countervailing cost to all the above is the potential cost, both explicit and implicit, to the individual or organization incurred in doing without access to needed information. Implicit cost is likely when one remains unaware of information that would carry value in a given situation. Consideration of costs implies also resources, such as motivation, familiarity, patience, procedural knowledge, time, or awareness of the range of sources available or of one's right to access. In addition, one must operate in a social environment that supports effective access to and use of information, to benefit from the access (Doctor 1991).

### Access to (Knowledge of and Ability to Exercise) Rights

Implicit in the idea of access to information is that it leads an informed citizenry to enjoy or exercise certain rights, such as the right of participation in the political process, as well as even supposedly inalienable rights. However, not everyone does know about, or is able to enjoy, their rights. Thus access to knowledge about, or access to the ability to exercise, one's rights, is a common (though usually implicit) theme across the literatures.

In some instances those rights are supposedly accessible through various services, including government services (Gandy 1988). However, the range of rights is not always known, and necessary information about locations and procedures is often difficult to obtain if access is not common among members of one's social network (Chatman 1991). Sometimes, access is most effectively gained through interactions outside one's network, with an individual or entity with whom/which one has weak (infrequent or indirect) ties (Granovetter 1973). Particularly with regard to access to rights through political channels, access includes the right of advocacy, interpretation, or debate. Those without privileged access are left to struggle for access to even being able to raise questions or issues of concern in their lives (Hall 1982).

Another right of common concern across the literatures is the right to privacy. Of equal consequence, and occasionally in conflict with privacy rights, are security or ownership rights. This tension can be illustrated in considerations of caller ID. Is the caller's right to security from revealing his telephone number more important than the privacy rights of the call's recipient, who may use the device to avoid intrusion by telephone marketers? These issues are potentially compounded when considered in the context of a huge network like the Internet, which facilitates the right to interconnect. Privacy rights can also be thought of as the right not to interconnect.

## Facets of the Information-Seeking Process

Directly or indirectly, all the literatures considered here have in common a concern with the information-seeking process. Traditionally, the information-seeking process includes a problem or question (situation) and an attempt to find information to address the problem or question (strategies), often assuming an intentional, rational, directed search for information on the part of an individual or organization. According to Marchionini (1995), information seeking depends on interactions among the seeker (who has mental models about the domains and the system), setting, task (a manifestation of problem/need), knowledge domains, system, and outcomes (feedback from the system, which typically alters the seeker's knowledge and influences the conceptualization of the problem, task, and subsequent search activities). In his model, the information-seeking process is a mix of systematic and opportunistic behaviors, involving the following steps (his figure 3.3, 50): (1) recognize/accept, (2) define problem, (3) select source, (4) formulate query, (5) execute query, (6) examine results, (7) extract information, (8) reflect/stop—all with many transitions and feedback loops, some occurring in parallel.

Because considerations of access to information in some literatures focus on what occurs prior to a search (context) and what occurs as a result of a search (outcomes), the traditional range of the information-seeking process is extended in this discussion to include four facets (see table 3.3): (1) the context or background in which the need for information arises, (2) the problem or situation that is to be addressed, (3) the strategies applied in seeking access, and (4) the use of information or formulation of a new situation that occurs in the outcomes facet. Because these facets are not necessarily sequential and may be iterative, we avoid the more familiar term, *phases*.

It appears rare for a research literature to consider the information-seeking process in its entirety, despite a few exceptions (Borgman 1999; Dervin 1992; Sonnenwald 1995). In those literatures that explicitly address the information-seeking process, the focus seems to fall primarily on the strategies facet, with some attention to situation and occasional treatment of the context in which access to information is sought or of outcomes (the latter two generally being treated more implicitly than explicitly).

## Context Facet

The context of access can be understood as the larger picture in which the potential user operates, an information system is developed and operates, and potential information may become available. Context includes all the precursors to information seeking, such as the social, political, economic, educational, and experiential environment of the individual (Borgman 2000; Johnson 1996; Rice 1987; Wilson 1997), including the user's demographic situation, organization, and the social, intellectual, and cultural background (Allen 1996). From other perspectives, it also includes the economic, political, and cultural context in which an information system is owned, developed, and operated; and the potential information itself in whatever abstract or concrete stage it or its potential exists. The setting includes physical constraints, lighting, time, cost, number, and type of participants possible, permissions to access or change content or process, social and communication relations among participants, self-confidence and familiarity with the situation, and organizational role (Marchionini 1995, 47).

Information is typically highly time-dependent: "Information believed to be correct at the time may well be regarded as misinformation at some later time—or vice versa" (Buckland 1991b, 111). The context of time includes the opportunity cost of

**Table 3.3**
Facets of the Information-Seeking Process

| Facet | Description | Examples |
|---|---|---|
| Context | The larger picture in which the potential user operates<br>The larger picture in which the information system is developed and operates, and potential information exists | Precursors to information seeking<br>Social, political, economic, experiential context of individual<br>Economic, political, cultural context of development, ownership |
| Situation | The particular set of circumstances from which a need for information arises<br>Awareness (however vague) of a need for information | Gap, visceral need, discomfort, anomalous state of knowledge, information need, conscious need<br>Experience and standing with particular set of circumstances: relative status, perspective, cognitive, affective, physical resources<br>Range of system choices |
| Strategies | The dynamic process of addressing the situation, both planned and serendipitous<br>Formalized need, plan of action, query statement, problem statement<br>Interaction with system<br>Informal evaluation<br>Iterations | Focusing, clarifying, expanding, redirecting of understanding of need for information<br>Bridges, barriers, blocks, helps encountered on way to address situation<br>Learning, refining, reconfiguring, reiteration<br>Resources: knowledge of range of system choices, knowledge of costs/benefits of pursuing search |
| Outcomes | Retrieval and use of information<br>Evaluation<br>Possibility of new situation | Access to the value or benefit of using information<br>Broader understanding of evaluation requires accounting for use, and relevance to both context and situation |

spending time in a particular way, information's becoming outdated, consequences of not obtaining information at the appropriate time, poor feedback between system and user because of slow response time, preventing subsequent users from accessing information, associated costs such as travel and frustration, and switching to a faster but less reliable system (Buckland 1991b; van House 1983).

Groups exist within the social and value structures of organizations, so organizational influences determine how groups behave in given situation, how groups perceive situations, and what sets of alternative actions are understood to be available or accessible. (People are always embedded in social contexts, which makes distinguishing between individual and social influences on information-seeking behavior difficult.) Thus, one's organizational situation (whether management, occupational groups, other work groups) can constrain the accessibility one has to various information-seeking behaviors (Allen 1996). There are many new options for sources of organizational information in a rapidly changing environment of immediate competition and information growth (Christensen and Bailey 1997). In addition to accounting for the background and experience the user brings to a search, the context facet of the information-seeking process also accounts for factors of particular concern in the mass communication literature, namely, creation and production of information distributed via mass media channels or diffused (Rogers 1983) through a wide range of channels of communication.

Borgman (2000) identifies five developing contexts of a global information infrastructure. Each of these implicitly involves issues of accessing information and communication: (1) from metadata to data (providing access to multimedia full content as well as metadata); (2) from independent to linked systems (distributed environments, institutions, resources, requiring interoperability, data exchange, common formats and terminologies); (3) from searching to navigation (using multimedia features and networked environments, supporting browsing); (4) from individual to group processes (information creation and use, because they are highly socially situated and communicative, involve groups of users in various forms of collaboration, including virtual teams working across interdependent tasks—Borgman 2000, 161; Kraut and Galegher 1990; Majchrzak et al. 1999); and (5) from local systems to global systems (requiring language translation or some kinds of standardized or multilingual indexing, widely varying capabilities at users' access sites around the world, more universal character sets such as the 16-bit unicode).

### Situation Facet

Situation refers to the particular set of circumstances from which a need for information arises, along with the awareness, however unclear, that information may be useful in addressing the situation. The focus of most of the literature regarding the situation facet is that of the user or information seeker engaged in an intentional, directed search for information, but recent work relaxes the assumption of full awareness and intentionality. Included here are concepts expressed in the literature as a gap (Dervin 1983), visceral need and conscious need (Taylor 1968), problematic situation (Wersig 1979), anomalous state of knowledge (Belkin 1980), information field (Johnson 1996), discomfort, or information need. These terms all refer to the awareness or inkling that something in a process of sense making or problem solving or supporting an argument needs to be addressed, explained, challenged, supported, or expanded. It refers also to the awareness that information is required to take care of the something. The experience and standing of an information seeker in regard to the particular set of circumstances are part of this facet.

MacMullin and Taylor (1984) propose that information needs are a result of interactions among 11 continuous problem dimensions: (1) design/discovery, (2) well-structured/ill-structured, (3) simple/complex, (4) goals specific/ambiguous, (5) initial state understood/not understood, (6) assumptions agreed upon/not agreed upon, (7) assumption explicit/implicit, (8) pattern familiar/new, (9) risk great/not great, (10) empirical analysis applicable/not applicable, and (11) imposition internal/external. Taylor (1986) identified six general criteria that influence user selection of information: "ease of use, noise reduction, quality, adaptability, time savings, and cost savings" (Choo 1995, 39).

In a given situation, an information seeker may have varying expertise in the subject area; knowledge of the range of systems available to address the situation; experience with the operation of appropriate systems; resources to overcome potential economic, political, physical, and time constraints; and status to gain access easily. For example, a college librarian seeking information on an educational matter covered extensively in literature published in journals carried by the library where he works, finds himself with adequate background and experience to gain access easily. The same librarian, however, facing a different situation, such as how to find adequate medical treatment for his child recently diagnosed with a neurological difficulty, may find himself a novice with little or no experience.

Some information needs arise from failures of perception, either individual or collective. If they are individual, they can arise from inadequate knowledge structures, inappropriate or ambiguous social influences, or a combination of the two. If collective, they can arise from inadequate knowledge structures, inadequate group communication processes, inappropriate or ambiguous social and organizational influences, or combinations of the three (Allen 1996, ch. 4). Other information needs arise from a need to associate alternative decisions with potential outcomes.

These, too, can be individual or collective. If individual, the needs associated with alternative selection and evaluation are driven by inadequate knowledge structures, inadequate or conflicting social signals, or both. If collective, they are driven by inadequate knowledge structures, inappropriate or inadequate group processes, conflicting organizational values, or combinations of the three.

**Strategies Facet**

The strategies facet represents the dynamic process of addressing the situation and includes both planned and unplanned actions, directions, interactions, or discoveries. Although the entire process is potentially iterative, this is the stage most likely to be repeated, evaluated, revised, redefined, retried, adapted, or replayed. This is the facet in which the user focuses, clarifies, expands, reconfigures, or redefines her understanding of the situation, what is needed to address the situation, and how to go about addressing the situation. Psychological and cognitive styles may play a role here. For example, Julien (1999) found three primary styles among adolescents seeking career information: (1) rational (using multiple sources, basing actions on prior information), (2) intuitive (little purposive seeking, relating decision to enjoyment), and (3) dependent (passive, no sense of personal responsibility). (Part II of this book identifies ten patterns of browsing that may be considered strategies.) Agada (1999) and Chatman (1991) note that the strategies used by the urban poor were related mostly to short-term needs and lack of trust in outsiders. The dynamic nature of information seeking in general, and this facet of the process in particular, may well lead to adaptation or correction of the anomalous state of knowledge as the potential user encounters bridges, barriers, blocks, or helps (Dervin 1983) along the way. The user moves toward developing a formalized need (Taylor 1968), a plan of action, a query statement, or a problem statement, in short a more structured representation of the situation and what is required to address it.

On the other hand, the underlying strategy may seem highly irrational or may be largely situational. Decisions are often made without reference to predetermined criteria, and once data elements are defined, others may be added while few are removed (Solomon 1997a). That is, information sought and used is *retroactively* associated with decisions—it "accretes." The act of information seeking itself (not even actual information) often serves to justify decisions already made rather than to provide a basis for decision making (Feldman and March 1981; Solomon 1997a). Solomon (1997c) concludes that "sense making involves movement through time and space until a point of satisfaction is reached, time runs out, or something else diverts attention" (1135)—satisfying, not optimizing; expanding or contracting to fit time or resource limits; brushed aside by more pressing issues; avoiding sharing because it would violate previous commitments or confidences, or be in conflict with one's own self-interest, or lead to loss of credit or sounding foolish—resulting in the "self-construction of information poverty" (1136). "Sources of information are not so much selected as defined as appropriate organizationally for a constellation of reasons related to Weick's properties of organizational sense making" (Solomon 1997b, 1112).

Often, for example, informal communication is valued much more than formal written sources because it is perceived as more current, can be questioned, can be evaluated on the basis of associated nonverbal cues, may be associated with sources of power, and can provide forums for extracting and enacting cues, evaluating plausibility and social impacts, and creating group identities. So, one's reference group and recent consequences play a large part in organizational information sharing.

For example, in Solomon's study (1997a, 1105–1106), projects that had not been priority-ranked were quickly added, "followed by laborious information gathering and processing, and then attempted use, which identified inconsistencies, inaccuracies, and missing information. The repeated jump to an answer without analysis of the question led to costly attempts to make sense when the answer and the question did not satisfactorily match." Thus, Solomon concludes that information systems can both limit and focus future action, especially when information seeking and collection is not grounded in an understanding of the potential biases of past decisions.

It is in this strategies facet that the information seeker is likely to interact with the information system, whether that system is a college admissions office, a restaurant, an automated teller machine, a library, an interoffice message system, or an online database. That very interaction may require the user to evaluate his mental model of the system and thereby change or adjust the expectations he holds for that interaction. In the course of negotiating strategies, the user may learn something new or encounter new data that raise new questions (Kuhlthau 1985), reevaluate the search or the interaction, or redefine the situation and start over again in formulating strategies (Johnson and Rice 1987).

Part of the evaluation process of the strategies facet includes weighing the costs and benefits of pursuing the search. This can be influenced by resources available, such as motivation, time, convenience, tolerance for uncertainty, or delayed gratification, or a worldview that sees the potential for addressing the situation as more or less likely. Such informal evaluation of the potential risks and value is facilitated if the user already has a clear understanding of the problem situation and an awareness of the range of system choices available to address the situation. A more formal evaluation is not possible until access is gained and the information is used and evaluated.

**Outcomes Facet**

Outcomes include retrieval and actual use or consumption of information as well as evaluation and possible redefinition and reiteration of the process. The outcomes facet of the information-seeking process, though implied in discussions of access to the value or benefit of using information, is rarely examined explicitly in research on information seeking, except for extensive focus on precision, recall, relevance, and satisfaction. Several information scientists and communication researchers (Belkin and Vickery 1985; Dervin and Nilan 1986; Tague and Schultz 1989) have called for including outcomes in evaluating information retrieval services but have also pointed out practical difficulties in attempting to do so. In the literature on mass media, however, some studies do explicitly examine how mediated communication (and, by implication, information) is used in everyday life (Kubey and Csikszentmihalyi 1990; Radway 1984) or how it is adopted, adapted, and reinvented (Johnson and Rice 1983; 1987; Rice and Rogers 1980; Rogers 1983).

Outcomes include both product and process. The product (document, feedback, citation) may play a secondary role as an object evaluated to assess the success of the system. Process outcomes may be the affective experience of conducting the search, or changes in the user's problem definition or expectations, such as what one can do in the process of searching, such as realizing one now has the ability to sort lists, produce high-quality output, find associations among otherwise disparate information, and manipulate the system interfaces (Marchionini 1995, 15). Constraints on the potential consequences of new electronic environments for information seeking range from physical, economic, and technical to intellectual property, copyright, the legal authority of different representations (both in terms of copies and digital alterations as well as the essence of a document that can be hyperlinked in different ways by different users), and whether information is viewed as a commodity/resource or as a right (Marchionini 1995).

The organizational communication field probably provides the most pervasive coverage of outcomes. For example, information seeking is associated with satisfaction, performance, achievement, social integration, socialization, reduced message distortion, and commitment (Glauser 1984; Morrison 1993a; 1993b). Alternatively, insufficient access to organizational information is associated with loss of control, increased collusion between coalitions, imbalances in information distribution, power from controlling information, information hoarding, decreased accountability, and multiple demands on attention (Johnson 1996). As attention directed toward some information takes away from attention directed elsewhere, information distribution can have multiple consequences throughout the organization (Smithson 1989). Information systems and institutions may have better or worse access to feedback about service provision, and what they do have access to may or may not correspond with, and may or may not provide the same kinds of feedback as, users' experiences. For example, lowered levels of accessibility to books may decrease user demand, thus ironically increasing a library's sustainability (Buckland 1991b, ch. 13).

Most literatures assume that decreasing ignorance is necessarily a desired as well as likely benefit of access to information. However, information seeking may not always reduce ignorance. It can increase ignorance by widening the scope of awareness about what is known socially but not personally (Kerwin 1993), and ignorance may be intentionally fostered to reduce information-processing demands or to manipulate actors (Johnson 1996; Singer 1980). Further, ignorance may have multiple benefits, such as simplifying environmental enactment, decision justification, and wider commitment through flexible interpretation of ambiguity (Eisenberg 1984; Kellerman and Reynolds 1990; March 1994; Smithson 1989; Weick 1979). As Johnson (1996, 77) summarizes, additional information may increase uncertainty by identifying more alternatives; foster groupthink (Janis 1971); be susceptible to personal biases toward confirming, simplifying, and symbolizing rationality (Feldman and March 1981); delay or foreclose the decision process (Saunders and Jones 1990; Swinehart 1968); reinforce centrally held beliefs in threat or crisis situations (Staw, Sandelands, and Dutton 1981); be constrained by available resources, leading to satisficing (Hickson 1987; March 1994); be used to emphasize problem solving rather than situation assessment and assumptions (Nutt 1984); and increase confidence even while reducing performance because of overload (O'Reilly 1980).

Often providing free systems and materials implies improved access. However, it can also mean more difficult access to the evaluation of authoritativeness, integrity of source, and accuracy. This is because commercial institutions not only have the staff and expertise to assess and enforce these attributes but also depend on achieving these criteria in order to meet their customers' requirements and thus obtain future business (Borgman 2000, 196). In free systems, the costs of assessing the materials are borne by the user, who has no economies of scale in creating or finding these metadata.

Including outcomes in evaluating the information-seeking interaction accounts for relevance to both the situation and the context of the user. If, indeed, the value

**Table 3.4**
Potential Interactions of Mediation with Access

| Potential | Examples with System | Examples with User |
|---|---|---|
| Intensifying | Acceleration, embedding of difficulties (crazy systems)<br>Increase in surveillance potential<br>Increase in capability to match data from different sources<br>Increase interactive capabilities | Potential for those with access to gain further advantage, and those without, further disadvantage<br>Compounding of power balances/imbalances (panoptic potential)<br>Potential for greater access |
| Compensating | Facilitates convenience in system of otherwise limited availability (time, distance, scheduling)<br>Facilitates access when system design is limited (e.g., interface, indexing, organization) | Facilitates boundary spanning for those otherwise limited in space, time, mobility, flexibility<br>Facilitates ease of use when procedural or cognitive knowledge, or experience are limited<br>Facilitates interaction across interpersonal and structural bounds |

of information cannot be known until it is used, then it is necessary to account for outcomes or use in the evaluation of the information-seeking and retrieval process in order to account for the entire process, including access to value. Outcomes may include learning, focusing, reinventing, or redirecting the situation, thus generating a new search, or they may influence strategies and serve as the catalyst for adaptation and further iterations of the strategies facet. Outcomes tie the information-seeking process together, closing the loop among the facets and potentially being influenced by, and influencing, the context, situation, or strategies facet.

## Mediation and Technology

Technology and mediation arise frequently as issues or concerns in the literature on access to information. Mediation occurs when our natural individual abilities to create, transmit, receive, and process visual, auditory, olfactory, gustatory, or tactile messages are extended, expanded, or enhanced technologically by media, or interpersonally by human intermediaries (Ruben 1993, 227). Analysis of the literature indicates that mediation has the potential for two primary influences or constraints on access to information: it can intensify or compensate. Table 3.4 summarizes the two primary potential interactions of mediation with access, and includes examples of intensifying and compensating potential for both the information system and a user seeking access.

**Potential Interactions Between Mediation and Technology**

Lievrouw (1994) argues that technology establishes an "information environment" with regard to access to information. The more traditional communication technologies (such as the mass media), because of a number of factors including economies of scale, tend to operate in an "informing information environment." This means that information is disseminated as messages from a limited number of sources to multiple receivers (the familiar broadcast/mass media). Information in this environment is mediated not only by technology (television, newspapers, radio, or books, for example) but also by human gatekeepers such as producers, journalists, announcers, columnists, librarians, or museum curators. Newer point-to-point communication technologies tend to be less expensive than traditional mass communication systems to operate, are more likely to be used by individuals to interact with other individuals or small groups, and are somewhat less likely to require human intermediaries (although bulletin boards are mediated by sysops, mailing lists by list owners, and so on). These technologies, frequently relying on a personal computer equipped with a modem and communication software, are more conducive to an "interactive" information environment (Culnan and Markus 1987; Lievrouw 1994; Sproull and Kiesler 1991; Zuboff 1988), in which the information seeker is frequently a participant in the interactive process of communicating with others on a network, bulletin board, mailing list, users' group, or e-mail system.

**Intensifying Potential**

The intensifying potential of mediation operates when selected characteristics of the user or the system are intensified with use of the mediation. For example, McGee and Prusak (1993) note that the potential of organizational information systems to decrease centralization through broader access to information communication might also reduce an organization's overall focus on strategic issues, as local tactical and operational issues are more salient to local units with increased control. Singer (1980) points out the potential for technology to accelerate or embed difficulties of an information system. Consider, for example, a comment such as, "No, we can't accommodate your request—the computer isn't set up that way"; one (technological) system is intensified over another (social) system.

In the context of the workplace, technology has the potential to intensify surveillance capabilities (Gandy 1993; Marx and Sherizen 1986; Zuboff 1988). The panoptic potential (Botan and McCreadie 1993) of communication and information technologies increases both the likelihood that surveillance will be carried out and the capability for matching of data from different sources (such as insurance records and employment histories) to produce a new set of data that would not otherwise exist (Gandy 1993), leading to the exclusion of classes of individuals or groups from eligibility to participate in the workplace or in society.

The intensifying potential may also be positive. For example, technologies can increase the possibilities for access to information (Frenkel 1989), as was the case with the advent of the printing press or the telephone or, more recently, with the public availability of community online systems such as the PEN (Public Electronic Network) project in Santa Monica (Rogers, Collins-Jarvis, and Schmitz 1994). Through PEN, all citizens, including Santa Monica's significant homeless population, can gain access to a wide range of opportunities for information, communication, advocacy, and the potential for participation in the political process. If we return to the example of matching data, other possible outcomes of new sets of data are the ability to provide crucial services or avoid dangerous interactions among medical treatments. In the workplace, feedback from information systems can be used to "informate" activities to the benefit of workers and customers (Zuboff 1988).

Whether the intensifying of a particular mediation is positive or negative depends on the perspective from which it is considered. For example, H. I. Schiller (1989) argues that technologies facilitate corporate control of culture. From the perspective of those with concerns for the rights of individuals, this may seem to indicate a danger. On the other hand, from the corporate perspective, this may be in keeping with a long-range marketing plan to improve service to customers and may, indeed, appear very desirable.

**Compensating Potential**

Mediation and technology are often viewed as compensating for potential limitations or barriers to access, spanning boundaries of time or space, or overcoming physical, social, cognitive, or other constraints on access to information and communication.

Technologies can bring information to those unable to travel because of physical limitations or limitations imposed through responsibilities such as childcare or a work schedule that is incompatible with hours of operation of a particular information system. It is not long ago that one had to arrange to visit a financial institution during banking hours in order to carry out simple transactions such as the depositing or cashing of checks. Now, because of the spread of ATM machines, although safety concerns may present a barrier, hours of operation no longer limit when such transactions can be carried out, even when the user is thousands of miles away from the home institution.

Similarly, mediation can compensate for limitations in procedural knowledge of the user or for a system design that is less than transparent. Consider a typical visit to a library. Depending on the need and experience of the user, access to the information sought may require as little mediation as a few minutes with a technological interface (online catalog) and a glance at a conveniently located map of the building to find the location of an information source. It might be more complex, requiring a lengthy interview with the reference librarian, an extended search of several online databases with the librarian acting as intermediary, then again, with guidance from the librarian, directions to locating information sources available in the building, and additional guidance in filling out requests for interlibrary loans. Follow-up may be required for those items that are supposed to be on the shelf but are not, and for ideas on how to track down needed sources that are on loan. In other words, specific mediations can compensate for some limitations, but not for others.

Mediation and technology can compensate also for interpersonal or structural barriers to access to information. For example, in computer-mediated communication, individuals may overcome interpersonal barriers such as shyness to interact with others when they would be far less likely to do so face-to-face (Rice and Love 1987). Think of the increased access for those with limited hearing brought about with the offering of telecommunications for the deaf and disabled (TDD).

In an organizational context, upward communication is far more likely through computer-mediated communication than in traditional face-to-face contexts. From the perspective of the mailroom clerk, this may appear desirable. At last he has a means to convey that brilliant idea to the head of the corporation. From the perspective of the CEO, however, who is deluged with hundreds of e-mail messages daily, she may long for the days when a closed door and a good secretary assured some quiet work time, and hierarchical status helped to filter information.

### Influences and Constraints on Access

Factors such as survival, identity, history, relations with the environment, and extraction of cues "structure and support what, where, when, why, and how information behaviors are employed in sense making" (Solomon 1997b, 1109). For several decades researchers have been aware that the quantity or quality of information available from a system is frequently less important to users than is the degree of ease with which they gain access to the information (Taylor 1968). Most studies interested in access, such as to information systems, have focused primarily on physical access or access to other individuals (Culnan 1983; 1984; 1985; Gerstberger and Allen 1968; Hart and Rice 1991; Hiltz and Johnson 1989; Rice and Shook 1988). Buckland's summary of motivations for becoming informed includes (1) personal values and motivations, (2) information needed for various situations (professional, physical, social), and (3) cultural influences and social pressures. Buckland couches the allocation, provision, and use of information systems in cognitive, economic, political, and managerial contexts (see, for example, his figure 15.4, 161). Providers thus have their own values and motivations—distinct from users'—depending on aspects such as commercial/free, sponsorships, policy, and political influence.

In general, the research literatures discuss six categories of influences and constraints on access to information: physical, cognitive, affective, economic, social, and political (Rice 1987), summarized in table 3.5.

Two broad, integrative concepts reflect this increasing awareness of the multidimensionality of influences and constraints. The concept of an "information use environment" (Taylor 1991) addresses the contexts in which specific groups of individuals operate and how these contexts influence information behavior and choices. Information behavior includes the flow, use, and perception of information within a group. An information use environment is characterized by (1) groups of people, (2) their organizational and environmental settings, (3) the types of problems and possible resolutions they are faced with, and (4) their typical handling of information in problem-solving activities (Katzer and Fletcher 1992; Taylor 1991). A related concept is the "personal information infrastructure," one's complex of knowledge, mental models for systems and knowledge domains, specific and general cognitive skills (including self-reflection and monitoring), prior experience with content domains and systems (including computer systems, books, and other people), attitudes toward information and knowledge seeking and acquisition, and resources that influence how we seek and use information (Marchionini 1995, 11). Cognitive factors include general intelligence, and special knowledge and skills relating to the domains, system/medium, and the information-seeking process itself (such as how knowledge is organized, experience with types of reasoning, the task requirements, professional norms and strategies, available and appropriate strategies and resources) (Marchionini 1995, ch. 4). Attitudes include "motivation, confidence, tenacity, tolerance for ambiguity and uncertainty, curiosity, and preferences for social interaction and media" (61).

**Physical Influences/Constraints**

**Geography and Demographics** Physical access to information is described in several different ways. Some assume that those who live in rural areas find access to information more difficult than those in urban areas (Hudson 1988), while others dispute this (Larose and Mettler 1989). It is commonly agreed, however, that the potential of telecommunications and telecommuting can serve to ease some of the geographic and demographic limitations to access to information, and can add to flexibility in transcending geographic constraints to access in the context of employment (Kraut 1989) and beyond.

**Environment and Ergonomics** The environment can be thought of as part of the information flow network (Archea 1977). The physical arrangement of the environment regulates distribution of and access to information, particularly with regard to the workplace or other environments in which more than one individual functions. The very way in which information is organized can influence access (Budd 1987), as discussed in part II of this book. Within the environment, the orientation of furniture, partitions, sources of light, and so on, determine what is visually or audibly accessible and what is hidden. In this regard, environment accounts principally for information that is most likely to be accessible through observation of or interaction with others. The same considerations apply to the environment when relying on senses other than sight. If the environment is very noisy, and the primary source of information is one that requires listening, access is hampered; alternatively, if it is very quiet, one has easier access to one's own or others' spoken interactions (whether directly or indirectly).

**Space** Space can serve physically to influence or constrain access to information along dimensions of distance and proximity, openness and security, and clarity or obstruction. Distance and proximity arise as physical influences or constraints on access to and interpretation of information (Archea 1977; Davis 1984; Reinsch and Beswick 1990; Rice and Aydin 1991). In general, that which is closer in space, especially if it is visible, is more likely to be accessible (Rice 1988) and, in particular, proximity to a system tends to increase likelihood of its use (Hiltz and Johnson

**Table 3.5**
Influences/Constraints on Access to Information

| Influence/ Constraint | Examples/Components | Implications |
|---|---|---|
| Physical | Geography, demographics<br>Environment: arrangement, orientation<br>Space: distance/proximity, open/secure, clear/obstructed<br>Display: medium, format, information-processing capabilities | Can lead to perceived availability or convenience, likelihood of system use<br>Influenced by physical abilities, limitations, geographical flexibility, complex power relations |
| Cognitive | Understanding: identifying need<br>Awareness: of means of addressing, of rights, entitlements, procedures<br>Literacy: verbal, quantitative, technical<br>Facility/skill: system, command language, protocol<br>Matching of user and system: content and language, mental model and expectations, learning style, organization of information | Requires matching between user and system, between user and representation of information<br>Leads to questioning: notion of query statement as valid representation of need for information, notion of relevance<br>Influenced by educational, biological, social background/experience |
| Affective | Attitude toward information seeking, computing, interacting<br>Confidence/fear/trust<br>Comfort/discomfort<br>Motivation level | Influenced by perceived convenience, dependability, availability<br>Influenced by relative status, perceived control over situation, experience, resources, familiarity |
| Economic | Benefits: profitability, affluence, solutions, public good externalities, ancillary social value<br>Costs: price, money, time, inconvenience, discomfort, going without, risk (loss of money, time, face)<br>Value, potential for value added: not known until information is used | Can lead to control of information: content, privacy, security concerns<br>Influences compounding effect, reinforcing link between socioeconomic class and informational class<br>Influenced by market forces, economies of scale, class membership, educational and social background, policy |
| Social | Cultural norms: privilege, struggle<br>Class membership and background<br>Social networks, electronic networks<br>Education: learning, skill level, competence<br>Competence: communication and technology<br>Experience: expert/novice, familiarity with system, situation | Influences type of information to which one has access, linking socioeconomic and informational class<br>Compounding effect influences access to privilege/lack over time<br>Influences whether individual is able to use access to information effectively |

**Table 3.5** (continued)

| Influence/ Constraint | Examples/Components | Implications |
|---|---|---|
| Political | Power, including knowledge, with special implications in democracy<br>Control: of information flow, of individuals, of public debate, of policy<br>Equity, participation: ability to understand and be understood | Influences individual's ability to exercise political rights and power<br>Influenced by communication competence, resources, social environment, existence of a right, and awareness of that right |

1989). However, it cannot be assumed that physical proximity and information access necessarily follow one another (Culnan 1984). Other factors may come in to play, such as timing, ease of use, and experience.

Whether a space is open or closed can influence access to information. Closed can also be thought of as secure. Therefore, another way to think about this is to consider whether information is publicly available or available only with access to a secured or locked area or system. If the latter, the user will likely need resources, such as security clearance, a key, or a password in order to gain access. In an open area, one might feel uncomfortable or embarrassed, or suffer performance anxiety, thus reducing perceived access. The same open area might influence another user differently, however, leading to ease in locating appropriate sources of assistance and thereby increasing perceived access.

A broader conceptualization of space considers organizational structure—its physical structure, its positional and formal structure, its informal relations within and across organizational boundaries, and the structuring of meaning through symbols and jargon (Rice and Gattiker 2000)—as a major influence and constraint on access to information. Johnson (1996), as do others, argues that organizations must manage the inherent dilemma of making information accessible while also limiting, filtering, and delegating its creation and diffusion. Thus, upward and downward flow of information is heavily influenced by superior-subordinate relations (including openness and trust) (Jablin 1985). Internal organizational structures serve both to facilitate and to constrain access (Kanter 1983; O'Reilly 1978), though usually indirectly, unintentionally, and without full knowledge of the consequences. Examples of such structuring include unit integration, specialized units, lateral relations, teams, information systems, mission and vision, outsourcing, slack resources, and self-contained tasks (Galbraith 1973; 1974; Johnson and Rice 1987). Macrolevel organizational structures, such as hierarchies, networks, and markets, also heavily influence access to information, often as an intentional internal or competitive strategy (Johnson 1996). Indeed, theories of organizational and market structure are fundamentally about the relative costs (such as transaction costs) of access to information within an organization compared to those of the market (Bradach and Eccles 1989; Nohria and Eccles 1992; Powell 1990).

The features and contents of a system and the needs or capabilities of the user must match in order for one to gain access to information (Culnan 1985). Of course, obstructions can arise in multiple forms, not all of them physical. The physical capabilities of the user, however, can influence what is accessible. For example, much information for those in wheelchairs is physically obstructed. On the other hand, if the same information can be provided through mediation, such as over the telephone, or uploaded to a computer network to which the same user has access, or delivered through an intermediary, an alternative, clear path is accessible.

**Display** Along somewhat the same lines, the form in which information is displayed (heavily determined by the interface) must also match the needs of the potential user for access to occur. Browsing for information, for example, requires that the potential sources of information be on display in some manner (visual, aural, tactile, olfactory) for scanning or consideration by the potential user (see part II). Similarly, the medium must match the physical abilities of the user; print is an inappropriate physical display of the information for blind users. In that case, a human or computer reader, or an audiotape, might provide adequate access to the same information. Alternatively, what is displayed or displayable in organizational communication situations (such as clothing, décor, acceptable talking distance, symbols of status) also influence access (Davis 1984).

### Cognitive Influences/Constraints

**Awareness** To gain access to information, a user must be aware that the means of addressing the situation are available (Chatman 1991; Gandy 1988; Harris and Dewdney 1994; Mulgan 1991). In order to pursue information about a local school district's budget, for example, a citizen must first be aware that budgets are prepared and published. An additional component of this factor is awareness that as a citizen one is entitled to request copies of such budgets and that it is one's right to attend and participate in meetings of the school board of directors. Awareness refers also to procedural knowledge, or awareness of how to move forward or of what steps to take to gain access to information (Budd 1987; Rice 1988). Awareness, therefore, includes awareness of means of addressing the situation, awareness of one's rights and entitlements with regard to access to that information, and awareness of how to proceed in the information-seeking process. Awareness also means the ability to identify tacit knowledge and to create shared cognition of that knowledge (Polanyi 1997). Some information may be too overwhelming, disconnected, or contradictory (Harris and Dewdney 1994; Wilensky 1968).

**Literacy** Because print represents a significant proportion of displayed information, one's reading or literacy level is likely to influence access to information. Given the diffusion rate of technological mediation as the primary means of access to information, technological literacy becomes a major influence or constraint on access. Current research measuring prose, document, and quantitative literacy (Kirsch et al. 1993) indicates that nearly one half of the U.S. population, age sixteen and older, lacks literacy skills adequate for functioning in the workplace and thus has limited access, at best, to traditional sources of information.

**Facility and Skill Level** The facility or skill level required to use an information system influences the information seeker's ability to access information. This expertise includes general cognitive skills, expertise in the content domain, with the particular source, medium, or system, expertise in information seeking (unmediated and mediated, and across types of online systems such as reference, full-text, and numeric) (Marchionini 1995). It is also likely that both past experience and the design of the system will influence that level. Included are skill levels in navigating an interface or interface protocol (Rice 1988) and using the command language of a system (Culnan 1985).

**Matching** Matching between system and user is necessary along other dimensions of cognitive influence. For example, the needs of the user and the offerings of a system must match with regard to content and language. If the system is designed or programmed with a model of a user that is not at all representative of how the user operates, or if the user's mental model or expectations for a system are off base, the match is not adequate. A simple example that arises frequently in a county community college library occurs when a potential user enters the library expecting to find either highly technical information or the latest popular novel. Because the library's collection is built to support the two-year college curriculum only, the user is likely to be disappointed in either search, indicating that the match between user and system is not adequate.

Access is similarly influenced or constrained according to how well matched are the system and user with regard to information processing, learning, or intelligence styles (Borgman 1989; Gardner 1983; Kolb 1984). Learning styles of some users lend themselves far more successfully to processing visual information or to learning by doing rather than by reading. Also, learners develop through an epistemological maturation process (Perry 1970), and they may do so differentially according to factors such as gender (Belenky et al. 1986; Gilligan 1982; Jansen 1989). To the extent that higher mental functions are socially formed and culturally transmitted (Vygotsky 1978), human cognitive processes differ according to cultural phenomena (Luria 1976). A classroom is an ideal illustration of the potential influence or constraint on access to information of such a match or its lack (Belenky et al. 1986; Freire 1969). Students who learn more readily through doing than through reading or listening will be more likely to grasp the information at hand if the class is run as a workshop than in a reading and lecture format. Thus the degree of matching between what the user needs and can make use of most effectively, and what and how the system makes available its resources, can strongly influence the degree to which the interaction leads to access.

Another major form of matching is the extent to which the medium chosen to provide or obtain access to information and communication matches the information-processing needs of the task (Daft and Lengel 1986; Johnson 1996; Reinsch and Beswick 1990) and the individual (Dervin 1980; Schamber 1994).

**Understanding** One's understanding that a need for information exists and the level of understanding of that gap, problematic situation, or anomalous state of knowledge certainly influence the likelihood of gaining access to information to address it (Budd 1987; Dervin 1980). Closely tied to understanding or identifying the need for information is the understanding of the domain of interest, given the situation. The level of cognitive understanding of the domain of interest will influence what information is truly accessible in the sense that it is intelligible to the potential user, as every user is a novice in many domains and is also likely to be expert in at least one (Cuff 1980). Even given an understanding of the need that is closer to conscious than to visceral need (Taylor 1968), and a well-developed understanding of the domain, additional cognitive factors influence access.

### Affective Influences/Constraints

**Attitudes** Less has been written about affective influences and constraints on access. Emotions, feelings, and thoughts are important and changing factors, as people seek to understand a situation (Kuhlthau 1993; Solomon 1997a). Observation of students as they attempt to find their way in a library reveals that the students' own attitudes about their competence or experiences influence their attempts to gain access. Many are afraid of feeling or appearing "stupid" or inadequate. Attitudes toward information seeking and sharing (Dewhirst 1971), toward computing (Rice 1988), or about an information system's convenience (Culnan 1984), dependability (Culnan 1985), or availability (Culnan 1983) may all influence one's decisions about whether or not to pursue access in a given situation. Personal attributes such as creativity and high growth needs are associated with different information-seeking patterns (Varlejs 1986). An experience of "flow" (a balance among control, challenge, intuition, and enjoyment) may be associated more with some media for accessing information than with others, such as electronic messaging instead of voicemail (Trevino and Webster 1992).

**Confidence, Fear, Trust** Technology attitudes may influence, also, further affective components such as confidence, fear, self-efficacy, or trust (Hochschild 1983). Those who have had less than optimal experiences with seeking information in the past may be more likely to feel apprehensive or unsure as they approach another information-seeking situation. Confidence and fear are related to the degree to which an information seeker perceives herself to be in control of a situation. This in turn is related to relative status, experience, and supply of resources. Trust between interactants influences how information is exchanged and interpreted (O'Reilly 1978), how willingly a potential user pursues access, and how willingly an intermediary or information source facilitates the process. Affective influences enable some to manipulate the behavior of others or to manipulate messages or the information flow. It is the job of collection agency employees, for example, to manipulate others into feeling fearful, unworthy, and threatened, thereby making them more likely to reveal information about themselves or their financial situations (Hochschild 1983). In some instances, it may be the job of librarians or teachers to manipulate others into feeling confident and capable of gaining access to information. Motivations or attitudes toward obtaining or providing access to information and communication can include obsessiveness, rationality, defensiveness, avoidance of responsibility, tendency to blame, risk aversion, preference for ambiguity so as not to foreclose future actions, anxiety and arousal over implications of new information, distrust of others' expertise, insufficient shared trust, expectation of future interaction and reciprocity, professional standards, and loss of status in revealing ignorance (Allen 1969; Blau 1954; Eisenberg 1984; Feldman and March 1981; Kuhlthau 1991; Smith, Carroll, and Ashford 1995; Smithson 1993; Staw, Sandelands, and Dutton 1981).

**Comfort/Discomfort** Because every information-seeking situation is unique, it is rare for any user to move absolutely comfortably through the process (Kuhlthau 1991). For some, affective influences are sufficient to preclude their taking on the search process, or they may easily become frustrated or discouraged and give up the search without gaining access. Users are more likely to experience comfort in a familiar setting or situation, in using a familiar system or protocol, or in dealing with a familiar situation or content domain (Cuff 1980).

### Economic Influences/Constraints

**Benefits** Economic influences and constraints include three basic components: anticipated benefits, costs, and value. Anticipated and realized benefits of access are weighed against the anticipated, real, and perceived costs of access. Benefits can take many forms, such as profitability or, more abstract, gaining access to information that is used to address or seek a solution to a problematic situation and that then increases one's sense of self-efficacy. Benefits also include public good externalities, the additional benefits to the public good derived from information's availability or repeated use (Hall 1981), and ancillary social value, the additional value to society derived from information's availability or use (Bates 1988).

From another perspective, it is beneficial to gain access to creating, producing, or distributing information. This includes potential financial benefits, along with the benefit of determining what information is available for others. As the number of corporate owners of sources of information such as television and radio broadcasting, book and periodical publishing, and film and video production grows smaller (Bagdikian 1990), the number of perspectives and the range of ideas represented can become dangerously limited, leading perhaps to a very small group's gaining exclusive access to an enormous potential to influence and shape our culture (H. I. Schiller 1989).

**Costs** Some costs are explicitly monetary. For example, commercial online database searches involve various fees. In some instances these costs are absorbed by the system, in some they are offset through mechanisms such as selling advertising time or space, and in others the costs are passed along to the information seeker (individual or organization). Some previously commercial databases are now available free on the Internet; the Internet is an exciting marketplace to follow to see which of these and other business models will prevail. To watch television, a viewer either pays for programming through purchasing advertised products or pays for programming more directly through cable fees or subscriber donations; much less frequently do viewers pay for viewing specific programs.

Other costs may be less quantifiable. For example, it may be difficult to quantify the costs of time, inconvenience, and annoyance experienced while attempting to gain access to information, especially as the potential benefits may be difficult to determine in advance (March 1994; Rice and Shook 1988). Reinsch and Beswick (1990), for example, show that a variety of dimensions of cost come into play when deciding upon which medium to use (e-mail or voicemail) for different situations. For some, time spent waiting may also represent loss of income as well as the timely usefulness of the information, and therefore represents both a quantifiable and a social cost. There may be social, personal, and organizational costs to articulating some kinds of knowledge, keeping tacit what could otherwise become organizational memory (Boisot 1998). Of course, gaining access to information requires information about appropriate sources and channels, which itself requires access and has costs (Johnson 1996; O'Reilly, Chatham and Anderson 1987).

Clear goals and the motivation to achieve them exemplify a balance against costs (Budd 1987), so that those with greater motivation may be more willing to take on access costs (Chatman 1991). However, the individual's worldview may also influence how accurately he is likely to anticipate benefits. For example, nonelites tend to function with an emphasis on immediate gratification, so the benefits of access to information, if they are not immediately obvious, may be less likely to be trusted or anticipated (Chatman 1991). Motivation can serve as a balancing influence against affective constraints in a search. The situation or need for information may be of sufficient import to outweigh the uncertainty, lack of confidence, or discomfort. In fact, a feeling of discomfort is more likely to generate or motivate a search than is a comfortable situation. Motivational factors can include economic or political relationships, or health and family concerns, for example. They are influenced also by the user's perceived need for and store of resources.

Any consideration of costs also must take into account the potential cost of doing without information, or of not gaining access to information necessary to address a situation, solve a problem, or carry out a new project. This is one type of cost that can be described as risk (Culnan 1984).

**Value** If one weighs the costs against potential benefits and pursues the search, the ultimate objective of access to information is to gain access to the underlying or application value of that information. Value requires the ability to anticipate benefits and, in the case of information, is not fixed (Bates 1988) and requires use of the information itself (Arrow 1979). Use, however, does not assure that value is realized or understood. Access to the value of information requires the belief that such access is likely (Dervin 1989) and requires a match between expectations, needs, and abilities and what is offered. Value can be accessed by individuals as well as by social groups (families, work groups, or athletic teams). The need for access can be more urgent when the potential for value added is greatest (Murdock and Golding 1989).

### Social Influences/Constraints

**Cultural Norms** According to Hall (1982), there are two social groups with regard to access: those with privileged access and the power to signify terms of the debate, and those who must struggle to gain access. For those among the latter group, not only can it be difficult to gain access to relevant information, but such information may not exist at all. This occurs because others who are likely to be oblivious to issues of import to the latter group set the agenda and select what is to be reported on, debated, discussed, researched, or questioned. Cultural norms also influence which technologies are developed, sold, and implemented (Braman 1989). Symbolic norms about rationality and being informed foster levels and rituals of information access and use (Feldman and March 1981). To understand the role of technologies in access to information, they must be considered in the light of local social fields within organizations (Perin 1991), the organization's information-sharing norms and expectations (Dewhirst 1971; Miller and Jablin 1991), the larger social context and processes (Slack 1984), or as a social phenomenon that shapes and is shaped by its host society (Doctor 1991). The socialization process in organizations and other groups not only helps to establish the norms for accessing, sharing, and using information but also the value of seeking and providing feedback (say, about performance) (Ashford and Tsui 1991; Miller and Jablin 1991).

**Class Membership and Background** One's class membership has the potential to act as a social influence or constraint on access to information (Agada 1999; Harris and Dewdney 1994). Often one's social class influences the range of employment opportunities, which in turn influences the range of information to which one has access. This is illustrated among the poor, who demonstrate lower expectations about the likelihood of success in unfamiliar endeavors or situations (Chatman 1991) and are therefore more likely to continue in the most familiar surroundings, patterns, and occupations. Family, ethnic background, and gender can also influence or constrain access. The family's use of media is the strongest predictor of the likelihood that one will take advantage of access to information through a range of media including books, magazines, television, museums, newspapers, video, academic performance (Greenberg and Heeter 1987), or computer-mediated communication (Doctor 1991). Also, those who grow up in families in which members seek out information are more likely to be aware of information systems and of their rights with regard to access to information.

**Social Networks** Social networks influence who has access to what information or technologies (Albrecht and Adelman 1987; Gandy 1988; Mulgan 1991). In many instances, access to information comes about serendipitously, through unplanned encounters or conversations with others (Archea 1977; Kraut et al. 1990). The exception is when an information seeker is in a situation that requires information not normally or not frequently needed among the individual's social networks. In such a case, the individual is more likely to gain access to information through weaker ties (Granovetter 1973) than through those with whom he is more familiar. Similarly, participation in multiplex ties (overlap across different kinds of networks) increases variety, innovativeness, and freedom from local dependencies, though at the cost of loyalty, stability, and responsiveness. The organizational and library literature emphasize the network roles of the boundary spanner and environmental scanner (Choo 1995; Choo and Auster 1993), who strongly influence how the environment is "enacted" and thus what information is sought, how it is interpreted, and what actions are taken (Weick 1979). Influences of social networks on access to information are exemplified in considering the invisible college (Crane 1969), in which scholarly work is shared informally through interpersonal networks (even if mediated by computer networks—Weedman 1999) long before it appears in published form.

Social networks also influence the environment in which information, once accessible, is perceived or used. Social and work networks can influence one's attitudes and thereby one's expectations and use of systems to access information (Rice and Aydin 1991). Because of greater access, trust, and contextuality, people tend to seek information from known interpersonal sources in both social and organizational settings (Harris and Dewdney 1994; McKinnon and Bruns 1992). In order to gain access to the benefit of information (Doctor 1991), even given access to information, the individual requires a social and media environment that enables and supports effective use of that access (Haythornthwaite and Wellman 1998; Williamson 1998). Access through one's social network to advice, analysis, interpretation, and debate

**Table 3.6**
Common Issues/Concerns, by Research Literature

| Issue/Concern | Library Studies | Information Science | Information Society | Mass Communication | Organizational Communication | Economics of Information |
|---|---|---|---|---|---|---|
| *Conceptualizations of Information* | | | | | | |
| Thing: resource/commodity | | | | X | X | X |
| Data | X | | | | X | X |
| Representation | XX | XX | | | | |
| Communication process | X | X | X | X | X | |
| Mediation | X | X | XX | XX | X | X |
| *Conceptualizations of Access* | | | | | | |
| Knowledge | XX | XX | X | X | | |
| Technology | | X | XX | X | XX | |
| Communication | X | X | XX | | X | |
| Control | | | X | XX | X | XX |
| Commodities | | | | X | | XX |
| Rights | X | | X | | | X |
| *Facets of Information-Seeking Process* | | | | | | |
| Context | | | X | X | | XX |
| Situation | XX | XX | | | | |
| Strategies | XX | XX | | | X | |
| Outcomes | | | X | X | | X |

XX = issue is major concern or focus of research area.
X = issue is of some or implicit concern.
Note: Absence of X does not necessarily mean that the research literature does not cover this influence or constraint at all, just that coverage levels are low compared to those of the other research literatures.

**Table 3.7**
Influences/Constraints, by Research Literature

| Influence/Constraint | Library Studies | Information Science | Information Society | Mass Communication | Organizational Communication | Economics of Information |
|---|---|---|---|---|---|---|
| Physical | X | X | X | | XX | |
| Cognitive | X | XX | | | X | |
| Affective | | | | | X | |
| Economic | | | X | X | | XX |
| Social | | | XX | XX | X | X |
| Political | X | | XX | X | | X |

XX = issue is major concern or focus of research area.
X = issue is of some or implicit concern.
Note: Absence of X does not necessarily mean that the research literature does not cover this issue or concern at all, just that coverage levels are low compared to those of the other research literatures.

is often required to make the best use of access and to participate as a citizen (Agada 1999; Grainovetter 1983; Murdock and Golding 1989).

**Education** One's educational background includes learning, skill level, and competence as well as formal schooling. An individual with a higher level of education is likely to encounter fewer constraints in attempting to gain access to information, in part because educational level not only influences access directly but also is likely to influence one's social network and levels of communication and technological competence. One who has learned to cope with new situations or problems is more likely to have developed the skills necessary to do so again. Learning and skill level are both cumulative, particularly with regard to access to information (Budd 1987). Again, however, there are exceptions according to the situation from which the need for information arises. Higher education can preclude knowledge of or access to other kinds of information, such as practical or manual expertise.

**Competence** Given awareness of the means of addressing and the right to address the situation, competence in expression as well as in print and technological literacy comes into play. Those more able to express their need for information are more likely to gain access (Budd 1987; Gandy 1988; Taylor 1968). Both communication competence (Gandy 1988) and technological competence can influence or constrain access to information. Competence compounds over time and use (Doctor 1991). As is true of education, the degree to which competence influences or constrains access varies by situation (Cuff 1980).

**Experience** One's level of experience and expertise will be situation- and domain-specific. Repeated use, especially successful use, and often physical use (Hayles 1999), is likely to increase one's level of expertise with any given system as well as with system use in general (Rice 1988). Familiarity and successful past use of an information system increase the likelihood of a user's having developed appropriate techniques to gain access to information (Culnan 1984).

### Political Influences/Constraints

**Power** Limitations to access to information carry grave implications for a participatory democracy (Gandy 1988). Power influences policy, how it is developed, and who it favors. In a democratic society, an informed citizenry is in a stronger position to counter those who would develop policy unfairly. As Buckland (1990) explains, Francis Bacon, around 1600, wrote not that knowledge is power but rather that ignorance is a source of weakness. Knowledge, being the opposite of weakness, is therefore a source of power. Conversely, power can be used to limit access to information, thereby limiting others' access to knowledge, a source of power.

**Control** Political influences and constraints on access to information can be used to control information, such as through copyright or privacy laws (Mulgan 1991), telecommunications policies, or control of information systems and flows of information. Control of the marketplace can also influence access to information through control of cultural institutions, which can serve as a vehicle for control of the course of public debate or the setting of the public agenda. Questions arise as to who controls access to information about the individual in the form of data gathered through monitoring the individual's workplace performance or through pre-employment screening, which may require blood or urine samples from the prospective employee.

**Equity and Participation** Democracy requires equitable access to advice, analysis, interpretation, and debate as well as to some goods and services that are necessary resources for citizenship (Murdock and Golding 1989). Equity and participation require not only access to information but also access to the right and the means to inform others (Dervin 1989). Levels of communication competence can thereby influence one's ability to use information resources to improve one's quality of life (Gandy 1988).

### Summary

Tables 3.6 and 3.7 summarize the major common issues, and influences and constraints, that emerge from the review of the six research literatures.

# 4

# Unique Aspects Across Research Literatures, and a Preliminary Framework of Access

## Unique Aspects Across Research Literatures

This chapter identifies some assumptions and primary issues about accessing information and communication unique to each research literature, and proposes a preliminary framework based on the common and unique aspects.

### Library Studies

The literature of library studies tends to view the issue of access to information from the perspective of the user, a shift from an earlier focus on the institution (library) or the information system (stacks, online catalog, commercial database). In general, the users studied are those seeking print information in the setting of a library building, using subject headings or key words to represent the reality of the need for information. A further shift is moving the perspective toward understanding the information-seeking process as movement through space and time in an attempt to make sense of one's world (Atwood and Dervin 1982). In recent years, library studies has moved outside the library context and beyond traditional print sources, such as to Internet searching and multimedia materials. These changes are a reason that areas such as library studies, information science, and information democracy (and even economics of information) are converging into a field called by some social informatics.

This focus on users carries its own limitations, however, particularly as it applies to an issue of significant concern in library studies—information democracy. The limitations are tied to the failure to account for the contexts, situations, and potential strategies of nonusers and therefore for providing services appropriate to the needs of a broader segment of the population, despite library studies' historical concern with freedom of speech, as applied to collection development and protection of patrons' circulation records. For example, Chatman (1991) writes of working-class individuals seeking employment, who are likely to trust and attend only to interpersonal sources of information, not to written announcements, especially scholarly or scientific publications. To account theoretically for factors involved in access to information, the field of library studies needs to broaden thinking about who is seeking information, what information means (Chatman 1987), and the cultural and organizational contexts of information seeking (Durrance 1989).

**Information Science**

In information science, research tends to focus on the nature of information itself (Belkin 1978; Belkin and Robertson 1976) and on how elite users go about seeking citations to and abstracts of highly technical or scientific documents (Bamford and Brownstein 1986). In studies of the latter, the facets of the information-seeking process under consideration are generally limited to situation and strategies. In particular, the focus is generally limited to cognitive processes, from query formulation through retrieval of a list of bibliographic references to print documents. Evaluation of the information-seeking process is based principally on a narrow definition of relevance, derived from matching of a query statement with citations.

This research area does attend to issues related to reducing or otherwise addressing "anomalous states of knowledge" (Belkin, Oddy, and Brooks 1982a; 1982b). However, as defined, an anomalous state of knowledge assumes far greater user understanding of the situation than is often the case among those facing challenges or questions in their everyday lives. The approach of this research area is based on several assumptions: first, that a query statement is a reasonable representation of one's need for information, and second, that the research area's narrow definition of relevance is an acceptable measure of performance. In addition, it assumes that access to a citation or bibliographic reference is an adequate representation of access to information, and that it is sufficient to account for cognitive processes as the primary source of influence or constraint on the information-seeking process and on access to information.

Critics have suggested that those designing systems need to explore human behavior more fully, to include influences in addition to the cognitive (Brown 1986), in part, to help avoid unintentionally creating barriers to access (Budd 1987). Models of information retrieval need to account for differential access (Borgman 1989) and differential levels of experience (Cuff 1980; Daniels 1986; Kling 1980). Others suggest a need to account for the contexts within which a particular user encounters a situation and a need for information (Chatman 1991; Dervin and Nilan 1986) and, at the other end of the information-seeking process, to account for the evaluation of information that is retrieved and used, especially as it may apply to gaps, challenges, needs, or questions encountered in everyday life (Belkin and Vickery 1985; Chatman 1987; 1991; Tague and Schultz 1989). According to Marchionini (1995, 27–28), a central assumption in information-seeking research is that "life is active, analog, and accumulative.... We learn by 'bumping into the environment.'" Further, because life is analog—continuous and periodic—we have to develop mental and physical structures that limit and focus the flow of information.

**Information Society**

The literature on the "information society" and new technologies tends to view access to information as access to technologies, through which one can gain access to information, power, or control. The focus is on the relationship of technology to human communication (Dordick 1987; Slack 1984) and commerce (Schement and Curtis 1995) and related social issues such as information democracy. This literature also addresses issues associated with the diffusion of innovations, including technologies that influence access to information (Rogers 1986). In terms of the information-seeking process, this perspective is more likely than others to account for the context and general outcomes of access to information, but not necessarily for the situation or strategies facets.

This perspective tends to rely on a number of assumptions, including that society is experiencing a revolutionary transformation because of the overwhelming significance of information, computers, telecommunications networks, and digitization (Bell 1973; Beniger 1986). These assumptions raise issues of power and distribution of privilege in society, such as, for example, that class membership may determine the type of information to which one has access, and that information policy is a factor in determining the impact of new technologies on specific classes (Braman 1989). In addition, technology tends to be viewed as a social phenomenon that shapes and is shaped by the host society (Doctor 1991). Communication and technological competence (or the lack thereof) are related and compounded with time and practice (or lack of them). Personal privacy is becoming a central issue because of increased accessibility through online information services and databases, and is pitted against organizational and national security, and marketing and service interests.

As is true in library studies, the focus of this perspective on information democracy assumes a commitment to equitable distribution of information and its benefits as well as equitable distribution of the benefits of information age technology

(Bourque and Warren 1987; Doctor 1991). There is a tendency to assume also that technology makes information available equally, plentifully, and universally, and that technology can span space and time (Hudson 1988; Kraut 1989; Larose and Mettler 1989), and in so doing, expand access and information flow (Hiltz 1986).

Critics assert that a mechanistic model prevails (Jansen 1989) and argue against such a model of communication because it presents technologies as causal rather than as social phenomena (Slack 1984). Some call instead for general cultural analyses of uses of technologies (Sproull, Kiesler, and Zubrow 1984) or argue that the assumption that technology provides information equally, plentifully, and universally is misleading and irresponsible (Gillespie and Robins 1989; Lievrouw 1994).

**Mass Communication**

The literature of mass communication that explores access to information is most strongly focused on the context of access to information, especially the context in which the information system operates and how those who control the system then set the cultural agenda or context for others. This view assumes that who controls the media influences what is produced and distributed (Compaine 1985; Herman and Chomsky 1988), and that the focus of inquiry belongs on the production and distribution of information (Bagdikian 1990; Coser, Kadushin, and Powell 1982). To some degree, this view also assumes a position of technological determinism (Innis 1951; McLuhan and Fiore 1967; Meyrowitz 1985).

Others assume that hegemony serves to explain cultural consensus building through the media (Gitlin 1980). It is easy to oppose an argument that is part of the public agenda. It is far more difficult, however, to change the terms and logic of the debate, particularly without privileged access to establishing the terms in the first place (Hall 1982). Further, there is concern that privatization of information, and the consequent narrowed range of access, threatens the rights of individuals (H. I. Schiller 1981; 1989). An additional view assumes that taking the perspective of the audience member and how she makes use of information may change the understanding of the information provided through the media (Radway 1984).

**Organizational Communication**

Issues of access to information of concern in the literature of organizational communication tend to focus on managing information; that is, on information flow and physical access to information systems, or to information in the form of messages or data. Unlike the other literatures, organizational communication research sometimes considers the benefits of *limiting access*, such as to managerial time or to proprietary or confidential information, by means of gatekeepers and other organizational structures. Privacy and security issues, and the influence of technology on the workplace and its functions, are also of concern.

Several assumptions prevail with regard to access to information in organizational communication. The first is that given physical access to information systems or messages, access to information necessarily follows (Allen 1969). A second assumption is that the environment and setting play a role in determining information behavior (Mick, Lindsey, and Callahan 1980), including that interpersonal behavior depends on exposure of information about oneself to others and access to information about others because of relative spatial location (Archea 1977). This view assumes each person to be at the center of a dynamic field of information behavior, continuously adjusting to the surrounding field. Choo (1995) reviews theory and research that conceptualizes management as conversations—to create, manage, and begin commitments, and establish action contexts and possibilities, through linguistic acts. Thus organizational members participate in recurring conversational networks.

Some assume that management styles drive applications of technology (Garson 1988), and that technology can facilitate a panoptic relationship already of concern in issues of privacy, monitoring, and security (Botan and McCreadie 1993; Gandy 1989; Zuboff 1988). Tension between the assumptions that more information is better and that privacy issues are of concern is indicative of other tensions that arise in issues related to access to information, such as the tension between information democracy and privatization of information.

Some critics argue that an obsolete understanding of communication processes and power relations prevents our seeing the corporate domination of available information and processes of public decision making (Deetz 1992). Others question any restriction of the flow of information in a democratic society (Allen 1988) and are met by those who raise concerns about national security, privacy rights, or worker alienation (U. S. Congress 1987). The assumption that access to information necessarily and causally follows from physical or system access has not been supported (Culnan 1984), thereby strengthening the argument for investigating additional influences and constraints on access, such as the relationship between perception of availability and use of a system (Culnan 1983), or the relationship between the ability to formulate a query and the perception of accessibility (Culnan 1985). The assumption that more information is better has been challenged by the argument that the major problem for managers is not lack of data but reducing the equivocality in information (Daft and Lengel 1986).

**Economics of Information**

The primary foci with regard to access to information in the literature on economics of information include the free market and privatization; information democracy; considerations of cost, benefit, and value; and again, privacy and control (McCain 1988). The notion of value requires the study of the information-seeking process through to the outcomes facet, in order to determine whether the user gains access to the value of information in a given situation (Mulgan 1991, 172). This perspective offers explicit considerations of the weighing of social as well as economic costs and benefits, which provides an important addition to understanding influences and constraints on access to information. A political perspective emphasizes distribution of control capacities and the availability of resources such as competence and time rather than simple access to information (Mulgan 1991).

Assumptions of this perspective are that information can be viewed as a thing/commodity, but that information is unlike other goods and services (Arrow 1979; Bates 1988); that access to information is tied to the ability of the individual to participate fully as a citizen and the ability of the institution to succeed in the economic market; and that information carries with it the potential for public good (Hall 1981). Some proponents of this perspective assume that when some goods and services are necessary resources for citizenship activities, then political rights can fall victim to the vicissitudes of the marketplace (Murdock and Golding 1989; Schement and Curtis 1995). Some critics see as untenable the notion of information as a commodity rather than as part of the human communication process (Budd 1987).

**Summary**

Table 4.1 summarizes the primary issues, foci, and assumptions of each research area, making explicit some of what has implicitly led to differences among the research areas with regard to their treatment of issues of access to information. We note, of course, that other research areas can also offer perspectives that contribute to an understanding of access to information. In particular, research in developmental psychology and learning theory can provide insight into identifying influences and constraints on access to information. These research areas, along with feminist research perspectives, also underscore the argument for viewing the phenomenon of interest from a variety of perspectives in an effort to account for a full

**Table 4.1**
Unique Perspectives by Research Literature

| Research Literature | Primary Issues, Foci | Assumptions |
|---|---|---|
| Library studies | How users seek documents in library<br>Information democracy | Documents address questions of users<br>Subject headings represent reality<br>Bibliographic sources meet needs for information |
| Information science | Elite users seeking citations to technical, scientific documents<br>Nature of information | Access to citation equals access to information<br>Relevance as defined is acceptable measure of performance<br>ASK or query statement is reasonable representation of need for information<br>Cognitive processes are sufficient focus of inquiry |
| Information society | Relationship of technology to human communication<br>Information democracy<br>Privacy | Society is experiencing a transformation that will change social structure<br>Relationship of technology to human behavior and societal context is appropriate focus of inquiry<br>Technology can make information available equally, plentifully, and universally |
| Mass media | Access to control over information production, distribution<br>Cultural agenda setting | Who owns and runs the media determines what is produced and disseminated<br>Access to control over production and distribution is appropriate focus of inquiry |
| Organizational communication | Information flow<br>Privacy/security<br>Physical access | Physical access to information sources equals access to information<br>More information is usually better<br>Issues of privacy are of concern |
| Economics of information | Free market, privatization<br>Information democracy<br>Cost, benefit, value | Information, if viewed as commodity, operates differently from other goods and commodities<br>Individuals require access to information to participate fully as citizens |

theoretical understanding. They also support the need for sensitivity to issues of privilege with regard to access.

## A Preliminary Framework of Access

This section integrates the analyses of common and unique perspectives into a preliminary framework of access.

Because each research literature has its own foci, theoretical concerns, and methodological approaches, a comprehensive understanding of the concerns, influences and constraints, and implications of access to information will come only from combining the insights, both common and unique, across multiple literatures. Tables 3.6 and 3.7 showed that no literature explicitly covers all of these issues, and no issue is covered by all of the six literatures. The present integration of reviews of six research literatures has identified several overlapping dimensions of the general concept of access to information.

First, there are several conceptualizations of information itself (thing, data in the environment, representation of knowledge, and part of the communication process). Each of these focuses on different aspects of information and makes different assumptions about the nature of participants, communication, content, and meaning. Second, several conceptualizations of the notion of access to information appear across various literatures (knowledge, technology, communication, control, goods/commodities, and rights). Each of these emphasizes different aspects of the access process (such as form of knowledge, technologies as mediators, and economic value) and leads to different implications (concerning power, compounding effects, public and ancillary goods, democratic participation). Third, the research perspectives focus on different aspects of a general information-seeking process (context, situation, strategies, and outcomes). This broader scheme substantially extends what is usually a limited concern with one or two components, necessarily overlooking other important factors in accessing information, from implicit design obstacles to assessing the value of retrieved information.

Fourth, a variety of influences and constraints affect the nature and extent of access to information (physical, cognitive, affective, economic, social, and political). Few system designs, institutional structures, or research approaches attend to all of these influences and constraints, making access a much more complicated and obscured endeavor for all participants. Implications vary from false assumptions about the relationship of system use to access, physical access to evaluation, and compounding effects of competence and social networks. And fifth, each literature has unique assumptions and concepts that can both highlight specific concerns not considered by other literatures and limit our understanding of access (ranging from the physical form of information, cognitive processes, industry control, and tensions between privacy and freedom).

Figure 4.1 shows one slice of this multidimensional framework for understanding access to information, using the two dimensions that emphasize human behavior in the process of seeking to gain access to information: (1) the information-seeking process (horizontal axis), and (2) influences and constraints on access to information (vertical axis). No hierarchical relationship is intended among the influences and constraints, and although context and situation generally precede strategies and outcomes in the phases of the information-seeking process, the process itself is neither linear nor sequential and is likely to be iterative. At any stage in the information-seeking process, any of the influences or constraints may come into play. Other common issues and concerns identified in the literature can be considered once the two basic dimensions of the preliminary framework are clarified.

As the user seeks to gain access to information, she encounters influences and constraints on access that may be deeply embedded in the context. For example, in the context phase, social influences and constraints might contribute to the likelihood that a given individual generally operates in a milieu that views information and information systems as accessible, thereby influencing the user to see access to information in general as a viable possibility. In the situation phase, social influences and constraints might again contribute to the degree of familiarity of the same user with a particular set of circumstances and need for information. Social influences and constraints might, in the strategies phase, contribute to the likelihood of the individual's knowing the range of information sources available and how to navigate them. Finally, at the outcomes phase, social influences and constraints might contribute to the likelihood that the individual can make use of the information (i.e., understand and apply it) and gain access to the value of information retrieved or apply what is found to revising the search strategies, reframing the question, reconfiguring the tentative understanding of the situation, and returning to other components of the search process.

This initial framework aims to identify a full range of factors involved in the information-seeking process, emphasizing factors both common and unique across various literatures. Potential uses of such a framework would be as a diagnostic evaluation approach for systems designers, implementers and managers, and users.

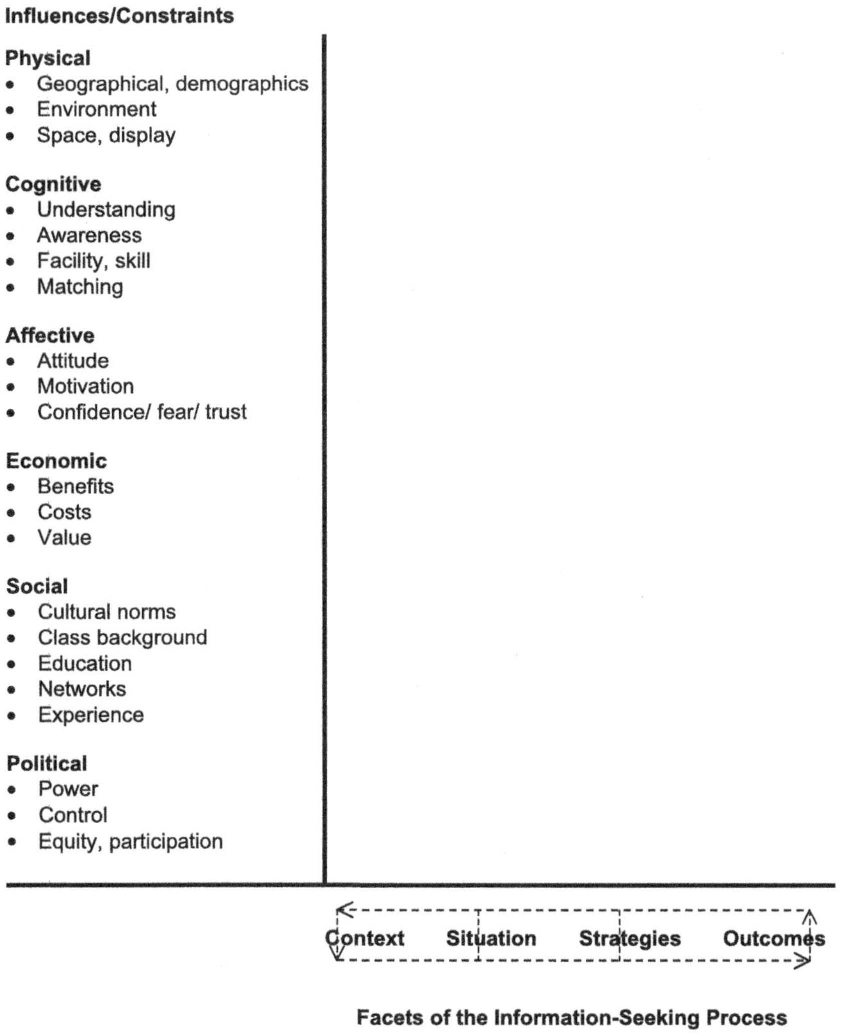


Figure 4.1
Preliminary Framework for Understanding Access to Information and Communication

What issues seem to be most hidden, missing, or underemphasized, and in what particular information-seeking components? What issues attract the most attention from research and theory precisely because they are considered commonly across several literatures? To what extent are theories of access comprehensive or biased in their coverage? Testing of this multidimensional framework would indicate whether additional dimensions are needed to fully capture the issues and perspectives surrounding access to information and communication in any particular situation.

# 5

# A Research Approach: Access

A case study approach provided a rich store of data against which to test how well the initial framework developed from the literature reviews reflected dimensions of access to information and communication for real users in situations from their own lives. An initial pilot study was followed by a primary case study. Content coding of survey documents provided a basis for adjusting the coding process and the framework slightly, and for verifying the dimensions of the framework derived from the literature. These results were used to revise the framework. Finally, a follow-up case study of a very different population was used to test the boundary conditions of the revised framework, leading to a final refined framework.

## The Pilot and Primary Case Studies

A small pilot study, based on reports from 21 students enrolled in January 1995, led the way to a more extensive main case study. Both studies relied on the same setting, a one-credit course on how to use the Internet. Convenience and access of the investigator determined selection of the setting for the pilot and main case studies. However, using case studies to enhance theory building relies on theoretical rather than statistical sampling, and the goal of theoretical sampling is to choose cases likely to replicate or extend the emergent theory (Eisenhardt 1989). Therefore, opportunities to replicate results or extend theoretical variance appropriately guide the approach to sampling.

The case sample for the initial pilot study included students from a variety of backgrounds, ranging in age from late teens to retired adults, who enrolled in a five-week course on how to gain access to information using the Internet. This pilot study was used to refine the operational procedures and the actual survey form.

The sample for the main case study was similar. The investigator taught both classes. Written surveys were assigned as part of a one-credit five-week introduction to using the Internet offered between August and December 1995. The course was offered at a community college in its early days of Internet use. The course predated popular and widespread access to the World Wide Web and easy availability of graphic interface access to the Internet, so students were searching for information using text-based search tools through serial connections almost exclusively. Conditions were primitive and frustration was common.

Participants included 38 students ranging in age from 17 to 82 years. Educational levels of the participants also ranged widely, from completion of tenth grade to graduate degrees, including Ph.D.s, an M.D. degree, and degrees in law. Twenty-one men and 17 women, all of the students enrolled, responded to the survey. Although students were not graded on their surveys, they were required to submit their notes, search logs, and surveys in order to complete requirements for the course and receive a grade.

The researcher asked that students document five searches on topics, questions, problems, or issues of their choosing as the final assignment for the course. The only limitation in their selection of a topic was that their investigation matter to them. One student submitted reports on seven searches, two students submitted six searches each, 21 students submitted five searches each one submitted four searches, three submitted three searches each, four submitted two searches each, and six submitted one search each. This represented a total of 38 participants and 151 searches. Students were not limited to using the Internet for their searches, though most chose that medium.

### Sense-Making Methodology

To garner the perceptions and to gain accounts of the behavior of users, participants, as part of their course assignment, documented their experiences, guided by an expanded interview protocol designed initially as part of the methodology of "sense making" (Dervin 1983). Several assumptions underlie the sense-making approach, which has been developed to study the human process of making sense of everyday life and which is built on a set of theoretically derived methods for such study. The core assumption of sense making is that discontinuity is a fundamental aspect of reality (Dervin 1992). This assumption is consistent with the situation phase of the preliminary framework, which posits that an individual encounters a set of circumstances from which a need for information arises. Others characterize this as an anomalous state of knowledge (Belkin 1980), a gap (Dervin 1983), a visceral or conscious need (Taylor 1968), a problematic situation (Wersig 1979), or discomfort. The assumption of discontinuity underlies several additional assumptions of sense making, which are again consistent with the proposed preliminary framework of this study. Consistent with both the preliminary framework and with the assumption of discontinuity, the sense-making approach assumes human actors in the process of making sense of their worlds. Both the sense-making approach and the preliminary framework depict the facets of the information-seeking process as a process rather than as a condition. The process is iterative and is not hierarchical. The data are elicited from the perspective of the actor rather than the observer.

Sense making guided the protocol for interviews with respondents. The method applied here, the micromoment time-line interview, asks the respondent to reconstruct a real situation in terms of what happened in the situation, then describe each step in detail. Dervin's interview protocol was expanded here to account for influences and constraints on access to information and for the context from which the situation or need for information arises.

**Interview Protocol**

The 21 participants of the pilot study were asked to describe and reflect on their experiences with seeking information about an issue of their choosing in the context of that course. They were asked to report on anything that facilitated or blocked their gaining access to the information they sought. Responses indicated that participants experienced difficulty with the conceptual nature of what this study seeks. Many of the participants reported nothing unless they gained access to information and then were more concerned with what they found than with the process of finding it. Therefore, a more structured survey protocol was used in the main case study in an effort to lead participants to report on the entire search process whether or not they found what they sought, increasing the likelihood of eliciting user-defined influences and constraints on access.

According to the survey protocol, as detailed by Dervin (1983), participants selected a real situation, challenge, or question of interest or import to them, about which they were seeking information. As they searched, they kept notes on their movements through time, space, and problems. The researcher requested that they keep notes on their thoughts and feelings along the way, on their decisions, on their challenges, and on their discoveries. Afterwards, in response to the survey, they detailed in writing each step in the search, reporting on what happened along the way.

In response to the survey and for each step of each search, participants described what questions arose at the time, what issues came up that led to their seeking to find out, learn, come to understand, unconfuse, make sense of, seek access to

**Table 5.1**
Interview Protocol

| Indicator Category and Associated Influences/Constraints | Interview Questions |
|---|---|
| Context | What set of circumstances led to your interest in this topic/question/problem? Include anything you think helps explain this. |
| Influences/constraints | Did anything contribute to the set of circumstances behind your selecting this topic/question/problem? What?<br>Did anything hinder you in the set of circumstances behind your selecting this topic/question/problem? What? |
| Situation | What were you trying to do when you selected this topic/question/problem?<br>Did you see yourself as blocked or hindered when you asked this question? How?<br>Is there anything else you can think of that explains why you selected this question? |
| Influences/constraints | Did anything help you arrive at this topic/question/problem? What?<br>Did you experience any difficulty in arriving at this topic/question/problem? What? |
| Strategies | Did this issue/question stand alone or was it related to other questions? How?<br>How easy did it seem to get an answer? Why?<br>How important was getting an answer? Please explain.<br>Did the importance ever change? How? Why?<br>Did you get an answer? When?<br>Was the answer complete or partial? In what way?<br>How did you get an answer?<br>What approaches did you try in seeking an answer?<br>Please describe the approaches whether or not you got an answer.<br>Did you get new questions? What were they? |
| Influences/constraints | Did anything help you in looking for an answer? What? How did it help?<br>Did anything make it difficult for you to look for an answer? What? How did it make things difficult? |
| Outcomes | What did you do with what you found?<br>What did you do if you didn't find what you were looking for?<br>Did it help you? How?<br>Did it make things difficult? How?<br>Was it worth trying to find? How or how not? |

**Table 5.1** (continued)

| Indicator Category and Associated Influences/Constraints | Interview Questions |
|---|---|
| | Did this (what you found or what you did if you didn't find anything) lead to any other questions, problems, ideas, changes? What were they? |
| Influences/constraints | Did anything help you in making use of what you found or deciding what to do next? What? How did it help?<br>Did anything hinder you from making use of what you found or deciding what to do next? What? How did it hinder you? |

information. For each question, participants responded according to the survey guide presented in table 5.1. Finally, because the literature refers repeatedly to the compounding effect of one's context and background (Braman 1989; Budd 1987; Doctor 1991; Gandy 1988; Greenberg and Heeter 1987; Mulgan 1991; Murdock and Golding 1989), participants were asked to respond to general questions (see table 5.2) about themselves and their households to provide additional context indicators.

### Field Notes, Search Logs, E-mail Messages

In addition, to draw on multiple data sources, the investigator gathered a set of field notes based on the discussions and questions of the class meetings and established a file of physical artifacts such as search logs and e-mail interactions between student and teacher. Field notes included observations on the access-related discussions, successes, difficulties, and questions of each class period. Students generated printouts of their search logs and turned them in as part of their class assignment. Further, the investigator captured the text of access-related e-mail interactions with students. The field notes, search log printouts and assignments, and the e-mail interactions were included in the case study database and were used to corroborate and augment evidence from the content analysis of the written interview protocol. All were reviewed for consistency with established categories and with an eye to identifying additional categories. These additional data sources corroborated the findings derived from analysis of the responses to the written surveys and suggested no additional categories other than mediative influences and constraints.

The reasons for selecting this approach were as follows:

- It seeks to elicit from the participants their perceptions or behavior in terms and categories defined and determined by the user rather than the researcher.

**Table 5.2**
Background Questions

| Question | Responses |
| --- | --- |
| How long have you lived in X County? | Years: |
| How many people 18 years of age or older live in your household, including yourself? | Adults: |
| How many children (people under 18) live in your household? What are their ages? | Children:<br>Ages: |
| Are you employed outside the house? | Yes No |
| Are you retired from your employment? | Yes No |
| If yes, what kind of job do (did) you have? At what kind of place do (did) you work? | Kind of job:<br>Kind of workplace: |
| What category describes the yearly income of your household? | $9,999 or less<br>$10,000 to $19,999<br>$20,000 to $29,999<br>$30,000 to $39,999<br>$40,000 to $49,999<br>$50,000 or more |
| What kind of job does/did your parents have the last time you lived at home? | Mother's job:<br>Father's job: |
| What is the last grade of school you completed? | Primary: 1 2 3 4 5 6<br>Secondary: 7 8 9 10 11 12<br>College: 13 14 15 16<br>Postgraduate: 17+ |
| What year were you born? | 19__ |

*The information on this sheet is confidential and will have no bearing on your class grade.*

• The overall aim of Dervin's research agenda parallels the aims of this study (namely, to seek to understand phenomena related to human use of information in the context of real lives), and the sense-making methodological approach has been developed in a programmatic research effort active since 1972.
• Perhaps most important, the combination of data collection methods and consequent production of multiple types of data for analysis constitute a triangulated approach, strengthening substantiation of theoretical propositions.

The participants' written accounts of their reported experiences in seeking to gain access to information based on a situation of their choosing provided both systematic data (through content analysis) and rich descriptive data (their written accounts). The interviews followed the same protocol as the written survey, but the face-to-face interaction provided the interviewer with additional, nonverbal cues and the opportunity for interaction, adding richness to the data of the follow-up study. In addition, the field notes, search logs, and e-mail interactions provided yet another view on the data and the constructs of the framework.

## The Initial Framework

The preliminary framework represents the theoretical propositions derived from review and analysis of the literature. The two dimensions of the framework include ten theoretical categories: four facets of the information-seeking process and six influences/constraints on access. Among the first tasks in the framework testing phase was establishing operational definitions for each of the ten categories of the preliminary framework and expanding the interview protocol. An aim of the initial test was to revise the operationalizations to develop explicit categories and to achieve high reliability in assigning text to categories. The researcher carried out the initial coding. A second trained coder analyzed samples of the texts of the written responses to the interview protocol to check for and improve on intercoder reliability, thereby contributing to establishing how well the empirical data fit the theoretical categories and whether the data suggested additional categories.

### Content Analysis

One requirement of content analysis is that the categories be mutually exclusive and exhaustive (Babbie 1986; Budd, Thorp, and Donohew 1967; Kerlinger 1986). The initial categories of the preliminary framework represented the theoretical propositions based on the categories, components, and examples developed earlier. Each was operationalized as described in the following sections. To meet the requirements of mutual exclusivity and exhaustiveness, the set included an additional "other" category for each axis of the framework.

The universe of content was the written responses to the interview protocol submitted by the students as part of their 151 search reports. The unit of analysis for the content analysis was individual searches that the user had carried out in attempting to address or investigate a question, an issue, a topic, or a problem. The texts were organized and analyzed using Nud*ist (Non-Numerical Unstructured Data Indexing Searching and Theorizing) software. The program allowed direct content coding of the responses according to the categories identified in the preliminary framework. For each of the 27 questions per document, coders assigned responses to facets and to influences and constraints. This unit of analysis is smaller than the individual participant. This was necessary, given that influences and constraints

**Table 5.3**
Operational Definitions of Categories for Content Analysis

| Category | Definition | Examples |
|---|---|---|
| Physical influences/ constraints | Physiological abilities or limitations of a user; environmental, spatial, and display characteristics of representations of information or of a space or system through or in which one might find information | Geography and demographics (Hudson 1988; Larose and Mettler 1989); arrangement (Budd 1987); orientation in an environment (Archea 1977); spatial proximity (Hiltz and Johnson 1989), security, or obstruction (Culnan 1985; Rice 1988); display (Chang and Rice 1993; Daft and Lengel 1986) |
| Cognitive influences/ constraints | User's understanding, awareness, literacy, facility or skill level, and information-processing style with regard to the situation and content, and with regard to the systems, procedures, and means available to address the situation<br>NOT formal education, competence, or experience | Understanding (Cuff 1980; Dervin 1980); awareness of means and procedures (Budd 1987; Chatman 1991; Gandy 1988; Rice 1988); technical, quantitative, verbal literacy or facility (Culnan 1985; Kirsch et al. 1993); learning, skill level, information-processing style (Budd 1987; Gardner 1983; Kolb 1984) |
| Affective influences/ constraints | User's feelings about self, system, and situation in information-seeking process<br>NOT motivation | Attitudes about self (Hochschild 1983), about computing (Rice 1988), about system (Culnan 1983; 1984; 1985); confidence/fear/trust in relation to situation and others (O'Reilly 1978); comfort/discomfort about situation, about process (Cuff 1980) |
| Economic influences/ constraints | Benefits, costs, and value (potential and realized) of information to user or provider; motivation to overcome costs, derive benefits<br>NOT power relationships<br>NOT emotion itself, only its costs, benefits | Profitability, affluence, solutions, public good externalities (Hall 1981); ancillary social value (Bates 1988); financial costs as well as costs of inconvenience, time, annoyance weighed against motivation (Budd 1987; Chatman 1991) or the cost of doing without information, including risk of loss (Culnan 1984) or the potential for value added (Murdock and Golding 1989) |
| Social influences/ constraints | Cultural norms, class membership and background, social networks, education and communicative competence, and experience with regard to particular situation<br>NOT literacy or technical facility | Privilege and struggle (Hall 1982); background and networks (Chatman 1991; Crane 1969; Doctor 1991; Gandy 1988; Granovetter 1983; Greenberg and Heeter 1987; Mulgan 1991); formal education, competence |

**Table 5.3** (continued)

| Category | Definition | Examples |
|---|---|---|
| | | in expression (Budd 1987; Cuff 1980; Doctor 1991; Gandy 1988; Taylor 1968); experience and familiarity with situation (Culnan 1984; Rice 1988) |
| Political influences/ constraints | Power and control relationships of actors, institutions, equity and participation NOT financial aspects | Control over how power is applied (Mulgan 1991); over participation as a citizen (Gandy 1988; Murdock and Golding 1989); over information flow (Mulgan 1991); over individuals |
| Context facet | Background and frame of reference of the potential user; background in which an information system operates | The individual's overall range of background experiences; overall climate of a system's ownership, development, operation |
| Situation facet | The particular set of circumstances from which a need for information arises, the awareness of those circumstances, and the awareness (however vague) of that need | Gap (Dervin 1983), visceral need and conscious need (Taylor 1968), problematic situation (Wersig 1979), anomalous state of knowledge (Belkin 1980), discomfort, or information need |
| Strategies facet | The dynamic process of addressing the situation, including a more structured representation of the situation and what is required to address it; interaction with a system; informal evaluation and iterations | Bridges, barriers, blocks, helps encountered on way to address situation (Dervin 1983); a more formalized need (Taylor 1968) and plan of action; query statement or problem statement; reevaluation (Johnson and Rice 1987); new questions (Kuhlthau 1985) |
| Outcomes facet | Retrieval and use of information; evaluation, possibly leading to new situation, iterations | Consumption or use of information (Kubey and Csikszentmihalyi 1990; Tague and Schultz 1989); adoption, adaptation, reinvention (Johnson and Rice 1983; 1987; Rice and Rogers 1980) |

for an individual can affect access differently in different situations. For example, the level of expertise or degree of experience for one situation may be extensive, while the same individual may approach another situation as a novice. Participants' reports on each search were coded with respect to facets of the information-seeking process and influences/constraints on access. This process of assigning evidence to the theoretically derived categories provided frequency counts of instances of categories across the units of analysis.

### Operational Definitions

Table 5.3 shows the experimental operational definitions for the theoretical propositions represented in the preliminary framework. They are based on the categories, components, and examples developed so far.

As noted, a number of cues for content analysis might be ambiguous without clear guidelines on where to assign particular terms. Experience, for example, could reasonably be assigned to cognitive rather than social. The rules of content analysis require mutual exclusivity. Experience is assigned here to the social category, given the focus of this research on the behavior of nonelites, whose experience might more likely be based on the workplace, the family, or social networks than on the academic. Motivation is assigned to economic influences and constraints because it balances potential costs of access.

### First Coding

The first pass at coding identified several difficulties. First, it became evident that although mediation had been considered independently of the influences and constraints on access to information, it was reported in participants' responses as an influence/constraint and was therefore added as a seventh influence/constraint. Second, a number of the interview documents included responses that were so brief (or missing altogether) as to be impossible to code meaningfully, so were assigned to the "other" categories. Third, the first test of intercoder reliability pointed out a need to assign coding in a more rigorous fashion, requiring more explicit operationalizations.

Because many of the responses indicated more than one influence or constraint, procedures for the first pass at coding allowed for the assigning of more than one influence/constraint category to a single response. Intercoder reliability testing revealed that such an unstructured approach made consistency in coding extremely unlikely. When the data were recoded, therefore, each response was coded according to one facet of the information-seeking process and one influence/constraint on

**Table 5.4**
Summary of Changes in Coding Procedures Resulting from Initial Coding

| Procedure | Initial Coding | Subsequent Coding |
|---|---|---|
| Assigning mediative responses | Not assigned or assigned to secondary category | Established as category and assigned accordingly |
| Assigning blank or monosyllable | Not assigned | Assigned to other |
| Assigning to category | Responses assigned to as many or few categories as were represented | Responses assigned to one facet and one influence/constraint |
| Assigning multiple categories | Responses assigned to as many or few categories as were represented | Responses assigned to predominant influence/constraint (one only) |
| Outcomes facet and operational definitions | Retrieval and use of information; evaluation, possibly leading to new situation, iterations | Retrieval and use of information; evaluation, possibly leading to new situation |

access to information. In the latter instance, if more than one influence/constraint were evident, the response was coded for the predominant influence/constraint. That meant that each of the 151 documents yielded 27 facet codings and 27 influence/constraint codings. Finally, the operational definition of the outcomes facet was refined slightly to delete "iterations," which was already identified as part of the definition of strategies. Therefore, if a search led to a new situation, coders assigned that report to outcomes, but assigned iterations of a search on the original situation to strategies. Table 5.4 lists the changes.

The first pass at coding also identified additional cues for coding. In other words, participants' responses provided additional instances of influences or constraints that fit into existing categories but that had not been explicitly spelled out as part of the operational definitions. For example, although memory, curiosity, and expectation were not explicitly identified in the operational definition for cognitive influences and constraints, that category could clearly account for them. Similarly, travel, health, and body were not initially listed under physical influences and constraints, but they belong in that category. Table 5.5 indicates the categories identified for each influence/constraint based on the literature along with the additions for each category.

A few additions took more than a moment's thought to place appropriately. "Timeliness," for example, was briefly assigned to physical. Ultimately, it was

**Table 5.5**
Additions to Operational Definitions

| Influence/ Constraint | Examples/Components | Additions |
|---|---|---|
| Physical | Ability or limitation | Health, body |
| | Geography, demographics | Locations, destinations |
| | Arrangement | Space |
| | Orientation in environment | Path, route |
| | Proximity | Equipment |
| | Security/obstruction | Printout, download |
| | Display | Format |
| Cognitive | Understanding | Decision, confusion, curiosity |
| | Awareness | Expectation, surprise, interest |
| | Literacy, facility | Exploration, experimentation |
| | Learning style, information processing | Attention, confusion |
| | Style | Syntax, language, specificity |
| | Skill level | Questions, answers |
| | | Remembering, forgetting |
| Affective | Attitudes | Laughter |
| | Confidence | Funny, humor |
| | Feat/trust | |
| | Comfort/discomfort | |
| | Feelings | |
| Economic | Benefits | Difficulty/ease, effort |
| | Costs | Timeliness, time, waiting |
| | Value | Worth, usefulness, waste |
| | Motivation | Persistence |
| Social | Cultural norms | Work, job, career |
| | Background | Social activities (dancing, music) |
| | Networks | Life events |
| | Education | |
| | Communication competence | |
| | Experience | |
| Political | Control | Participation |
| | Power | Government functions |
| | Equity | |
| Mediative (added after coding #1) | Not in initial list of influences/ constraints | Intensifying, compensating potential |
| | | Connecting, links |
| Other | Anticipated possibility of new category—only mediative | No answer |
| | | Nothing, no, yes |

moved to economic because of its relationship to value, benefit, and motivation. "Surprise" was assigned to cognitive because it assumes expectation, but assigning it to affective had been considered.

The facets of the information-seeking process did not require additions. They did, however, require careful re-readings of the operational definitions to clarify which examples belonged in which category. One of the difficulties was the distinction between questions generated from a search that constituted new situations and questions that shed new light on the original situation. The former example belongs in outcomes, the latter in strategies. Very little appeared that did not fit comfortably in an identified category. Aside from "no answer," "nothing," "no," and "yes," the only addition to the "other" category was "dumb luck." Table 5.5 shows the additions to the operational definitions.

### Recoding and Intercoder Reliability Testing

Following the first pass at coding, the recommended changes and additions were applied to the operational definitions. In addition, for each response, coders assigned one facet of the information-seeking process and only one influence/constraint. Ten interview documents served as the basis for intercoder reliability testing. The second coder trained on two of the ten documents, leaving eight documents, representing a sample of roughly 5 percent of the total as the sample for intercoder reliability testing. Results from this sample were compared with the primary coder's coding of the same interviews.

The confusion matrices in tables 5.6 and 5.7 summarize the results. The numbers in the cells represent how the two coders assigned categories. When both coders

**Table 5.6**
Confusion Matrix of Initial Coding: Facets of the Information-Seeking Process

| Coder 2 \ Coder 1 | Context | Situation | Strategies | Outcomes | Other | Total |
|---|---|---|---|---|---|---|
| Context | 11 | 3 | 0 | 0 | 1 | 15 |
| Situation | 3 | 35 | 2 | 1 | 5 | 46 |
| Strategies | 1 | 3 | 63 | 12 | 5 | 84 |
| Outcomes | 0 | 0 | 3 | 65 | 4 | 72 |
| Other | 0 | 5 | 0 | 0 | 16 | 21 |
| Total | 15 | 46 | 68 | 78 | 31 | 238 |

**Table 5.7**
Confusion Matrix of Initial Coding: Influences/Constraints

| Coder 2 \ Coder 1 | Physical | Cognitive | Affective | Economic | Social | Political | Mediative | Other | Total |
|---|---|---|---|---|---|---|---|---|---|
| Physical | 1 | 1 | 0 | 5 | 3 | 0 | 1 | 1 | 12 |
| Cognitive | 5 | 27 | 0 | 12 | 8 | 0 | 2 | 7 | 61 |
| Affective | 0 | 1 | 6 | 2 | 1 | 0 | 0 | 0 | 10 |
| Economic | 0 | 2 | 0 | 35 | 0 | 0 | 0 | 1 | 38 |
| Social | 1 | 2 | 0 | 5 | 18 | 0 | 3 | 0 | 29 |
| Political | 0 | 2 | 0 | 1 | 1 | 0 | 0 | 0 | 4 |
| Mediative | 3 | 0 | 0 | 2 | 0 | 0 | 17 | 0 | 22 |
| Other | 0 | 0 | 0 | 1 | 2 | 0 | 0 | 51 | 54 |
| Total | 10 | 35 | 6 | 63 | 33 | 0 | 23 | 60 | 230 |

assigned a response to the same category, a number is added where like categories intersect. For example, cell 1,1 represents 11 instances in which both coders assigned a response to the context category. Cell 1,2, however, represents three instances in which coder #1 assigned a response to context, but coder #2 assigned the same response to the situation category. Ideally, all coding would fall along the diagonal from cell 1,1 to cell 5,5.

The Holsti formula (Wimmer and Dominick 1991, 173) yielded reliability coefficients of .80 for facets of the information-seeking process and .67 for influences/constraints. These results were less than ideal, even when taking into account the complexity of the coding scheme. Scott's *pi*, which corrects for agreement between coders by chance, was also applied. For facets of the information-seeking process *pi*=.73, and for influences/constraints *pi*=.59. In both cases, the initial coding revealed some initial conceptual ambiguities that needed clarification.

**Coding Clarifications** Analysis of the areas of disagreement (the off-diagonal entries in the confusion matrix) allowed identification of several patterns of differences between coders. These patterns guided development of further clarifications in the coding process, shown in table 5.8. First, if there was enough information from the question and answer to categorize the facet of the information-seeking process, even for monosyllabic responses, then coders assigned the response to the facet or influence/constraint rather than to "other." This condition arose more frequently for facets than for influences/constraints. This is likely because the questions

**Table 5.8**
Coding Clarifications Based on Intercoder Reliability Testing

| Condition | Action |
|---|---|
| If question cues sufficient to assign response | Assign response to facet, not other |
| If more than one influence/constraint evident and they are of equal importance | Assign response to influence/constraint first mentioned |
| If reference to knowledge of availability or to expectation | Assign to cognitive, not economic |
| If reference to human or electronic intermediary | Assign to mediative |
| If nature of ease or difficulty not specified | Assign to economic |
| If nature of ease or difficulty specified | Assign to category specified |
| If reference to human or electronic networks | Assign to social |
| If reference to lock outs for lack of authorization | Assign to political |
| If reference to lock outs for lack of connection | Assign to mediative |

themselves frequently provided enough information to be able to assign responses to facets but not enough to be able to assign for influences/constraints. Second, if more than one influence/constraint were present and of equal importance, then coders assigned the response to the influence/constraint that appeared first in the response. Third, expectation and knowledge of what was available on a given question or topic were assigned to cognitive, not economic. Fourth, mediative influences and constraints included human, electronic, or other intermediary, such as books, handouts, and posters. Fifth, when the nature of ease or difficulty was not specified, coders assigned the response to economic. If the ease or difficulty was attributed to another influence/constraint, however, coders assigned the response to the category of attribution. Sixth, coders assigned networks, whether electronic or interpersonal, as social influences/constraints. Finally, coders assigned reports of users' being locked out of systems for lack of password or authorization as political influences/constraints.

**Intercoder Reliability in Recoding** All interview responses (151) were recoded according to the additions to the operational definitions. Coders were retrained according to the additions to the operational definitions and the clarifications, producing nearly diagonal confusion matrices. This time intercoder reliability coefficients were far more encouraging. Holsti's formula yielded .95 for facets of the information-seeking process and .96 for influences/constraints. For facets of the information-seeking process, *pi* was .93, and for influences/constraints, *pi* = .94. These coefficients reflect reliable coding for the content analysis. The coding structure, definitions, and procedure demonstrated sufficient validity and reliability.

## Follow-up Case Study: Framework Refinement

Because this research approach uses the case study method to build a theoretical understanding of access to information, and because such an approach to theory building relies on theoretical sampling, the follow-up case study was selected to be significantly different from the pilot and main case studies, to extend theoretical variance. This allowed the framework, refined and extended based on analysis of the data from the main case study, to be retested to compare it against the behavior and perceptions of participants from outside the traditionally elite contexts of most related research.

Participants in the follow-up case study were enrolled in a program designed to prepare them to enter or reenter the work force. The program, Support, aims to work toward job training and placement with individuals on public assistance and thereby serves individuals who are likely to have been outside populations traditionally served by institutional information systems. The program's director provided names of participants willing to be interviewed.

In this case, the same question protocol was administered as a face-to-face interview rather than as a written survey. Three arguments drove the decision to interview rather than to elicit written responses to the interview protocol:

1. As no course assignment was required of this group, participants were more likely to complete an interview than a written assignment.
2. Some participants in this group may have had limited resources, such as time or facility in reading and writing. The interview approach was therefore more likely to allow for all participants to respond.
3. The additional data source was designed to contribute to a more complete understanding of access to information and further tested the validity and comprehensiveness of the framework.

The investigator conducted the face-to-face interviews with one participant at a time during the summer of 1996. Interview length ranged from 40 minutes to two hours. The four extensive interviews were tape-recorded and transcribed.

Results were analyzed and compared against the revised framework and used to develop a refined theoretical framework for understanding access to information.

# 6

# Results: Testing the Framework of Access

All categories of the framework occurred in the interview responses. Although a number of responses were assigned to "other," these represented empty or monosyllabic responses rather than new categories not accounted for by the framework. Examining intersections of categories demonstrated a significant relationship between (1) facets of the information-seeking process, and (2) influences/constraints on access to information.

## Frequencies and Examples

This section reports frequencies for the individual facets of the information-seeking process and for the individual influences/constraints, along with examples of each (summarized in table 6.1). The percentages represent the proportion of the total responses assigned to any category except "other." For facets, the total frequency was 3,729; for influences and constraints, 2,988. The difference in frequencies of the two categories reflects the fact that although it was often possible to identify the facet of the information-seeking process based on a brief or monosyllabic response, such coding was less possible in assigning influences and constraints, which were more often placed in the "other" category and thus not included in computing the percentages.

### Facets of the Information-Seeking Process

Of the facets of the information-seeking process, strategies occurred most frequently and context least frequently. Of the 3,729 non-"other" responses, 347, or 9 percent, represented context; 884, or 24 percent, represented situation; 1,572, or 42 percent, represented strategies; and 926, or 25 percent, represented outcomes.

**Context** Context is the background and frame of reference of the potential user or the background in which an information system operates. It generally implies

**Table 6.1**
Summary of Frequencies and Examples from Main Study

| Category | Frequency | Percent | Example |
|---|---|---|---|
| *Facets of the Information-Seeking Process* | | | |
| Context | 347 | 9 | The primary topic that I selected was esophageal cancer, since I was diagnosed with this condition in June and have undergone radiation therapy, chemotherapy, and reconstructive surgery over the past five months. |
| Situation | 884 | 24 | I hoped to learn about alternative treatments for cancer and possibly clinical trials that might be appropriate for me. |
| Strategies | 1,572 | 42 | I tried selecting what seemed to be the most likely telnet sites based on the names of the site. Once connected, I worked through the menus in attempting to find the most likely locations for the information. Much of this was trial-and-error in the beginning. |
| Outcomes | 926 | 25 | I found nothing. |
| Total | 3,729 | 100 | |
| *Influences/Constraints* | | | |
| Physical | 286 | 9.5 | The aspect that it was all graphical made it easier to receive answers. It made it easier to understand the search. |
| Cognitive | 1,034 | 35 | It seems to me with more knowledge of commands and accessing these listings they would be at my disposal. As a newcomer I found it [the system] discouraging, hard to use, and not all it's hyped up to be. Without the knowledge it is no good. |
| Affective | 135 | 4.5 | I was intimidated so far as to what is on line. |
| Economic | 575 | 19 | Time is all that hindered my searches. |
| Social | 511 | 17 | I wanted to try to talk to people with my same interests one-on-one for more information. |
| Political | 66 | 2 | To protect myself as a potential home buyer. And to be fully knowledgeable of my rights, options, and the real estate market. |
| Mediative | 381 | 13 | I first had problems with my home computer in responding to the system, but after speaking to fellow students I was able to connect. |
| Total | 2,988 | 100 | |

phenomena that predate the situation that arises from them. Reports of contexts varied. Some were relatively simple and spoke to a current context. Others revealed more of the past and provided greater detail, as illustrated in responses to the question What set of circumstances led to your interest in this topic/question/problem?

> When I was eighteen, I found my father was trying to get me involved in what I considered to be major fraud. Trying to move out, and having no girl friends willing to move out of home, I found myself living with my boyfriend. Soon we discovered I was pregnant; then we broke up and now he is nowhere to be found. In the midst of all of this I became a statistic as an unwed mother receiving public assistance. So I picked women on welfare as my research topic.

Several responses represented pressing issues of daily life. In general, the context indicated circumstances in the lives of the respondents and their frames of reference in seeking information and using an information system, for example,

> The primary topic that I selected was esophageal cancer, since I was diagnosed with this condition in June and have undergone radiation therapy, chemotherapy, and reconstructive surgery over the past five months.

Implicit in the reports was the context of the information system most of the participants used as the basis for the searches reported in this data set. Most used primitive electronic search tools and a serial connection to the Internet. They worked in a classroom or lab situation using monochromatic monitors and text-based information-seeking tools that required considerable knowledge on the part of the user to be able to navigate the information system. This context rarely appeared explicitly in the responses, but it was a shared context for the participants that did affect them in other facets of the information-seeking process, especially their reports on strategies.

**Situation** The situation is the particular set of circumstances from which a need for information arises. It includes also the awareness of those circumstances and the awareness of that need. Some examples of the situation facet were procedural in nature:

> We were trying to learn how to play a bunch of new songs by Pink Floyd for our friends this past weekend. We needed sheet music, and money was limited, so the only logical solution was to surf the Internet.

Others had longer-range goals in mind:

> The topic I searched was grants, as in money for college.

Many were interested in health and wellness issues, either for themselves or because friends or relatives could be affected:

We are continuing to monitor our cholesterol, since there is a tendency for it to rise too much. So, we are interested in anything related to cholesterol, especially factors that affect HDL and LDL cholesterol.

**Strategies** The strategies facet includes the dynamic process of addressing the situation, a more structured representation of the situation, and what is required to address it. Interaction with a system or systems, informal evaluation, and new questions that lead to iterations are also part of strategies.

Examples of responses assigned to the strategies facet are descriptions of a course of action, comments on what helped or hindered progress, or reflections on what might have been a more effective strategy. The differences were, for the most part, cued by the questions themselves. What approaches did you try in seeking an answer? and How did you get an answer? tended to elicit the descriptions of the process. Comments on helps or hindrances usually appeared in response to Did anything make it difficult for you to look for an answer? or Did anything help you in looking for an answer? Reflections on improvements generally were offered in response to questions such as What did you do if you didn't find what you were looking for? or Did the ease or difficulty change? How? Why?

Courses of action ranged from the simple and familiar to the complex and sophisticated:

I used a Boolean search in Veronica to locate files and books. In some cases I retrieved thousands of files through insufficiently specific searches. I remedied this with extensions . . . or by using more specific searches.

Comments on helps and hindrances revealed a number of examples that included instruction, experience, and persistence:

I found the instruction and handouts easy to understand. It helped me understand even more when I helped fellow classmates.

The ease and difficulty changed when I decided to be more specific about what team I wanted information about.

Reflections on possible improvements to a search strategy seemed to focus on planning and syntax:

Not finding anything taught me that I should have been better prepared. I should have had the descriptors from the Medline search. I should have researched the descriptors used in Index Medicus; I should have had the names of some researchers and sites that are doing research. These may have helped me with authors and keyword searches.

Since most participants chose to try out the search tools introduced in class, these data may reflect an unusually high frequency of mediative difficulties. It is likely that reports of a wider range of strategies, not limited to the tools of the classroom, would ordinarily appear. In fact, as discussed later in this chapter, the actual frequencies of strategies intersecting with mediative influences and constraints do significantly exceed expected frequencies.

**Outcomes** The final facet of the information-seeking process, outcomes, includes retrieval and use of information, and evaluation. Retrieval, use, and evaluation can lead to new situations. As discussed earlier, most of the emphasis in studying information seeking has been on the situation and strategies facets. Little has been considered in the literatures with regard to context and outcomes, yet 34 percent of the responses in this study fall in those facets. In response to the question What did you do with what you found? comments ranged from terse to detailed:

> Read it, and just smiled.
>
> I wrote the lyrics down, combined them into my version and got them calligraphed on posterboard and hung them up in my room.
>
> All the information I have gathered, I have used to my advantage to continue working on personal photography projects. I have realized that my future in photography has already been changed, because new, young photographers are already showing their work on the Internet and gaining recognition and getting jobs. I need to learn all that I can about the Internet to possibly have a gallery site for myself.

Outcomes are of particular interest with regard to the nature of information as a thing or commodity. By having failed to account for the use of information—the actual outcomes—we have neglected to account for a major portion of access to the value of information. In many instances, outcomes reflected a level of satisfaction with the search, as expressed by the respondent. Ordinarily, this was in response to questions about whether or not the search had been worthwhile. Satisfaction, therefore, was frequently expressed in terms of economic influences and constraints.

### Influences and Constraints

The influences and constraints on access to information and communication derived from the extensive review of the literature that laid the groundwork for the preliminary framework included physical, cognitive, affective, economic, social, and political. In the course of carrying out the initial coding, the data illustrated the need for one more category—mediative influences and constraints. This was not particularly surprising in that one of the questions posed, prior to data analysis, was how to account for mediative functions in access to information. Mediation had been discussed extensively in the literature and was identified as a dimension of access. The question was whether it should be included as an influence/constraint or whether it was a separate dimension that interacted with other phenomena of access. Given the participants' responses, it seemed clear that mediation operates in a manner similar to other influences and constraints on access to information. The operational definition for mediative influences/constraints is the extension, expansion, enhancement, or limitation of natural individual abilities through interaction with technological or human intermediaries (Ruben 1993). Examples include intensification and compensation (Lievrouw 1994); acceleration, embedding of difficulty (Singer 1980); linking (Rogers, Collins-Jarvis, and Schmitz 1994); and facilitation (D. Schiller 1989).

As was true of the facets of the information-seeking process, nearly everything assigned to "other" represented no response or responses so terse as to make it impossible for the coder to determine a meaningful assignment. No new influences or constraints emerged from the data, and all categories derived from the literature appeared in the responses. Discussion and examples of each of the influences and constraints on access to information follow.

**Physical** The physiological abilities or limitations of a user, along with environmental, spatial, and display characteristics of representations of information or of a space or system through or in which one might find information, make up the category of physical influences and constraints on access to information. Examples of physical influences and constraints showed up in response to a variety of questions. Some had to do with display features:

> The aspect that it was all graphical made it easier to receive answers. It made it easier to understand the search.

Others were more literal, referring to physical presence or distance:

> I spend a great deal of time with computers and have an interest in the effects of being so close to the terminal screen.

An interesting aspect of assigning influences and constraints is that in some instances the designation applies to participants' discussions of their search procedures, whereas in other instances the focus is on the topic of the search. Physical influences and constraints, for example, cover the gamut from reference to physical health or difficulties and limitations, to electronic space. A number of the participants selected topics related to health or physical activity:

> I need to lose weight and I like to dance.

or to virtual physical space or limitation:

> Since my e-mail box is small ... I figured that by opening another account I wouldn't have to worry about not having enough room for any important information.

Physical influences and constraints occurred in 286, or 9.5 percent, of the responses. The comments from participants were, for the most part, consistent with the operational definition and examples derived from the literature. Specific illustrations of physical influences and constraints appeared in the responses. Several examples had not been addressed in the literature that provided the basis for establishing the categories, such as references to equipment; to the products of an electronic search, namely, printouts and downloads; and to travel, such as locations or destinations. The other examples—path, route, and format—appeared in the literature but for the framework were included under other explicitly listed subcategories. Health and body, for example, were implied under ability or limitation. Path and route could fall under geography, arrangement, or orientation in the environment, depending on participants' meanings.

**Cognitive** Cognitive influences and constraints include the user's understanding, awareness, literacy, facility or skill level, and information-processing style with regard to the situation and content, and with regard to the system, procedures, and means available to address the situation. More than 1,000 responses, or 35 percent, referred principally to cognitive influences or constraints.

Participants commented on what made the process harder or easier:

> The difficulty of syntax for connection and subscribing made it a little difficult.
>
> I realize that not all systems are the same, but I was unaware of what to even type after that didn't work.

Cognitive influences/constraints appeared, also, in reports of what respondents were trying to accomplish in their searches:

> It seems to me with more knowledge of commands and accessing these listings they would be at my disposal. As a newcomer I found it [the system] discouraging, hard to use, and not all it's hyped up to be. Without the knowledge it is no good.

In general, then, cognitive influences and constraints appeared most frequently in descriptions of the topic or problem of the search and in explanations of the participants' interactions with the system.

Again, comments from participants were consistent with the operational definition and with the literature that served as the basis for developing the categories of the framework. As was the case with physical influences and constraints, although specifics from the responses were added to examples of the category, most had been discussed in the literature but were included under subcategories. Syntax, for example, was discussed under literacy and facility, expectation was part of awareness of what was available, and so on. The comments affirmed the validity of this category as defined. The high frequency of responses that fell under this category gave it further support.

**Affective** The user's feelings about herself, the system, and the situation in the information-seeking process fall under affective influences and constraints. Examples include attitudes, confidence, fear or trust, and comfort or discomfort. Participants mentioned affect in only 4.5 percent, or 135, of the responses. Since the surveys in this study represent reports submitted to a teacher in an academic environment, it is possible that participants were less likely than the general population to report on their feelings. They appeared more comfortable with reporting on their procedures and the cognitive aspects of their decisions on how to proceed.

Affect influenced the importance of a search as well as the strategies a participant tried. His attitudes towards himself were influential, but the search experience also influenced the view of self:

> It was very important for me to get an answer because I am afraid of this specific disease and want to know all I can about it.

> How could I get so lost? I am an intelligent individual who holds a responsible position in my company and if this is so simple, where the X%#$@ am I?

Not much appeared in the responses as additions to this category—only humor and its expressions, such as laughter, emerged from the data as new components. Again, it is worth asking if affective influences and constraints truly represent an independent category or if they are more appropriately a subset of economic influences and constraints. Affect, though clearly influential in the information-seeking process, usually occurs as a cost, a benefit, a motivator, or an indicator of the value of the search and its outcome.

**Economic** The benefits, costs, and value (both potential and realized) of information to the user or provider, and the motivation to overcome costs and derive benefits, constitute the economic influences and constraints. Other nonfinancial costs, such as time, inconvenience, or annoyance, are also considered to be economic influences and constraints. Nineteen percent, or 575, of the responses represented economic influences and constraints.

Many of the examples illustrated the benefits the user sought through the search:

> Wanted to shop around to save money, and this search provided a way to find the lowest price through the state insurance department.

> Competing in today's job market is quite an awakening. It makes the "clue phone" ring, if you know what I mean.

Others illustrated costs or benefits of a system:

> Time is all that hindered my searches. It hindered it in that these are not the fastest systems and take a lot of time to transfer information.
>
> [The Internet] seemed to be the way to go for immediate info on this subject. No waiting for correspondence on the mailing lists. No waiting at the library for a book. Just punch in the relevant data and you'll get something!!

Others commented on the value of what they found or failed to find and revealed the unique nature of information as an economic entity. It is affected by timeliness, and the user has no access to the value of the information until he consumes it.

> Difficult. So much information to use and some of it out of date. Until I attempted to get the information some of it was unusable.
>
> It was not worth the aggravation and frustration I experienced.

As noted, the distinction between affective and economic influences and constraints is not entirely clear. Aside from that, the data affirm that economic phenomena do influence or constrain access to information. Again, additions to the examples were not surprising. Time and timeliness were evident in the literature, and persistence simply supported that motivation is a valid subcategory of economic influences and constraints.

**Social** Cultural norms, class membership and background, social networks, education and communicative competence, and experience with regard to a particular situation compose social influences and constraints. Social networks include networks of interest and activity, such as shared interest in musical groups or social acquaintances. Seventeen percent, or 511, of the responses reflected social influences or constraints. Examples illustrated the various components of social influences and constraints, including networks, experience, background, and education:

> Exploring NASA is fundamental to my interests in the space program because I have worked for NASA in the past and have a son who is an astronaut.
>
> I like to dance. I have friends that are promoters and djs, and I have been to many raves. I tried to find out the dates of upcoming raves.
>
> One of the board members, who is a social worker at a continuing care retirement community, needs this information and asked me for help.

Networks, both interpersonal and electronic, featured prominently in the comments on social influences and constraints. The frequency of another component, education, may reflect the setting of the case study in that all participants were enrolled in a course. Again, both the frequency of occurrence and the components referred to in the examples affirmed the validity of social influences and constraints and illustrated that, for the most part, the operational definition and examples adequately accounted for the phenomena of social influences and constraints on access.

The additions from the comments—work, job, and career; social activities; and life planning and events—were illustrative. Work, job, and career fell in the realm of social influences and constraints when the concern on the part of the individual was how to prepare for or select a career.

**Political** Political influences and constraints include power relationships of the actors and institutions. They also include equity and participation as a citizen. Although political influences and constraints were mentioned less frequently than any other influence or constraint (66 times, or 2 percent), this may result less from the prevalence of such influences and constraints on access to information and than from the classroom setting of this particular case study. In other words, it is possible that if the interview protocol had been administered in a workplace rather than in a classroom, more of the situations would have focused on workplace structures, proprietary information, and access through status. Examples referred to rights of participation in political processes and to failure to gain access to certain databases or sites because of lack of authorization. The first example explains what the participant was trying to accomplish in her search:

> To protect myself as a potential home buyer. And to be fully knowledgeable of my rights, options, and the real estate market.

> I tried to track down users of e-mail. No such luck. This is because most of the sites I was trying to reach have installed fire walls, because of their size in the industry; [they were] designed to do the job they did on me.

In both of these examples, the participants were looking for information that could lead to advancement in life. They illustrate power relationships of actors and institutions as well as participation rights. The data from the follow-up case study, participants of which fall outside the realm of those with privileged access to information, may shed light on the extent to which political influences and constraints pervade the process outside of a classroom setting.

**Mediative** Based on Ruben's (1993) definition of mediated communication, mediative influences and constraints include the extension, expansion, enhancement, or limitation of natural individual abilities through interaction with technological or human intermediaries. A teacher, a librarian, a friend, a gopher menu, or a book all qualify as mediative influences or constraints. Thirteen percent, or 381, of the responses made reference to mediative influences or constraints. Examples include human, print, and technological guidance or connectivity:

> I first had problems with my home computer in responding to the system, but after speaking to fellow students I was able to connect.
>
> I e-mailed my teacher asking for some help, and she e-mailed me back an address and I tried it to see if it worked. It did.
>
> The textbook helped in giving me preliminary sites to look through. From there, there were some references in the files I downloaded. Not many people can sit down and come up with ftp sites off the top of their head, so a textbook or small guide is very handy for things of this nature.

As noted earlier, this category was added in response to the data. Earlier on, mediation was identified as a potentially intensifying or compensating phenomenon in relation to access to information. It was not clear until mediative influences and constraints appeared frequently in the interviews that this was properly a category under influences and constraints. The data provided evidence that mediative influences and constraints occur with considerable frequency. It is possible, however, that the frequency in this case study is higher because of the classroom setting. Again, the theoretically extreme, follow-up case study sheds light on this question.

## Addressing the Research Questions

What have the data shown so far about the research questions under consideration in this chapter?

All categories of the framework were represented in the data, and this suggests that they do capture or organize participants' perceptions of access, certainly across situations and individuals. However, as noted, although participants were free to use and report on any setting, most carried out their searches using tools of the Internet introduced in class. Thus, the follow-up case study, in which participants were interviewed outside a classroom setting, will shed further light on whether the framework applies across settings.

As noted also, mediative influences and constraints were added to the framework to better reflect participants' responses and to improve the ability of the framework to capture or organize participants' perceptions of access to information. Aside from mediative influences and constraints, however, the data suggested no further additions to the framework, with the exception that they did extend each of the categories beyond what was identified by a review of the literature.

### Category Intersections

For every response, coders assigned one facet of the information-seeking process and one influence/constraint. Since we have been looking at the two dimensions of access to information identified in the literature that best reflect human behavior, it seemed reasonable to investigate whether the two dimensions operate independently or not. Excluding those intersections that included one or more "other" responses, the matrix produced 2,985 instances of intersections between facets and influences/constraints. A chi-square goodness-of-fit test applied to these intersections indicated a significant association between the rows (facets of the information-seeking process) and columns (influences/constraints on access to information) (chi-square = 472, d.f. = 18, $p < .001$).

Table 6.2 illustrates the analysis. First, the actual frequencies of each set of intersections are presented. Each intersection represents an instance in which a particular response was assigned to a given facet and a given influence/constraint. The intersection of context and physical, for example, occurred 31 times; the intersection of strategies and political occurred 22 times. Next, a summary of expected frequencies is provided. Expected frequencies were computed from the frequencies in the margins of the table of actual frequencies. Third, the chi-square values are shown. Those intersections demonstrating a large difference between expected and actual values include the one between context and cognitive (26.0), context and affective (20.8), context and economic (16.3), context and social (128.32), situation and economic (19.8), situation and mediative (12.8), strategies and physical (15.6), strategies and affective (19.5), strategies and social (54.2), and strategies and mediative (37.1).

Table 6.3 provides a summary of the chi-square values of intersections and examples of responses representing each intersection. Given a probability level of .01, at 1 degree of freedom, as would be applicable to any single cell of the chi-square analysis, a chi-square value equal to or exceeding 6.6 would be significant. Therefore, those intersections with a chi-square value of 6.6 or greater are included in the table, along with examples of each qualifying intersection.

### Discussion

We begin with discussion of those intersections where the actual frequencies significantly exceeded predicted frequencies.

**Context and Social** Given the operational definitions of the context facet (the background and frame of reference of the potential user; the background in which an information system operates) and social influences/constraints (cultural norms, class membership and background, social networks, education and communicative competence, and experience with regard to the particular situation), it is not overly surprising to see a high frequency of responses coded for both. After all, context is

**Table 6.2**
Chi-Square Analysis of Intersections from Main Study: Actual, Expected, and Chi-Square Values

| | Physical | Cognitive | Affective | Economic | Social | Political | Mediative | Total |
|---|---|---|---|---|---|---|---|---|
| *Chi-Square Analysis of Intersections: Actual Frequencies* | | | | | | | | |
| Context | 31 | 51 | 30 | 26 | 131 | 4 | 22 | 295 |
| Situation | 82 | 185 | 41 | 68 | 163 | 22 | 46 | 607 |
| Strategies | 90 | 561 | 29 | 330 | 129 | 22 | 264 | 1,425 |
| Outcomes | 82 | 242 | 35 | 146 | 88 | 16 | 49 | 658 |
| Total | 285 | 1,039 | 135 | 570 | 511 | 64 | 381 | 2,985 |
| *Chi-Square Analysis of Intersections: Expected Frequencies* | | | | | | | | |
| Context | 28.2 | 102.7 | 13.3 | 56.3 | 50.5 | 6.3 | 37.7 | |
| Situation | 57.9 | 211.3 | 27.5 | 115.9 | 103.9 | 13.0 | 77.5 | |
| Strategies | 136.1 | 496.0 | 64.5 | 272.1 | 243.9 | 30.6 | 181.9 | |
| Outcomes | 62.8 | 229.0 | 29.8 | 125.6 | 112.6 | 14.1 | 84.0 | |
| *Chi-Square Analysis of Intersections: Chi-Square Values* | | | | | | | | |
| Context | 0.3 | 26.0 | 20.8 | 16.3 | 128.3 | 0.9 | 6.5 | 199.1 |
| Situation | 9.9 | 3.3 | 6.7 | 19.8 | 33.6 | 6.2 | 12.8 | 92.4 |
| Strategies | 15.6 | 8.5 | 19.5 | 12.3 | 54.2 | 2.4 | 37.1 | 149.6 |
| Outcomes | 5.9 | 0.7 | 0.9 | 3.3 | 5.4 | 0.3 | 14.6 | 31.0 |
| Total | 31.7 | 38.5 | 47.9 | 51.7 | 221.5 | 9.7 | 70.9 | 472.0 |

**Table 6.3**
Summary of Chi-Square Analysis of Intersections with Examples

| Intersection | Chi-Square | Example |
|---|---|---|
| Context/ Social | 128.3 | I looked up alcoholism because it runs in my family and I would find it interesting to hear other people's stories. |
| Strategies/ Social | 54.2 | Actually, the answer came to me via discussions of people ... and what they found that helped them. |
| Strategies/ Mediative | 37.1 | I ended up sending a "please help me" message to my instructor. I was delighted at the quick reply. I also had to call the help line. |
| Situation/ Social | 33.6 | I am a freelance photographer and I ... wanted to find what the visual community was doing in other parts of the country. |
| Context/ Cognitive | 26.0 | I am involved in emergency medicine, and AIDS is a great threat to each of us. The more I know about this, the better off I am. |
| Context/ Affective | 20.8 | Regarding the selection of the cancer issue, perhaps the only thing is the embarrassment of admitting that I have cancer. |
| Situation/ Economic | 19.8 | I was trying to get some advice from people who had used the two radios, since the purchase constitutes a significant investment. |
| Strategies/ Affective | 19.5 | The importance was there, but accepting my limitations, I didn't have my hopes up. |
| Context/ Economic | 16.3 | I'm currently seeking to transfer to a university. I do not have an extensive bank account, so I'll have to borrow the money. |
| Strategies/ Physical | 15.6 | The lack of disk space caused me to have to consume and assimilate the data right away before I could do something else. |
| Outcome/ Mediative | 14.6 | I got this answer from what could be called the knowledge person source. I relied on another person's knowledge. |
| Situation/ Mediative | 12.8 | Trying to find out how to get into cyberspace. Asked around. Used e-mail. Used gopher. |
| Strategies/ Economic | 12.3 | Time hindered me. I came extra days to work on it, but found it hard to find information. |
| Situation/ Physical | 9.9 | I was trying to find more definitive information and the best site within a reasonable distance for an examination and treatment. |
| Strategies/ Cognitive | 8.5 | I found the directory but was unable to access the information there because I wasn't aware of what to do next. |
| Situation/ Affective | 6.7 | This topic is a bit humbling. I also have my own conclusion about the public assistance program. It's a frustrating oxymoron. |

likely to draw on one's experiences, education, and other components of social influences and constraints. That actual frequencies (131) were more than twice expected frequencies (50.5), however, warrants a closer look.

In several instances, the context was work-related. For example, in response to the question Did anything contribute to the set of circumstances behind your selecting this topic/issue/problem? one answer included

> Having been laid off from my past contracting position. I've been looking for work.

In others, education contributed to the context, though in the next example, social concerns are also part of the topic:

> Last fall I took a psychology class and I had to keep a journal. In the journal I found that I kept writing about children in our society today and how violent they have become. Children have become so desensitized to violence that they treat it as a natural part of everyday life. I wonder what the causes are because there is not one single cause but a combination of them.

Most of the responses that were jointly coded for context and social can be described as work-related, education- or classroom-related, or related to one's social network (that is, one's group of friends or family, or network-related to shared interests).

**Strategies and Mediative** The next most significant relationship in which actual frequencies exceeded expected frequencies is that between the strategies facet and mediative influences/constraints. Again, the operational definitions shed light on the relationship between the two. Strategies are defined as "the dynamic process of addressing the situation, including a more structured representation of the situation and what is required to address it; interaction with a system; informal evaluation; possibly leading to a new situation; iterations." Mediative influences and constraints are "the extension, expansion, enhancement, or limitation of natural individual abilities through interaction with technological or human intermediaries." Given the definitions, it does not seem unreasonable that someone seeking information would use mediative approaches in carrying out search strategies. As was the case with the context and social interaction, however, actual frequencies (264) far exceeded expected frequencies (181.9). Examples illustrate the relationship:

> The things that usually helped me were either helpful people who offered other places to go or straight answers right there, or pointers in files that I found that gave other sites and people to go and ask or question if I had any problems or whatnot.
>
> I also had to call the help line a few times from home. The first problem I had was not being able to log in. I was told that the line was down and to try again tomorrow. I was very pleased that the computer lab called me back so quickly.

Since the participants were students in an introductory course on how to use the Internet in the early days, when the interface was text-based and awkward, they may well have been more likely to ask a human intermediary for guidance and to use technological intermediaries, since that was a focus of the course. That aside, however, a significant relationship between the strategies facet and mediative influences/constraints is likely to show up even in a different setting, since it makes sense that a user would seek guidance and use search tools while addressing a situation or interacting with a system.

**Situation and Social** The next most significant relationship between facets and influences/constraints is that between situation and social. The actual frequency (163) of the intersection between the situation facet and social influences/constraints significantly exceeded the expected frequency (103.9). These comments illustrate the relationship:

I wanted to find other artists my age to find out what they are doing and what I could possibly learn from them.

I wanted to get my brother into computers so I got him into e-mail.

Social networks and life situations, which fell under the definition for social influences/constraints, were frequently important influences on the situations participants selected. Education was another common influence on the situation, as in the next example, from a student, whose aim was to

find information for a chemistry paper.

Although education-influenced situations might be more prevalent in this main case study than in the follow-up case, where the participants were not students, the social networks and life situations suggest a significant relationship across settings and individuals.

**Context and Affective** Affective influences and constraints intersected with the context facet 30 times. Expected frequency was less than half that, 13.3. Affect tended to come into play with context regarding emotional connections in participants' contexts and how they viewed themselves or coped with their lives. When asked about the set of circumstances behind their selecting a particular topic or issue, participants wrote

Wanting to care for people emotionally as well as physically.

My original topic was dance or music. I love to dance and I like music. They help me relax and clear my head when I have a problem or need to think.

Although actual frequency significantly exceeded expected, 30 occurrences represents only a little more than 1 percent of the total number of responses, so it will be helpful to view the results of the follow-up study to see if a similar significant relationship holds.

We turn now to considering those intersections that indicated frequencies significantly lower than expected.

**Strategies and Social** The expected frequency for the intersection of the strategies facet with social influences/constraints was 243.9, whereas the actual frequency was only 129. Again, looking at the operational definitions, it seems reasonable that social influences and constraints might come into play less in strategies than in other facets. In fact, however, social intersected with strategies only two times fewer than it intersected with context (131) and more than it intersected with outcomes (88). The primary examples of this intersection reveal a reliance on experience or education or on communicative competence or networks in addressing the situation or interacting with the system:

*How easy did it seem to get an answer?*
Really easy because of past experience.
*Did anything make it difficult for you to look for an answer?*
I'm still very new at this.
*What approaches did you try in seeking an answer?*
I telephoned both of my children and told them that I had sent them e-mail. I have and will continue to try to call my son back.
E-mailing other subscribers.

The highest frequencies of influences/constraints in intersections with the strategies facet fell under cognitive (561), economic (330), and mediative (264). Perhaps the gap between expected and actual frequencies with strategies and social is more reflective of the statistical basis for establishing significance and the high frequencies of other categories in the set than it is based on a logical connection or lack thereof between strategies and social influences/constraints.

**Context and Cognitive** The intersection of context with cognitive influences/constraints occurred 51 times, significantly fewer than the expected 102.7. For many of the same reasons that context and social intersect with higher than expected frequency (131), it makes sense that context and cognitive would intersect less frequently. The user's background and frame of reference are more likely to be related to experience, education, and networks than to understanding, awareness, literacy, facility or skill level, and information-processing style. Some examples did, nevertheless, illustrate this intersection. Most focused on users' background interests that provided the frame of reference for their searches:

*Is there anything else that explains why you selected this topic?*
Simply that since the information super highway we all call the Internet is fast becoming the way everyone finds information, I wanted to see just how simple and quick it was to acquire information about acquiring information. If you don't have the basics, you can't go any further, and then you are back to the beginning with nothing to show for it.

*Did anything contribute to the set of circumstance behind your selecting this topic/question/problem?*
My interests in good movies, new and old.
I had worked for a medical center and had done a lot of electronic transmission of insurance forms. This introduced me to the electronic transmission age but everything was done by rote rather than with an interest in learning the why and what if questions I am interested in.

## Summary and Conclusions

Primary findings indicated that all categories did appear in participants' observations, though it was necessary to add one new category, mediative influences and constraints (see table 6.1). Responses assigned to the "other" category, included to allow for factors not accounted for by the framework, represented blank responses or responses so short as to provide insufficient evidence for assigning to a category rather than data suggesting new categories.

Among the facets of the information-seeking process, context occurred in 9 percent of the responses, situation in 24 percent, strategies in 42 percent, and outcomes in 25 percent. In most research on the information-seeking process, the focus has been on the situation and strategies facets. That 34 percent of the responses in this study referred to context or outcomes indicates the importance of including these two facets for future study of the process. In particular, outcomes need to be considered because it is only in the use of information that one has access to its value. The findings on outcomes, which represented one quarter of the responses, also indicated another aspect of the user's making sense of the world in that one can view the user not only as a consumer or user of information but also as a maker of meaning or producer of information.

Among the influences and constraints on access to information, physical represented 9.5 percent of the responses, cognitive 35 percent, affective 4.5 percent, economic 19 percent, social 17 percent, political 2 percent, and mediative 13 percent.

Data for both dimensions supported the categories of the framework as defined and extended. The categories reflected participants' perceptions of access to information. The data suggested the addition of the mediative influence/constraint category (see table 6.1).

Next, this chapter considered intersections among categories of facets of the information-seeking process and influences and constraints on access to information. A chi-square goodness-of-fit test indicated a significant association between the facets and the influences/constraints (see table 6.2). Several intersections of a facet with an influence/constraint stood out as highly significant: context and social (128.3), strategies and social (54.2), strategies and mediative (37.1), situation and social (33.6), context and cognitive (26.0), context and affective (20.8), situation and economic (19.8), and strategies and affective (19.5). In each of these examples, a chi-square value of 6.6 or greater indicated that the relationship was statistically significant. Table 6.3 summarizes all such intersections.

Overall, findings supported the framework as defined and extended. Chapter 7 presents findings from the follow-up case study, designed to extend theoretical variance and provide the basis for refining the framework.

# 7

# Results: Refining the Framework of Access

This chapter reports on the follow-up case study, selected to extend theoretical variance by comparing the revised framework with the behavior and perceptions of participants from outside the traditionally elite foci of most related research. Methods described for the prior analysis were replicated in the follow-up study, with the exception that the interview protocol was face-to-face. Results were analyzed and compared against the revised framework, leading to a refined framework. In addition, this chapter presents an in-depth analysis of one interview that was particularly rich in detail and insight. The follow-up study supported the framework as extended by analysis of the data from the main study, and it clarified several questions that arose from that analysis with regard to the affective and political categories. Finally, this chapter presents the refined framework, applying the findings of the primary (main) and follow-up case studies.

## Research Methods

Because the aim of part I of this book is to build a theoretical understanding of access to information and communication, and because the case study method as applied to theory building relies on theoretical sampling, the follow-up case study represented an example designed to extend theoretical variance. Every effort was made, therefore, to select participants for the follow-up case study from outside the population of elite users of information and, if possible, from among nonusers.

### The Research Setting

Participants in the follow-up case study were referred through a program that we will call Support, the aim of which was to help those on public assistance become self-supporting (the names of the agency and the participants have been changed). The program provided training in life skills, such as how to identify a career direction, how to search for job openings, how to prepare a résumé, how to dress for and conduct oneself in a job interview, and so on.

The director of the program provided the researcher with the names of eight Support participants who had indicated their willingness to be interviewed. Of the eight, the researcher was able to interview four. Of the four individuals not interviewed, one, despite a number of attempts, was never reached. One was in the middle of moving at the time of the interviews and was unable to schedule a time to meet. Two others were homeless, and although they were willing to be interviewed, scheduling was difficult. One made an appointment but did not keep it and did not return follow-up attempts to reach her. The other left the area.

The four participants who did give interviews were mothers of young children. They were in their twenties and thirties. Three of the interviews were conducted in the participants' homes. The three participants interviewed at home lived in the same subsidized housing complex. The fourth interviewee was living with her mother and opted to be interviewed in the researcher's office.

Interviews, using the same interview protocol as in the main case study, ranged in length from 35 minutes to two-and-a-half hours. As in the main case study, participants were asked to select a real situation, challenge, or question of interest or import to them, about which they sought information. This time, however, the interviews were carried out face-to-face by the researcher. This was in part to eusure that participants would complete the interview protocol. In this follow-up case study, participants offered their time on a voluntary basis; they were not enrolled in a course for which the interview was a requirement. Second, there was some likelihood that a participant might not be able to read, although that did not turn out to be the case. Third, employing an additional interview approach triangulated the sources of data, contributing to a more complete understanding of access to information and further testing the validity and comprehensiveness of the framework.

Those who participated were extremely generous in telling their stories. They were exhausted and pressed for time because of the multiple demands on their lives, yet they were not only willing to talk but appeared genuinely pleased at the opportunity to make their perspectives known.

### Data Analysis

As with the main case study, the interview texts were entered into the Nud*ist program and content-coded according to the identified categories. Again, the units of analysis were the responses to each of the 27 questions per interview, for each of which coders assigned responses to one facet of the information-seeking process and one influence/constraint on access to information. In many instances, the responses were so rich as to represent multiple categories. This time, only nonresponses were assigned to the "other" category.

Coders followed the assigning rules detailed in chapter 5. Because of the clarifications and adjustments to coding procedures developed from the multiple passes at coding the main case study, intercoder reliability for the follow-up case study data was very high. For facets of the information-seeking process, Holsti's formula yielded a reliability coefficient of .98, and the *pi* index (which corrected for agreement by chance) yielded .97; for influences and constraints, Holsti's formula and *pi* were both .98.

Analysis of the interview texts indicated that the categories of the extended framework adequately accounted for the phenomena of interest. The stories of the women in the follow-up case study added additional depth to several of the categories. "Prayer" and "faith," for example, were prominent in the responses from this group, whereas they hadn't appeared in the 151 documents of the main case study.

*How did you get an answer?*
A lot of work and a lot of prayer.

Although they might have been added to several categories, including economic, because they frequently served as motivators or balances to costs, or to cognitive because they were frequently referred to as belief, "prayer" and "faith" as well as "self-doubt" were ultimately assigned to the affective category. They seemed most consistent with deeply held feelings of the user.

"Worry" was another common reference:

And now I'm trying to go back to school, and day care—just juggling and then trying to have a life in between that. Right now I'm just worried about school. And I'm worried about who's gonna take care of my daughter. I'm hoping at times I will somehow figure it out.

"Worry" was assigned according to the source of the concern.

"Indignity" and "degradation" arose for the first time in this set of responses, as in the following example:

The indignities are really the worst. The worst. It will knock you down faster than anything else. Because you're like, so much more.

They were assigned to political because they usually arose in the context of power relationships.

The following section reviews proportional distributions and examples from the various categories and reports on themes that ran throughout the interviewees' responses.

## Frequencies and Examples

Examination of the distributions represented in each of the categories of the framework based on the follow-up case study further addressed the two research questions that guided the prior two chapters. The interviews in the follow-up study were rich in detail. However, because the follow-up study was based on only four interviews, results were considered in terms of percentages, or proportions of the whole, to provide a reasonable basis of comparison between the distributions in the main and follow-up studies.

No responses were assigned to the category of physical influences/constraints. This result is a bit misleading, because many of the responses in the follow-up case study interviews were extremely lengthy. Coders assigned each response to the dominant influence/constraint and to the facet of the information-seeking process, as determined by the clarifications to the coding process described in chapter 5. In several instances, interviewees did refer to physical influences or constraints. They also referred to other influences or constraints within the same response. This example, which was coded as economic, from a participant who was a recovering alcoholic, illustrates this complexity:

> It meant survival.... It was a matter of I was gonna be able to make it and survive or do I just give up and say, oh well. You've made your bed. Lie in it. That's another voice I kept hearing in the back of my mind. And then I thought, uh, uh, that's not true. I'm sorry. We are human and we do make mistakes and some things we just don't have, like I didn't ask to be an alcoholic. And I know my husband didn't ask to be an alcoholic. It's like that commercial we have on TV. What did you used to dream? Did you wanna be a drug addict when you grew up? No. No. We didn't ask for this.

Had alcoholism been the main point of this response, it would have been categorized as physical. Because it focused on survival, however, and survival was mentioned first, along with the discussion of weighing costs and benefits, it was categorized as economic. Other examples of physical influences and constraints mentioned in the interviews included a daughter's asthma, the implications of attention deficit hyperactivity disorder for one of the interviewees, children's accidents, equipment breakdowns, transportation difficulties, and challenges of distance and proximity.

With the exception of physical, all categories were represented. Fifteen responses in each set of categories were coded as "other." In every instance these represented "no response." If they are removed from consideration, there were 100 responses in each set of categories.

**Facets of the Information-Seeking Process**

Of responses assigned to facets of the information-seeking process, 20 percent represented context, 17 percent represented situation, 40 percent represented strategies, and 23 percent represented outcomes. This distribution is quite similar to that from the main case study: 9 percent context, 24 percent situation, 42 percent strategies, and 25 percent outcomes, with only context being noticeably different, and strategies and outcomes representing almost identical distributions between the two studies.

Among influences and constraints, there was greater variation between the two data sets. For the follow-up study, as noted, no responses were assigned to physical. Of the other categories of influences and constraints, 14 percent were assigned to cognitive, 11 percent to affective, 26 percent to economic, 25 percent to social, 14 percent to political, and 10 percent to mediative. Compare these with the distribution for the main case study: 9.5 percent physical, 35 percent cognitive, 4.5 percent affective, 19 percent economic, 17 percent social, 2 percent political, and 13 percent mediative. Thus, the four follow-up cases exhibited noticeably less overall mention of physical and cognitive, and noticeably more overall mention of political, influences and constraints.

**Context** The interviewees tended to provide more background for their investigation, and their backgrounds seemed to bear significantly on what they chose to explore. The following represents a typical, though briefer than most, example of a context statement:

When my children's father left the family. And then my older daughter [left] and at that point I was dependent on my family and I was really sick during my pregnancy. So when my mom found out that I was pregnant and that he had left me, that's when I was out of a job and started going on welfare and then he moved out of the state, so that's another fight about it. And now I'm trying to go back to school, and day care—just juggling and then trying to have a life in between that.

**Situation** The proportion of responses coded for the situation facet was somewhat lower in the follow-up study than in the main study. Again, there was greater emphasis on context and, further, situations tended to be broader and directed more toward general life goals than toward a specific question or issue. The following example, which focuses on deciding the next step to take in life, illustrates the situation statements typical of the follow-up study:

Just the back and forth as to what can I do? What can't I do? Which would be best and a lot of second guessing and doubting with nobody to fall back on. If I made the wrong choice, not only was I hurting myself, but maybe more toward hurting them. I have my parents to talk to, but I kept getting, well, it's your life, and you have to make good decisions and I had an ex-husband who wasn't worth and isn't worth anything, but ... so it was on me. Lots of pressure.

**Strategies** Strategies represented almost the same proportion in the two studies. Because participants in the follow-up case study tended to pursue situations that involved larger decision-making issues than was the case in the main case study, the type of information they sought was less likely to be found in the more traditional sources than that sought by participants in the main study. Similarly, because participants in the follow-up study were not enrolled in a class and were not being introduced specifically to electronic means of seeking and finding information, their strategies were far less likely to rely on that setting or on such means. Participants were more likely to rely on word of mouth, social networks, and human intermediaries. This is consistent with Chatman's (1991) analysis of information-seeking behavior. The following examples illustrate strategies typical of the follow-up study:

It wasn't really easy. Articles and journals—there was a lotta information, but, uh, actually the person-to-person interviews, which I also needed for the research paper [for a community college class] was very difficult. I just had to use some other mother's experience 'cause I couldn't get ahold of any officials who would talk to me.

Um, I would run back to Sharon [at the Support organization]. I still run back to Sharon. A lot of listing out pros and cons. I had the choice of moving at one point and I even spoke with them [children] about it before I knew what it was going to be, anyway. A lotta asking questions of other people out there—anybody who would talk to me or answer questions.

**Outcomes** Outcomes also represented similar proportions in the two studies. The outcomes of the follow-up case study revealed a common thread. First, participants came to see themselves as deserving of answers:

I found a lot of locked doors and I had to maneuver around 'em for the keys, but I didn't really find anything dead end. Just kept buggin'. Right now I'm buggin' the state rep to get welfare to review a policy because he [son] starts kindergarten.

Several of the women spoke of having found voice and how, once found, they would not give it up. In terms of outcomes, they were concerned not only with how to use what they had retrieved but also with how to be heard, now that they knew enough to speak and knew they were worth listening to. In the analysis of the literatures of the various research areas, only mass media research considered information from the perspective of providing and disseminating it. The idea of voice, however, is a dominant theme in the literature (see chapter 3). The participants were not thinking in mass media terms, but they were definitely viewing themselves as makers of meaning, creators of information for others. For example:

> And I was talkin' to my sister, and she said, "Well, you'd better just keep your mouth shut," and I said, you know, "Well, you know me. And especially now I'm getting educated? Uh, uh, it's like gonna be so hard. You're gonna have to rip my lips off, 'cause I don't know. Mmmm mmmmm. There's no way I'm shuttin' up."

As noted in chapter 4, most research on information seeking has focused on the situation and strategies facets of the information-seeking process. Given that 34 percent of the responses in the main case study and 42 percent of the responses in this follow-up case study represented context or outcomes, it seems essential that these facets also be included in future research for a full understanding of the process. Further, given the increasing use of interactive means of communication or information seeking, such as the World Wide Web, it is becoming ever easier for users of information also to be creators and distributors of information. This is a significant contribution of including the outcomes facet in the framework. Information is not simply something one seeks. It is also something one can create and make available to others, illustrating the potential for information use to lead to ancillary social value (Bates 1988).

### Influences and Constraints

More than half of the responses represented economic (26 percent) or social (25 percent) influences or constraints on access to information. Also, whereas political influences and constraints accounted for only 2 percent of the main case study, in the follow-up study, 14 percent of the responses represented political influences and constraints. As noted, although no responses were coded as representing physical influences or constraints, the category was represented, but not as the predominant component of any given response. Examples of each category follow.

Table 7.1 illustrates the intersection of facets of the information-seeking process with influences/constraints on access to information. A chi-square goodness-of-fit test applied to these intersections indicated a significant association between the rows (facets) and the columns (influences/constraints). Applying a probability level of $p<.01$, a chi-square value equal to or exceeding 34.8 indicates a significant relationship between rows and columns at 18 degrees of freedom. The value of chi-square in this analysis was 34.6. Table 7.1 reports actual frequencies of the intersections, expected frequencies, and chi-square computations for each intersection and for the sets of categories. The numbers in the cells of table 7.1 represent frequencies rather than percentages.

**Table 7.1**
Chi-Square Analysis of Intersections from Follow-up Study: Actual, Expected, and Chi-Square Values

| | Physical | Cognitive | Affective | Economic | Social | Political | Mediative | Total |
|---|---|---|---|---|---|---|---|---|
| *Chi-Square Analysis of Intersections: Actual Frequencies* | | | | | | | | |
| Context | 0 | 0 | 3 | 8 | 7 | 0 | 2 | 20 |
| Situation | 0 | 1 | 0 | 6 | 8 | 1 | 1 | 17 |
| Strategies | 0 | 5 | 4 | 9 | 6 | 9 | 7 | 40 |
| Outcomes | 0 | 8 | 4 | 3 | 4 | 4 | 0 | 23 |
| Total | 0 | 14 | 11 | 26 | 25 | 14 | 10 | 100 |
| *Chi-Square Analysis of Intersections: Expected Frequencies* | | | | | | | | |
| Context | 0 | 2.8 | 2.2 | 5.2 | 5.0 | 2.8 | 2.0 | |
| Situation | 0 | 2.4 | 1.9 | 4.4 | 4.3 | 2.4 | 1.7 | |
| Strategies | 0 | 5.6 | 4.4 | 10.4 | 10.0 | 5.6 | 4.0 | |
| Outcomes | 0 | 3.2 | 2.5 | 6.0 | 5.8 | 3.2 | 2.3 | |
| *Chi-Square Analysis of Intersections: Chi-Square Values* | | | | | | | | |
| Context | 0 | 2.8 | 0.3 | 1.5 | 0.8 | 2.8 | 0 | 8.2 |
| Situation | 0 | 0.8 | 1.9 | 0.6 | 3.2 | 0.8 | 0.3 | 7.6 |
| Strategies | 0 | 0.06 | 0.04 | 0.2 | 1.6 | 2.1 | 2.3 | 6.2 |
| Outcomes | 0 | 7.2 | 0.9 | 1.5 | 0.5 | 0.2 | 2.3 | 12.6 |
| Total | 0 | 10.9 | 3.1 | 3.8 | 6.1 | 5.9 | 4.8 | 34.6 |

**Physical** None of the responses represented physical influences and constraints. This is less a function of physical factors' not appearing in the responses and more a function of the length and complexity of the responses. For example, in the following response, the daughter's physical condition was, indeed, influential. The overriding influence/constraint, however, was economic. This is typical of many of the responses.

> *What set of circumstances led to your interest in this topic/question/problem?*
> Divorces. Two kids. She's [daughter] chronic asthmatic. I could not figure out how to make $600 in medicines, $600 in rent, and $900 in day care on a seven dollar [an hour] job. It just doesn't work. So I just wanted something more to be able to take care of them [the children]. When I started she [daughter] was six months old.

Even though no responses in this follow-up study were coded as physical, this influence/constraint was well represented (9.5 percent) in the main case study, and there was sufficient mention of physical influences and constraints in the follow-up study to support its retention as an independent category of the framework.

**Cognitive** Fourteen percent of the responses were assigned as cognitive influences and constraints. This is a noticeably lower proportion than the 35 percent of the main study. The discrepancy is probably a result of the settings of the two studies. The main case study was carried out in a classroom setting, whereas the follow-up case study was conducted with participants facing larger social and economic challenges. Their responses reflected these challenges.

It is interesting to note that the investigation of intersections of facets with influences/constraints revealed that only one intersection was statistically significant: the outcomes facet with cognitive influences/constraints (with a chi-square value of 7.2, where 6.6 or greater indicates a significant relationship at 1 degree of freedom and a probability level of $p<.01$). Among this group of participants, cognitive influences/constraints occurred at the outcomes facet more frequently than at any other facet. There were no cognitive influences/constraints coded in context, one in situation, and five in strategies. The cognitive outcomes tended to represent what the participant had learned or new questions that had arisen from the process of exploring their issues:

> Every question leads to more questions. Again, back to the career, back to the school, back to the kids. Even in discipline [of the children], are you doin' the right thing? Uh, are they gonna be traumatized by the time they're 15? 'Cause I used to bust on my mother that she was the meanest thing and I'd never be like her and now she turns around and says I'm more rotten than she ever was as far as how strict I am with them. The questions are, am I doing the right thing? Am I too hard?

**Affective** For this group, affective components—how they viewed themselves, the system, or the situation—played a larger role in information-seeking and meaning-making behavior than in the main study (11 percent compared to 4.5 percent in the main study):

I didn't feel that I had the ability to do it. I knew I always had a lot of common sense and I knew I wasn't stupid, but I kinda breezed through high school and I didn't really put that much into it 'cause my parents had a business and I was kinda workin' for them, so it was kinda a lot was taken away from high school years, but again, it was something that had to be done. It was more a lack of confidence in my own abilities to do it.

Affective influences/constraints were distributed fairly evenly across context (27 percent), strategies (36 percent), and outcomes (36 percent) (see table 7.1). There were no instances of affective influences/constraints coded at the situation facet. The previous example reflects affective influences at the context facet. The example that follows reflects affective influences in intersection with the strategies facet:

The more I did well, the more that I knew I was doin' the right thing. I would get kicked back five steps and I'd pull myself all the way forward again. But once I at least caught up to where I was before, the doubt kind of slipped off and I kept on going.

At the outcomes facet, affective influences/constraints tended to reflect growth, acceptance, and appreciation of self:

*Was it worth trying to find? How, or how not?*
Definitely. Definitely. Because I feel so much better about myself. I know that I'm a capable person. I'm not a worthless piece of dirt and, um, and I can give that to my children. So no matter what happens, I can give them that gift.

Examples of affective influences and constraints in the follow-up study seemed to represent users' perceptions of self, system, or situation rather than, as posited in the discussion of the main study, feelings that served usually as motivation, cost, or benefit. Although further study and consideration are required, the results of this follow-up study support continuing to treat affective influences/constraints as an independent category rather than as a subcategory of economic influences/constraints.

**Economic** Economic influences and constraints occurred more frequently than any other influence/constraint. Twenty-six percent of the responses reflected economic concerns. In some instances, economic concerns are expressions of financial pressures:

*Did anything hinder you in the set of circumstances behind your selecting this topic/question/problem? What?*
Poverty. You don't get the same response from a lot of people when they find out that you're on welfare.

Other examples illustrate other types of costs and responsibilities:

> Self-doubt comes back every once in a while. Time. Lack of time to try and pursue information. Most offices seem to close by five. I don't usually get home most nights 'til six and no access to the Internet, so you can't pull any information that way. So, yeah, lack of time, lack of money to be able to have somebody watch the kids so I could have the evening hours or . . .

Economic influences/constraints occurred most in the strategies facet (35 percent), next in context (31 percent), then situation (23 percent), and least frequently in outcomes (12 percent).

**Social** Social influences and constraints occurred in 25 percent of the responses, almost as high a distribution as economic. Again, this reflected the life concerns of the participants, which were evident in every facet of the information-seeking process. For example, the backgrounds or cultural norms of the participants influenced or constrained access in the context facet. Social influences and constraints, particularly as they related to work, social network, or life path concerns, occurred most frequently at the situations facet:

> *Did anything help you arrive at this topic/question/problem? What?*
> I am finally making it. Well, I'm not making it, but I have a job and I'm making it a little and I'm not gonna be happy at that and I'd rather be able to go back to school. Then, when I'm out of school I know I'll be in a career that I like. Um, doing something—packing boxes, or whatever—I won't be happy, so I knew I wanted to go on. But I wasn't happy in the relationship I was in, anyway. Lots of problem situations I've gotten myself into.

Other social concerns reflected education and family responsibilities.

**Political** As anticipated, political influences and constraints represented a larger proportion of the responses in the follow-up study than they had in the main study. Political influences/constraints were most prevalent in the strategies facet, representing 64 percent of the examples, and generally reflected power relationships or attempts to gain access to participation:

> *Did anything make it difficult for you to look for an answer?*
> Yeah. The stone wall. No answer on whether they ever planned on implementing a full-day kindergarten, you know, to get busing.

The next example represents the workings of a political construct, medical assistance, and also illustrates how difficult it is for one lacking political clout to gain access to information without something to span the boundaries of power and control:

I had to be referred in an emergency situation—if you were admitted through the ER and then they referred you to someone who would accept it or you were taken on a rotation basis. One doctor in all of Doylestown for that month would take MA [medical assistance] cases and.... If you were lucky enough to find that one each month who was taking it, then you would have a doctor from then on, but the only way I would find doctors is through the answering service I worked for. I just started answering for 'em and some of them were very personable in talking with them, and I'd just come out and say, you know, "I'm on MA. Do you take it? Do you know anybody who does?" And most said eventually that they would take it, only because I was working for the answering service. They'd come out and say it's not our turn to have it.

These examples lend support to recognizing political influences/constraints as an independent category that helps capture participants' perceptions of access to information across situations, individuals, and settings.

**Mediative** The final category, mediative influences and constraints, occurred in 10 percent of the responses. Whereas in the main study mediative influences tended to favor technological intermediaries, in the follow-up study human intermediaries played the more important role, as both helps and hindrances:

So I got into the GED program and I got through ... lo and behold, I got a 313 on my GED.... It was workin' out good. And Linda.... and Sharon—they ran the program through [College A] and they were, like, great. They were the best two to put together 'cause they got along so well and they were very, very helpful and encouraging, and they wouldn't let us quit. They wouldn't let us quit, and they just said, "Trust us! Go through the book, and you'll do fine." But, um, I think because I was still floatin' around, I wasn't sure what was gonna happen at that point. I was getting very panicky. They said, "We know where you need to go now." So they sent me over to Sharon [at Support] and this woman is such a gift! She is such a wonderful lady. It's just amazing. That job was meant for her. She is, aaah, I can't even tell you—she is like an angel. And she would just laugh and tell her stories, and she's just amazing.

### Summary of Follow-up Study Distributions

Analysis of the data of the follow-up study indicated that the categories as defined and extended from the main case study adequately and accurately captured or organized participants' perceptions of access to information across situations, individuals, and settings. Further, the data did not suggest additional dimensions for the framework, though they did suggest a few additional components.

Distribution of the coding categories among facets of the information-seeking process was similar to that of the main case study, with strategies and outcomes representing almost identical distributions, and the distribution of context and situation almost evenly divided in the follow-up study. In the main study, situation occurred nearly three times more frequently than context.

Among influences and constraints, variation between the two data sets was greater. In the follow-up study, physical influences/constraints were not represented. This, however, appeared to be a consequence of the richness of the data rather than of an absence of the category; there was sufficient mention of physical influences/constraints to support the retention of this category in the framework.

Context played a larger role in the follow-up study than in the main study. Participants' backgrounds guided what they chose to explore. The situations category tended to represent broader, more life-goal-directed circumstances than in the main study. Strategies represented almost the same distribution in both studies. Strategies in the follow-up study were more likely to rely on word of mouth, social networks, and human intermediaries than in the main study, which was carried out in a classroom setting. An important finding of analysis of the outcomes facet was the metaphor of voice, and of the participants' interest not only in consuming information but also in finding channels through which to be heard. Participants came to view themselves as makers of meaning and creators of information who deserved a hearing from others.

Given that 43 percent of the responses in the follow-up study represented the context or outcomes facet, any comprehensive theoretical model of access to information must account for the full process of background for, access to, use of, creation of, and distribution of information.

Table 7.1 presents a chi-square goodness-of-fit analysis of the data from the follow-up study. The test indicated a significant interaction between rows (facets of the information-seeking process) and columns (influences and constraints on access to information).

Cognitive influences and constraints, particularly at the outcomes facet, represented what the participant had learned or new questions that had arisen. Affective components played a large role in follow-up study participants' information-seeking behavior. Affective influences tended to represent users' perceptions of self, system, or situation rather than a subset of economic motivation, costs, or benefits. Economic influences/constraints occurred more frequently than any other category, illustrating financial pressures as well as other costs, benefits, and responsibilities of the participants. Social influences and constraints were almost as prominent, reflecting the life concerns, such as job or career, education, family, and social networks, of the participants.

Political influences and constraints represented a significantly larger proportion of the distribution in the follow-up study than in the main study. They reflected power relationships or attempts to gain access to participation and lent support to retaining political influences/constraints as an independent category in the framework.

Finally, mediative influences and constraints, added as a result of the main study, occurred in 10 percent of the responses. In the follow-up study, mediative influences tended to refer to human intermediaries rather than to electronic or technological intermediaries as was usually the case in the main study.

Overall, results of the follow-up study validated the categories of the framework as capturing or organizing participants' perceptions of access to information across situations, individuals, and settings. Although the study results did not suggest additional dimensions for the framework other than the addition of mediative influences/constraints, the follow-up study did suggest a few additional components for categories of the framework.

## Amy's Story

In addition to specific examples of the categories, the data revealed themes that ran through the women's stories. The comments of one of the interviewees, we'll call her Amy, offered rich illustrations of the categories as well as the themes. Her responses were also indicative of the complexity of this data set. The response to one question alone was three full pages of single-spaced type. As was true of the four participants in the follow-up study, Amy was extremely generous in providing details of her story.

### General Themes

To introduce Amy, here is her opening response. It is presented in full to give a sense of how she tells her story. The themes of *care*, *diggin' and buggin'*, and *voice*, noted in italics in her response, are discussed in detail in subsections that follow.

*Please describe the issue you are exploring. [What I want you to do first, if you don't mind, is just think of some situation for which you really needed information. Now that could be how you found Support—that's just one example. The only stipulation is that it be some instance that mattered to you, something where it was important for you to find information.]*
I think probably when I first made the decision to separate from my husband, it was very, very difficult to find out what was out there and in place for us as a mom and two kids in order to get a roof over our heads. I had no clue how we were gonna make it, what we were gonna do, and I was even ready to agree to $50 a month, just as long as, you know, we made the break, and I knew the information was out there, but it wasn't very easily accessible. *I'm*

*the type of person I keep diggin' and diggin' until I get to the bottom of it and, um, just I was led through a path through the phone book and all kinds of places and eventually I was hooked up with the right information*, but it's frustrating for a person who's not used to doing that or maybe their situation was even worse where they didn't have that kinda time 'cause I felt that that time to me was a luxury and I was fortunate that I had access to a phone and I was able to make the calls that I needed to make. Otherwise, I can't imagine. I can't imagine what would happen for someone that was, you know, in a physical abuse situation or they had to leave immediately. Basically, all you're left with is the street because if you don't know what's available to you, you're out of luck. You're pretty much out of luck. It's there. You just have to uncover it. But it's tough to find the information but it was amazing. I know God was working in my life because everything came together. I mean they even changed the laws up at domestic relations and they started to do mandatory wage attachment. I had prepared myself for a fight over that. Um, my husband's an alcoholic and he's also into other, uh, drugs. What he's into now I really don't know but um umm ummm umum um, oh yeah, and I didn't know....

See, I have a hard time with my words and stuff and I didn't know if I would be able to sit in front of a judge and explain to him, well, this is an alcoholic and if you trust an alcoholic with money and they, you know, they'll agree to it, I mean the intentions are there, but by the time it comes down to payin', you know you get all the ... all the excuses at the end and so I really didn't want to have to do that and so I was very lucky I didn't have to. I didn't have to 'cause the laws had changed right when we went through the system. But it's really very difficult 'cause you start to feel like, maybe you're doin' somethin' wrong and, um, in your quest to survive you feel like you have to beg for every little thing that comes your way and it's the most degrading experience. I mean, I wouldn't want to be rich and be ignorant to everything that's goin' on and so I know I have to go through this for a reason and it's makin' me a lot stronger—if it doesn't kill me along the way [laugh/groan]. But, uh, um, it's a very very degrading process. When I went for, um, my protection from abuse order I had to bring my son with me. I had no babysitters. And I brought my son to the courtroom and we waited for hours and hours and hours. And you try occupying a $2\frac{1}{2}$-year-old outside in a waiting room. I mean, we did fantastically well, and he was amazing, but I just had to keep runnin' and he found where if he would walk past a certain point—ooh, they all start to run, now, and so he was playin' that game for a while. And then finally they called us in and I walked into the waiting—like, there's a little foyer right before you get into the courtroom and I gotta back up a little bit. They told me, well, we're not going to see any more today. And I said, there's no way—we've waited here all day. I cannot do this again with this child. It's not fair. We have to be seen today. I was promised. I'm on the list. We're gonna be seen. So they called us into the little waiting room, into the little foyer and the guard there said, "You can't take that [pointing to the child] in there." And it took every ounce of, of I don't know what, to hold back and keep from ... from decking that man right there on the spot. I just couldn't believe that he even ... that he even spoke to us in that manner. I ... I ... I just ... just, I don't know. It's been an experience. It's absolutely been an experience, but inside the court it went okay because I just, you know, I told the judge what was in my heart and why I felt we needed to be protected and everything went fine at that point, but that was just like the first of many battles that we ... that we've had to fight along the way, and we've *had* to fight. We really have had to fight, and, um, I ... my husband doesn't see the kids. He hasn't seen them since January. I'm taking my daughter in for counseling now. All of us need it because it's difficult enough to have two adults raising children.

It's even that much more difficult for one because you ... you're everything. You're doin' everything. You're mom, you're dad, you're chauffeur, you're activity director, you're laundress, you're cook, you're a student—all of this—and it's like ... like eventually the nut's gonna crack. It ... it and you try so hard and it ... I'm particularly in isolation because my mom ... my mom is older and sick and she lives in the Northeast and my dad is older and sick and he's in a nursing home and that was another, like, that's another part of my life that was very difficult, too, because I wanted to be able to take care of him. I never wanted him to be there, but that was out of my hands. But, um ... uh ... it's just ... it's very difficult. It's very difficult.

And someone that hasn't walked this path has no idea what we have to put up with. It's not fair. It's not fair and ... and ... they gotta do something. They have to change the system and Clinton, as far as I'm concerned, he sold out when he signed that bill [on welfare reform]. He sold out! We're out of immediate danger, but what about the women who are still being violated at home? They have no way out if he ... if he slams the door shut. *But now that they're teaching me to speak, I'm never gonna shut my mouth again!* I had no access to a lawyer. Everything I did I had to do on my own. Well, there's wonderful organizations like WomanHelp. They were amazing. They were amazing and you wouldn't believe what kind of doors my son opened. You wanna know how fast we'd get into a judge's chambers and out again? Bring a two-year-old into the office. Oh, you're havin' a problem? Ok. Hah. Because they say they'll fidget, but, I don't know it was ... it was good when I brought [my son] with me 'cause it made the whole process faster.

But, oh, WomanHelp was absolutely amazing. Absolutely amazing because I needed ... needed to know that everything was gonna be okay and they walked me ... once I found them they walked me through the whole process. It was just incredible. Incredible. It's ... it's out there. You just have to know where to go and, um, I don't know. You just have to keep your faith 'cause ... everything started comin' together for us. It's not ... it's not easy, but we can, we're doin' it, we're doin it. And, um, I'm finding less there's people that's in the system. People on the outside don't even have a clue what goes on and I'm ... I ... I get resentments because I know where I was and I know where I am now and I don't appreciate someone saying I'm lazy and I sit back and don't do a damn thing because that's not fair. I challenge them to try this for even one month. I don't think they could even make it for 48 hours. I really don't. I really don't. And don't misunderstand me. *I love my children with all my heart, and it's not like this is a sacrifice. 'Cause this is what I need to do. I mean, these are my kids and this is my job, to make sure that they're gonna be healthy, reasonably healthy and safe. And that's all that I'm tryin' to do is give them a fairly decent healthy childhood so they can grow up to be fairly decent healthy adults*, and it's amazing, it's like you wanna say, hello, is anybody out there? Can't you see what's ... I mean, like it's all over the place. All over the place. And welfare isn't even a dent in what kind of money they're spending, but they found that they've got so much emotions tied into it and that's where I don't know, I have no idea where they're goin' and what they're doin' but they're in for ... they have no clue what's gonna happen. I mean, it's gonna get worse instead of better. There's gonna be more crime. There's gonna be more people on the streets. So I don't know. I know maybe there's good in it, too. I don't know. I know it needed to be reformed. It definitely needed ... the system definitely needed to be reformed. Um, but to cut people off. I don't know. I don't think it's right. I really don't think it's right. There's too much ... there's still too much ... there's wealth in this country. I believe in fair share. My sociology class. I'm definitely a believer in fair share and equal distribution. Kinda like, okay, you have enough for this many years, now we're gonna make sure everybody has enough just to survive, and then we can start over again. 'Cause I don't know where it's leading to. I really don't. And high tech is going to marginalize people even more. Because if they don't have access to technology, they're gonna be left on the sidelines. They're eliminating the middle class by downsizing. It's ... it's very scary. It's very scary. And it's real hard to stay positive and I try not to ... I try not to project but I mean the more I'm learning, the more it's opening my eyes, and it scares me. It makes me want to scoop up my children and run for a cabin in the woods and scoop up all the rest of 'em because it's going to be a fight. And we owe it to 'em to leave 'em a legacy of something that they can be proud of. They're gonna be so angry. That's why they are, I think, that's why a lotta children are angry. They're ... they're ... I don't know.

## Care

One theme, care of others, stood out in all four interviews. This theme, referring usually to caring for children, appeared most prevalently in context and situation statements of the interviewees. Gilligan (1982) noted that an ethic of care was common among the women and girls she interviewed in her investigation of moral development. She pointed this out in contrast with an ethic of justice that seemed to be more prevalent among the boys interviewed in an earlier study (Kohlberg 1981) and argued that moral development may progress differently, depending on whether one's moral judgment is based on a framework of care or justice.

The situations the participants investigated were nearly all care-based. One interviewee reported three different situations. Even the most traditional of the situations, the one on which she planned to write a paper for school, was focused on care-taking in that she was investigating the possibility of all-day kindergarten so she would have reasonable care for her son in the coming year. She used both traditional information systems and social networking in her attempt to pursue the question.

*What set of circumstances led to your interest in this topic/question/problem?*
My very survival, I guess. My survival and my kids' survival.... When I married my husband, I married him for better or worse, and we were gonna be on the rockers together when we were 80 and 90 years old and that was it. And I love my husband today. I still have hope for him. And I also love myself today. And I know that I can't do anything to change him.... I just know that all of a sudden I knew that I could not stay here any longer 'cause I just got this whole picture of the scenario that the children were gonna grow up seein' this kind of, uh, this kind of a lifestyle and this was gonna be normal to them and that was it. I said no. No no no no. And I didn't know how I was gonna do it. I just knew if we stayed in it we were still gonna be in the rat wheel. Forever. And from that point on I just worked my way through.

The most important thing to me was being able to support my kids and myself and with my very limited education I just knew, because I already had a taste of the work force, and I already knew that I wasn't going to get very far on minimum wage.

Care was a consistent influence, whether it meant the participant's care for others or others' care for the women. Care-taking, especially from Support, was frequently mentioned as a helpful influence, as illustrated in the following examples from two participants:

*Did anything help you arrive at this topic/question/problem? What?*
Sure. Just the test that she [director of Support] provided. The emotional backing, the kick when you needed it. She was the biggest thing that made me get started.
*Did anything help you in looking for an answer?*
Well, um, Sharon, up at Support. I wouldn't be here without Sharon. She helped me quite a bit.

This ethic of care influenced strategies participants used in addressing their situations and also frequently led to a struggle for independence on the part of the participants. The ultimate goal of independence was, in every instance, to provide for the children, get them off welfare, and set an example for them.

*What were you trying to do when you selected this topic/question/problem?*
To provide a normal life for them [children] without having to rely on anything. I wanted to show my older daughter that it can be done and *not* to walk in my footsteps. I wanted to show her that it can be different.
*Was the answer complete or partial? In what way?*
It depends on the circumstances. Or on what it is that I'm looking to get answers for right then. Um, like to find a way to pay for the roof over our heads, that was an answer. I found an answer, but it's just a temporary, and it's a false security because if they dangle the eviction over your head. That's not real to me. That's why it's so important that once I get out of here the only material thing I want is a piece of ground and a house. And I think you have rules no matter where you go, but I don't think like this. Ever. This is not fair. This is not fair. Not to do to a grown human being and not to do to little children. It's just not right. It almost forces them into some underground way of life. I don't know. It just forces you to feel like you have to do things on the sly. Not that I do, but you just kind of get that feeling about it because of the attitude that's presented to you. Like less than, and people are, like, lookin' at you like you are up to something that you're not supposed to be doin'. I haven't quite figured that one out, yet, but I try to keep a sense of humor about that, otherwise you'd slowly go wack-o, ga-ga. I am not kidding.

This ethic of care not only shaped the situations for the participants, it also served as a motivator when information was difficult to find once they knew something might be available to them. Several of the participants called this "diggin'" or "buggin'."

## Diggin' and Buggin'

As the women progressed through the information-seeking process, they seemed to discover two things. First, that answers or paths or choices might be available somewhere, and second, that if they were willing to go "diggin'" and "buggin'" they were more likely to gain access to what they needed or wanted. As Amy put it,

> I'm the type of person I keep diggin' and diggin' until I get to the bottom of it and, um, just I was led through a path through the phone book and all kinds of places and eventually I was hooked up with the right information, but it's frustrating for a person who's not used to doing that or maybe their situation was even worse where they didn't have that kinda time 'cause I felt that that time to me was a luxury and I was fortunate that I had access to a phone and I was able to make the calls that I needed to make. Otherwise, I can't imagine. I can't imagine what would happen for someone that was, you know, in a physical abuse situation or they had to leave immediately. Basically, all you're left with is the street because if you don't know what's available to you, you're out of luck. You're pretty much out of luck. It's there. You just have to uncover it.

The participants all seemed to need to dig and bug to find out about the Support program through the public assistance program. They reported similar difficulties in finding out about a number of programs or avenues, but they seemed to experience particular difficulty in this example, because the four participants in the follow-up study had young children and therefore were not required to move themselves along and off public assistance. They had to fight to find out about the program that helped them strive for independence for themselves and their families.

> The most important thing to me was being able to support my kids and myself … so when I had to … when I had to um reapply for food stamps, there was a paper that they gave me about Support, the Support Program. And, um, I was very much interested, because this is not the way I wanted to live my life. I wanted to be able to get back on my feet and move on and I, you know, I read through it and my … my son at the time was maybe a little over three and that made me exempt, but I … I still wanted to get involved. I said, well, can I still do this if my son is only three? And what I found out through the welfare office is they don't give you information. They let you ask. You know, there's a bazillion programs out there but unless you know that they exist, they don't offer it to you, they don't say, well, being in this position is only going to get you so far for so long. You may want to consider trying to move out and here's … here's what we have in place for you. Uh, uh. It's almost like I don't even know how to describe it, like I don't know. And the … the attitude … the attitude is of contempt. I don't know. It's bizarre and so I don't and so I asked and I prodded around and the employment and training counselor told me about the GED program through the college. And I asked him about the child care. He said child care would be provided and then I was really gifted and he told me that they would even pay for transportation and they said that if your car breaks down … there's a certain amount of money that you can have to help fix your car and I was like … I mean all … all the things that stop you from, like, moving forward—they were like they were there for you to make sure that you could … you know, keep on going.

Amy's persistence paid off. She did get the information. She did enroll in the program. She earned her GED. She is now working on earning her associate's degree. Her children are still young enough that she could still be simply on public assistance. But she went diggin' and buggin' and found far more than she expected. Diggin' and buggin' were essential strategies for Amy as well as for the other women. Persistence and motivation, components of economic influences/constraints, come closest to accounting for diggin' and buggin' in the framework.

Despite the challenges the participants faced, they were still privileged in a number of ways. Their knowledge that the program existed was key to their ultimately gaining access to information about it (i.e., they had access to knowledge of their rights and thus their ability to exercise them). Without that knowledge, without their sureness that they were entitled to the information, and without their personal drive to improve their families' lot and their persistence in pursuing the information, they never would have overcome the barriers and gained access to the information. Finding voice, the theme discussed in the next section, also gave them the means to gain access.

### Voice

The metaphor of voice ran throughout the interviews but was particularly evident in Amy's story. Part of the aim of her information-seeking process was, in a larger sense, to find and use her voice. Her earlier references to voice were to its absence, as in the following example:

> The decision to leave my husband—the difficulty? Hah! That was the hardest decision I ever had to make in my life. A man I slept next to for 17 years. When I realized that I needed to tell him what I thought was best. *I turned him over to talk to him and the words wouldn't even leave my mouth. I didn't know how to speak. There was no voice.* And I couldn't even imagine death being any more painful than havin' to tell—I mean, I had a lot of abandonment when I was a kid, so, I mean, that transferred over, so that was, yeah, hah, difficult? That's like an understatement. It was an understatement. Because I wasn't even sure if I had the right to take my children away from their father. I didn't know if I had the right to put them in jeopardy. I had no idea how I was gonna take care of them. Just something in my heart told me, my heart and my head just told me, that we cannot stay the way it is. We cannot stay. There's no way we're gonna make it this way. So we have to see what's on the other side.

Amy's journey, with all the influences and constraints on access, led eventually to very different references to voice:

> But now that they're teaching me to speak, I'm never gonna shut my mouth again!

That was Amy, reflecting on her position at present. On the future, she offered these comments:

> You know, I can only do so much. And then I'm gonna be ringing the phones off the hook....

Well, you know me. And especially now I'm getting educated? Uh, uh, it's gonna be so hard. You're gonna have to rip my lips off, 'cause I don't know. Mmmm mmmmm. There's no way I'm shuttin' up.

The final example illustrates the three themes. The point, to Amy, of using voice was one of care. She was willing to dig and bug until someone heard her. To do this, she had to learn first that she had a voice, and then that she was worthy of being listened to.

And guess what? Now I have a mouth and a voice, and if it gets to the point where they really give me a hard time, I will go knocking until somebody listens. You know, it may not get us anywhere, and we may end up on the street. But at least maybe somebody will hear it, and the next person coming up will have it a little bit easier, because that's not right. That's not fair, at all.
*Was it worth trying to find? How or how not?*
Definitely. Definitely. Because I feel so much better about myself. I know that I'm a capable person. I'm not a worthless piece of dirt and, um, and I can give that to my children. So no matter what happens, I can give them that gift.

Again, in terms of outcomes, participants were concerned not only with how to use what they had retrieved but also with how to be heard, now that they knew enough to speak and knew they were worthy of being listened to. As noted, the metaphor of voice is a dominant theme in the literature (see chapter 3). The participants came to view themselves as makers of meaning, creators of information for others.

## The Refined Framework of Access

The refined framework takes into account the two dimensions that emphasize human behavior in the process of seeking to gain access to information: the facets of the information-seeking process and influences/constraints on access to information and communication, as developed from analysis of the literature and proposed in the initial framework. Because the data from the main case study indicated such a need, the framework was extended by adding a mediative category to the influences/constraints dimension. Components of each influence/constraint category have been expanded and detailed in accordance with participants' reports in the studies.

In addition, based on the follow-up case study, the information-seeking process dimension has been refined to reflect the importance of the context and outcomes facets and to emphasize the potential for an outcome to include the making of meaning and the creation and production of information, often through communication, thereby underscoring the iterative nature of the process. The representation of facets of the information-seeking process has been refined to underscore that it is not necessarily a linear process, that it is iterative, and that any facet can intersect with any influence or constraint.

In addition to the study results, this chapter reported on recurring themes of the follow-up study, themes of care, diggin' and buggin', and voice. For the participants in the follow-up study, care was usually the underlying focus of the situations they reported, and diggin' and buggin' represented common strategies. The metaphor of voice, illustrated especially through Amy's story, indicated the journey from voicelessness (frequently in the context facet) to finding voice, to a determination to be heard. That participants came to view themselves as makers of meaning and creators of information adds to the significance of the outcomes facet in understanding access to information and underscores the iterative nature of the process.

# 8

# Summary and Implications of the Framework of Access

Part I has identified underlying dimensions of accessing information and communication applicable across situations, systems, research literatures, and research processes. The accompanying typology made explicit many of the implicit, common, and unique assumptions about access, and has the potential to contribute to the integration of research on access to information and communication across literatures. Although this particular research tested only two dimensions of the framework, this chapter proposes a synthesizing framework that seeks to account for the range of dimensions identified in the literatures of the research areas reviewed, categorized, and synthesized so far.

## Research Questions

To develop a framework and taxonomy identifying the underlying dimensions of access to information, part I considered five research questions.

### 1. What Are the Common Issues and Concerns Implied by Discussions of Access-Related Issues in Several Relevant Research Areas?

Four major issues or concerns common to the six research areas were identified, indicating the range of factors implied in discussions of access to information and communication: (1) the conceptualizations of information, (2) what is implied by the various conceptualizations of access to information, (3) components of the information-seeking process, and (4) the potential interactions of mediation and technology with access.

**Conceptualizations of Information (Table 3.1)** In this conceptualization, information is viewed as a *thing* (resource/commodity) that can be produced, purchased, replicated, distributed, manipulated, passed along, controlled, traded, and sold.

Information as *data in the environment* includes objects, artifacts, sounds, smells, visual and tactile phenomena, activities, events, or the phenomena of nature. As a *representation of knowledge*, information tends to be conflated with its material carrier, or artifact, such as a document, book, or periodical. It might also be a video or audiotape, a CD, or a home page on the Internet. Information as *part of the communication process* is a part of human behavior in the process of moving through space/time to make sense of one's world.

**Conceptualizations of Access to Information (Table 3.2)** Access to *knowledge* was the most common conceptualization of access to information. It can include withholding of information as well as sending or seeking information. Such access can lead to access to power, to decision making, and to citizenship activities, and influence socioeconomic opportunities and quality of work life or life in general. Access to *technology* is, for some, considered requisite to access to information and may include a range of media, such as movies, newspapers, books, magazines, music, academic performance, television, or other information delivery systems. It is a common, but mistaken, assumption that access to technology necessarily results in access to information. Further, access to technology can also lead to an increase in monitoring or surveillance.

Access to *communication* can mean access to content, comprehension, retention, or understanding. Communication competence is required for participation in society's social, economic, and political systems. Access to *control* can imply control over who gains access to what to whose advantage (Braman 1989). It can mean access to control or loss of it, depending on which party holds control. Access to control can also mean influencing policy that affects subsequent access to information. The primary assumption of access to control is that power, control, information, and knowledge are linked.

Consideration of access to *goods and commodities* underscores the unique nature of information in that context. The general principles of supply and demand as they relate to cost or value do not hold when applied to information. The value of information remains unknown until it is consumed. Information is durable in that, unlike other commodities, consumption does not imply depletion. In addition to traditional economic costs, the potential costs of seeking or gaining access to information include the time spent weighing the costs and potential benefits of a search, or the time to carry out the process. Risk represents another potential cost. Consideration of costs implies resources, such as motivation, familiarity, or patience.

Information is requisite to *participation* in a democratic society. Access includes advocacy, interpretation, or debate. Without such access, an individual may lack the resources required to benefit from access. Of equal consequence, and occasionally in conflict with privacy rights, are security and ownership rights. These contradictory rights illustrate the tension between openness and security or between public access and privacy. Viewing these rights from perspectives represented by the various potential participants reveals a number of trade-offs and balances inherent in the notion of access that occur throughout the information-seeking process.

**Facets of the Information-Seeking Process (Table 3.3)** The *context* facet includes the background and frame of reference of the potential user as well as the background in which an information system operates. This facet is less well covered in the literatures than the next two.

The *situations* facet covers the particular set of circumstances from which a need for information arises, the awareness of those circumstances, and the awareness of the need. The theoretical heritage of the situation facet includes gap (Dervin 1983), visceral need and conscious need (Taylor 1968), problematic situation (Wersig 1979), anomalous state of knowledge (Belkin 1980), and discomfort or information need. The dynamic process of addressing the situation, including a more structured representation of the situation and what is required to address it, falls in the *strategies* facet. Strategies also include interaction with a system and informal evaluation. Here the terminology has been of bridges, barriers, blocks, or helps encountered on the way to address a situation (Dervin 1983), a more formalized need (Taylor 1968), or a plan of action. Other examples are query statement or problem statement, reevaluation of an initial adoption agenda (Johnson and Rice 1987), and new questions (Kuhlthau 1985).

Finally, the *outcomes* facet entails retrieval and use of information, its evaluation, and the potential for new situations. Examples include consumption or use of information (Kubey and Csikszentmihalyi 1990; Tague and Schultz 1989); and adoption, adaptation, and reinvention (Johnson and Rice 1983; 1987; Rice and Rogers 1980). The data from the studies underscore the importance of including outcomes in any theoretical understanding of the information-seeking process and access to information.

**Potential Interactions of Mediation with Access (Table 3.4)** The initial review and analysis of the literature identified technology and mediation as a common issue of concern in discussions of access to information. Although the notion of mediation is often thought of as reliant on technology, as the term is applied here it also accounts for interaction with human intermediaries. Technology and mediation commonly were understood as phenomena that could intensify existing influences and constraints on access or compensate to span gaps in space, time, or ability. Although identifying technology and mediation as a common issue/concern in discussions of access to information was helpful, based on the data of the primary (main) case study, technology and mediation were added as an additional influence/constraint on access to information rather than as an independent dimension.

**2. What Are the Influences and Constraints on Access to Information?**

Analysis of the literatures of the six research areas identified seven categories of influences and constraints on access to information, summarized in table 8.1, which updates table 3.5.

**Physical Influences/Constraints** Components of physical influences and constraints included geography and demographics, environment and ergonomics, space, and display. Data from the case studies suggested the addition of several components that arose in participants' responses and that were indicative of their perceptions. Health, body, locations, destinations, path, route, equipment, printout, download, and format were added based on the case study data.

**Cognitive Influences/Constraints** Understanding, awareness, competence, facility or skill, and matching of the user with the system were identified as components of cognitive influences and constraints. Additional examples derived from the interview data include decisions, confusion, curiosity, expectation, surprise, interest, exploration, experimentation, attention, syntax, language, specificity, questions, answers, remembering, and forgetting.

**Affective Influences/Constraints** Affective factors derived from the literature include attitudes; confidence, fear, and trust; comfort and discomfort; and motivation level. The last was included in economic influences/constraints as a resource and was therefore explicitly excluded from the operational definition of affective influences/constraints. Data from case studies added laughter, humor, funny, prayer, faith, and self-doubt to the components or examples of affective influences and constraints. The primary (main) case study raised the question of whether affective influences/

constraints might more appropriately be considered a subset of economic influences/constraints because most of the examples of affective indicated a cost, benefit, or motivation. In the follow-up case study, however, affective influences and constraints represented a greater proportion of the responses and indicated attitudes, especially about self, thereby supporting the argument for maintaining affective as an independent category of influences and constraints.

**Economic Influences/Constraints** Three basic components constituted economic influences and constraints as drawn from analysis of the literature: anticipated benefits, costs, and value. Motivation served as a fourth component of economic influences/constraints. These terms refer to economic benefits, costs, and value but also to other examples, such as time, inconvenience, and discomfort. Case study data introduced the following additions: difficulty or ease, effort, timeliness, time, waiting, worth, usefulness, waste, and persistence. Worry was assigned according to the source of concern, which, in the follow-up case study, was frequently economic in nature.

**Social Influences/Constraints** Social influences and constraints included cultural norms, class membership and background, networks (social and electronic), education, communicative competence, and experience. The case study data added work, job, career, social activities such as dancing or music, and life events.

**Political Influences/Constraints** The final original category of influences and constraints on access to information included political factors, such as power, control, equity, and participation. The case study data added governmental operations or activities as well as indignity and degradation, the latter two of which implied a power relationship.

**Mediative Influences/Constraints** Technology and mediation were discussed in the section on common issues and concerns. As a result of the first analysis of the data of the main case study, a seventh category, mediative influences and constraints, was added. Its components included connecting and links, as well as intensifying and compensating potentials.

Tables 3.6 and 3.7 summarize the common issues and concerns and the influences and constraints according to the degree to which each research area treats them.

**Table 8.1**
Influences/Constraints on Access to Information

| Influence/ Constraint | Examples/Components | Additions from Study Data |
|---|---|---|
| Physical | Geography, demographics<br>Environment: arrangement, orientation<br>Space: distance/proximity, open/secure, clear/obstructed<br>Display: medium, format, information-processing capabilities | Health, body<br>Locations, destinations<br>Path, route<br>Equipment<br>Printout, download<br>Format |
| Cognitive | Understanding: identifying need<br>Awareness: of means of addressing, of rights, entitlements, procedures<br>Literacy: verbal, quantitative, technical<br>Facility/skill: system, command language, protocol<br>Matching of user and system: content and language, mental model and expectations, learning style, organization of information | Decision, confusion, curiosity<br>Expectation, surprise, interest<br>Exploration, experimentation<br>Attention, confusion<br>Syntax, language, specificity<br>Questions, answers<br>Remembering, forgetting |
| Affective | Attitude toward information seeking, computing, interacting<br>Confidence/fear/trust<br>Comfort/discomfort<br>Motivation level | Laughter<br>Funny, humor<br>Prayer, faith<br>Self-doubt |
| Economic | Benefits: profitability, affluence, solutions, public good externalities, ancillary social value<br>Costs: price, money, time, inconvenience, going without, risk (loss of money, time, face)<br>Value, potential for value added: not known until information is used | Difficulty/ease, effort<br>Timeliness, time, waiting<br>Worth, usefulness, waste<br>Persistence<br>Worry assigned according to source of concern (usually economic) |
| Social | Cultural norms: privilege, struggle<br>Class membership and background<br>Social networks, electronic networks<br>Education: learning, skill level, competence<br>Competence: communication and technology<br>Experience: expert/novice, familiarity with system, situation | Work, job, career<br>Social activities (dancing, music)<br>Life events |

**Table 8.1** (continued)

| Influence/ Constraint | Examples/Components | Additions from Study Data |
|---|---|---|
| Political | Power, including knowledge, with special implications in democracy<br>Control: of information flow, of individuals, of public debate, of policy<br>Equity, participation: ability to understand and be understood | Government<br>Indignity, degradation |
| Mediative | Not in initial list of influences/ constraints (see table 3.5) | Intensifying, compensating potential<br>Connecting, links |

### 3. What are the Assumptions and Primary Issues or Foci of Each Research Area That Lead to the Differences among Them?

For library studies, the primary foci were access to print documents and information democracy. For information science, issues of paramount interest included access to citations by elite users and the nature of information. The most important issues in research on the "information society" included the relationship of technology to communication and information democracy. Mass media research focused on access to control of production and distribution of information and cultural agenda setting. In organizational communication, the primary foci included information flow, the tension between privacy and security, and physical access. The final research area, economics of information, focused on the free market and privatization and on information democracy. Also of interest in economics of information were the costs, benefits, and value of access to information.

Table 4.1 summarizes the underlying assumptions of each research area, which have led to differences among the research areas with regard to their treatment of issues related to access to information. For library studies, the assumptions include that documents address users' questions, that subject headings represent reality, and that bibliographic sources meet users' needs for information. Assumptions that underlie information science include that access to citations equals access to information, that relevance, as narrowly defined, is an acceptable measure of system performance, that an anomalous state of knowledge (ASK) or a query statement is a reasonable representation of a need for information, and that cognitive processes are a sufficient focus of inquiry.

In research on the "information society," assumptions included that society is experiencing a transformation that will change the social structure, that the relationship of technology to human behavior and one's societal context is an appropriate focus of inquiry, and that technology can (but may not) make information available equally, plentifully, and universally. For the literature on the mass media, assumptions included that what is produced and distributed is determined by those who own and run the media, and that access to control over production and distribution is an appropriate focus of inquiry. In organizational communication, key assumptions were that physical access to information sources is the same as gaining access to information, that more information is better, and that issues of privacy are important issues of concern. Finally, analysis of the literature on economics of information revealed the assumptions that information, if viewed as a commodity, operates differently from other goods and commodities, and that individuals require access to information to participate fully as citizens.

### Preliminary Framework

An aim of surveying the literature to answer the first three research questions was to develop a framework and taxonomy identifying the dimensions of access to information. Analysis of the literature identified five sets of categories related to access to information: the conceptualization of information, what is implied by conceptualizations of access to information, components of the information-seeking process, the potential interactions of mediation and technology with access, and the influences and constraints on access to information. Among these, two sets of categories represented dimensions of access most illustrative of human behavior in seeking to gain access to information: (1) the information-seeking process, and (2) influences and constraints on access to information. The preliminary framework aimed to account for human behavior in seeking to gain access to information. Along the way, the individual encounters influences and constraints on access that can block or facilitate access. No hierarchical relationship is intended among the influences and constraints, and the process is neither necessarily linear nor sequential. Figure 4.1 shows the preliminary framework.

### 4. How Well Does the Framework Capture/Organize Participants' Perceptions of Access to Information across Situations, Individuals, and Settings?

### 5. Do the Study Results Suggest Additional Components or Dimensions for the Framework?

The pilot and main case studies involved obtaining responses from Internet users in a classroom setting. Among the facets of the information-seeking process, context occurred in 9 percent of the responses, situation in 24 percent, strategies in 42 percent, and outcomes in 25 percent (see table 6.1). The outcomes facet, representing one quarter of the responses, needs to be considered in any theoretical understanding of the information-seeking process. It is only through the use of information that one gains access to its value, including the possibility that the user will produce new information or ancillary social value as a result.

Among the influences and constraints on access to information, physical represented 9.5 percent of the responses, cognitive 35 percent, affective 4.5 percent, economic 19 percent, social 17 percent, political 2 percent, and mediative 13 percent (see table 6.1). These findings support the framework's comprehensiveness in representing participants' perceptions of access to information across situations and individuals because, although they extend the descriptive aspects of the framework, they do not suggest additional dimensions of the framework other than the addition of mediative influences/constraints.

Data from the follow-up case study, involving nonelite users and nonusers of traditional information systems, further supported the dimensions of the framework and extended the understanding of access to information. Of responses assigned to facets of the information-seeking process, 20 percent represented context, 17 percent represented situation, 40 percent represented strategies, and 23 percent represented outcomes. Among influences and constraints in the follow-up study, none of the comments illustrated primarily physical instances. Of the other influences and constraints, 14 percent were assigned to cognitive, 11 percent to affective, 26 percent to economic, 25 percent to social, 14 percent to political, and 10 percent to mediative. Analysis of the data of the follow-up study indicated that the categories, as defined and extended from the main study, adequately and accurately captured or organized participants' perceptions of access to information across situations, individuals, and settings. Further, the data did not suggest additional dimensions of the framework, although they did suggest a few additional components.

The distributions of the coding categories among facets of the information-seeking process in the follow-up study were similar to those of the main case study, with strategies and outcomes representing distributions almost identical to those in the main case study. The distributions of context and situation were almost evenly divided in the follow-up study. However, in the main study, responses coded for situation occurred nearly three times more frequently than those coded for context. Among influences and constraints, variation between the data sets of the main and follow-up studies was greater. In the follow-up study, physical influences/constraints were not represented. This, appeared to be a consequence of the richness of the data rather than of an absence of the category, as responses tended to be extremely lengthy and complex, frequently including references to multiple influences and constraints.

Context played a larger role in the follow-up study than in the main study. Situations tended to be broader, more life-goal-directed circumstances than in the main study. Strategies represented almost the same proportional distribution in both studies. Strategies in the follow-up study were more likely to rely on word of mouth, social networks, and human intermediaries than in the main study, which was carried out in a classroom setting. An important finding of analysis of the outcomes facet was the metaphor of voice, and of the participants' interest not only in consuming information but also in finding avenues to be heard. Given that 43 percent of the responses in the follow-up study and 34 percent in the main study represented the context or outcomes facet, any comprehensive theoretical model of access to information must account for the full process of background for, access to, use of, creation of, and distribution of information.

## Limitations of the Study

The chief limitation of this part I study was the difficulty of observing or interviewing *nonusers* of information systems. Every attempt was made, both methodologically and procedurally, to carry out a follow-up case study that would investigate the behavior of nonelites. The aim was to extend theoretical variance as well as to contribute to a broader understanding of access, one that included potential users and nonusers as well as users of information systems.

Although the follow-up study succeeded in accounting for the behavior of nonelites to some extent, it was evident from the responses of the four participants that although they met the criterion of being economically disadvantaged, they were still advantaged in other ways. For example, the four who participated overcame a number of barriers—exhaustion, multiple responsibilities, time limitations—to arrange to meet with the interviewer. Participants were exceptionally verbal. They were exceptionally determined to improve conditions for themselves and their children. They were exceptionally motivated and did not allow barriers to stop them. They were resourceful and imaginative and, through their journeys, had grown exceptionally aware of their rights to participation and their own worth. They had found their voices and were proud to use them. Would the results of the follow-up study have been so consistent if the researcher had managed to meet with the other four proposed interviewees who, though willing to be interviewed, did not participate because they could not overcome the barriers that accompanied lack of housing, lack of a telephone, and lack of time and money?

Another limitation was that the setting of the pilot and main case studies likely guided the strategies employed and the manner in which several of the influences and constraints affected participants. Because it was a classroom setting in which students were introduced to the various resources of the Internet, and because the tools available to the students at the time of the interviews were primitive, there was probably a greater focus on electronic means of communication and the accompanying technological challenges and difficulties. To some degree, that limitation was countered by the broad variation in age, socioeconomic standing, experience, education, and background of the participants in the main study, but future research can aim to address these limitations.

Beyond these limitations are the limitations inherent in a study of this breadth. Several dimensions of access to information were identified from the literature, but only two dimensions were initially tested.

## Synthesis of Elements of a Framework of Access to Information

Although it was the aim of the studies reported in part I to test the two dimensions of the framework that most represented human behavior in the process of accessing information and communication, several other dimensions of access to information emerged from analysis of the literature of the research areas considered. The model that follows is a preliminary attempt to synthesize the multiple conceptualizations of information, and the multiple dimensions of access to information, initially derived from the comprehensive research literature reviews. The case studies, however, also allow one to consider these conceptualizations from the users' perspectives.

Amy, for example, tended to view and use information as part of her communication process, as a factor in her making sense of and taking charge of her world as she moved through space and time. Access to information for her carries multiple conceptualizations and implications, including in particular, knowledge, communication, control, and participation. The conceptualization of access to information appears to be closely related to outcomes in that they represent how the user conceptualizes the potential goal of any search for information.

Future testing of the dimensions and their relationships from multiple perspectives will contribute further to an understanding of access to information and can enhance understanding of the relationship between theory and research on the one hand and practice and application on the other.

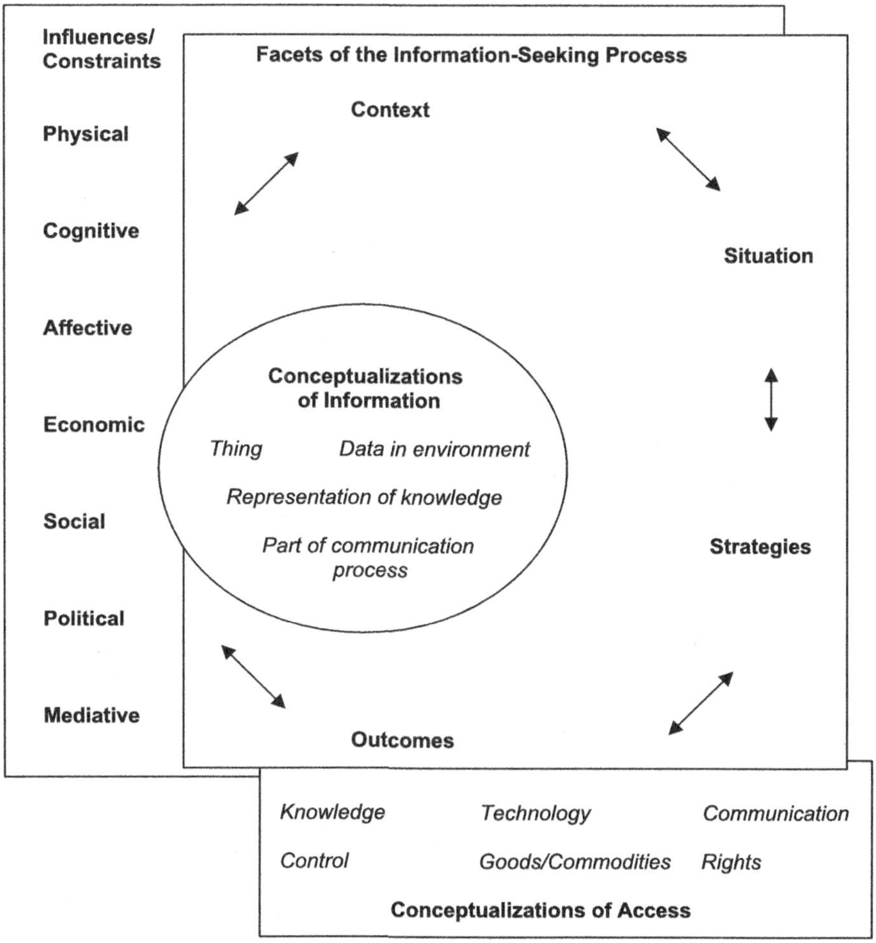


**Figure 8.1**
Synthesis of Elements of a Framework for Understanding Access to Information and Communication

It might be that just as technology and mediation fit among influences and constraints on access to information, the relationship between the conceptualizations of access and conceptualizations of information might indicate a need to synthesize them in some way. Or, it might be that testing of the comprehensive model will verify that conceptualizations of access and conceptualizations of information are independent dimensions. The former represent the aims or conceptualizations of the user and his desired outcomes, whereas the latter represent theoretical perspectives.

The model in figure 8.1 seeks to account for the dimensions of access derived from the literature by positing a continuum from theory to practice, with the latter focusing on human behavior and influences in seeking to gain access to information. As has been stressed throughout this study, perspective is key, in that if one focuses on pragmatic facets of the information-seeking process, aspects of the more theoretical dimensions—conceptualizations of information and conceptualizations of access to information—are implicit and underlie the facets. If one focuses on the conceptualization of information, the real-world influences and constraints underlie those conceptualizations.

Questions remain as to the relationships among the dimensions and whether the theory-to-practice continuum is a valid construct. Given the results of this study, the model might also account for production of information or making of meaning and the connection between seeking to gain access to information and doing something with what the seeker finds or does not find. Again, future research can test the dimensions and their relationships.

# II

# Browsing Information and Communication

# 9

# Perspectives on Browsing in Six Research Literatures

According to *Webster's Third New International Dictionary* (Merriam-Webster 1986), browsing is

1. To look over casually (as a book): SKIM/he lazily browsed the headlines
2. To skim through a book reading at random passages that catch the eye
3. To look over books (as in a store or library) especially in order to decide what one wants to buy, borrow, or read
4. To casually inspect goods offered for sale usually without prior or serious intention of buying
5. To make an examination without real knowledge or purpose
6. Browsing room: a room or section in a library designed to allow patrons an opportunity to freely examine and browse in a collection of books

From these definitions we begin to sense the intriguing nature of browsing, which refers to both purposive information-seeking behavior (definition 3) and seemingly nonpurposive information behavior (definitions 2, 4, 5).

Marchionini (1995, 8) distinguishes between *analytical strategies for information seeking*, based on planning, use of query terms, and iterative adaptations of the query based on evaluation of intermediate results, and *browsing strategies for information seeking*, heuristic, opportunistic, associated with recognizing relevant information. Browsing is primarily interactive and collaborative with the information source or system and involves less cognitive but greater attention demands than do analytical retrieval strategies; it cannot easily be conducted by an intermediary. Browsing is "informal and opportunistic and depends heavily on the information enviornment" (Marchionini 1995, 100). He identifies four primary strategies: scanning, observing, navigating, and monitoring. These are more dependent on interactions between the user and system than are analytical strategies; the information-seeking subprocesses may occur more simultaneously; and there may be much more iteration and feedback. Further, the user typically makes quick relevance judgments during the examination process. Referring to the work of Belkin, Marchetti, and Cool (1993), Marchionini presents five dimensions along which information-seeking strategies might vary between analytical and browsing: planned/opportunistic, goal-driven/data-driven, deterministic/heuristic, formal/informal, and discrete/continuous (73).

Conceptualizations of browsing are treated in a variety of literatures, including

1. Library user studies (library use and information-seeking studies)
2. End-user computing and information science (information retrieval study; interface design; operations research)
3. Consumer research (consumer shopping behavior; eye movement research)
4. Audience research (audience studies, e.g., TV-viewing patterns)
5. Organizational research (information-scanning strategies; managers' information behavior; organizational communication; information communication)
6. Environmental planning and architectural design (environmental perception and cognition; wayfinding)

The following sections review these related literatures to identify common as well as unique dimensions of browsing and to answer a specific set of research questions underlying a framework of browsing.

## Library User Studies

The notion of browsing in the library community originated in the discussion of collection management policy—closed stacks vs. open stacks—in the 1930s. With a closed-stack library system, users need to specify what they want in order to obtain the materials from the intermediaries (librarians) because the collection is inaccessible to them directly; but users do not always know exactly or are unable to specify what they want. In an open-stack system, patrons are exposed to the materials directly for free examination without having to specify what they want. In other words, they are able to browse.

Browsing as a specific subject for research in the library literature can be traced back to the Project Intrex in the mid-1960s, when experiments on browsing were suggested to find out how a university library system in the future might support browsing as a library function intended to foster unplanned discovery through planned facilities (Overhage and Harman 1965). Since then, browsing has been related to direct access to shelves in the library (Hyman 1972), collection and space management (Lawrence and Oja 1980; Boll 1985), serendipitous findings or creativity (Bankapur 1988; Bawden 1986; Celoria 1968; Davies 1989; O'Connor 1988; Swanson 1987; 1989), and search strategies (Bates 1989; Ellis 1989). It has also been related to improving information organization and provision techniques via shelf classification (Baker 1988), display arrangement (Baker 1986), and online public access catalogs (Akeroyd 1990; Hancock-Beaulieu 1989, 1990; Hildreth 1982; 1987). Two major reviews of browsing have been done by Hyman (1972) and Ayris (1986). However, the literature is still divided on issues such as the conceptualizations, importance, influence, and consequences of browsing.

Hyman (1972) surveyed 521 librarians and library educators and showed that most (80 percent) agreed that "browsing provides a valuable learning experience" but less than half (45 percent) thought that "browsing is essential for academic libraries above beginning level." Greene (1977) surveyed faculties at George Technology University and showed that browsing was the most commonly used, but least valuable, way of securing books for research purposes. Considering browsing as at-the-shelf discovery of library material, Lawrence and Oja (1980) showed that 32 percent of the books selected for use were not specifically sought, and that 47 percent (the largest category) of users of unknown items were engaged in open-ended browsing. Browsers did not appear to see themselves as having a well-articulated purpose and thus could not articulate a need for the material. Boll (1985) defines shelf browsing as a type of selective scanning that is a useful retrieval strategy for a casual search but unreliable for research, which often requires a comprehensive search. Many researchers and librarians considered browsing to be a unidimensional concept and often thought of it as the opposite of "searching" (Herner 1970); the latter was considered purposeful and the former was not. The debate on the value of browsing in this community thus centered around varying judgments on the "intellectual purposefulness" or educational value of such a "random" activity. At the same time, some observers recognized that browsing could be both purposeful and nonpurposeful (see Hyman 1972).

Although browsing as a search strategy has been historically undervalued by librarians, researchers in different literatures, including humanists, scientists, and social scientists, have testified to the need for browsing. Browsing has been reported as an important way of selecting fiction and nonfiction books by public library users in several use and user studies (Ayris 1986). Browsing has been valued as a way to gain access to and examine an information source without the need to specify the intent to intermediaries (e.g., librarians). "Browsing is a more flexible and adaptable means of searching than is submitting queries, and is well suited to distributed environments" (Borgman 2000, 157). It allows navigation and traversal from one access point (such as metadata) to another, as it is easier to recognize than to recall information, especially when the resource is outside the user's knowledge domain. In research communities, the concept of browsing often refers to examining materials beyond the researchers' research focus or research boundaries for exposure to interdisciplinary information sources, or in order to monitor specific information sources to keep up with an area of interest (Bawden 1986; Ellis 1989; Larsen 1988; Menzel 1966).

### What Is Browsing?

In general, one set of descriptions portrays browsing as non-task-oriented, referring to the unplanned nature of browsing and the lack of a specific plan of action for conducting an information search or reaching a goal, if, indeed, one is present (Apted 1971; Bankapur 1988; Buckland, cited in O'Connor 1988; Larsen 1988; Overhage and Harman 1965).

In an opposing set of descriptions, the terms *formal* and *systematic* in the library literature imply a planned course, sometimes involving the use of bibliographic tools, for achieving a goal. This group of definitions describes browsing as a form of subject access—looking for something or some things in an area of potential interest—and portrays a more task-oriented browsing activity (Ellis 1989; Hildreth 1982a, b; O'Connor 1988; Overhage and Harman 1965, 119).

Most of these definitions, partly because of their time frame, have a limited conceptualization of the nature or type of the information resources (i.e., they are limited to books, documents, and bibliographic information). Choo (1995) notes, for example, that traditional library and information science research tends to consider scanning only in a narrowly defined set of resources (library documents or database) and users (patrons), and to focus on the search, rather than viewing, aspects. It is not clear whether and how various objects sought might influence browsing behavior. Nevertheless, these descriptions suggest that the nature of browsing is likely to be associated with the resource involved, people's purpose (e.g., for pleasure, discovering pertinent information, making judgments), internal knowledge about search goals (e.g., not known or vague) and action plan (e.g., systematic or without a plan). The majority of these definitions also suggest that one of the characteristics of the browsing process is scanning (e.g., sampling or reading here and there; see Morse 1973, 246).

### What Is the Nature of Browsing?

Apted (1971) discusses three forms of browsing: (1) specific browsing, when a user makes a literature search through a bibliographic tool but does not start with a formal search strategy; (2) general purposive browsing, planned or unplanned examination of sources, journals, books or other media in the hope of discovering unspecified new but useful information; and (3) general browsing, random, nonpurposive, passing-time browsing. Herner (1970) derived three similar categories: (1) directed browsing, (2) semidirected or predictive browsing, and (3) undirected browsing. Thus according to Apted and Herner, different forms of browsing emerge according to

1. Types of resources the user interacts with (bibliographic tools, books, journals)
2. Purpose of examining a resource (discovering information, passing time)
3. Specificity of search goal (unspecified, vague search, low in document specificity)
4. Presence or absence of a plan (random, planned, unplanned, without planning)

Note that bibliographic tools are distinguished from other, nonbibliographic, types of materials. The former provide meta-information or information indicating search paths for finding information content. The latter refer to resources that contain information content itself.

Levine (1969, 35) characterized browsing according to the browser's knowledge of or familiarity with the external information store or environment she interacts with, as follows: (1) random browsing through an unknown collection, (2) quasi-random browsing through an area of a building or a collection previously explored, and (3) semi-deterministically in a limited physical area or bounded intellectual area. This description, like Herner's, implies that the way people go about browsing (i.e., directed, patterned, or undirected movement) is influenced by their external knowledge (including experience) within the information space (see also Stone 1982). In turn, Lancaster (1978, 181) points out that the individual's original need for information tends to be modified during the course of browsing.

## What Are the Dimensions of Browsing?

**Randomness and Movement** While Hyman (1972) notes that browsing has the connotation of casual inspection in a superficial manner, Bates (1989) contends that browsing is usually associated with a sense of random visual movement. However, as discussed, movement during browsing could be either directed or undirected. Thus, randomness does not have to be an essential characteristic of browsing.

**Searching and Browsing** Many researchers contend that browsing is "exploratory, vague, nonspecific and has associated activities of exploring, scanning and extending," while nonbrowsing is "exclusive, specific and has associated the activities of getting, focusing and narrowing" (Batley 1989; Celoria 1968; see also literature review in Hyman 1972).

While conceptually it may be useful to make such distinctions in some circumstances, it is difficult theoretically and empirically to draw a clear line between browsing and nonbrowsing in these terms. Indeed, browsing has been loosely described as searching where the initial search criteria are only partly defined or where the search goal is not exactly known beforehand (Cove and Walsh 1987; Gecsei and Martin 1989). For instance, a distinction has been made between the analytic (preplanned) search and the browse (exploratory) search (Liebscher and Marchionini 1988; Marchionini and Shneiderman 1988, 71; Pejtersen 1989).

Rigby pointed out that "most activities involve, however, a combination of the two approaches in widely varying proportions" (cited in Hyman 1972, 116–117). Further, what appears to be a preplanned or specific search (e.g., a title or author search) may turn out to be an exploratory search, a concept that is usually associated with subject access (Hancock-Beaulieu 1989; 1990). Thus, as Herner perceptively suggested, it may be more realistic to conceptualize browsing as a multidimensional and multilevel concept than as a dichotomous concept opposed to searching.

Based on this discussion, four prominent dimensions of browsing have emerged:

1. *The act of scanning.* Browsing embodies an act of scanning, which has been variously described as looking, examining, or sampling where the person's body or eyes move smoothly at will. Scanning is one of the four primary tasks accomplished by users of information systems as they interact with those systems (Allen 1996, ch. 7): scanning, evaluating, learning, and planning. Scanning may not be linear process, is certainly not a simple task, and uses a variety of cognitive resources. In the process of scanning, users employ their existing knowledge of a topic and of index terms describing the topic, use their understanding of data formats to direct attention, and are limited by their perceptual abilities (such as scanning or reading speed).
2. *Presence or absence of a purpose.* In the information context, browsing as a scanning process acquires the meaning of a purposeful act characterized by the presence of an intention. Although a purposeful act can be goal-directed or non-goal-directed, the presence of an intention suggests that the concept of browsing cannot be adequately described by behavioral characteristics alone.
3. *Specificity of search criteria or search goal.* One useful way to conceptualize browsing is to place it on a continuum according to the specificity of search criteria, if any, imposed on the object sought. At one end of this continuum, the objective of browsing is well defined; at the other end, the objective of browsing is not defined. In the middle, the objective of browsing is poorly defined.
4. *Knowledge about the resource or object sought.* Because individual differences play an important role in determining the quality of the interactive process and performance results, another way to conceptualize browsing is to differentiate various

types of browsing based on the browser's prior knowledge about and experience with the resource, whether knowledge of search paths or knowledge of content.

### Types of Browsing

Marchionini (1995) identified three main types of browsing: (1) directed, specific, systematic or repetitive browsing of an object, such as a list; (2) semidirected and predictive, allowing improved definition of the problem through multiple attempts; and (3) undirected, with little goal or focus. Kwasnik (1992) compared browsing of paper, a command-driven system, and a hypertext system, concluding that browsing seemed to consist of six kinds of actions: (1) orientation (understanding the structure and content), (2) place-marking (noting important objects), (3) identification (evaluating relevance), (4) resolution of anomalies (assessing ambiguous objects), (5) comparison (of multiple objects), and (6) transition (moving to other objects). It should be noted that one may move from one type of browsing to another in a single information-seeking episode (Belkin, Marchetti, and Cool 1993). It is an important empirical challenge to devise a way for recognizing when and how one type of browsing occurs and leads to another. Based on the interdisciplinary reviews, two broad types of browsing can be identified.

**Goal/Purpose-Based Browsing** In an informational context, browsing has been classified into three categories (Cove and Walsh 1987; see also Apted 1971; Herner 1970; Hildreth 1982; Levine 1969; McAleese 1989):

Type 1 Search browsing (directed browsing) (specific, goal-oriented browsing): a closely directed and structured activity where the desired product or goal is known

Type 2 General-purpose browsing (semidirected or predictive browsing) (purposive browsing): an activity of consulting specified sources on a regular basis because it is highly probable they contain items of interest

Type 3 Serendipity browsing (undirected browsing) (not goal-oriented): a purely random, unstructured and undirected activity

Note, then, that instrumental as well as recreational browsing is possible (Dozier and Rice 1984). Indeed, despite the fact that undirected browsing is commonly observed, most researchers in the library and information science field assert that information seeking in general tends to be purposive and goal-oriented (Apted 1971; Gecsei and Martin 1989).

**Method/Technique-Based Browsing** Evans (1990) describes these three types of browsing in relation to the level of information the searcher has about the item or the probable location of the item. Thus, as noted, in addition to knowledge of the content of the item sought, the searcher's knowledge of search paths (or structure of the contents) that lead to the item can also be an important factor distinguishing one type of browsing from the other.

Others have categorized browsing based on the methods used to go through the search paths of an information space. Zoellick (1986) describes four different browsing methods: (1) sequential browsing: moving to the next or previous document in a collection, (2) structural browsing: moving (not necessarily sequentially) between parts of a document based on the structure of that document (e.g., the previous chapter, the next hierarchy), (3) keyed-access browsing: using some type of access key to move between documents (e.g., an index by author, or key word, or subject heading), and (4) linked browsing: following explicit links within or between documents (e.g., footnotes or citation trails).

Similarly, Bates (1989) argues that browsing and searching, although separate activities, occur in an integrated fashion. She describes six widely used search strategies that are associated with the nature of browsing or may evoke browsing behavior: (1) footnote chasing (or backward chaining), (2) citation searching (or forward chaining), (3) journal run (browsing central journals in an area of interest), (4) area scanning (browsing the materials that are physically collocated with materials located earlier in a search), (5) subject searches in bibliographies, and (6) author searching. As noted by Bates (1986b) in the discussion of "area scanning," research has shown that two commonly mentioned purposes in the use of the subject catalog are to select books on a subject (as in keyed-access browsing) and to find the shelf location of a classification category in order to make book selections in the stacks (as in structural browsing). This implies that some browsing methods are more likely to be used for certain types of searching tasks or purposes. Somewhat related to Bates's (1989) concept of area scanning, or what she calls "berrypicking," is "pearl growing"—expanding through iterations from a small but familiar set of core materials to more diverse and less directly associated materials (Borgman, Moghdam, and Corbett 1984). To find out what methods are more effective for what purposes/tasks is another empirical issue warranting investigation.

### What Influences Browsing?

More broadly, Marchionini (1987, 70) suggests four factors distinguishing different types of browsing techniques: (1) the object sought: the objective of browsing may be well-defined or ill-defined, (2) the individual searcher characteristics: experience and knowledge about objects sought, (3) the purpose of the search: for pleasure, fact retrieval, concept formation, interpretation, evaluation of ideas, keeping abreast of developments in a field, and (4) the setting and context for conducting the search: this influences the extent and type of browsing.

**Objects** As far as "the object sought" is concerned, there seems to be a difference between browsing real objects and browsing representations (or surrogates). Some researchers describe this as the difference between the direct shelf (real) approach and the catalog (representation) approach (see Hyman 1972, 123–125), which differ in (1) the desirability of seeing objects and related objects physically grouped, (2) the value of visual contact with grouped objects, (3) direct location of an object, and (4) the greater number of attributes of a book that can be examined in a direct shelf approach.

Levine (1969) described the nature of browsing as a sensory experience of physical materials considered accessible in their entirety to one or more of the senses. For instance, one may aurally "browse" through (scan) a number of radio stations to select one. Thus, there may be different information requirements for different types of objects sought (e.g., image-based vs. text-based) to support effective browsing. For example, O'Connor (1985) argues that surrogates for moving image documents can and should include more information than the traditional catalogs, by including picture or sound.

**Individual Characteristics** Individual differences in browsing may include motivation, purpose, knowledge, experience, and other aspects such as learning pattern (Allinson and Hammond 1989), cognitive style (e.g., mental model and expectation) (Borgman 1989; Hulley 1990; Marchionini 1989; Marchionini and Liebscher 1991).

**Contexts/Settings** Browsing as a sensory experience involving the assimilation of new information into one's personal knowledge store (Levine 1969) and as an interactive process with possibility of obtaining feedback from the environment (Marchionini 1987) is subject to the influence of external as well as internal factors.

In Ayris's review (1986), some factors associated with "browsability" (a term that implies effective browsing as measured by items found and used) emerged. In academic and research libraries, these factors include collection size, subject divisions, subject discipline, work activity, and medium. In the public library context, another set of factors influencing browsing activities has been identified: the book blurb, nature of text, display, user's educational level, interfiling policy as well as organization/classification scheme. Two noticeable factors of a context are (1) information organization (such as classification schemes, subject divisions), and (2) display (such as shelf arrangement, screen display, formats of materials) (Baker 1986a; Hildreth 1982a; Huestis 1988; Egan et al. 1989; 1991).

A more macrolevel context comprises the browser's "information field" (Johnson 1996), "information use environment" (Taylor 1991), and surrounding social, work and media networks (Erdelez 1996; Haythornthwaite and Wellman 1998; Marchionini 1995; Savolainen 1995; Williamson 1998). Thus, one's experience, potentially accessible contacts and communication channels, and preexisting cognitive and emotional associations make one predisposed to finding useful information even when there is no intended information seeking going on.

### What Are the Consequences of Browsing?

**Serendipitous Findings** One of the consequences of browsing in the library and through journals is finding something of interest or some things that are not originally sought, although the conditions that lead to such results are not well understood (Ayris 1986; Bawden 1986; Ellis 1989).

**Modification of Information Requirements** Through browsing, the individual becomes aware of unforeseeable, useful information that may lead to a change of the individual's state of knowledge and subsequently influences or, more specifically, clarifies, her original information need (Allen 1996; Lancaster 1978; Hildreth 1982; Marchionini 1995; Oddy 1977; Stone 1982).

## End-User Computing and Information Science

In this literature most authors tend to dichotomize the concepts of searching and browsing; searching refers to seeking for a specific item whereas browsing refers to identifying something of interest or something on a general topic (a nonspecific search behavior). Table 9.1 compares several studies on searching behavior in computers, showing four distinct types of information-searching behavior regardless of the variation in terminology.

As a general trend in this research area, browsing has been used as a supplementary search technique in traditional information retrieval systems, and information retrieval techniques have been applied to traditionally browsing-based systems such as hypertext and e-mail systems. An adaptive system is expected to be able to support both types of search strategies (Allinson and Hammond 1989; Bates 1990; Savoy 1992).

**Table 9.1**
A Comparison of Browsing Models in Information Retrieval Studies

| Browsing Type | Canter, Rivers, and Storrs (1985) | Cove and Walsh (1988) | Batley (1989) | Aigrain and Longueville (1992) | Carmel, Crawford, and Chen (1992) |
|---|---|---|---|---|---|
| Type 1: Looking for a target item | Searching | Search browsing | Seeking | Search | Searching |
| Type 2: Looking for items that share some characteristics | Browsing | General-purpose browsing | Focus browsing | Generalization | Reviewing |
| Type 3: Finding out what is there | Exploring Scanning | | Open browsing | Exploration | Scanning |
| Type 4: Incidental | Wandering | Serendipity | Wandering | | Scanning |

In response to information retrieval problems during the period from the late 1950s through the late 1970s, brought about by the traditional query-based, command-driven computer interface (Sparck Jones 1981), browsing as an alternative search technique was first proposed by Oddy (1977). He based his design of an experimental interactive system on the assumption that information retrieval was better served through an interactive process such as user-machine dialogue. The implication is that during such a process, users must be exposed to the information (both specific items as well as clustered items) before they can attempt to recognize what they want. Fox and Palay (1979) introduced the first online library catalog to provide an explicit browsing capability. They identified two major disadvantages of browsing in stacks and card catalogs: (1) the existence of only one physical location of a book confines shelf browsing to a single area, and (2) the physical separation of alternative classifications in card catalogs hinders browsing. Their BROWSE system, they claimed, provided "richer" browsing capability than that found in a typical library and its card catalog by (1) making an item accessible under more than one classification and classification system, and via access points such as author, key words, or other meaningful descriptors, and (2) easing the movement between the access points. Hildreth (1982) grouped browsing capabilities offered in ten commercial online catalogs into two broad categories. One category is related to *term selection*, such as displaying a list of thesaurus terms for scanning, and the other is related to *result manipulation*, such as giving a list of references; each group is intended to facilitate presearch and postsearch tasks, respectively. They can be conceived as purposeful, goal-directed, and structured types of browsing.

With the development and applications of hypertext technology, browsing capabilities have been recognized as one of the central characteristics of a hypertext system, allowing a nonlinear organization of text by providing machine-supported links within and between documents in the database. Conklin (1987) describes these browsing capacities in terms of three ways that such a database can be browsed: (1) by following links and opening windows successively to examine their contents, (2) by searching the network (or part of it) for some string, key word, or attribute value, and (3) by navigating around the hyperdocument using a browser that displays the network graphically. The "richer" browsing capabilities now go beyond classification hierarchies to include the ability to scan the lower-level attributes of an item (such as content words) and to look at structural aspects of the database content displayed as relational graphics in a computer system. Particular features supporting browsing may include "probes," "zooms," and "filters and templates" (Marchionini 1995). Although there is no generally accepted operational definition of browsing, studies of browsing functions (in the sense described) in various information retrieval systems have become a research priority as applications of hypermedia systems increase.

As a whole, studies of browsing in computer-based systems have focused on issues of information overload in electronic messaging systems (Hiltz and Turoff 1985), identification of search techniques used in information retrieval systems (Akeroyd 1990; Belkin, Marchetti, and Cool 1993; Canter, Rivers, and Storrs 1985; Zoellick 1986), and disorientation in hypermedia environments (Foss 1989; McAleese 1989). Differences between the use of printed materials and their electronic counterparts have been investigated in an attempt to improve user interface design by increasing "browsability" of a system (Hildreth 1987a; cf. Hyman 1971) and to devise better techniques of information representation and organization (Egan et al. 1991; Marchionini and Liebscher 1991).

### What Is Browsing?

Several definitions of browsing in the context of human-computer interaction in particular have been offered (Cove and Walsh 1987, 183; Gecsei and Martin 1989, 237; Tuori 1987, 4). Although the terminology varies, four conceptual elements recur in these descriptions of browsing, with examples of terms from the definitions: (1) *scanning*, which is variously described as "search casually," "looking," "inspecting," or "examining"; (2) *resource*, which refers to "a body of information" or "database"; (3) *goal*, in terms of "intent," "search criteria," "search goal," or "what one wants"; and (4) *knowledge*, indicating the state of the individual's knowledge: "without ... clearly predefined," "not exactly known," "partly defined," or "not knowing."

In addition, *path* ("shaped on the way," "structure," "information map") and *content* ("contents of a database") are considered as two distinct aspects of both resource and knowledge. Although in most cases, the person's inadequate knowledge about the search goal is content-based, Tuori's definition suggests that the person's indeterminacy may be related to his knowledge about search paths of a resource. Further, in Cove and Walsh's description, the phrase "not knowing ... until one finds it" implies the concept of recognition in the process of browsing.

All of these descriptions of browsing activities point to some common behavioral and cognitive characteristics. Behaviorally, it is looking and examining. Cognitively, it is purposive but is characterized by the lack of a well-defined goal or specific intention for conducting such activity. These definitions, however, imply the existence of such a goal or intention. Note that in these descriptions, terms such as *goal*, *intent*, and *search criteria* are used interchangeably, referring to the nature of the expected outcome of browsing rather than to the process of browsing itself. The characteristic of the nonspecific goal has been associated with inadequate knowledge about the content or search path of the resource. It should also be noted that, as in the library literature, there is still a lack of consensus among researchers in this field regarding the use of the term *browsing*, as some definitions are medium- or resource-specific (McAleese 1989, 7).

**What Is the Nature of Browsing?**

Gecsei and Martin (1989) suggest that learning the content and path/structure of a database is what takes place when people browse. Similarly, in an attack on the traditional output-oriented information retrieval paradigm, Hildreth (1987a) argues that most end-users do not have a well-defined output product in mind and asserts that the process of searching and discovery is more central to end-user searching objectives and satisfaction than to the delivery of any predefined product.

Belkin, Marchetti, and Cool (1993) conceptualize an information-seeking model along four dimensions: (1) method of interaction (scanning, searching), (2) goal of interaction (learning, selecting), (3) mode of retrieval (recognition, specification), and (4) resource considered (information items, meta-information). The concept of browsing is not explicitly addressed but is implied in some complex of values on those dimensions, which involves "scanning" as the method of interaction (Belkin et al. 1995). Scanning refers to "looking around for something interesting among a collection of items," which can be content-focused (information) or search path/structure-focused (meta-information).

Arguing that browsing is the most important form of searching for casual use, Tuori (1987, 4) proposes a taxonomy of searching in which an approach to searching is characterized by the following four aspects: (1) intention (the degree to which the person begins with a well-defined goal or intention), (2) structure (the real or apparent structure of the information space; i.e., search paths), (3) language (the characteristics of the language by which a person communicates with a system), and (4) modality of interaction (a variety of forms of expression or channels of communication). Defining browsing as examining a body of information without the need for a clearly predefined path, Tuori contends that it offers a useful approach for an initial, exploratory search, especially by inexperienced or occasional users, and that a system is more browsable if it does not create great demand on users along these four aspects.

Thus, browsing, in human-computer interaction research, has been considered an "interactive search strategy" (Marchionini 1987), involving scanning a resource, and is characterized by the presence of a goal but a lack of well-planned search strategy, with ill-defined search criteria at the beginning of the interaction with the resource.

### What Are the Dimensions of Browsing?

**Extent or Form of Feedback** In addition to the dimensions common in library literature, such as scanning, purpose, goal, knowledge, resource (path and content), research in computer science and information retrieval has shown that feedback is an important feature in human-computer interaction, especially in browsing (Marchionini 1987, 69). However, there may be significantly different types or levels of feedback, i.e., displays of different representations of organizational schemes or contents. Thus, the extent or form of feedback presented to the human browser can be considered as the unique dimension of browsing in this context.

### Types of Browsing

**Content/Path-Based Browsing** Canter, Rivers, and Storrs (1985) derive a taxonomy of five browsing strategies based on studies of the paths chosen by hypermedia users: (1) scanning: covering a large area without depth, (2) browsing: following a path until a goal is achieved, (3) searching: striving to find an explicit goal, (4) exploring: finding out the extent of the information given, and (5) wandering: purposeless and unstructured globe-trotting. There seems to be a different focus in each strategy in terms of the degree of content or search path orientation. Studies of browsing in image-based databases have similar findings. Batley (1989) finds four types of browsing while using a system: seeking, focused exploration, open exploration, and wandering. Aigrain and Longueville (1992, 521) derive similar categories: search (seeking one target image), exploration (wandering until one discovers contents of specific interest), and generalization (obtaining new image from already selected images by using implicit or explicit links).

**Facility/Function-Based Browsing** The notion of browsing in the sense of recognition-based, direct exposure to information resources has led to concern about what to display and how to display multiple levels of information. For example, graphics-based displays make the structure of the database content or search paths and their relations explicit to the user for manipulation, which may not be available in character-based systems. In a review of ten commercial online public access catalogs, Hildreth (1982a) groups online support for browsing into two broad categories, including features for (1) term selection, and (2) result manipulation and displays.

In an evaluation study of a hypertext learning support system, Allinson and Hammond (1989) found four major navigation tools used for various types of users' tasks: (1) the tour (users select and then are guided around a sequence of frames until the tour ends; users can leave or rejoin the tour at any point) was mostly used for study of unfamiliar material; (2) the map (to see where users are in relation to other display frames) was mostly used for browsing and study of partially familiar material; (3) the hypertext links were mostly used for study of familiar material; and (4) index (directed access to key word–coded frames or tours) was mostly used for information search and seeking references. This study shows that a particular tool is or could be usefully associated with a specific user's task in relation to a purpose. When compared with Zoellick's definitions of different browsing methods (1986), it is clear that the map is associated with "structuring browsing," the index is used in "keyed-access browsing," hypertext links are associated with "linked browsing," and the tour is associated with "sequential browsing." More recently, Agosti, Gradenigo, and Marchetti (1992) suggest similar functions that may facilitate browsing in a hypertext environment: sequential reading, associative reading, semantic association, and navigation. Thus, the users' tasks and purposes affect not only the way people engage in browsing in terms of the strategy used (Canter, Rivers, and Storrs 1985) but also the tool or function chosen. Further, users' knowledge or lack of knowledge about the material affects the tool chosen.

**Medium/Resource-Based Browsing** Each medium or resource has a number of unique attributes, such as format and organization structure. Based on the assumption that browsing may be medium-specific, types of browsing have been grouped by the nature of the resource, such as shelf browsing, catalog browsing (bibliographic tools, directories), full-text browsing (journals, encyclopedias), and computer browsing (Overhage and Harman 1965; Ayris 1986). However, as discussed later, it may not be media per se that lead to various types of browsing behavior but rather the display or structure or, more generally, the interface inherent in each medium that constrains or facilitates various types of scanning activities.

### What Influences Browsing?

**Full-Text Systems** Several studies have compared various computer-based full-text systems to print media such as newspapers (Dozier and Rice 1984; Egan et al.

1989; 1991; Joseph, Steinberg, and Jones 1989; Marchionini and Liebscher 1991; Marchionini and Komlodi 1998; Shneiderman et al. 1989; Zerbinos 1990). They found that (1) users gradually changed their expectations and strategies applied from the familiar print medium to the new computer medium; (2) some kinds of search accuracy and search time are better in computer systems and some are faster in printed media; (3) hypertext systems invite browsing while imposing lower cognitive load compared to search-term systems; (4) browsing in computer environments can result in incidental learning or serendipitous findings; (5) there are possibly more "false alarms" (identifying topics not actually in the browsed material) in electronic systems; (6) users tend to browse or scan more in newspapers but search for specific information in videotext systems, reinforcing the role of "noninstrumental" reading, especially in media that do not have hierarchical menu-based database structures; (7) online technical manuals do not easily support flipping pages, referencing back and forth, and scanning an entire table; and (8) users with domain expertise (content knowledge) tend to spend more time browsing than do those who have search expertise (search-path knowledge).

Some systems seem to invite more scanning than others. The use of system features such as fast and easy paging through sets of text, and highlighting query terms in the text, encourage browsing in the computer environment (Marchionini and Komlodi 1998). When compared with browsing in printed materials in the sense of nonsequential reading, the speed and screen size of a computer-based system play an important role (Lelu 1991). Card, Moran, and Newell (1983) report that although how fast a person can read text is a function of the reader's skill and the conceptual difficulty of the material, speed-readers skim. One study shows that speed of reading stories from computer screens and books does not differ significantly, but skimming (defined as "proceeding at a rate three to four times faster than normal reading in order to grasp a general sense of the content or to retain only the main points") is 41 percent slower from the computer screens than from books (Muter and Maurutto 1991). A speedy communication interface, multiple windows, and a large screen are needed to support skimming in computers (Muter and Maurutto 1991).

**Bibliographic Information Retrieval Systems** Hildreth (1987) notes a difference between a product/output-oriented search and a process-oriented search in online public access catalogs (OPACs), suggesting that much end-user searching can best be described as "exploratory, circuitous, and fully interactive," characteristics that have also been attributed to browsing activities (Belkin, Marchetti, and Cool 1993;

Liebscher and Marchionini 1988). This concept of the exploratory and interactive nature of information retrieval is especially important when we look at browsing as a form of subject access, characterized by the absence of predefined products or a well-defined goal in the user's mind.

Studying social scientists' information-seeking behavior, Ellis (1989) emphasizes that systems should provide aids for browsing activities in order to facilitate the identification of relevant sources in an area of interest, through (1) identification, (2) familiarization (becoming aware of the availability of the sources of material in an area), and (3) differentiation (developing a knowledge of the differences between sources of materials).

Hancock-Beaulieu (1990) compares subject-searching behavior at shelves and at both printed and online catalogs. She considers shelf browsing to be subject-searching behavior to find information on a particular topic. From the behavioral perspective, she finds that 82 percent of all cases are unstructured shelf browsing, an activity in which the user does not follow an entire class number sequence but pursues a nonlinear course through the stacks and backtracks to the area that has already been covered. The other 18 percent is accounted for by structured browsing, which progresses in a linear fashion with little backtracking. Users, having found references, did not use the given class numbers to further their search by browsing the classified sequence of the microfiche catalog nearby or the online catalog. However, about one third of about 50 percent of the users who follow up specific references at the shelves from the online catalog and find them to be relevant also select other items in the same area on the shelves. Hancock-Beaulieu notes that the constraints of screen displays make viewing references in the online catalog for a subject search more akin to structured shelf browsing and concludes that users need to do subject searching but do so mainly at shelves rather than at catalogs.

From a cognitive perspective, Akeroyd's (1990) analysis in the evaluation of three OPAC system interfaces indicates four reasons why people engage in browsing activities at OPACs: (1) to make amends for problems at the input stage, such as browsing forwards or backwards to the correct position, (2) to establish the scope of the terminology, such as browsing in subject indexes, (3) to expand the scope of retrieved documents, such as browsing a hierarchical classified list, and (4) as a focusing device to specify a subset of a retrieved set in a Boolean set. However, he points out one fundamental problem with text-based bibliographic systems: the lack of user recognition of the overall size of the file because there are no physical indicators as there would be in a card catalog or some online catalogs. As Soderston (1986) asserts, the user's disorientation when using a computer results from the fact that the display screen is a digital form of information, with each screen perceptually divorced from its surrounding context.

As the recognition of the importance of browsing increases, some researchers have begun to prescribe what browsing facilities should be provided for system users (Bates 1989; 1990; Hildreth 1987b). Ellis (1989) suggests that OPACs make available any type of information in the database for browsing, including a list of authors, journals/books/proceedings, tables of contents, cited works, subject terms, and broad subject headings. Others have focused on improvement of index browsing, classification browsing (Huestis 1988; Losee 1992), and subject headings browsing (Massicotte 1988). Although it is generally assumed that classification browsing can be facilitated in online catalogs, both the Hancock-Beaulieu and Akeroyd studies show that "classification search" in online catalogs is seldom used, whether as an initial search step or as a follow-up procedure after a specific reference is found. The classification numbers are understood by the user simply to be a location mark rather than a summary of a subject content; few users are likely to make a conceptual link between classification number and the hierarchical subject relationship.

**Electronic Messaging/Filtering Systems** Although not explicitly addressed, the notion of browsing as an information retrieval strategy or a screening technique has been applied in research in computer-mediated communication such as e-mail systems and electronic bulletin boards. Hiltz and Turoff (1985) propose that one way to cope with information overload as commonly experienced by many e-mail users would be to devise better retrieval facilities such as classification of messages according to various common attributes or personal interest profiles for the purpose of selecting messages of interest. However, based on their belief that no automated routine can simultaneously filter out all useless and irrelevant communications and still ensure the receipt of all valuable communications, they argue that one important feature of the system should be the flexibility it allows users to structure communications they send and organize information they receive according to their own criteria, such as key words, date, and sender's name.

Malone et al. (1987) propose three approaches for organizing information to facilitate filtering and selecting information in an electronic messaging environment, including (1) cognitive filtering by characterizing the contents of a message and the information needs of potential message recipients, (2) social filtering by supporting the personal and organizational interrelationships of individuals in a community, and (3) economic filtering based on cost-benefit assessments or explicit/implicit pricing mechanisms. Typical filtering and selecting processes would include dealing with "junk mail," scanning electronic bulletin boards, and examining a table of contents to decide which articles to read in a journal.

Malone (1983), in a study of how people organize their office desks, suggests that computer-based systems may help with the difficulty of classifying office material by doing as much automatic classification as possible (e.g., by the explicit fields or headers such as subject and sender of an e-mail message) and by allowing multiple classifications of a given document. An important function of desk organization is to remind the user of things to do, not just to help the user find desired information; thus the notion of information access on the basis of spatial location instead of its logical classification is a feature that might profitably be incorporated into computer-based information systems. It is interesting to note that the functions of finding and reminding seem to parallel searching and browsing (see Schank 1982 for a theory of reminding).

**Visual/Image-Based Systems** Borgman and her associates (1991; 1995) in designing a children's interactive science library, model the physical library environment on the screen, including visual displays of bookshelves, floor maps, and walking paths for locating a book. They purposely remove the keyboard, thus forcing users to browse by means of interacting with the system with the mouse only. They find that in comparison with a previous study of a Boolean-based system, a browsing, direct-manipulation interface for children is in general a superior approach to information retrieval, being more usable and favored across the population, and less sensitive to children's level of computer experience. The use of an image of library shelves and their physical layout to facilitate browsing in electronic environment has been emphasized (Bates 1989; Beheshti 1992). Antonoff (1989) describes the Prodigy videotex system, which models the physical shopping mall environment. Interview data showed that the small text window and speed problems created difficulties in browsing.

### What Are the Consequences of Browsing?

**Finding and Learning** Two major positive results are finding what one wants and accidentally learning the contents of a database during the course of finding information (e.g., Egan et al. 1991).

**Disorientation** Disorientation arises from unfamiliarity with the structure and coceptual organization of the document network, originating from the cognitive demands placed on the user (Foss 1989). On the other hand, disorientation may occur because of elements of the interface design such as the lack of contextual cues (Soderston 1986). This problem has drawn researchers' attention to the study of human spatial behavior in psychology (Hulley 1990). A number of approaches to making browsing more effective by avoiding the problem have been proposed, such as the provision of a history tree to keep track of the user's movement through the system or a layout display of the document network (Agosti, Gradenigo, and Marchetti 1992; Foss 1989; Lelu 1991; McAleese 1989).

**Information Overload** Browsers may experience information overload, which, according to Foss (1989), stems from general inexperience with learning from browsing, which leads to difficulties with remembering, consolidating, and understanding the semantic content. On the other hand, information overload may simply be due to the mode and amount of information presented in a single information-seeking episode (Hiltz and Turoff 1985; Malone et al. 1987) or may be related to attributes of information such as complexity or relevance (Losee 1995; Iselin 1989). Various techniques to deal with this problem in electronic environments have also been proposed, such as categorization and ranking of electronic messages (Losee 1995) or providing a "summary box" for keeping the user's annotations during hypertext browsing (Foss 1989).

### Consumer Research

The notion of browsing is a recent concept in consumer research. There are three characteristics of the literature on browsing in this area:

1. Browsing behavior has been investigated as a distinct consumer shopping behavior related to but not equated with buying behavior.
2. Some attempts have been made to quantify the concept of browsing (Bloch and Richins 1983; Bloch, Ridgway, and Sherrell 1989; Jeon 1990).
3. Eye movement research has been shown to be a potentially useful approach to the study of browsing behavior (for specific applications to information system research, see Marchionini 1995, 159).

Although there seems to be no direct dichotomy like the use of browsing vs. searching in the library and information science literature, the contrast between window-shopping and purchasing is similar to that between browsing and searching. Both purchasing and searching can be considered as selecting something available, and both can be stimulated by initial browsing. Further, browsing in the information context may lead to both recreational and informational benefits. In this sense, these two distinct sets of literature give parallel demonstrations of the same phenomenon.

### What Is Browsing?

Bloch and Richins (1983, 389) define the concept of browsing as "the in-store examination of a retailer's merchandise for informational and/or recreational purposes without an immediate intent to buy," and, with others (Block, Ridgway, and Sherrell 1989; Jarboe and McDaniel 1987; Jeon 1990), have developed measures of customer browsing involving the following dimensions: (1) the context dimension: "in-store," (2) the behavioral dimension: "examination," "looking around," (3) the resource dimension: "merchandise," (4) the motivational dimension: "purposes," "just for fun or recreation," "to get information," "to look at new models," and (5) the cognitive dimension: "intent." The three dimensions common to the previously reviewed literatures are scanning (behavioral characteristic), resource (specifically, the content aspect of the resource), and goal ("intent" or the lack of it). Note that such scanning behavior is considered to be purposeful but not necessarily goal-directed or task-oriented.

### What Is the Nature of Browsing?

According to Bloch and Richins' (1983, 389) definition, browsing is "both a form of leisure activity and a form of external search behavior" that can occur independently of specific purchase occasions/intentions. They suggest that the search aspect of browsing may be pleasurable in and of itself and can be done to satisfy epistemic or curiosity motives. Further, the phase "without immediate intent to buy" stresses the lack of a purchase plan at the time of browsing, suggesting the indeterminate nature of browsing. Indeed, browsing as a distinct shopping behavior can be directed or nondirected (Salomon and Koppelman 1992). However, the concept of browsing has been more associated with nondirected shopping behavior described as on-going information acquisition, which is not directly tied to a specific purchase plan. It is "informal, ongoing, and nonstructured" (193), implying the unplanned nature of such nondirected shopping behavior or information acquisition process.

### What Influences Browsing?

In one survey, browsing was found to be positively associated with the degree of interest in the class(es) of products, the propensity to engage in other forms of search behavior relating to the product class (measured by number of product-related magazines read regularly or subscribed to), the degree of knowledge concerning the product class, and the degree of word-of-mouth activity (Bloch and Richins 1983). In a similar study, Bloch, Ridgway, and Sherrell (1989) found support for the concept that consumers browse to obtain two benefits: (1) to get information, and (2) for recreation. The receipt of such benefits is affected by two factors: (1) retail environment, and (2) product involvement levels, both of which in turn influence the consumer's browsing activity. Two major outcomes of such browsing activity are found to be (1) product knowledge, and (2) opinion leadership. In Jeon's (1990) study, in-store browsing is related to pre- and post-shopping mood, psychological situation, and impulse buying. One of his conclusions is that in-store browsing is directly influenced by the pre-shopping mood and affects both the psychological situation and the consequent impulse-buying behavior, which in turn influences post-shopping mood.

Shim and Mahoney (1991) study the characteristics of teleshoppers and show that (1) most teleshoppers are recreational users (shopping through videotex services for fun), and (2) teleshoppers are less concerned with convenience and time than non-teleshoppers. They suggest that those who are under time pressure may not "browse through" the electronic shopping system, implying those who teleshop are more likely to engage in browsing behavior in using the system.

Buckley and Long (1990) identify features of teleshopping and the system, knowledge, and goods variables that contributed to problems with usability in such system as Viewtron's videotex. System variables include the jargon used in the system, the organization of goods, the extent of the description of goods, and the modality of description of goods; these correspond to what Tuori (1987) identifies as interface factors influencing the extent to which people are able to browse. Knowledge variables include knowledge of brand names, general knowledge of transaction domain, knowledge of natural language and computer systems, and general knowledge of transactions. Goods variables such as delivery delay, availability of goods, and range of goods are also reported as obvious sources of problems in the use of such systems. Consumer eye movement research techniques could be usefully applied to the study of the user information evaluation process, such as browsing to judge the relevance of retrieved citations (Choo 1995, 106–110; Drucker 1990; Howard 1991; Smead, Wilcox, and Wilkes 1981; von Keitz 1988; Young 1976). As in the library user studies, the differences between browsing real objects and surrogates (such as shopping catalogs, which cannot show all the object's attributes) have also been noted (Buckley and Long 1990; Grover and Sabherwal 1989).

### What Are the Consequences of Browsing?

The consumer research literature suggests that possible results of in-store browsing include recreational enjoyment, information gathering, opinion leadership, and impulse buying.

## Audience Research

Although it has not been explicitly investigated as such in audience research, browsing (in its broadest sense as a sensory experience characterized by short attention given to each object the person is exposed to) can take place with different media (or objects); that is, it is also likely to occur in the process of mass media exposure. Indeed, although the word *browsing* has not been much used in the mass media literature, the notion of browsing is implicitly embedded in the study of audience selectivity and involvement in television viewing in which "zapping" and "grazing" have emerged as new viewing patterns. When browsing behavior can be considered a part of mass communication consumers' behavior, uses and gratifications research provides insights to answer the question of what motivates people to browse. The literature lays out several useful theoretical foundations that a study of browsing behavior may incorporate, each of which describes some dimensions of a phenomenon that the others do not fully account for. Methodologically speaking, variables related to media use may also be included to investigate browsing activity.

### What Is Browsing?

Heeter and Greenberg (1988) show that people browse during remote channel switching (called zapping) or in the process of passive television viewing. Zapping initially referred only to the use of a remote control device to switch away from commercials, but the use of the term has broadened to include other types of active channel switching while viewing, such as zapping shows partway through them and "grazing" interesting images and segments across multiple programs (Arrington 1992; Dorr and Kunkel 1990; Heeter and Greenberg 1985). Such interaction with television may indicate "a complex consciousness that derives satisfaction by sampling information in small, seemingly random chunks" (Arrington 1992, 13). Characterized by this description, zapping or grazing reflects the notion of browsing common to other literatures in that it is a scanning process and involves a resource (TV channels and schedules can be considered as search paths of the resource, and TV programs on each channel can be considered as contents of the resource).

**What Is the Nature of Browsing?**

According to Heeter and Greenberg (1985), zapping is not an idiosyncratic behavior aimed at TV commercials but one among several systematic approaches to watching television. People who constantly change channels are found to use TV more as an accompaniment to other activities in the household. Similarly, in Perse's (1990) study, zapping is found to be a ritualistic viewing pattern characterized by the audience's higher selectivity before and during television exposure and less involvement during exposure.

**What Influences Browsing?**

In their surveys of the selection process of TV viewers, Heeter and Greenberg (1985) show that zappers can be differentiated from nonzappers through the following characteristics: they have more remote control channel selectors, do less planning of their TV viewing, are more likely to watch programs that they do not watch regularly, and are more likely to change channels between and during shows and at commercials. In other words, zapping tends to be associated with more search paths facilitated by a convenient display interface such as a remote control, the viewer's lack of a prior viewing plan, and the notion of serendipity (being drawn to the programs not originally sought). Two primary reasons for channel switching reported in the same study are (1) to see what else is on the TV, and (2) to avoid commercials. Other reasons include boredom, variety seeking, and multiple-show viewing.

In terms of demographic variables, Heeter and Greenberg (1985) find that sex and age were important predictors. Men are more likely to zap than women, and young adults are more likely to do so than older adults. Zappers are also familiar with more different channels and exhibit more reevaluation behaviors during program viewing. In Olney's study (1989), attitude toward commercials, emotional response, and related contents are antecedents that influence commercial zapping behavior during viewing.

To test whether the TV audience is active or passive and to what extent medium versus content influences TV viewing patterns, Hearn (1989) conducted a field experiment involving 156 adults using questionnaires and diaries as instruments. His findings show that content does play an important role in influencing viewing behavior, suggesting that not all TV viewers are unselective or situation-dependent. He concludes that viewers can be distinguished by their motivations for TV viewing in terms of viewing orientation (either content or medium) and experienced freedom (either high or low). Both entertainment motivations and avoidance/boredom motivations tend to be medium-oriented. The former is related to high-freedom viewing and the latter to low-freedom viewing. People motivated by information/surveillance needs tend to be content-oriented with high-freedom viewing, whereas the satisfaction of social needs may be the main function of content-oriented low-freedom viewing.

To the extent that the notion of browsing can be conceived as a type of viewing, the findings in this literature might also have implications for understanding browsing behavior in other contexts. For instance, the semistructured, patterned browsing observed in library settings may be associated with a specific medium such as a set of journals (Ellis 1989) or a particular section of the book stacks (Morse 1970) because of the high possibility of finding potentially relevant information; it is a behavior motivated by an information/surveillance need.

On the other hand, along with findings in other contexts such as in-store shopping (Bloch, Ridgway, and Sherrell 1989) and newspaper reading (Zerbinos 1990), the distinct characteristics of zappers and nonzappers suggest that some people may tend to browse more than others. Whether those who tend to browse in one context are the same group of people who tend to browse in other contexts, or whether people would demonstrate similar browsing behavior across contexts, are open questions.

### What Motivates People to Browse?

Four theoretical approaches potentially relevant to browsing have been used in the study of mass media audiences, including psychological, social/structural, cultural, and phenomenological approaches. These perspectives address the underlying motivations of human information behavior in general and media exposure in particular.

**Psychological Perspective** McGuire (1974) notes that in the psychology literature two major dimensions underlying human motives have been proposed. The first dimension includes cognitive motives, stressing the person's information processing and attainment of ideational states. The second includes affective motives, stressing the person's feelings and attainment of certain emotional states. McGuire (1974) subdivides each of these two dimensions into (1) growth vs. preservation needs of human beings, and (2) the internal vs. external goal orientations of human striving. These subdivisions are further divided according to a breakdown of human nature into active vs. passive models to form 16 categories of human motives that generate communication-relevant human needs. Note that the motives of browsing suggested in consumer research are echoed here in that "obtaining information" (informational need) can be considered a cognitive motive while "for recreation" (recreational need) can be considered an affective motive.

McGuire (1974) grants that initial exposure to mass media might be largely the outcome of chance and situational factors (e.g., availability) but argues that human needs and gratifications are significant determinants of the typical continued exposure to given types of materials, basing this on the theory of reinforcement. The implications are that some browsing behaviors may be initially due to situational exposure, while others may be patterned through positive reinforcement.

In answering the question of why people want exposure to media, some researchers contend that four functions are fulfilled by communication (Wright 1974; Littlejohn 1989): (1) surveillance of the environment or new activities (knowing what is going on), (2) interpretation of the events surveyed and prescriptions for reactions to them (having options or solutions for dealing with societal problems), (3) transmission of social values and other elements of culture to new members of the society (socialization and education), and (4) human amusement or entertainment. To the extent that the concept of exposure is related (or a prerequisite) to browsing behavior, it seems that surveillance, education (or more generally, learning), and entertainment can also be conceived of as high-level motivations or functions of browsing activities. Throughout this chapter, browsing has been construed as a monitoring, screening, and learning strategy as well as a recreational activity.

**Social/Structural Perspective** Motivational incentives for browsing do not have to be psychological. Marchionini (1987) notes that there are three primary reasons why people browse. One is that the information system (such as an open-stack library), that is, the display or general interface, may support and encourage browsing. The other two are related to cognitive factors. First, browsers cannot or may not have defined their search objective. Second, it takes less cognitive load to browse than it does to plan and conduct an analytical optimized search. To a certain extent, people are subject to the influence of physical structures and social systems that are largely beyond their control. The implication is that people are not confined only by individual factors but also by situational or social structures. To fully account for the variation in human information-seeking behavior, both individual and situational dimensions need to be taken into account.

As far as the debate between situational and individual factors is concerned, some empirical studies of media use in an organizational context suggest that individual differences tend to be less influential than situational or contextual factors in media selection, and may be influential only when situational factors allow people to exercise individual preferences (Trevino, Lengel, and Daft 1987; Trevino, et al. 1990; Rice, Chang, and Torobin 1992). The implication is that browsing can be either a proactive choice for exposure to a resource or externally or contextually induced behavior, depending on whether the situation constrains or facilitates such browsing activity.

**Cultural Perspective** To study the cultural aspects of communication activities, specifically popular culture, some researchers argue that the motivations for mass media consumption include a peculiar kind of aesthetic satisfaction, self-contained within the consuming experience itself—a satisfaction that differs in kind from the functionalists' utilitarian needs (Day 1979; Dozier and Rice 1984; Stephenson 1986). People may engage in such activity in a nonpurposive way, such that the creation of particular moods or feelings through an immediate experience with popular art should be apprehended in its own terms. That is, they are intrinsic rather than extrinsic experiences (Noble 1987). This approach stresses the context of media use and the rules and meanings that apply in given cases.

**Phenomenological Perspective** While the popular cultural approach suggests that some human actions are not purposive and are engaged in for their own sake, the phenomenological perspective emphasizes the idea of media use as a rational, goal-directed activity. Phenomenologist Alfred Schutz (1967) makes a distinction between conscious behavior and unconscious behavior. According to Schutz, "An action is conscious in the sense that, before we carry it out, we have a picture in our mind of what we are going to do. This is the 'projected act'." Within this perspective, media use is regarded as an act of free choice by an actor who seeks to gain some immediate or delayed future benefit, to be or do what he wishes. Researchers are typically concerned with situations in which media use appears to be purposeful and in which the actor is able to explain his choices. Consequently, to find out why viewers, listeners, or readers attend to media, one must ask them, and their answers are the only relevant explanation of the actions in question. However, unconscious media exposure implies that people may not be always aware of, and therefore not able to fully articulate, what they attempt to do or what they are doing or why they are doing it.

### Organizational Research—Environmental Scanning

Although the word *browsing* has not been used by many researchers in management and organizational communication literature, the notion of browsing has been documented in studies of environmental scanning and informal communication as a form of information seeking. It is also reflected in the concept of "management by wandering around" (Peters and Waterman 1984), which emphasizes casual access and unpredictable exposure to social links and environmental information of an organization for effective management.

**What Is Browsing?**

Aguilar (1967) defines the activity of environmental scanning as "scanning for information about events and relationships in a company's outside environment, the knowledge of which would assist top management in its task of charting the company's future course of action." To Coates (1986), environmental scanning is "a process of systematic surveillance and interpretation designed to identify events, elements, and conditions of the environment that have potential relevance and impact for an organization." In general, these descriptions portray a goal-directed, structured approach to identifying relevant information in the areas of interest from the organization's point of view. However, it is individuals in the organization who do the scanning.

**What Is the Nature of Browsing?**

In Auster and Choo's (1991) investigation of executive scanning behavior, environmental scanning is considered as a form of information-seeking behavior of executives involving both the perception of information and simply being exposed to information. In other words, the activity of scanning for information can be a result of proactive behavior or a situation-induced behavior. Recognizing that scanning behavior can be either active or passive, formal or informal, they maintain that from the point of view of the individual manager, environmental scanning is often a personal, informal activity that is an intrinsic part of the managerial function.

Still, four types of scanning activity in organizations have been identified (Saunders and Jones 1990): (1) "undirected viewing" (general scanning without a particular purpose), (2) "conditioned viewing" (search of an identified area), (3) "informal search" (limited, unstructured effort to obtain particular information for a particular purpose), and (4) "formal search" (deliberate, planned search to obtain specific information for a particular purpose). This categorization of scanning tasks is similar to the model of browsing identified in library and information literature in which three types of browsing have been proposed (Cove and Walsh 1987). The fourth type is equivalent to "search browsing," where a specific goal is present, while the second and third types of scanning can be equated with "general-purpose browsing," where information-seeking behavior is guided by a vague goal in mind and is characterized by scanning information in a predictable pattern. The major variation in this categorization lies in a different conception of purposelessness. Unlike "undirected browsing" in library and information science literature, which is taken to mean a time-passing activity with no conscious browsing goal in mind, undirected viewing from an organizational point of view implies a purpose of environmental surveillance or monitoring, although specific goals for such scanning may not be present.

Environmental scanning includes both looking at (viewing) and looking for (searching) information (Choo 1995, 72), ranging from undirected viewing/exposure and conditioned viewing to informal search and formal search, at multiple levels (from macroenvironment to specific task), at varying time horizons (short-term to long-term). Thus "scanning is a form of organizational browsing" (85). Daft and Weick's (1984) scanning/interpretation model identified information needs, information seeking, and information use, within four types of scanning/interpretation modes, based on assumptions about the environment (unanalyzable, analyzable) and organizational intrusiveness (passive, active): (1) unanalyzable/passive (undirected viewing), (2) unanalyzable/active (enacting), (3) analyzable/passive (conditioned viewing), and (4) analyzable/active (discovery).

Several underlying dimensions of these scanning or browsing activities can be identified, including the act of scanning, a resource as the object of scanning, a goal or purpose (or the absence of it), and knowledge about the search criteria (e.g., "specific information," "an identified area"), and the presence or absence of a plan of action in terms of scanning/search strategies (e.g., "planned" or "unstructured").

**What Influences Browsing?**

According to Auster and Choo (1991), scanning behavior can be measured by multiple indicators such as scope (or level of interest) of scanning, amount of scanning, and use of environmental information, all of which are influenced by informational variables such as perceived environmental uncertainty, perceived source accessibility, and perceived source quality. They also suggest that use of environmental information gained by managers can be related to the four decisional roles or activities of managers in the decision-making process of each activity. Thus, the extent to which managers engage in environmental scanning is influenced by environmental characteristics and source characteristics as well as individual factors. Note that in consumer research, Bloch and his associates (1989) propose a similar framework that depicts the influence of both environment and resource. Further, two similar variables of the individual—product involvement (e.g., "level of interest") and amount of browsing—are used to measure scanning behavior in consumer research.

### Organizational Research—Informal Communication

In informal communication, browsing tends to be an activity that is often unplanned and not goal-directed. At the group level, studies of information-seeking behavior among scientists show that informal communication such as hallway chatting, or after-meeting discussion is an important component of knowledge creation processes, especially in collaborative scientific work (Poland 1991). Doty, Bishop, and McClure (1991, 28) describe one important aspect of such informal communication as "generating new ideas through serendipitous, interactive contact with external sources of expertise," which is not normally available from formal communication such as recorded documents. One may argue that such unintended exposure in a social environment is similar to the act of browsing bookshelves, interacting with author's ideas in the book picked up on the way to finding something else, and deriving serendipitous findings. The difference is that the objects of browsing in this case are people instead of books, and of course these people are not organized sequentially according to some classification system (except possibly by where their offices are located) nor are they, typically, stationary.

#### What Is Browsing?

Root (1988, 27) proposes the concept of "social browsing" to describe "a dynamic process of informal, in-person, mobility-based social interaction" and suggests that "social browsing is a fundamental mechanism for developing and maintaining social relationship in the workplace." Kraut et al. (1990, 160) describe the informality of conversation as "the degree to which the conversation was scheduled or spontaneous." They operationalize a conversation's "degrees of spontaneity" on a four-level continuum from formal to informal. The four categories are described as follows: (1) a conversation that was previously scheduled or arranged, (2) one in which the initiator set out specifically to visit another party, (3) one in which the initiator had planned to talk with other participants at some time and took advantage of a chance encounter to have the conversation, and (4) a spontaneous interaction in which the initiator had not planned to talk with other participants. They name these categories "scheduled," "intended," "opportunistic," and "spontaneous," respectively. They found that "the more spontaneous the conversation, the more informal it was likely to be" (160). Thus, the notion of browsing in this context refers to casual access to social links and unpredictable exposure to many possible social interactions and to the implied knowledge available through these interactions.

It is interesting to note that if we replace the word *conversation* with the phrase "search or scanning task," and conceive "the other party" as the "resource" to be consulted, Kraut et al.'s continuum still applies. That is, a search task can be arranged (such as a prescheduled online searching for a specific purpose), or intended (such as scanning a new journal when it arrives on a regular basis), or opportunistic (such as looking for information pertinent to another goal while searching the same material to find a particular fact for the current project), or spontaneous (such as serendipitous finding of something of interest while looking for something else).

**What Influences Browsing?**

Based on Allen's concept of physical "proximity" (1969), Kraut and Galegher (1990) and Kraut et al. (1990) show how geographic separation may impair workers' ability to effectively browse the social environment, resulting in a significant and consequential reduction in the frequency of informal communication, which in turn affects the quality of intellectual teamwork. Within the same location, some research evidence indicates that employees' interpersonal experiences as well as visitors' perception of the organization are affected by the organization's physical layout, suggesting that an organization's physical structure influences its membership and information processing in organizational contexts (Walsh and Ungson 1991). As Haythornthwaite and Wellman (1998) report, increased interaction is also more likely among people who have multiplex network links (which cover more than one topic) with each other and who typically use more than one communication channel to communicate with their network members. Further, in their study of a university research group (faculty, staff, and students), unscheduled encounters were the most frequent form of interaction for receiving work, giving work, collaborative writing, and providing major emotional support. Interestingly, close friends and friends had many more unscheduled encounters than acquaintances or work-only interactions. Thus spontaneous interactions represent a consequential form of organizational browsing.

With new technology, it is possible that people can "browse" others online and potentially have an unplanned conversation with another person. Kraut and Galegher (1990) propose the concept of electronic hallway or sidewalk where people in different locations can meet spontaneously or have unplanned interactions mediated by video technology. In a number of empirical studies of patterns of contact and communication in scientific research collaboration, Kraut et al. (1990) demonstrate how the findings of informal communication research can be applied to the design of an audio-video communication medium to facilitate social browsing, although the implied knowledge inherent in social interaction in a public space, such as whether the other party is in a mood to have a face-to-face conversation, cannot be transformed easily into electronic environments (Fish et al. 1993).

The random examination of materials arranged for use in the library setting can be considered as an analog to the unplanned scanning of people in the social environment. That is, (1) the object of browsing can be seen as moving from information and real objects to people as a database; (2) the "interactivity" in browsing increases as the medium changes from real objects (including information items such as printed materials), to computers and to people; and (3) the concept of "links" (or associations and relations) changes from document links to social links (between people). What is being sampled changes from physical attributes and written (formal) knowledge attributes to include informal or conversational information attributes, and social and organizational attributes.

In a larger context, Drucker and Gumpert (1991) point out the difference between public and electronic space in terms of the degree of sensory and emotional involvement, and the influence such difference may have on unpredictable social interaction. As research in informal communication shows (Kraut et al. 1990), the psychological distance experienced in electronic communication may be potentially different from that when people communicate with each other in physical environments. Therefore, Drucker and Gumpert (1991) assert, computer-mediated interaction and face-to-face interaction, while functionally equivalent, are contextually and experientially dissimilar. However, it should be noted that although its impact is still to be fully understood, the development of new technology and its potential applications in many aspects of life may modify Drucker and Gumpert's conclusion. The emerging concept of "virtual reality" or "cyberspace," a system that allows people to simulate operation (movement) in the real world without physically being in the real place and that is capable of creating multiple sensory "feelings" in people, may blur temporal and spatial distinctions between public and electronic environments.

### Environmental Planning and Architectural Design

In the environmental planning and design literature, the notion of browsing is often implicitly assumed in discussions of (1) perceptual experience in visual communication, which can be guided or confined by architectural and display design, and (2) "wayfinding" in a complex environment, which emphasizes an understanding of human spatial behavior in order to facilitate spatial learning and problem solving through spatial planning and signage systems. In this context, the notion of browsing is examined in its broadest sense as a scanning process (usually visual) and has been related to environmental perception and cognition. Such a notion has its theoretical roots in environmental and cognitive psychology. Arthur and Passini (1992) provide a set of concepts relevant to the discussion of the nature of the scanning process:

1. Perception is the process of obtaining information through the senses, [which can be differentiated from] cognition that is related to understanding and being able to manipulate information (33).
2. Recognition is remembering an item in the presence of the item; recall is remembering an item in the absence of the item (31).
3. Cognitive map is an overall mental image or representation of the spaces and the layout of a setting (23).

**What Is Browsing?**

According to Arthur and Passini (1992, 33), "environmental perception is based on a process of scanning and glancing. When moving through a complex setting, the eye scans the visual field. This preattentive perception serves to identify objects or messages of interest." The authors suggest that identification as a result of scanning is derived through recognition from stimulated association (see also Pryluck 1976, 37). Harbison (1988, 3–4) describes a similar concept, "simultaneous perception," as "a stream of consciousness ... which keeps us linked to our surroundings.... Simultaneous perception helps us experience our surroundings and our reactions to them, and not just [our] own thoughts and desires." In these descriptions, the notion of browsing is related to a form of environmental communication, or "environmental browsing," which involves the process of scanning and requires attention to the external resource. Exposure to the resource as a prerequisite is implied, which may lead to the identification of something of interest through recognition.

**What Is the Nature of Browsing?**

According to Harbison (1988, 34–35), although people have always responded to light, colors, sound, and smells in their surroundings, experiencing a city in terms of "simultaneous perception" involves (1) changing the way we look at things, diffusing our attention and also relaxing its intensity—a change that lets us start to see all the things around us at once and yet also look calmly and steadily at each one of them; (2) deciding, once or many times, whether to keep our attention on our own thoughts and plans or accept whatever our surroundings have to give us—whether to experience ourselves or what's around us; and (3) taking our attention away from some routine assumptions and expectations about what is there and what comes next. In other words, simultaneous perception involves an interplay of the individual's state of knowledge (such as without "routine assumptions and expectations") and the environment.

Sightseeing is an example of browsing in terms of such perceptual experience. People create an image of a city by scanning an environment in which a large amount of information is presented without completely absorbing all the information. This holistic view of something is very important in the early stage of information seeking where exploration is crucial for the later focus formulation stage (Kuhlthau 1993). How, then, do people construct the image in the sightseeing process, which to some extent is similar to the process of watching motion pictures (Friedberg 1991)? Pryluck (1976) attempts to answer this question by theorizing that people create meanings in motion pictures and television through cognitive processing of three components: (1) environmental experiential data directly perceived and processed, (2) reports about data processed in a sign system, and (3) an individual's memory store of knowledge and belief. The course of synthesis is partly determined by stimulus information, but it also depends on individuals' past experience, expectations, and preferences. These nonstimulus variables influence the choice of one figure rather than another for attention as well as the details of the construction that then takes place.

### What Influences Browsing?

Harbison (1988) notes that we seem to use simultaneous perception constantly to monitor our surroundings on a subconscious level for information that helps us maintain ourselves and go about our business. He suggests that orientation is one component of this everyday subconscious use of simultaneous perception. However, when we get lost and try to find out where we are or to find our way out of a place, orientation can be a goal-directed activity and thus a conscious use of such perception. This point has been made by Wyer and Srull (1989), who distinguish automatic from controlled cognitive information-processing activities, or what is often called conscious vs. subconscious information processing. According to them, certain well-learned cognitive activities are performed virtually automatically, without conscious awareness of the cognitive steps involved in them. That is, in many instances, information is acquired and processed without any specific goal in mind (the free flow of thought). In other instances, there may be the spontaneous initiation of goal-directed processing in the absence of external demands (28–29).

The implication for browsing activities is twofold: (1) one type of browsing is primarily perception-based without any specific goal or objective in mind at the moment of processing external information, unless obtaining the perceptual experience itself is considered as a goal; and (2) another type of browsing is goal-directed. Such goal-directed behavior can be stimulated either before or, as the phrase "spontaneous initiation" suggests, during the process of perceptual browsing, with or without external demands.

As a goal-directed activity, wayfinding, involving environmental perception and cognition, refers to the process of reaching a destination, whether in a familiar or unfamiliar environment; it is "a cognitive process for solving problems of movement in space" (Downs 1979, 19). Reaching a destination—the process of wayfinding—depends on how one understands the physical layout of the environment and organizes one's spatial behavior within it. Four linked operations are crucial to the successful solution of a wayfinding problem: (1) maintaining orientation, (2) making choice of a route, (3) keeping on the right track, and (4) recognizing the objective. It serves as a good analogy to information seeking in the electronic environment. For example, a destination that a person tries to reach can be a node in a hypertext information system in which choice of route refers to the choice of a link between the nodes.

People's spatial behavior in an environment depends on the nature and characteristics of the environment as well as on personal preference. Environmental characteristics influencing people's spatial behavior may include size, physical audiovisual attributes, location and layout (O'Neill and Jasper 1992). Browsing as an audiovisual communication process is influenced by the physical structure and layout of an environment because these determine what browsers can be exposed to and have access to within the environment in a specific time and space (Archea 1977; Drucker and Gumpert 1991; Harbison 1988; Walsh and Ungson 1991). Personal preference, in turn, depends on the individual's mental model or cognitive map of the environment.

Two basic learning processes operate simultaneously and give rise to two types of cognitive representation or two methods of organizing information in an environment. One of these, "nondimensional learning," generates sequential or route maps and suggests a linear design style for the wayfinding system. The other process, "dimensional learning," produces a spatial or cognitive map and encourages a spatial design style (Arthur and Passini 1992; Downs 1979; Sanoff 1991). Research shows that initial learning of a spatial environment necessarily involves nondimensional learning, that is, sequential images are a prior development in the formulation of a spatial image (Sanoff 1991). Thus, as Downs (1979) suggests, the two types of learning and the two forms of representation are not mutually exclusive but are stages in a general learning process. Graduation from nondimensional learning (knowledge of how to get there) to dimensional learning (knowledge of where things are) takes place as a direct result of time and repeated use of an environment. Similar conclusions can be found in a few empirical studies of people's interaction with electronic environments. For example, when searching unfamiliar materials or subjects, people tend to follow the "tour" (a sequential learning). As their knowledge about a subject area increases, they navigate electronic space using different tools such as "links" and "indexes".

Seeing wayfinding systems as information systems, researchers in this area (Arthur and Passini 1992; Pollet and Haskell 1979) suggest that the design of an efficient wayfinding system—and thus information systems in general—should support both wayfinding and learning based on the understanding of wayfinding as spatial problem-solving activity and the process of learning in a spatial context. Information system design based on such understanding will take into account people's spatial behavior, architecture and signage systems, and the interaction of both within a spatial context.

For example, based on the findings of architectural design research, legibility—the extent to which an environment looks as if one could explore it extensively without getting lost—has been proposed as a design principle of environmental planning to facilitate environmental perception and cognition (Harbison 1988). Landmarks serve as "anchor-points" allowing people to retain and mentally structure environmental information. Other important spatial elements in the architectural design of wayfinding systems, including entrances, exits, paths, and circulation systems, may also contribute to the legibility of an environment (Arthur and Passini 1992).

As more and more applications of information technology attempt to model physical environments (e.g., virtual reality, electronic libraries, or shopping malls) research on spatial cognition and wayfinding may contribute not only to a better understanding of browsing physical places and browsing in electronic space but also to better system design. Wayfinding systems in the form of interactive video displays such as SITEGUIDE have indeed been implemented to address two commonly asked questions by first-time visitors in public settings: How do I get where I want to go? and What is there here that might interest me? (Arthur and Passini 1992). Analogically, these questions are also frequently raised by the users of information systems when they place themselves in a complex electronic environment. For example, Bates (1986b) points out that one of the most neglected areas in designing online public access catalogs is the lack of orientation tools by which the user can get a feel of how the system works in order to move about easily and comfortably during the interaction with the system.

Browsing for wayfinding purposes in such systems demonstrates many of the concerns addressed in library and information science. Not accidentally, some researchers concerned with human information seeking in electronic environments also stress the desirability of "legibility" (using graphics, colors) for better browsability of the system to avoid disorientation and information overload problems (e.g., Conklin and Begeman 1989) and emphasize the importance of perceptual factors in the design of interactive information displays (Scrivener 1983). Others demonstrate working models to support browsing in a hypermedia system that is built upon an understanding of how spatial information is represented in cognitive models, applying the concepts of contextual cues, landmarks, and multisensory imagery of spatial arrangement (e.g., Hulley 1990). Browsing in an electronic environment is often associated with the problems of disorientation and information overload. The same problems occur in complex physical environments such as cities or buildings. As Canter, Rivers, and Storrs (1985) remind us, it is beneficial for information system designers to recognize the direct parallels between navigating concrete environments and navigating data.

### Summary

Each of these six literatures looks at browsing from a specific, unique perspective. Nevertheless, some common dimensions have emerged. For example, the concept of social browsing in organizations may appear at first to be quite different from the concept of browsing as a search strategy in the library environment. However, to the extent that people can be considered as an information source or database (and in fact, much research has shown that individuals as information sources are preferred by most people in the information-seeking process), the implication is that social browsing—casual access to social links and unpredictable exposure to possible social interactions and the implied knowledge available through these interactions—may share characteristics with browsing other information resources such as books or computer databases in a library for casual access to document links or unpredictable exposure to possible interactions with documents of interest. One may begin to understand the commonality across these two contexts in terms of the object of browsing (person vs. print) and means of interaction during browsing (visual and oral communication vs. written communication), for example.

Most of the literature discussed points to some salient characteristics of browsing:

1. The ability to expose oneself to and sample (not necessarily systematically) from many information stimuli, which may be otherwise inaccessible

**Table 9.2**
Dimensions of Browsing, by Research Literature

| Dimension | Library User Studies | Information Science | Consumer Research | Audience Research | Organizational Research | Design |
|---|---|---|---|---|---|---|
| *Behavior* | | | | | | |
| Scanning, movement | X | X | X | X | X | X |
| *Cognitive* | | | | | | |
| Purpose | X | Y | X | X | X | Y |
| Goal | X | X | X | X | X | X |
| Plan | X | | Y | | X | |
| Knowledge | X | X | Y | Y | Y | |
| Experience | X | X | | | | |
| *Resource* | | | | | | |
| Content | Information and objects | Information | Goods | Programs | People/events | Scene/ environment |
| Paths | Meta-information and spatial | Meta-information | Spatial | Channels | Spatial | Spatial |
| Feedback | | X | | | | |

X = dimensions explicitly discussed; Y = dimensions implicitly assumed.

**Table 9.3**
Factors Influencing Browsing, by Research Literature

| Factor | Library User Studies | Information Science | Consumer Research | Audience Research | Organizational Research | Design |
|---|---|---|---|---|---|---|
| *Individual Characteristics* | | | | | | |
| Purpose/motive | | | X | X | X | |
| Goal | X | X | | | X | X |
| Plan | Y | | X | X | | |
| Knowledge | X | X | | Y | | |
| Experience | X | X | | Y | | |
| Interest | | | X | | X | |
| Mood/emotion | | | X | X | | |
| Expectation | Y | Y | | | | |
| Time/money | | Y | X | | X | |
| *Contextual Factors—Environment* | | | | | | |
| Atmosphere | | | X | | X[b] | |
| Uncertainty | Y | | | | X[b] | Y |
| Interface | | | | | | |
| Display | X | X | Y | | | X |
| Organizational structure | X | X | | | X[b] | Y |
| *Contextual Factors—Computer-Specific* | | | | | | |
| Language | | X | X | | | |
| Modality | | X | X | | | |
| Screen size | | X | X | X | | |
| Speed | | X | | | | |
| Feedback | | X | | | | |
| *Contextual Factors—Object/Resource* | | | | | | |
| Real things | X | | X | | | |
| Representations | X | X | Y | | | |
| Other attributes | X | Y | X | X | X[a] | |

X = dimensions explicitly discussed; Y = dimensions implicitly assumed.
a. In environmental scanning literature.
b. In informal communication literature.

**Table 9.4**
Consequences of Browsing, by Research Literature

| Consequence | Library User Studies | Information Science | Consumer Research | Audience Research | Organizational Research | Design |
|---|---|---|---|---|---|---|
| Serendipitous finding | X | | | | | |
| Modification of information requirements | X | X | | | | |
| Finding the target information | | X | | | | |
| Learning | | X | | X | | |
| Disorientation | | X | | | | |
| Information overload | | X | | | | |
| Cost of time | | X | | | | |
| Enjoyment | X | | X | X | | |
| Information gathering | | | X | X | X | X |
| Opinion leadership | | | | X | | |
| Impulse buying | | | | X | | |
| Monitoring/surveillance | X | | | | X | X |

X = dimensions explicitly discussed.

2. The ability to sample as easily as one wishes
3. The reduced burden of specifying what is needed or intended (individuals may directly interact with informational stimuli that are potentially useful to them)
4. The linking of information stimuli (or making associations), which is manifested in or constrained by the underlying organizational structure (or paths) of the items browsed

On the other hand, in terms of motivations for browsing in the information-seeking context, even in a situation where undirected browsing is taking place, an expectation to gain something (i.e., information) in the course of browsing or in the future is often presumed. The emphasis is placed on instrumental browsing as opposed to recreational browsing. Indeed, most researchers in the library and information science field agree that information seeking in general tends to be purposive and goal-oriented. However, recreational browsing is as important as instrumental browsing in consumer and media audience research.

**Table 9.5**
Evaluation of Successful Browsing, by Research Literature

| | Library User Studies | Information Science | Consumer Research | Audience Research | Organizational Research | Design |
|---|---|---|---|---|---|---|
| *Criterion* | | | | | | |
| Effectiveness | X | X | | | | |
| Efficiency | | | X | | | |
| Satisfaction | | | Y | Y | | Y |
| *Measurement* | | | | | | |
| No. of books checked out that were not known beforehand (circulation statistics) | X | | | | | |
| No. of unknown items found or used (self-report data) | X | | | | | |
| Target items found (search accuracy) | | X | | | | |
| Time spent (search efficiency) | | X | | | | |

X = dimensions explicitly discussed; Y = dimensions implicitly assumed.

The presumptions in the literature about the user's motivation in browsing tend to reflect the paradigmatic biases of the specific literatures and lead to the controversy regarding the value of browsing. What is needed is to evaluate the consequences of browsing from the user's perspective, especially in terms of the user's motivations to browse. Further, most researchers adopt experiments and surveys as methodologies, both of which are subject to the criticism that they lack ecological validity. That is, the users under investigation are not connected to the immediate events or environments in which the browsing activities are taking place (Dervin and Nilan 1986). Future research needs to take this limitation into account.

Based on these reviews, we can identify six general dimensions of browsing. First, there is a *behavioral* dimension, which is related to behavioral characteristics. Such characteristics can refer to physical movement, such as "looking over," "inspecting," "making an examination," "skimming." Second, there is a *motivational* dimension, which is related to why people engage in browsing behavior, such as "in order to buy, or borrow, or read," "without prior intention of buying," or "without purpose." Third, there is a *cognitive* dimension, which is related to the mental state of the browser. One such aspect is knowledge, for instance, "without real knowledge." Fourth, there is an *object or resource* dimension, referring to the object of browsing, which can be physical items (e.g., goods) or symbolic information/text (e.g., headlines). Fifth, there is a *context* dimension, indicating where browsing behavior is taking place, such as in a store or a library. Sixth, the *organization* dimension suggests that a specific and physical arrangement within a context (i.e., a separate room and its display in a library or in a public space) may be associated with more browsing or successful browsing. These definitions suggest that, behaviorally, browsing is examining or inspecting or looking over a resource, and it can be characterized on a continuum from absence, vagueness to explicit presence of, knowledge, purpose, or intention.

In conclusion, the concept of browsing is multidimensional. Four tables summarize the concepts identified in this chapter. Table 9.2 shows some dimensions of browsing in each literature. Table 9.3 lists factors influencing browsing identified in each literature. Table 9.4 provides a cross-literature look at the consequences of browsing. Table 9.5 summarizes the criteria and measurements for evaluation of successful browsing suggested in each literature.

# 10

# A Preliminary Framework of Browsing

This chapter provides descriptions of various constructs used in part II, elaborating and defining dimensions important to an understanding of browsing in various contexts. It presents a taxonomy of browsing and proposes a summary model of browsing incorporating this taxonomy.

Marchionini's model of browsing considers five interactions among the information-seeking factors of "task, domain, setting, user characteristics and experience, and system content and interface" (1995, 107). The object is characterized, first, by the extent to which it is easily specified with singular attributes or is a complex of multiple attributes, and second, by whether those attributes are externally defined (as through a system's display or index) or exist within the mind of the user. Browsing would be maximal when the attributes are ambiguous, both in the system and in the user's mind. Third, the extent to which the system organizes the objects, and fourth, the extent to which the system provides feedback to the user also influence the level of browsing. Fifth, the user's personal information infrastructure (analytical or browsing strategy, entry points, search tactics, cognitive and emotional states) and the particular situation influence the level of browsing through their effect on extent of interactivity and extent of cognitive demand.

So, for example, scanning is associated with high external definition, known internal definition, high organization, low interactivity, and low cognitive effort (Marchionini 1995, 111, his table 6.2). Linear scanning occurs when a user is browsing a list or when a user is within the object's local area. Selective scanning involves partitioning sections of the search space (e.g., looking at an article's reference list or searching every third track on a CD), perhaps to assess coverage or general accuracy.

Observing is associated with low external and fuzzy internal definition, low organization and feedback, and subsequent high cognitive effort. This approach might involve multiple senses and defer most to environmental initiatives, so identifying the relevant neighborhood is an important first step in "observe" browsing. In between are "navigate" browsing (what might be called incremental information seeking, heavily influenced by system feedback) and "monitor" browsing (useful in resources with weak structuring, and most successful when associations are stimulated).

Marchionini's model is somewhat similar to our proposed model, and indeed was influenced to some extent by our previous work (Chang and Rice 1993). Here, we extend this general approach and provide some more specific components.

## Behavioral Characteristics

Although the term *browsing* is usually applied to "the actions of moving about a library and dipping into books, picking out bits and pieces of information of all kinds" (Cove and Walsh 1988, 31), the notion of browsing has been construed as a shopping activity, a viewing pattern, and a screening technique in addition to a search strategy. In the most fundamental sense, these various interpretations of browsing share a central characteristic: they are *scanning* processes.

> Scan: (v.) 1. to examine closely, esp. in search; 2. to look at quickly without careful reading. (n.) an act of scanning, esp. a searching look (*Longman Dictionary of Contemporary English* 1978, 991).

> Scan *vb* ... to examine by point-by-point observation or checking ... to investigate thoroughly by checking point by point and often repeatedly ... to glance from point to point often hastily, casually, or in search of a particular item (Merriam-Webster 1993, 1041).

### Scanning

From a behavioral perspective, browsing is characterized by the act of scanning as an individual moves through an information or a physical environment. The two senses of scanning—the close examination or the quick glance—reflect two different approaches to looking through a surrounding or a resource in which multiple layers of information or objects are presented; scanning implies multiplicity of the scanned object.

Various descriptions of scanning behavior, based on the second meaning of the term, include skimming, glancing, or looking around. Although looking is the most common form of scanning discussed in the literature, scanning does not have to be visual and may involve more than one sensory faculty (including auditory, olfactory, and tactile sensations). Indeed, the immediacy of sensory involvement has been used as a criterion to differentiate different types of browsing systems called "browseries," organized in different ways (Overhage and Harman 1965). For example, the immediacy of sensory contact in browsing through a printed collection is good, compared to browsing microforms containing images of documents.

While scanning for orientation, which serves to identify landmarks, signposts, or other environmental cues, is typically characterized by quick glances observable from head rotation, scanning in exploration within new surroundings, which serves to acquaint the individual with the range of a resource environment and to familiarize her with the potential resources, seems less hasty than scanning as glancing or skimming. When Lancaster (1978) describes the mechanics of browsing in the library, he talks about the individual's movements between resources such that one resource encountered may lead to another. This is a kind of exploratory scanning. Once the probable location of potential resources is found, scanning within a potential resource for assessment tends to be more thorough so that comparisons can be made regarding the quality of the resource and whether to use the resource. O'Connor (1993) explicitly describes a general algorithm for browsing, which consists of four elements: (1) making glimpses, (2) connecting attributes, (3) evaluating connections, and (4) evaluating the search. By "making glimpses," he may well mean scanning. Further, instead of discussing browsing as a search strategy, he construes it as a sampling strategy. In sampling, as O'Connor suggests, overlaps between the individual's internal representations of an anomalous state of knowledge and the attributes of external resources are evaluated. Assessment through sampling characterizes typical browsing activity such as looking through a number of books at the shelf or examining a number of items in order to decide what to borrow or purchase.

The concept of sampling for selecting "worthwhile and useful information" is analogous to the original meaning of browsing, such as in a deer's "grazing" behavior (Cove and Walsh 1988). In the literature, it has been used in describing the notion of browsing in scanning TV programs, reading materials at the shelf, electronic information, or commercial products. Two implications can be derived from this last type of scanning.

Sampling implies *ongoing assessment*. Assessment is a step before the individual decides whether or not to seek the item (in the case of looking at representations) or to utilize the resource (in the case of looking at the item itself). Sampling depends on what is made accessible and how it is organized and displayed for examination. For instance, ongoing assessment is easier when walking through the library stacks than when browsing an online catalog, in which it is hindered by the size and speed of screen; in addition, online browsing is dependent upon the user's knowledge of computer procedures, which in turn puts an extra demand on the user.

Sampling implies *control of exposure.* Sampling implies interaction between the individual and the resource. Randomness in scanning refers to the possibility of making an alternative choice of route for the next move within a relatively short time during the interaction. For example, the difference between a card catalog and shelf displays lies in the depth of detail or the higher possibility of sampling attributes that one might examine in the shelf condition. Thus, the individual's control over exposure to resources during scanning is important. In this sense, watching home shopping programs on TV does not provide as great a potential for browsing because viewers cannot move where they want to go, compared with in-store shopping. Browsing is possible in any information system in which the user has active and relatively rapid control of the items she wishes to examine as well as initiative over and control of the depth of penetration (Overhage and Harman 1965).

**Movement**

The most general form of browsing behavior is scanning a resource in a manner that allows continuous movement, whether random or structured. Continuous movement at will is an overt characteristic of scanning behavior. In such movement, exposure to new information or objects is made possible and thus allows learning/discovery to occur.

One extreme along this dimension is "directed movement," when the person moves toward a specific destination (place or object). The other extreme is "undirected movement," when the person moves without a specific destination. In between is "movement by interruption," when movement toward a specific destination is interrupted by unexpected information stimuli, which might lead the movement to a new destination without returning to the original. Such movement by interruption can be considered as varying by degree of interruption and can be measured by the time spent on the detour activities or the number of interim stops.

Since the scanning process implies control of movement by the person, activities in which people steadily receive information from moving images (e.g., home shopping programs on TV rather than window-shopping behavior) would thus not be considered pure scanning activities.

Although in many cases scanning and movement are observable, in other cases, they are difficult to judge, especially when only eye movement is involved. Thus, behavioral characteristics are necessary but not sufficient for the concept of browsing to be useful. Judged by behavior alone, browsing cannot be practically or meaningfully differentiated from more deliberate efforts such as searching, reading, viewing, or other types of information-seeking behavior or, for that matter, mindlessness. Rather, teleological questions including people's motives, goals, and knowledge must be asked to derive adequate descriptions of various scanning activities. In this sense, browsing should be viewed as a cognitive rather than a (strictly) behavioral concept.

### Motivational Characteristics

Human information-seeking behavior occurs within meaningful contexts as people conduct purposeful activity. In this sense, nonpurposeful scanning activities such as random eye movement without the presence of human motives are not browsing and thus are not included for further discussion. Marchionini's (1995, 103) review of motivations for browsing includes (1) developing an overview of physical or conceptual space, (2) monitoring a process (such as while driving a car, searching bookshelves, or keeping up-to-date in a scientific area), (3) shifting or sharing cognitive load (relying on recognition and physical manipulation instead of initial formal query formulation), (4) clarifying a problem (reducing an anomalous state of knowledge, closing a knowledge gap, inspecting retrieved terms in order to devise a more contextual search), (5) developing a more formal information-seeking strategy (browsing retrieved results to identify the relevant knowledge domains), (6) discovering or learning (either specific knowledge not formally structured, or becoming aware of associated approaches or knowledge), and responding to environmental invitations (such as in museums and shopping malls).

The human motives depicted by McGuire (1974) may explain, in general, why people engage in communication activities (such as looking through a journal) to fulfill high-level functions such as surveillance, seeking entertainment, and learning. Yet, the complexity of human motivation needs to be examined in more detail, taking into account lower levels of goals or immediate purposes. Thus, we may have different layers of human motivation for browsing. At the highest level, two general types of motivation are extrinsic and intrinsic motives; either can be a cognitive orientation or an affective orientation. Further, a continuum of well- to ill-defined goals (with, at one extreme, no goal) can be placed at the lower level of a human motivation hierarchy.

#### Motivation (Purpose)

At the highest level, human motives for browsing can be broadly described according to the extent to which browsers are aware of or expect a desired outcome. Intrinsically motivated behaviors are behaviors for which the controlling, external contingencies have not yet been identified, that is, they lack any apparent reward contingencies or are without expectations about the presence of extrinsic rewards (Deci and Ryan 1985, 186). Curiosity-based behaviors and play are classic examples of intrinsically motivated behavior. The psychology literature has provided vivid evidence that curiosity leads people (especially children) to engage in a wide range of exploratory, manipulatory, and experimental behaviors, whereas play is compelling and satisfying in its own right. Both are characterized by the absence of external incentives or goals and by being active and natural (122). On the other hand, extrinsically motivated behaviors are instrumental in that a desired outcome or reward is expected or has been identified. Information-seeking browsing for problem solving and task-oriented browsing (such as finding a full citation of a publication or buying a gift for a friend's birthday) are typical extrinsically motivated behaviors.

Further, based on the kind of gratifications one may derive from browsing, two types of motivation or purpose can be categorized into cognitive motives and affective motives (McGuire 1974). Information-related browsing behaviors (i.e., browsing for obtaining information) tend to be influenced by cognitive motives. They are more likely to take place in the information seeking and retrieval context, such as in a library where people look for information. They are driven by information seeking or information use. Affective motives tend to lead one to engage in browsing activities that are recreational in nature (i.e., browsing for fun). Although cognitive aspects can also be gratified in such browsing, its focus is not information-driven. Note, however, that both cognitive and affective gratification can be present as a result of a single browsing activity (cf. Bloch, Ridgway, and Sherrel 1989; Joen 1990). It tends to be a matter of degree rather than a dichotomy.

Thus, although the literature reviewed about library user and consumer shopping behavior suggests two distinct types of motivation for browsing—informational and recreational—they are not mutually exclusive. For example, during in-store shopping, one may gain information about a product that one plans to buy in the future while simply looking around in the store for fun. Similarly, one may scan the shelves in a public library to look for some fiction for recreational reading over the weekend and feel that such information-related activity is enjoyable. Indeed, the cognitive gains from seemingly nonpurposive or affect-oriented scanning activities make browsing a fundamental human behavior important to even serious creative endeavors such as scientific innovation.

Being able to make such distinctions allows us to ask: What makes browsing entertaining and what makes information-oriented browsing successful or satisfactory? Answers to questions like these may suggest different system design requirements.

### Goal

The browser may carry out but not necessarily express a goal. A goal is what the person intends to accomplish in the scanning activities. For example, a goal during the person's interaction with a resource can be learning or selecting. Further, depending on the nature of task to be accomplished, such a goal can be well defined, semidefined or ill defined with respect to the content and path of a resource.

**Well- or Ill-Defined Goals** At one extreme along this continuum is the well-defined goal: knowing what one wants, how to find it, and where to get it. If one knows what to find and how to find it but does not know the exact location of the item, scanning may be observed during the location of the item.

When the person's anomalous state of knowledge extends to the question of what paths to follow in order to find that specific item, he may also engage in scanning activity to explore the possible paths that may lead to the item, apart from any information or communication content. On the other hand, in many cases, one may engage in scanning activity on familiar paths because one knows that there are usually some things of interest along these paths, but one does not have a specific search criterion to begin with or does not know exactly what to look for until one sees something along the way. Scanning in a path-specific situation in a search for either specific or nonspecific content, such as scanning a journal's table of contents to locate a specific article or to look for something of interest, is often associated with serendipitous findings, which may or may not relate to the original goal, are perhaps useful only for future needs, but are still of interest or importance to the browser.

At another extreme, one may have only a general goal in mind (e.g., find some information on this topic to write a report, or get a gift for a friend's birthday) without having specific ideas of what to look for, how and where to look for something of interest or use. In this situation, scanning activity may be observed for such non-content-specific search.

Non-content-specific scanning activity includes a distinct type of habitual browsing behavior that takes place within a familiar search path as a function to fulfill one's surveillance need or curiosity (e.g., scanning newspapers without a specific purpose, neither looking for specific contents nor any search paths). To the extent that one may engage in such habitual behavior without being aware of the presence of a goal, browsing of this type may become an ongoing, intrinsically motivated behavior of the browser that appears to be purposeless (e.g., window shopping as one walks home along a street, having a radio or TV on in the background). From a learning perspective, one explanation for such habitual activities is that people have lifelong unanswered questions regarding events taking place in a culture, which drive them to learn from situation to situation; these lifelong concerns, varying across people, refer to what are commonly called personal interests. To the extent that the very experience of a scanning process is emphasized, it includes a type of browsing that is goal-free, and experiencing the scanning process is considered satisfactory in itself (Friedberg 1991).

In most instances, browsing has been characterized by the presence of an ill-defined goal associated with a situation in which one's initial search criteria are only partially known or vaguely defined. Such search criteria can be either content-related in terms of what to look for or path-related in terms of how and where to look. Although uncertainty about the location of an item is not usually associated with browsing, scanning in locating an item does provide a condition in which accidental learning may take place because of exposure to other items in the neighborhood of the targeted item, especially when the targeted item is surrounded by similar items according to some sort of classified organization, or by new items when the searcher's categorization is not matched by the categorization or structure of the resource space.

**Non-Goal-Directed** On the other hand, one distinct type of purposeful scanning activity, which can be characterized as non-goal-directed behavior, is mainly externally induced. Perceptual readings of an environment or a resource in which one is present is an example of such scanning activity. Several researchers have described how cultural institutions such as libraries and museums (Carr 1991), grocery stores, or shopping malls (Friedberg 1991) are purposefully designed to invite browsing of this type. An important question that is closely related to creativity and serendipitous findings is whether and how unplanned, non-goal-directed browsing activity turns into a goal-directed activity.

### Cognitive Characteristics

Information structures are designed to facilitate access to contents. Thus, the object or resource (what a browser wants to find or interact with) can be broadly categorized into two components: contents and structure. Contents refers to any tangible goods such as music recordings or abstract concepts or information such as literature on activity theory or a stock price quote. When one scans contents, one is looking for "know-what," in contrast to when one scans to learn structure for "know-how." Analogically, contents are the destinations to which one goes. Paths of the structure are how one gets there. Note that what a browser wants to find is not to be confused with what a browser actually finds or interacts with. For example, one may want to find a specific publication (content) and fail, instead finding out how to use the system (path/structure), which may be useful in influencing future searches. Scanning activities differ depending on how familiar one is with or how much knowledge one has about the destination (object), where it is and how to get there.

**Browser's Knowledge (Contents vs. Structure)**

Two types of a browser's knowledge about how and what she can accomplish or gain from browsing are relevant. The first type is *expertise* knowledge, which is closely related to the browser's knowledge about the contents of an object or a subject sought. For library and information system users, this is domain knowledge; in the shopping context, product-related knowledge; in TV viewing, knowledge about programs on TV; and in the organization, knowledge about social events and organizational resources (e.g., people in the organization, their expertise).

The second type of knowledge is *pathway* knowledge, which is closely related to the knowledge of system structure or search paths. Research that compares information-seeking behavior of intermediaries and end-users indicates that end-users with high expertise knowledge tend to browse more compared to intermediaries who have more knowledge of search paths or system structures. Bloch and Richins (1983) found that consumer browsing is positively related to the degree of self-perceived knowledge concerning the product class; the more product knowledge a user has, the more frequently browsing takes place with respect to the product. Both types of knowledge can be affected by the browser's experience over time. For example, one may learn both the search paths or structure of a database and its contents because of frequent use. Indeed, one usually needs to know the search paths in order to know the contents. And some systems make search paths and contents explicit to browsers while some don't. As a user's knowledge is accumulated from the experience of using an environment over time, a closely related concept—the user's expectations—will also change over time. Expectations affect the subsequent evaluation of any human endeavor.

Another type of knowledge, not directly related to a resource, is *location* knowledge, or knowledge of where the item or resource sought is located. Consider the following example of looking for an item in the library. In order to see whether a library holds a specific item, one needs to know there is a record, organized by author, subject, or title, which allows one to search by that category. Having the idea that one needs to search library catalogs and knows how to search in them is path knowledge. The question of where the card catalogs or online catalog terminals are physically located requires location knowledge. One's physical movements on the way to the library catalogs allow exposure to other resources, such as new-book displays, to which one may or may not respond. In other cases, one goes directly to the catalog site. Then after getting the information, one needs to know where the item is located in the library stacks and how to get there. It is possible that one remembers the exact location of the item needed in a library or department store; in this case, there will be no scanning activity involved. More often, one knows the path along which the item is placed (e.g., on a specific shelf or on the newspaper racks), in which case locating the item entails scanning the neighborhood along the path. In the process of scanning the neighborhood, the searcher is exposed to other resources (in the case of traditional library stacks, books on a similar subject), which in turn increases the possibility that serendipity may occur. Note, however, that in a full-text computer system, knowledge about the location of an item may be irrelevant because the computer will bring up the full text of the item requested (as well as other items not as relevant). Nevertheless, in a material world, there is always a need to know where things are located.

Because the environment is not static (e.g., reshelving changes the location of an item, new items are added along the old path, new interfaces and menus structures are implemented), the individual's knowledge about a resource is often incomplete, varying in degree. Thus, the individual's knowledge about contents and paths as well as location determines the types of browsing activities he may engage in as well as the extent to which he may browse.

Discussing a schematic view of information-seeking behavior in which a search is categorized according to whether it is active or passive and whether it is directed or undirected, Bates (1986a, 92) considers browsing an active but undirected search in that the person "is committing actions in an effort to acquire information, but the information-seeking behaviors are not directed to any readily specifiable information." She states further that "the searcher cannot say what is being sought because there is no particular thing that is wanted." Information seeking of this type is preparatory in essence. The kind of information needed is, in Bates' words, "the kind we do not know we need" or even know that it exists; however, it is important and "valuable for our survival" (93).

To Bates, the "exploratory paradigm" is suited to browsing as such and not to passive searches—either directed or undirected; passive searches (e.g., "keeping my eyes open for ..." or "open to whatever impinges on my awareness") may be conceived as other types of browsing equivalent to indicative and invitational browsing, respectively. The passive directed information seeking is indicative in that "the person knows what is wanted and is alert for it if it should come along" (92). Such a monitoring function can be an ongoing information-gathering process. The passive undirected information seeking is invitational in that the form of information seeking is "receptive," externally induced information-seeking behavior. In this sense, invitational browsing is an information "gathering" or "acquiring" activity rather than an information-seeking technique. It does not begin with a search activity; a search begins when one has something specifiable to look for.

Bates suggests another kind of information is the kind we know we need. Thus, we purposefully seek for that information in an active directed search such as most online retrieval systems are designed for. However, there is a third kind of information, the kind we know we do not need now but may need in the future.

It is important to note that all these different types of human information-seeking behavior may take place spontaneously. Because the human mind is capable of parallel processing, when we keep our eyes open for something of interest, we are open to whatever impinges on our awareness and are more likely to discover what we want. In other words, while scanning a resource, one can purposively look for a specific thing while being on the lookout for something of interest when it comes along. Although each type of information seeking and each goal accomplished may occur in sequence in time and space, the possibility of fulfilling multiple, near- and long-term goals by scanning may explain why people engage in such browsing activities.

### Planning

The accomplishment of a goal can be planned or unplanned. The role of planning in human information-seeking behavior is addressed by Suchman (1987) and is an important aspect of browsing. Planning, which is often considered a sequential, intentional, rational process, is subject to continuous revision driven by feedback loops and is constrained by individuals' cognitive abilities, social factors, resources, and context, and thus may involve considerable browsing (Allen 1996, ch. 7).

Because people often have multiple goals or long-term as well as short-term goals in an information environment, and because there is an inherent uncertainty in information retrieval, people may accomplish some goals without an advance plan of how to achieve them by taking advantage of the situations they are in. Thus, although browsing can be a planned activity, it is often a situated action (Suchman

1987). In a situated action, one explores things without a plan, interacting with the resource and letting one thing (or idea) suggest another or taking advantage of the resources available in the context within which the activity is situated.

Applying search theory to a search task in which multiple targets were contained in a set of false targets, Janes (1989, 12) concludes that "a semiadaptive search plan (one which uses information gained during the process of searching) outperforms a nonadaptive plan, which does not take advantage of such information." Janes's finding suggests that the information-seeking process is better construed as a situated learning process (Brown, Collins, and Duguid 1989). What characterizes typical scanning behavior is a vague idea of what is to be found and where to find information that is potentially of interest. In this sense, it is probably reasonable to state that no information-seeking tasks can be fully anticipated and preplanned. This situation tends to bring about the notion of serendipity often associated with browsing activities. However, although accidental discovery is an important aspect of browsing, it is only one aspect. An increasing number of researchers in this area stress that such accidental discovery is not blind luck but rather a result of the patron's mindfulness to what the external resource has to offer (Carr 1991; O'Connor 1988).

Based on the preceding discussion, the concept of browsing can be construed as having two main dimensions: (1) motivation (purpose, goal), and (2) cognition (knowledge, plan) in a scanning process, with subdimensions: (a) the purpose can be either active information seeking or passive information gathering; (b) the goal can be directed or undirected; (c) the knowledge can be knowing what is needed or that what is being sought is not known; and (d) the plan can be either explicitly designed or not.

## Resources

Two of the criteria differentiating one type of browsing from another with respect to a resource are (1) form (things themselves vs. their representations), and (2) focus (content vs. structure) of the resource sought or scanned.

### Form: The Thing Itself and Its Representation

A representation is a surrogate for the thing itself. Representation converts the intangible into the tangible. "Indexes, abstracts, physical and mathematical models, classification schemes, statistical summaries, and catalog entries are all examples of representations of objects" (Buckland 1991b, 124). Compared to surrogates like catalogs, things themselves, such as books or documents, have more attributes to potentially show (though some attributes may be made more explicit in the representations) and allow browsers some sensory experiences that browsing their surrogates does not. "The representational structure of an interface refers to the organizations of information and the physical mechanisms required to manipulate the structure" (Marchionini 1995, 44). For example, in a book, representational structures include linear book pages, chapter divisions, tables or figures, footnotes, tables of contents, and indexes. These interface structures both facilitate and constrain search potentials. One initial challenge for browsing is identifying/selecting the "entry point," which may be accomplished randomly through representations that provide information objects for examination or through iterative opportunistic examination (Marchionini 1995, 101).

However, the thing sought can be the information contained in an article whose physical location need not be a printed journal or document but may be a full-text unit in a computer-based information system. Although the thing itself, in most cases, refers to a physical object in the material world that occupies a single physical space and thus a single category in a classified arrangement, it can be conceived of as a particular manifestation of retrieval media available at a particular time in human history. The possibility of separating content from media changes the way people perceive, seek, and use information (Rice 1987).

Although real objects occupy physical space, which makes comparison of multiple items more difficult, they are readily accessible to the browser and thus offer spontaneity for the browser to examine the item's attributes according to his own criteria. Real objects, having more spatial cues (shape, color, texture, physical placement), make browsing easier to follow and aid later memory recall of the information. On the other hand, a physical card catalog can bring together as many items as possible in one physical place for browsing and may allow easier comparison of some attributes between different kinds of items (books) that are physically separate from one another on the actual shelves.

As a special case of the difference between the thing itself and its representations, textual information itself can be the object sought or browsed. The typical surrogates/representations of such textual information are library catalogs. As suggested in chapter 9, browsing library stacks has different effects than browsing library catalogs. In online catalogs it is possible to have different levels of representation, such as a citation, a full MARC record, or an abstract. It is also possible to arrange information in online catalogs in different ways to allow various kinds of browsing to take place (e.g., by classifications, by title, by subject headings), which may not be possible in browsing library stacks because of the physical constraints of the material world.

The differences between browsing physical items and representations may have important implications for the concepts of virtual, digital, and paperless libraries (Lancaster 1978). These differences also raise the question of what happens when what was previously physical is now online, since the role of physical movement and authentic activity (in contrast to cognitive activity) may have substantial effects on cognition and learning (Brown, Collins, and Duguid 1989).

**Focus: Content and Structure/Path**

One may scan contents or paths, depending on one's knowledge about one's purpose and goal as well as on the resource and interface involved. Indeed, it seems that most systems emphasize content-based browsing. In reality, scanning for orientation is path-focused. As information structures are increasingly complex and may vary from system to system, path-based browsing activities may become commonplace, since information seeking and evaluation depend very much on what contents and paths are available and made explicit to users.

The literature shows that television viewers engage in zapping for orientation to see what is available and for evaluation before selecting a particular channel or program. In the case of wayfinding or hypertext browsing, the presence of maps or relational graphics helps users to see relations between the current position and its neighborhood, and to decide what path to take to reach the desired destination.

The efficiency and effectiveness of a search relies on a determination not only of what and where the destination is but also of how to get there. In a large-scale, complex environment, the nature of the process is as important as the result. Yet, in traditional information retrieval systems, little attention has been paid to such issues (Bates 1986a, c). With new technology such as hypermedia, where search paths are made more explicit to system users via maps or graphics, this is technically feasible and desirable. Belkin, Marchetti, and Cool (1993) identify several problems associated with the "browsing task." These problems include (1) not knowing the structures, nodes, and relationships of the resource, (2) not finding appropriate entry points to the resource, (3) not understanding one's location in the resource structure, and (4) not being able to move appropriately within the resource structure. They also propose some suggestions for system support to cope with these problems, including a structured display of the resource with an explanation of link types and a display of interaction history as well as the display and immediate availability of all traversals within the structure.

## Contextual Factors

"When the context of cognition is ignored, it is impossible to see the contribution of the structure in the environment, in artifacts and in other people to the organization of mental processes" (Hutchins, cited in Brown, Collins, and Duguid 1989). One of the two distinct situations in which one attempts to find an intended resource takes place when the individual is driven by the internal goal of finding a resource that is out of perceptual awareness. The other situation is when she is driven by the sight of a resource (Bell 1991). Thus, cultural institutions such as libraries and museums are purposefully designed to invite the attention of visitors (Carr 1991). During scanning, two important factors influence the visibility of a resource: *display or interface design*, and the *structure of organization*. Moreover, the duration of a scanning activity is also influenced by economic resources such as time or money available.

### Interface (Display)

Although interface normally refers to the point where a user and an information/communication system interact, more generally interface refers to the contact point between the user and a resource. The issues of interface are primarily related to the layout or displays of a spatial unit, whether a physical space or an electronic space. Since one characteristic of browsing is being able to gain access to and move about in a space as easily as possible, interface design affects scanning and movement behavior to a great extent.

For example, in an organization, hallways are primary interfaces for social browsing, and their layout influences the frequency and quality of members' social interactions (Kraut et al. 1990). In the library, shelf paths are the interfaces of collection browsing. Collections that are not grouped by related concepts (e.g., government documents arranged by geography) are not as browsable as classified bookshelves (Boll, 1985). In this sense, a good interface should bring related items together and facilitate the browser's association.

As to the computer interface, Tuori (1987) suggests that a system is more browsable if it does not create a great demand on users for specification of intention, knowledge of organizational (file) structure, and the language used to communicate with the system as well as modality of interaction. For instance, there is a major difference between scanning and movement in a computer and that in a library. Apted (1971) and Hancock-Beaulieu (1989) note that browsing in a computer environment is more like "specific browsing" (although this may be true in fewer instances with hypermedia, the Internet, and graphical browsers), whereas browsing in a library requires only a vague specification of topic ("general purposive browsing"), something that is not even necessary for a random walk. In computer browsing, users have to adjust their ideas from "shelf arrangement" to "computer procedures," which are often not transparent.

Furthermore, scanning via the computer interface is not the same as scanning via a physical interface; the former is mainly a cognitive activity, whereas the latter also involves physical movement such as walking or head rotation. For example, comparing various versions of an electronic library catalog system using the browsing metaphor, Borgman et al. (1995) report that adding the feature of "browsing physically adjacent items" seemed to confuse the children who were the subjects in their experiments. One explanation might be that movement in a physical setting also gives people a sense of place, multisensory stimulation, and social/recreational gratification, which may not be obtainable in electronic environments (Salomon and Koppelman 1992). Still, little is known about whether and how such spatial experience in a physical setting is different from that in electronic environments. Research is needed to explore the implications of such physical movement (or browsing in physical places) for understanding human information-seeking behavior in electronic information system environments in all areas that have technological applications, including browsing library stacks, in-store shopping, organizational scanning, and communication as well as wayfinding.

**Organization (Structure)**

Organizational arrangement and physical proximity of what is displayed influences the type and level as well as the ease of browsing.

**Organizational Arrangement** The alphabetical sequence of journal displays makes them easy to scan, but items placed next to each other alphabetically on a periodicals shelf sometimes do not present an apparent logical connection. With a similar linear physical structure, the classified arrangement of library stacks makes associative browsing easier by bringing logically related items together. On the other hand, both types of arrangement are constrained by limited alternative search paths (e.g., by descriptor terms) that can be made available without such physical constraints as in an online database. Thus, one design issue is to determine what types of organizational structure can be best used to facilitate browsing.

Another issue is whether and how the organizational structure is made explicit to the user/browser. In many instances, the problem of entry point arises because the organizational structure is not transparent to the browser. This is a problem especially to those who do not have knowledge of how many layers of information are in the system, what is available, and how to get to where they want to go.

**Physical Proximity** There are two important aspects of the concept of physical proximity, one related to "depth of penetration" and the other related to the "least effort principle." First, the display of items in a physical place often allows immediate access to the items for further inspection and thus increases the possibility for the browser to do sampling. The possibility of sampling at various depths of detail makes an important difference in terms of the consequences of browsing real objects versus browsing representations. In the latter case of representations, one often needs to take an extra step to locate the item's physical place in order to "try it on" or to make a value judgment. This extra step often leads to a different kind of browsing (e.g., to gain orientation to find the location of an item) or leads to disappointment, which may not occur when scanning in a physical context (for instance, when the item identified through a representation is not actually on the expected shelf). Although the user may still find that the needed item is not available, a person surrounded by other items will tend to look around the neighborhood to see what else is available, something that is less likely to happen in the case of online interaction that has not been designed to support browsing. During interaction with formal online retrieval systems, typically either one gets what one wants or not; there are no extra attention-catching messages available on the screen about related contents. However, Web pages on the Internet have radically changed this experience (Erdelez 1996), allowing users to encounter novel information as well as providing too many distracting and peripheral images and links.

Making a trip to a library or a shopping mall costs time and energy. People may take advantage of physical proximity to look around the neighborhood even when their purpose is to accomplish a specific goal. They may engage in a kind of opportunistic browsing to see what is there and may find something that is useful but unexpected before they encounter it.

### Feedback: Form and Extent

Browsing as an interactive, iterative process depends on whether and what kinds of feedback are available. In some instances, feedback is instant and effective. For example, if a person's knowledge can be conceived as a database, one may browse that knowledge store by engaging in a face-to-face communication allowing instant feedback and can easily change to whatever topics either communication partner

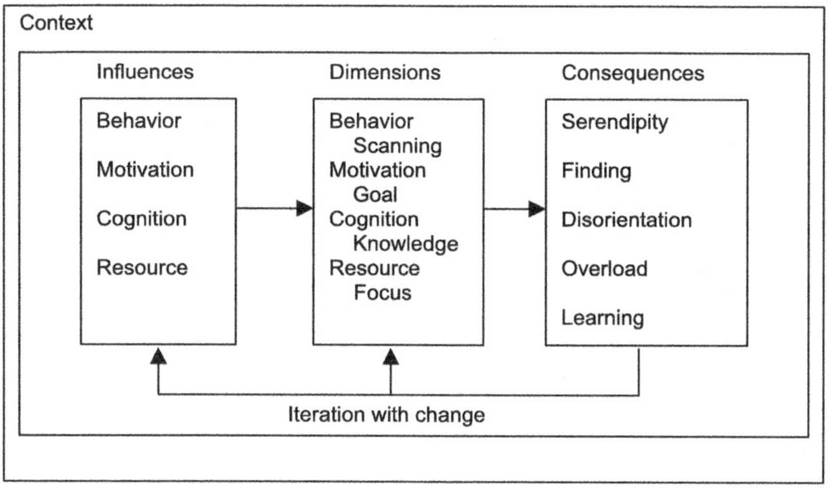


**Figure 10.1**
Preliminary Framework of Browsing

**Table 10.1**
Dimensions and Subdimensions in a General Model of Browsing

| Contextual | Behavioral | Resource | Motivational | Cognitive |
|---|---|---|---|---|
| Structure (organization) | Scanning | Form (item/ representation) | Purpose | Knowledge |
| Interface (display) | Movement | Focus (content/path) | Goal | Plan |
| Feedback | | | | |
| Economic factors | | | | |

wishes, making "choice of alternative routes" much easier. On the other hand, a menu-based system requiring the user to specify each command step by step for repeated searches may make the iterative process more time-consuming, and thus make the system difficult to browse or ineffective for browsing purposes, such as talking with Star Trek's Dr. Spock in his excessively logical moments. Evaluating in general plays a role in browsing, as users must decide on what they receive during the process of perceiving the resource, in terms of relevance, prior knowledge, compatibility with one's biases and expectations and with one's relevant social influences, and assessment of both the form (representation) and the content (Allen 1996).

**Table 10.2**
Tentative Taxonomy of Browsing

| Dimension | Extremes |
| --- | --- |
| Purpose (e.g., recreational or informational) | Intrinsic ↔ Extrinsic |
| Goal (e.g., learning or selecting) | Nondirected ↔ Directed |
| Content (e.g., physical item or information) | Nonspecific ↔ Specific |
| Structure (e.g., physical pathway or meta-information) | Non-path-specific ↔ Path-specific |
| Location (e.g., position on a shelf or a list) | Nonspecific ↔ Specific |

**Table 10.3**
Using a Motivational Dimension—Goal—to Analyze Situations

| Domain | Well-Defined Goal | Semidefined Goal | Ill-defined Goal |
| --- | --- | --- | --- |
| Library | Find a book by an author | Find books on a subject | Find something interesting |
| Shopping | Find an item of a brand of a category (e.g., Tide detergent) | Find an item in a category (e.g., any liquid detergent) | Find something for cleaning (e.g., soap) |
| TV | Choose specific channel and program | Choose a specific channel | Watch whatever catches the eye or ear |
| Organizational communication | Talk to particular person at specific time (formal meeting) | Talk to someone sometime | Talk unexpectedly in a hallway (informal conversation) |

**Table 10.4**
Interaction Between Goal and Resource/Content

| Resource \ Search Path/Structure | Well-Defined Goal | Ill-Defined Goal |
| --- | --- | --- |
| Well-Defined Content | Know how and what to look for | Know what but not how to look for |
| Ill-Defined Content | Know how but not what to look for | Unsure about what and how to look for |

In the literature, two common forms of feedback are (1) relevance feedback, and (2) orientation feedback. Relevance feedback is content-related (such as displaying a list of citations), whereas orientation feedback is structure/path-related (such as displaying the semantic structure of a database). The extent of feedback is related to "the depth of penetration" or level of browsability, ranging from citation only, citation with abstract, MARC format, all the way to full text, with or without pictures or sounds.

### Economic Factors

The term *economic* is used here to refer to time and money or the degree of effort that one needs to put forth in order to accomplish one's goal or purpose. The time available influences the level of browsing in terms of time spent. Timing of feedback also influences the extent to which one may browse. The money involved, such as online charges or money available during shopping, may also be an influential factor. The effort is confined by the limitation of people's energy and attention as well as other factors such as the perceived importance or usefulness of the resource. As mentioned earlier, the least-effort principle suggests that people do not always seek optimal results. Given the fact that browsing often takes place without knowing what will be found, it is conceivable that it will be encouraged when one is not required to invest much effort to do it.

## Models and Examples

For a quick reference of the dimensions discussed in this chapter, figure 10.1 shows a preliminary framework of browsing derived from the literature analysis. It depicts the possible relationships among influences, dimensions, and consequences. Table 10.1 summarizes the subdimensions under each component of the general model. Table 10.2 lists the common dimensions identified under the browsing component, again based on the literature review. Table 10.3 gives an example of using one aspect of the motivational dimension—goal—to analyze various situations in which browsing behavior takes place. Table 10.4 shows the possible interaction between two dimensions to form the prototypes of browsing behavior.

# 11

# A Research Approach: Browsing

The difficulties associated with the empirical investigation of browsing were expressed in the INTREX project in which a series of experiments on browsing was proposed (Overhage and Harman 1965). The authors noted that the absence of normative data on browsing habits in existing libraries made description, measurement, or evaluation of such a seemingly undirected activity problematic. Questionnaires, record keeping, personal diaries, user choices between alternatives, and subjective estimates of probabilities or costs involved in browsing have all been suggested as sources for data collection. Licklider (1965) suggests that researchers look at the user's account of browsing activities and define the conditions or courses of action within the domain of browsing. The one thing consistent throughout the literature is a call for the investigation of people's goals and motives during the processes of information seeking in general (Belkin et al. 1990; Roberts 1982) and browsing in particular (Ayris 1986; Boll 1985; O'Connor 1993). Thus, the design of this study of browsing behavior focuses on the identification of browsing activities and the conditions, including goals and motives, that lead people to engage in those activities. It seeks to answer the following two questions: What is the nature of browsing? and What motivates people to browse?

Given the ambiguity and complexity of the topic, this research lends itself to a triangulation methodology (Eisenhardt 1989). In this research, this entails empirical studies of real persons in real situations using multiple methods. The empirical study is mainly exploratory in nature. The hope is that the results of this empirical study and the subsequent new model will aid in the development of meaningful hypotheses for testing in the future. The aim for this research is to create a useful and robust framework for helping us understand browsing behavior in various situations. The preliminary taxonomy of browsing based on the literature analysis (chapter 10) is revised in chapter 12 to reflect the insights derived from the case studies. The following sections provide the sources of the data and describe the data analysis methods and procedures.

### Data

The data for the empirical part of this study is based on 33 cases selected from the 150 cases collected in a research project initiated by Nicholas Belkin and Tefko Saracevic (1991) at the School of Communication, Information and Library Studies (SCILS), Rutgers University, entitled "Design Principles for Third-Generation Online Public Access Catalogs: Taking Account of Users and Library Use." The project "aims to discover what people attempt to do in libraries ... and why, and how these activities relate to their more general goals and other characteristics and their degree of success in their information activities" (Belkin et al. 1990, 69). For the sake of convenience, this project is referred to here as the OPACs Project. This research was supported by the U.S. Department of Education, College Library Technology Awards No. R197A80263-88 and by an External Research Award from OCLC October 1988–March 1991.

The next sections describe the rationale and the field sites in which the data were collected, and the data collection procedures of the project. More detailed descriptions of the research design, methodology for acquiring the data, and the survey instruments of the OPACs project appear in Belkin et al. (1990).

#### Data Sources

The data used in the current study were collected for the OPACs Project in four library settings during 1989–1990. The project is characterized by a research design that takes into account the goals and general context of library users, and by a triangulation methodology using questionnaires, observations, and interviews to investigate people's generic information behavior in real-life situations. Library settings provide an appropriate context for the current study for the following reasons:

1. Library users are heterogeneous in terms of socioeconomic variables, knowledge and experience, purpose of visit, and other variables of interest.
2. Library environments encourage a variety of information seeking, retrieval, and use behavior by providing a wide range of information resources and facilities (varying within and across libraries).
3. The library encounter and activities are representative of other, similar real-life situations in which people may find themselves (e.g., reading newspapers or journals at home).

The four settings in which data were collected represent three types of libraries: the academic library (two settings), the public library (one setting), and the special library (one setting). The first of the academic libraries, labeled L, serves as an academic support unit for science and medicine. The other academic library functions as an academic support unit for the social sciences and humanities. The targeted users for these facilities include students, faculty, and staff. Both academic libraries are depository libraries and are also open to users outside the academic community. Chang participated in the data collection from the one academic library chosen among the two for inclusion. The public library, labeled W, serves as a public resource located in a county of New Jersey and is open to any resident of its service area. The special library, labeled F, is a research library and an information center for a banking company, providing information services for the company's employees. All four libraries have online public access catalogs available to their users and use standard classification schemes, such as Library of Congress or Dewey Decimal Classification Systems to arrange books on the shelves. Other materials are organized alphabetically (e.g., journals and newspapers) or according to some other criteria (e.g., current journals are separately placed from bound journals that are back issues, or rental books are separately displayed from other types of materials whose use is not charged for). In this study, only a subset of data from each of the three libraries was used.

### Data Collection Procedures

Research subjects were self-selected to the extent that they stated their purpose of their visit and agreed to participate. The interviewer approached a patron who entered the library and explained, first, the purpose of this project (i.e., to study patrons' use of the library) and next asked whether he would be willing to participate. If he agreed, the interviewer then asked, "What is the purpose of your visit today?" Only those who first agreed to participate and then whose purpose involved using library materials were recruited. Thus, people who came to the library to return the books, read materials of their own, and so on, were not included. If the patron did not agree or was not qualified to participate, the next person who walked into the library was then approached and interviewed in the same manner until someone who was qualified and agreed to participate was recruited. The response rates at libraries W, F, L were about 26 percent, 65 percent and 50 percent, respectively.

A financial incentive was given to subjects for their participation. A brief pre-search interview followed by a brief self-reported questionnaire was administered to discover the general background of the individual as soon as she agreed to participate. During the presearch interview, the interviewer asked, "Specifically what is it that brought you to the library today?" to elicit more description about the purpose of her visit and recorded the answer on the presearch interview form. In addition to questions regarding the patron's general background, the brief presearch questionnaire asked the patron to state the types of library material she intended to use.

The patron was then followed around from about 3 meters away and her behaviors and location in the library were noted. If the patron wanted to use the OPACs, she was directed to the designated terminal in which search logs with answers to online pre- and postsearch questions were captured. A postsearch self-reported questionnaire followed by a semistructured interview was administered once the subject completed whatever she had to do during that visit. The postsearch interview follows the following protocols. The interviewer would describe to the patron each activity he observed her doing based on what was recorded in the field log, asked her intention with that activity, how successful she was in realizing that intention, and why she felt that way about it. For example, the interview would use the protocols: "I observed you do [an actual behavior]; what was your intention with that activity?" and "How successful were you with that activity?" The subject then commented on her intentions and evaluated the success of the specific behaviors observed. The interviewer also asked the patron to state the reasons why she gave a particular success rating by prompting with the question: "Why do you feel that way about it?" In cases where OPACs were used, successive screens were played back to the patron, and each screen recording was treated as a separate activity and interviewed in the same manner.

The resultant data include observation logs, audiotapes from interviews, transcripts, structured and open-end questionnaire data, and computer search logs (when users used the online public access catalog in the library).

### Data Collection Instruments

Four kinds of instruments were used to collect data: the activity recordings, OPACs search logs, interview forms, and questionnaires. There were two set of questionnaires. The presearch questionnaire explored the user's purpose for the visit and types of resources intended for use. The postsearch questionnaire inquired about the reasons that brought the users to the library, their overall evaluation of the quantity, value, and importance of the materials found during the visit, and the importance of their success in achieving their purpose. The postsearch questionnaire also included biographical questions about the individuals, such as their level of education, occupation, age, and experience in using libraries, computers, and library catalogs. The original sample sizes from the W, F, L libraries are 38, 24, and 40 cases, respectively. Eleven cases were randomly selected from each of the three libraries, so 33 cases out of the 102 cases from the three libraries were used for this study.

## Analysis Methods and Procedures

### Analysis Methods

This empirical study is guided but not limited by the preliminary theoretical model as proposed in chapter 10. In this empirical research, browsing activities were identified and analyzed within the whole spectrum of library activities in which people engage. That is, in order to understand what constitutes browsing behavior, other kinds of information-seeking activities or nonbrowsing activities were also identified and examined. Specifically, subjects' scanning behavior and motivation, the resource interacted with, and cognitive aspects as suggested in the preliminary theoretical model were looked for in order to verify and clarify those constructs in the preliminary model by establishing the empirical evidence.

As in part I, content analysis was used (Wimmer and Dominick 1991). Enumerative and synthetic classification methods were used to identify categories and develop the coding schemes inductively and, iteratively, based tentatively on the dimensions and categories identified in chapters 9 and 10. A content analysis was conducted to identify and categorize the subjects' library activities, the resources involved, and motivation behind a given activity, as recorded in observation logs and transcripts of interview. The field observation logs were analyzed to uncover the behavioral characteristics of browsing and the resources involved by content analysis of the patron's library activities, as stated in the transcript as well in the sentence: "I observed you do such and such [repeat the data in the observation logs]; what was your intent with that activity?" in order to derive behavior and resource categories. Pre- and postinterviews were analyzed to reveal motivational and cognitive aspects of browsing by content analysis of the data in response to the questions What is the purpose of your visit today? at the entrance interview and What was your intention with that activity? during the postinterview to identify themes across cases and to derive goal categories in relation to a given activity.

### Analysis Procedures

The analysis was conducted in three stages. In the first stage, 10 cases across the libraries were selected for analysis to develop initial coding schemes. In the second stage, the coding schemes were then applied to 23 new cases across the libraries. The coding schemes were modified as more and more of these 23 cases were added for analysis through the iterative process of data analysis. The procedures used for analysis are as follows.

**Identification of Units for Analysis**

*1.* Each case was seen as being composed of a sequence of movements. Movements are distinguishable by the interviewer's question: "First I observed you to go . . .; what was your intent with that activity?" or "Next, I saw you go . . .; what was your intent?" Within a movement, there are episodes. Each episode constitutes the basic unit to be analyzed and is defined as a set of activities conducted toward either an identified intention or, with some identified objects, as perceived by the interviewer. Thus, an episode is first identified by movement between physical or logical places in a library setting. These movements were recorded in the observation logs as "Going to X," where X represents some area in the library such as the New Nonfiction area, Fiction area, Current Journals Room, bookshelf 363s, and so on. A new episode within a movement begins when either the goal or the object under consideration changes and it is distinguishable by a question similar to movement: "I observed you do . . .; what was your intent with that activity?"

*2.* All episodes within a case were numbered sequentially and each number was used as a reference point in later analysis. An example legend used for an episode is W014#1<1>, where W indicates the type of library, 014 is the case number, #1 represents the first movement, and <1> indicates the first intention or object within the movement. The relationships between case, movement, and episode can be described as follows. A case is composed of one or more movements, which are indicated by either a physical place or a logical place. A movement is composed of one or more episodes, which are defined by either a goal or an object.

*3.* For each case, the episodes that were considered browsing in its most general sense, as discussed in chapter 10, were first identified. That is, the episodes that involved "scanning a library resource" were considered potential browsing activities to be further analyzed. Scanning is operationalized as looking or moving through a resource. A resource is something that people use to solve problems, to cope with difficulty, to pass time, or to entertain themselves. In a library context, it may refer to individual items in a collection or library collections as a whole, including books, journals, and reference tools. It may also refer to facilities such as CD-ROM or computerized catalogs, or other search aids such as signs and floor maps. Thus, although many information-seeking behaviors were observed in the library setting, some of these behaviors had no direct connection to the activity of scanning and so were not included for further analysis. Talking with people (a librarian, a friend), using a copy machine, or looking at one's notebook, are examples of activities that were not included.

**Content Analysis**

*4.* The next step was to describe the characteristics of each episode involving scanning a resource with respect to those theoretical dimensions discussed in chapter 10, based on the observation logs and interview data. Take W004 as an example.

In the observation logs of W004#1<1>, the following was recorded:

Go directly to New NonFiction area.
Scan the shelf, select a book, look at the jacket, put back.

This instance was then described as characterized by direct movement to a known location, and involving looking through a series of books on the shelf, selecting an item, and examining jacket of the item. The behavioral characteristics were direct movement, looking, selecting, and examining. The resource involved was books. Location knowledge was implied.

In the transcript, the interviewer asks, "The first thing that I saw you do was go right over to the nonfiction area and browse. Looks like you selected a book from the shelf, looked at jacket in the front of the book, and you kept it at that point. Can you tell me what your intention was then?" The user responds: "Well, I guess as soon as I began looking at the book and after seeing the jacket and the subject, I decided that it might be a book that I would like to read." From the dialogue, the subject's goal was "to find" biographies to read, as also reflected in next two following episodes. The object was "biographies."

5. Commonalities across episodes that corresponded to theoretical dimensions were then identified. In the observation logs, the next two episodes were

Scan, look at cover, return. Scan, look at front pages, keep it.

The same behavioral characteristics were noted. That is, looking at the shelf, selecting a book, and examining part of the book. The resource involved was books.

In the transcript, the interviewer asks, "Okay, you continued to browse there, you selected a book, looked at the cover and put it back on the shelf, selected another, looked at the jacket, and found a book, and you kept it. What was your intention at that point?" (#1<2>) The user responds, "I guess I mostly lean toward biographies, the book I probably put back was not biographical." Interviewer: "And then you picked another book, which you kept." (#1<3>) User: "Yes, that was a biography, too." Interviewer: "So your intention for that book was to find a biography." User: "Yes, which I find is entertaining, is recreational for me." From the dialogue, the goal was "to find." The object was "biographies." The resource involved was books.

In this manner, behavioral and motivational characteristics as well as the resource involved were identified. Similar characteristics were then grouped together to derive the categories for each aspect. For example, with this case, behaviorally, three distinguishable acts are "looking," "selecting," "examining." Motivationally, one type of goal is "to find." One type of object is books in a genre.

6. Unique characteristics of each episode were also noted whenever they occurred. Take W004 as an example again.

In the transcript for the next episode, the following appears. Interviewer: "Okay, the next thing you did is you came up here to the second floor, Current Magazine area, and you began browsing [the shelf], looked at a magazine, looked at the cover, and then put it back on the shelf and continued browsing [the shelf]. At that point, what was your intention?" (#2<1>) User: "Probably to look for a health magazine

**Table 11.1**
Example of Data Analysis Procedures Followed for Case F007

| Data from Observation Logs | Data from Interview Transcript | Steps 1–3: Identification of Units for Analysis | Coding | Step 4: Descriptions from Data Analysis | Step 5: Identification of Related Constructs |
|---|---|---|---|---|---|
| Go over to loose periodicals section | I: "The first thing you did was go to the loose periodicals section, where the periodicals are on the shelves." | The first movement: an instance of physical movement | Movement #1 | Direct movement to a known location | 1. Knowledge (location) |
| Scan shelves and leave | I: "And I saw you kind of scan the shelves in the area. what was your intent with that activity?"<br>U: "Um, to locate the Treasury Bulletin." | The first episode, involving scanning a resource<br>User's goal is identified in statement "to locate . . . " | Episode #1⟨1⟩ | Instance characterized by going to an identified location, looking through a series of journals on the shelf<br>Goal is to locate | 2. Scanning a series of items<br>3. Resource: journals<br>4. Goal: to locate<br>5. Object: a specified journal |
| To reference desk; talk to librarian | I: "Okay, the next activity I observed you doing was going to the reference librarian and speaking with him for a little bit. What was your intent at that activity?"<br>U: "Just to ask him where the Treasury Bulletin was located." | The second movement<br>This activity did not involve scanning a resource<br>No further analysis | Movement #2 | | |
| Both go to loose periodicals section; select a volume; flip through it | I: "And, okay, after you spoke with him, then you both went back to the periodicals section and I saw you select a bound periodical volume and just do a real quick flip through that. What was your intent with that activity?" | The third movement<br>New episode, involving scanning a resource, an instance of changing user's goal | Movement #3<br>Episode #3⟨1⟩ | Instance characterized by looking through pages of a selected journal<br>Goal is to make sure the needed information is | 1. Behavior: selecting and examining<br>2. Resource: a part of a journal<br>3. Goal: to confirm |

**Table 11.1** (continued)

| Data from Observation Logs | Data from Interview Transcript | Steps 1–3: Identification of Units for Analysis | Coding | Step 4: Descriptions from Data Analysis | Step 5: Identification of Related Constructs |
|---|---|---|---|---|---|
| | U: "Um, that I was not looking for, I just looked at it to make sure that it had the tables that I needed." | | | included | 4. Object: specific tables |
| To reference area; scan shelf briefly | I: "Okay, after that, you went back to the reference area and did a quick scan of the reference shelves. What was your intent with that activity?"<br>U: "I thought the Treasury Bulletin might be on the reference shelves." | The fourth movement<br>New episode, involving scanning a resource | Movement #4<br>Episode #4⟨1⟩ | Instance characterized by direct movement to another resource area, looking through a series of items on the shelf | 1. Knowledge: location<br>2. Behavior: looking<br>3. Resource: journals<br>4. Goal: to locate<br>5. Object: a specific journal |
| To journals area; librarian gives journal to patron; flip through journal, to the front, flip through again | I: "Okay, then you went back to the journals area; by that point the librarian had located the journal you were looking for, and I saw you flip through it real quick and then go back to the front and flip through it again. What was your intent with that activity?"<br>U: "I was, I had located the table that I wanted but I was looking at some additional tables to see if they might help and to see how much it was, to see if I could copy it or if I should take the journal back to the office with me." | New episode, involving scanning a new object, an instance of changing object from one journal to another<br>User's goal was identified here | Movement #5<br>Episode #5⟨1⟩ | Instance characterized by looking through parts of a journal, identifying a specific piece of information, and examining some tables in that journal<br>Goal is to locate, then evaluate the information | 1. Behavior: looking, identifying, examining<br>2. Resource: parts of a journal<br>3. Object: a specific table, and useful tables<br>4. Goal: to locate, and to evaluate |

**Table 11.2**
Cases for Initial Analysis

| Library | Case No. | No. of Episodes |
|---|---|---|
| W | 004 | 5 |
| W | 014 | 17 |
| W | 037 | 11 |
| W | 059 | 4 |
| W | 079 | 8 |
| F | 001 | 6 |
| F | 009 | 5 |
| F | 015 | 6 |
| F | 021 | 10 |
| F | 023 | 4 |

**Table 11.3**
Number of Cases from Each of Three Libraries (W, F, and L), and Number of Episodes Analyzed

| W Cases ($n=11$) | Episodes ($n=90$) | F Cases ($n=11$) | Episodes ($n=55$) | L Cases ($n=11$) | Episodes ($n=88$) |
|---|---|---|---|---|---|
| 004 | 5 | 001 | 6 | 001 | 3 |
| 014 | 17 | 004 | 3 | 004 | 11 |
| 019 | 15 | 005 | 1 | 009 | 6 |
| 028 | 3 | 006 | 3 | 023 | 7 |
| 032 | 5 | 007 | 6 | 026 | 13 |
| 037 | 11 | 009 | 5 | 036 | 16 |
| 059 | 4 | 019 | 2 | 040 | 4 |
| 078 | 9 | 021 | 10 | 048 | 11 |
| 079 | 8 | 023 | 4 | 049 | 6 |
| 085 | 7 | 030 | 8 | 062 | 5 |
| 088 | 6 | 031 | 7 | 072 | 6 |

and there weren't any. Looked at the Mother Earth News, that was it, and decided that there weren't very many interesting articles for me in that. So then I continued on down to the Newsweek, and I took two of those."

Similarly, direct movement to a known location is noted. The behavioral characteristics in this instance are scanning a series of journals on the shelf, selecting one item, and examining the cover of the item. The resource involved is a journal. The object is a health journal. Note that although the patron's intention was "to look for a health magazine," he couldn't locate any. Thus, the goal of examination of that selected journal was "to evaluate" the item in order to decide whether it is of interest to read, as expressed in the statement, "... and decided that there weren't very many interesting articles for me in that," and resulted in returning the item to the shelf. This is an instance of identifying a unique characteristic of an episode with respect to motivational or goal aspect. Additionally, the commonality of the resource under consideration across those episodes was noted as "information object." In this manner, instances of specific behaviors were identified and grouped into categories. Those related categories were then grouped into more general categories. These initial categories were modified as more and more episodes from subsequent cases were applied.

7. During the analysis, steps 4–6 were conducted iteratively for all cases. Each time a new episode was described and analyzed, it provided either empirical descriptions of some new dimensions important to understand browsing, or it provided empirical evidence for existing dimensions. Table 11.1 summarizes the steps followed.

Note that *browsing* and *browse* were sometimes used interchangeably by the interviewer to refer to a patron's behavior of moving through a space while looking at the shelf, or when the patron was observed flipping through an information object. As did other descriptions that reflected the interviewer's observation of the patron's behavior, it served only as a means of describing an activity that was later explained and clarified by the patron's statements of his activity and associated intent. That is, although the interviewer's perception about what user intended to do might not correspond exactly to the user's intent, it was not of major concern because the user would point that out in responding to the interviewer's question. Thus, whenever it occurred, it was taken as an instance of "scanning a resource," like other potential browsing activities involving scanning, for further analysis.

### Characteristics of Cases

Table 11.2 shows the first ten cases included for analysis. Altogether, 33 cases, including 233 episodes, were analyzed. Table 11.3 shows these cases according to the settings from which they were selected and the number of episodes used in each case from each setting.

Two different levels of analysis were conducted on these cases. First, the cases were analyzed by episode. The patron's scanning behavior and intention were analyzed to identify empirical evidence in relation to the theoretical constructs proposed in chapter 10. Next, the cases were evaluated by person/case. The patron's purpose for the visit and her subsequent activities in the library were analyzed to identify and interpret emerging patterns of browsing.

Based on the results of steps 4–7, a new model of the browsing process is proposed, described, and elaborated, with empirical evidence, in chapter 12.

# 12

# Results: Testing the Framework of Browsing

This chapter reports the results from the content analysis of the 33 cases. It operationally defines the pertinent theoretical constructs of browsing by providing empirical examples and describing the nature of each dimension. It defines the dimensions of browsing, describes a taxonomy of browsing and discusses the use of the taxonomy.

## Dimensions of Browsing

### Definitions of Theoretical Constructs

The analysis of patrons' behavior identified four basic criteria that can be utilized to describe browsing activities: (1) the level of scanning activity, (2) the specificity of information provided by the resource, (3) the definiteness or specificity of the patron's goal, and (4) the specificity of the object sought.

In the following sections, notation such as Xnnn#y<z> refers to the source of example empirical support for a given concept as shown in the transcript, where X indicates the type of library, nnn is the case number, #y represents the movement, and <z> indicates the episode within the movement.

### Scanning

The term *scanning* in its simplest form refers to "looking through" a series of items. Therefore, the act of looking constitutes the most basic level of scanning. If we examine further, we can see that there are three additional levels: identifying, selecting, and examining. The intensity of attention or personal involvement increases as we move from looking to examining.

**Looking** This activity involves looking through the book stacks, journals shelf, or newspaper racks, or alternatively, it may involve paging through the list of citations in a computerized or card catalog in the library (L009#3<1>).

**Identifying** Identifying refers to recognition of something of interest, either intended beforehand or not (F009#2<1>; F030#1<1> and <2>; F031#3<2>).

**Selecting** Selecting refers to the action of taking down an item (e.g., a book, video, journal, or newspaper) or stopping at a particular item among a series of items under consideration (e.g., an article in a journal or newspaper) (F005#1<1>; F019#2<1>; W004#1<1>; W037#3<1>).

**Examining** Examining refers to the process of looking at various parts or a certain part of an item (e.g., the table of contents, index, or paragraphs of a book, introduction or figures of an article) to accomplish a goal (W004#2<1>; W014#8<1>; F007#5<1>).

The term *sampling* is often used to describe the two activities of selecting and examining to the extent that they often occur simultaneously in the process of scanning.

### Resource

The term *resource* refers to the information object scanned and can be further differentiated according to the nature of the information object. In the process of this research, four categories were identified.

**Meta-information** Meta-information is information about information, such as descriptors in an index and abstract (W019#2<1>), the-back-of-the-book index (L049#2<1>), the section index of a newspaper (F023#1<2>), signs or floor maps in the library functional areas (L036#2<1>), table of contents in a journal or book (F004#3, L062#2<1>), citations in an OPAC or card catalog (L009#4<1>), or citations in an index and abstract (L036#4<1>).

**Physical Information Objects (PIOs)** PIOs include the whole items in which information is contained, such as books (F009#1<1>), journals (W078#1<1>), newspapers (F001#1<1>), videos (W085#1<1>), or folders (F023#2<1>).

**Logical Information Objects (LIOs)** LIOs are similar to PIOs but include independent entities or sections of information found within physical items, such as articles in a journal or newspaper (F023#1<1>), columns in a journal or newspaper (W037#2<1>), or sections in a journal or newspaper (F023#1<2>).

**Information** The actual information provided in any resource, including numbers, such as "sports statistics" (W078#3<1>); facts, such as "the size of a particular enzyme" (L009#4<1>); report or stories, such as effects of an event (F001#1<1>); news, such as market news (W037#1<1>), advertisement, such as "airline ads" (W037#1<4>); graphics, such as pictures (W019#5<1>); or informed opinions or analysis such as journal or newspaper columns (W037#2<1>).

### Goal

This section concerns what the library patrons intend to do during the process of scanning a resource. Based upon the transcripts, the possible goals of scanning activities can be divided into six general categories, of which looking for information is only one.

**Goal 1: To Locate** Locating is, for example, to find a specific information object (W059#1<1>); to find a set of items or pieces of information with certain attributes (L036#4<1>); or to find a prespecified piece of information (F004#3: "trade figures"). This category is characterized by looking for some "thing" or "things" in the library, a process generally referred to as information seeking or searching.

**Goal 2: To Evaluate** Examples of evaluating are to see if the treatment of a book contains the right details (W014#8<4>); to see if the book includes the topics or information of interest (L049#2<1>; W014#8<3>); to see if the item is worth reading further (W014#6<2>); to see if the item is useful or helpful (L004#6<2>); or to see if the item is interesting to read (W004#2<1>; W085#1<1>). Any activity in which the patron is trying to judge the relevance, value, or utility of the item retrieved falls into this category.

**Goal 3: To Keep Up** Keeping up includes to keep up with recent development in other fields (L009#3<1>); to keep up with recent developments on a topic (L001#1<1>); or to bring up-to-date about an event or an intellectual area (W037#1<2>; F006#1<3>). Sampling selectively by reading a portion of a whole item or its parts according to some criteria characterizes this category.

**Goal 4: To Learn** Examples of the learning goal are to get a flavor of the book (W014#8<2>); to read something of interest (W019#5<1>; F030#1<1>); to know or know more about a specified event (F001#1<1> and <2>); or to find out a fact

**Table 12.1**
Attributes as Criteria for Evaluation

| Attribute | Case and Episode |
|---|---|
| Topic | F001#1⟨1⟩ |
| Genre | W004#1⟨2 and 3⟩ |
| Novelty | W037#3⟨1⟩ |
| Diversion | W059#2⟨1⟩ |
| Currency (time value) | W004#1⟨1⟩ |
| Names | F023#1⟨1⟩ |
| Presentation format | F023#2⟨1⟩; F001#1⟨4⟩ |
| Information quality | F001#1⟨4⟩; W059#2 |

(L009#4<1>). This category involves reading, absorbing, or using selectively what is contained in an information object.

**Goal 5: To Satisfy Curiosity** This goal includes "to see why someone would write a book (on that) and whether it was worthwhile reading" (W079#5<1>). This kind of goal involves momentarily pursuing an object incidental to one's original goal because the appearance of the object arouses one's curiosity.

**Goal 6: To Be Entertained** Examples are "to see what catches my eye" (W037#3<1>; W037#6<1>); to read something interesting or diversionary (L026#9<2>); or to browse to kill time (W079#2<1>). In this category, the subject is looking for enjoyment, or seeking novelty or a temporary diversion from routine.

Table 12.1 provides examples of evaluation attributes from specific cases, and table 12.2 provides several excerpts from cases and episodes indicating evaluation as a goal.

### Object

The object criterion refers to the type of object the patron is trying to obtain. This is distinguished from the resource criterion because a person may scan various types of resources in order to obtain an object.

**Specific Item** This includes meta-information (W019#2<1>: a heading "school trend fashion"); information objects (W059#1<1>: "a best seller"); or information (F023#1<1>: "analysis of commodities prices").

**Table 12.2**
Examples of Goal of Evaluating

---

To evaluate: Value Judgment

[F007#5:76–77]
"Looking at some additional tables to see if they might help and to see how much it was . . ."

[L004#5:54–55]
"I was just looking for the contents of the book to see if it would help me any, and it didn't help me any."

[L023#3⟨2⟩:124–126; ⟨3⟩:151–152, 156–157]
"I just read that briefly. Just like some of the figure and . . . some of the material and method. And then I decided this is an important work."
"I just read just briefly and see they have figure and some of the methods, like this. I thought this is the one I want."

[W014#8⟨5⟩:147–148, ⟨6⟩:157–158, 161]
"The book had certain history and information and diagrams that I felt I could use in the future for other work that I was doing."
[After he selected a book, looked at it, put it back, stated:] "I don't think it lasted long the interest."

[W014#8⟨3⟩:129–130]
"I paged through it and read to see if any information was in the book and that the writing on that type of thing was of interest. It wasn't as interesting as I thought."

---

**Items with Common Characteristics** These include a topic (L062#1<1>: "helicopter rotor"; L001#1: "nursing administration"); a genre (W004#2<1>: "biographies," "fiction"); an event (F023#1<1>: "bankruptcy filings"); a method (for "selecting a column"); a name (species, companies, securities); a time value (historical or recent); a diversionary value (W059#2<1>: "diversion readings"); novelty (new to patron); or other attributes (W019#7<2>: "school fashions"; W059#2<1>: "good").

**Items in a Specific Location** Examples of defined locations are a column or section in a newspaper (Science Section of *New York Times*) and a predefined location in a library (New Nonfiction area).

**General Knowledge** This includes the contents of a newspaper, journal issue, or book (W088#1; W088#2: "news").

**No Object or No Expected Outcome** An example is, "I wasn't setting out for anything" (W079#2).

## Taxonomy of Browsing

### Scanning

It is noteworthy that scanning as a nonverbal behavior (no need to express the intent or no statement in words) is considered a browsing activity, especially when it involves the more attentive acts of identifying, selecting, and examining. Scanning becomes even more like browsing when the whole process is performed iteratively. Thus, going directly to a resource area and scanning the bookshelf without retrieving any item may or may not be a browsing activity. If the person scans the shelf looking for a specific book, does not find it, and then leaves, this would not be considered an instance of browsing because what was looked for was prespecified and the patron's intent was to locate the specific item (finding it or not doesn't affect these criteria).

However, the same behavior could be conducted to identify what items are available in the library, or it could be simply a result of not finding anything of interest, both of which are considered browsing in the sense that no predetermined item was looked for; rather, a series of unknown items were scanned to identify something of interest. Similarly, the patron may scan the shelf and identify what is available in a library without retrieving any item for further examination. Thus, it is often difficult to tell, simply by observing, whether the person's behavior in such a situation constitutes browsing. When a patron scans the shelf and then selects an item and glances through the item, once or repeatedly, it seems as if she is conducting a browsing activity. If she moves from one resource area to another and conducts the same activity of scanning, selecting, and examining repeatedly, there is a strong tendency to identify this as a typical browsing activity. Thus, behaviorally, browsing is increasingly easier to recognize as the level of scanning involvement increases, that is, when a patron's behavior involves selecting and examining an item after looking through a series of items (see table 12.3). Furthermore, since all the other elements of scanning cannot be easily identified and tend to appear as looking activities (e.g., examining reading materials in a journal or newspaper), *scanning* is used hereafter to refer to the behavioral dimension of browsing to the extent that scanning is involved in conjunction with basic requirements of the other three dimensions, resource, goal, and object.

**Table 12.3**
Dimensions and Elements in the Taxonomy of Browsing

| Scanning | Resource | Goal[a] | Object[b] |
|---|---|---|---|
| Looking for | Meta-information | Locate | Specific item |
| Identifying | Object (whole) | Evaluate | Common items |
| Selecting | Object (part) | Keep up | Defined location |
| Examining | Information | Learn | General |
| | | Satisfy curiosity | None |
| | | Be entertained | |

Note: With greater levels of browsing (on a continuum from the first item in each column downwards to the last item), the specificity/intensity of action/attention (scanning) increases; the specificity of information (resource) increases; and the specificity of goal and of search criteria (object) decreases.
a. The relative frequencies of episodes for goals were locate, 44 percent; confirm, 5 percent; evaluate, 20 percent; keep up, 4 percent; learn, 15 percent; satisfy curiosity, 10 percent; and be entertained, 2 percent.
b. The relative frequencies of episodes for objects were specific item, 31 percent; common items, 45 percent; defined location, 1 percent; general, 21 percent; and none, 2 percent.

### Resource

The resource scanned refers to a series of information items under consideration. Four levels of a resource are identified according to the specificity of information provided for examination (see table 12.3). At one end, only meta-information (representations) of a resource is considered. Looking through a series of citations in a library catalog (e.g., to find items on a topic) is an example. Another level of resource under consideration is an information object as a whole, such as fiction, a video, or a book by an author. Scanning bookshelves in a fiction area (e.g., to find some items to read) is an example. Alternatively, a resource under consideration may be a series of logical information objects, such as articles in a journal or newspaper. Looking through a series of articles in a journal (e.g., "to get some idea of what is going on in a research area") is an example. At the other end, information itself is the resource under consideration. Information embedded in paragraph, a diagram, or a certain page (e.g., pages with pictures) is examined by scanning the texts of an information item. Scanning various parts of an article (e.g., to see if a specific method is included) is an example.

Depending on the form of a resource, it may be characterized by providing one or more levels of information specificity for consideration. The type of resource providing only meta-information is a representation of actual information objects. It does not allow various levels of examination as an information object itself does. For example, a patron who intended to find materials on a research topic expressed high uncertainty about the utility of items selected for examination in an OPAC (L062). In prototypical browsing as suggested in the library literature, the resource scanned refers to a series of information objects whose information allows various levels of examination, once selected. Nevertheless, browsing, in the sense of scanning a series of unknown items to identify something of interest, does take place in a meta-information resource. Further, with the advance of computer technology, scanning items in a meta-information resource such as a hypermedia online catalog also allows the patron to examine various levels of an item. Thus, browsing may involve any element in the resource dimension, but as we move along the resource continuum (see table 12.3), if the patron is allowed to examine deeper into the resource, her uncertainty about the appropriateness of the resource decreases as the amount of specifically related information increases.

### Goal

The goal dimension involves differing degrees of open-endedness to the criteria for valid information acquisition. *Specificity* and *vagueness* are often used in the literature in regard to this characteristic of browsing. One end of a continuum reflects the definite nature of a goal when the object intended is predetermined and well specified (see table 12.3). As one moves along the continuum, the specificity of the patron's goal decreases as what the patron intends to accomplish is increasingly determined by the information he encounters during the process of scanning. Thus, "satisfying curiosity" reflects a goal that is primarily indefinite to the extent that it is determined by external information objects. Prototypical browsing appears to occur when the patron's goal is to evaluate whether or not an item is of interest, is worth looking into, is useful, or has the right level of information on a topic. Evaluation means examining the unknown or unfamiliar object against some criteria, comparing the external information stimuli and internal criteria to derive a value judgment. Thus, an evaluative goal during the scanning process appears to be characteristic of prototypical browsing activities.

### Object

The object dimension refers to what the patron scanning a resource is seeking or expecting. At one extreme (see table 12.3), the patron's object, such as a book or journal, is specifically identified. That is to say, the specified item is the one and only one item sought, which can be a specified logical item such as an article seen before, or a piece of information such as "the size of a protein enzyme." At the other extreme, not only is the object to be sought not defined beforehand but also no specific location or content is determined at the outset. In between these two extremes, the patron knows that the type of object sought is at a specific location, but no item at that location is specified. Rather, scanning to see what is in the location is intended. A typical browsing activity often involves objects with common characteristics. That is, although patrons may or may not bring with them a specific idea of what will be of interest, no specific documents are sought. Rather, some attributes of a resource are examined upon encounter. Thus, as one proceeds along the object continuum, specificity of the object decreases. As we saw with the goal dimension, the object specificity involves differing degrees of open-endedness to the criteria for valid information acquisition. That is, specificity about what to look for decreases as one travels along the object continuum.

Thus, a four-dimensional taxonomy of browsing can be developed according to the level of scanning, the kind of resource scanned, the type of goal, and the type of object.

### Using the Browsing Taxonomy

Such a taxonomy derived from reviewing the literature allows us to categorize general examples from the literature as well as specific examples from our data.

Browsing considered as "a form of subject access to bibliographic information" (Hildreth 1982b) or looking into citations under a heading of interest or descriptor of an index and abstract to identify items on a topic (L036#4) are instances of *scanning meta-information to locate items that have common characteristics.*

Shelf-browsing in the public library to select a nonfiction book to read (Ayris 1986) or scanning the bookshelf to find new biographies to read (W004#1) are instances of *scanning information objects to locate items that have common characteristics.*

Browsing described as "sampling texts . . . to make one of two judgments: accept/reject document" (O'Connor 1988) or retrieving a book and flipping through the contents to see if the item is of interest or worth reading (W004#2) are instances of *scanning information objects to evaluate what is there in general.*

Browsing described as "glancing through a book in a casual way, reading passages here and there" (Bankapur 1988) or flipping through a book to see what it is like or to get the flavor of the book (W014#8<3>) are instances of *scanning an information object to learn something in general, something not specifically defined.*

Browsing described as "identifying relevant sources" (Ellis 1989) or selecting a journal and turning to a certain page and looking over the contents to see if the article is what is needed (L023#2) are instances of *scanning parts of an information object to evaluate whether the specific item is what is needed.*

Browsing to keep up-to-date in an area of interest (Bawden 1986) or looking through different issues of a journal to identify and examine articles on recent developments in a field or on a specific topic (L001#1) are instances of *scanning parts of an information object to keep updated on items that have common characteristics.*

Looking through a specific column or section in a newspaper and to keep up-to-date (e.g., the Science Section in the *New York Times*; the obituary column in the *Westfieldian*) (W037#2) is an instance of *scanning information at a given location to keep up with what is there.*

"General browsing" or passing time browsing (Apted 1971) or flipping through sections of a newspaper to see what is going on in the world (W037#1<2>) are instances of *scanning information to learn things in general.*

Browsing described as "an unprogrammed, recreational sampling of reading matter, done for pleasure and wonder" (Overhage and Harman 1965) or scanning bookshelves or a newspaper and examining what catches one's eye (W037#1<5>) are instances of *scanning information as a goal-free activity to entertain oneself.*

**Discussion**

When a patron is looking through a list of citations in an OPAC or card catalog to find the call number of a needed book in order to check it out, we tend to view such "scanning meta-information to locate a specific item" as a nonbrowsing activity. In this situation, what the patron needs is known and well specified. In addition, the value or appropriateness of the item sought does not raise a question in the patron's mind during the process (F004).

If the person is looking for a specific piece of information in a book, he may look through the item retrieved to see whether the needed information is these or not. In this situation, if he knows exactly what he wants and has strong confidence that the item examined is appropriate for use, examination of the retrieved item is only a matter of reassurance. Thus, we see him "scanning a physical information object in order to confirm a specific item." We would still say that he is not browsing. The same can be said if the person flips through the journal retrieved to see if the desired article is there. This is an instance of "scanning logical information objects to confirm a specific item" (F005).

When the patron examines a book not only to see whether certain information is provided in it but also whether the information is useful, he is "scanning an information object to evaluate something specific." In this situation, finding the specific book is not the end itself. Finding a specific information item serves only as a way of achieving a purpose. Case L040 illustrates such a situation. The subject, who was working on a computer project, located the book suggested by his professor on the shelf and then looked over the subroutine of a program in the book and decided that the information in it was not exactly what he was looking for. He then started "looking around the shelves to see if there were any other books on that subject in that area," selected other items not considered beforehand, and examined the contents of each item "to see if there is additional information" in relation to his computer project. In the latter situation, he was "examining information objects to evaluate items sharing common characteristics." The subject was not pursuing a specific item; rather, he was trying to find useful information to accomplish his task. Yet he had no specific items to look for except the one suggested by his professor. The content and value of the items selected for further examination were not known beforehand. We view this as an instance of browsing. The evaluation process is characterized by contrast and comparison. That is, in order to make a judgment about whether an item is useful, the subject compared what he considered a "useful program subroutine" with the information or characteristics presented in an item and contrasted it with other information objects examined.

A similar evaluation process can take place in relation to a location known to the patron. When the patron knows from previous experience that a specific location usually contains items of interest, she may go directly to that location and scan items in that location in order to find or learn something of interest. Such a location can be a bounded area of the bookshelf, such as a profession's aisle of the library's book stacks as indicated by call number (L049#3), a specific section in a newspaper as indicated by section heading (W037#1<1>), or specific columns in a newspaper as indicated by names of the columns (F001#1<4>). Patrons scan bookshelves, physical information objects, logical information objects, or information first to see what is presented in that location. The patron in these instances is more open to be influenced by the items encountered and is ready to select what appears to be of interest for further examination. Therefore, first we see the patron "scanning meta-information to learn about what is generally available" at the shelf. Then we see her "scanning information objects to evaluate items of interest" when she examines an item retrieved, or we see her "scanning logical information objects to learn something of interest" when she flips through a periodical and reads something interesting or useful. People engaged in browsing activities in a specific location known beforehand can be there simply to find out what is offered in the location rather than to look for something defined beforehand. That is, items are scanned because they are grouped together in that location. The characteristics and value of selected items are not known beforehand. Thus, the nature of browsing is evaluative. To evaluate, items are selectively examined to judge their utility. The object sought, if any, is likely to be induced by, as well as depend on, what is made available.

In some instances, patrons look for items that share at least one common characteristic—something "new." Items in a specific location may be featured by this characteristic of newness, for instance, New Book display or Current Periodicals Room. Such displays for new materials may be further divided into New Fiction area vs. New Nonfiction area or Current General Periodicals vs. Current Professional Periodicals. As the world is constantly changing, we see the patron "scanning information to keep up with general knowledge" about the world. Browsing through a newspaper is an example. Similarly, each specialized discipline or area of interest changes over time; hence, we also see patrons "scanning logical information items to keep up with something sharing common characteristics." Reading journal articles in a field of interest or on certain topics is another example. In essence, keeping up is a learning process. However, it differs from learning in that the patron has something in mind. The thing in mind can be a given set of periodicals devoted to reporting new developments in a field or research in progress, or it may be as broad as a specific location known to the patron that constantly provides new things in a wide range of interesting topics. Thus, browsing to keep up with something is often associated with some specific journals or newspaper and is likely to be a habitual behavior conducted periodically to serve as a way of ongoing information acquisition. Furthermore, a patron scanning periodicals to keep up with new developments of her professional field is likely to be made aware of information with future utility, for instance, material relevant to courses she may plan to take in the future, or other future projects (L001#2).

Similar activities can be conducted not to keep up with something but rather to read something of interest. The patron may select a few journals of interest after scanning the shelf and then flip through the pages to find something interesting to read. We first see the patron "scanning meta-information to locate items that share common characteristics" and then see him "examining information to learn about the contents in general." In this situation, the patron does not intend to read all the information provided in each information object. Rather, as one patron stated

(W037#3), "I picked up a few articles here and there"; this is characteristic of such activity.

On the other hand, if after scanning a series of items, the patron selects an information object and examines its contents because he is curious to see what it looks like, and does that in sequence with several items, we tend to view such "examining information objects to satisfy curiosity" as a typical browsing activity. Curiosity is the best teacher—it allows people to discover and learn things new to them.

The same activity may be conducted to judge whether the item examined would be useful for a research project or would be of any interest for recreational reading. Thus, we see a typical browsing behavior of "examining information to evaluate some things that share common characteristics." In this situation, the patron does not intend to read all the information provided during the process. Unlike "reading here and there" in a journal to learn something of interest, this browsing activity is to assess the value of the item in order to decide whether it is worth reading or learning.

Based on the preceding discussion, a typical nonbrowsing task such as case F005 (looking through the table of contents to find a needed article in a specific journal) can be described as scanning meta-information to locate a specific item, whereas a typical browsing activity such as case W004 (sampling books in the nonfiction area to find biographical items of interest to read) can be characterized by scanning information objects to evaluate the contents of items that have common characteristics.

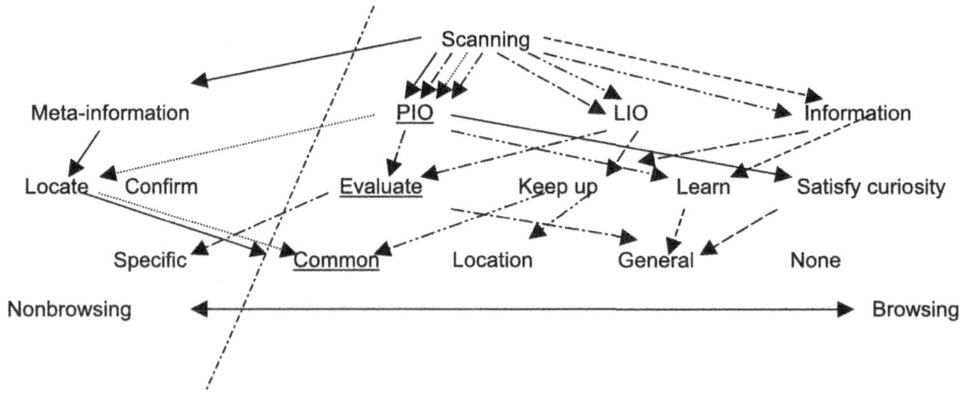


**Figure 12.1**
Graphic Representation of Examples in the Taxonomy of Browsing
*Note:* PIO = physical information object; LIO = logical information object. *Underlined* activities = general boundary between nonbrowsing and browsing.

As suggested in the literature, one of the central characteristics of browsing has been the vagueness of the person's goal or search criteria. Our analysis in the previous sections suggests that the difference between browsing and nonbrowsing lies mainly in the specificity of goal and object, because browsing, in the sense of scanning a series of unknown items, can involve any level of the resource dimension. However, this analysis suggests that the vagueness of goal can be usefully viewed as a non-information-locating or non-information-seeking goal in the process of scanning. That is, although a patron may intend to find or locate some information resource, the goal of his interaction with an unknown item identified during the process is often one of evaluating. Further, the vagueness of object sought can be explicitly described in terms of whether one is pursuing the only prespecified and well-defined item, which can be a (physical or logical) information object, or a prespecified piece of information. Thus, by making explicit the nature of various goals that people bring with them when they interact with library resources and the nature of object specificity, the specific elements identified within these four dimensions can be used to describe various types of browsing as well as nonbrowsing activities. Figure 12.1 portrays examples of types of browsing. The underlined components represent the region of the basic requirement on the continuum of browsing. However, it cannot be a specific countable value. That is, as one moves in figure 12.1 toward the right along any of the dimensions in the model, there is a tendency to consider any conceptual regions lying beyond these cut-off points (looking, information object, evaluate, common) as browsing. Conceivably, some combination involving the elements on the left side of the continuum (e.g., scanning meta-information to evaluate items sharing common characteristics) might also be considered browsing.

# 13

# Results: Motivating Themes and Patterns of Browsing

This chapter seeks to answer the questions How does browsing occur? and What motivates people to browse? by discussing the salient characteristics of patterns within each of five general themes underlying the patterns of browsing identified in chapter 12: (1) looking for a specific item, (2) looking for something with common characteristics, (3) keeping up-to-date, (4) learning or finding out, and (5) goal-free browsing. The sequences of the patrons' activities were examined to identify and describe the context in which the types of browsing described in chapter 12 took place. The patterns of browsing are characterized by the browsing process that the patron engages in, along with the four influence criteria (movement, resource, purpose, and knowledge).

## Looking for a Specific Item

### Nonbrowsing

This pattern is characterized by scanning to locate the only and unique position of a specific citation in a list, an information object on the shelves, or a piece of information within an information object, in order to achieve the purpose of the visit, such as checking out an item or looking up a fact.

Nonbrowsing is represented by case F004, in which knowledge of the existence of an intended item (in this case, a book used before) is present and its specific location in the library is looked for. The card catalog is used to identify the call number of the book sought (F004#1). The book was selected after it was located on the shelf (F004 #2). Finally, the specific piece of information needed (some trade figures in an appendix) was located in the book after the patron looked through the table of contents (F004#3<1>) and the appendix (F004#3<2>). The processes involved can be described: (1) scan meta-information (citations in the card catalog) to locate a specific item (in the card catalog), (2) scan meta-information (call numbers) to locate a specific physical information object (PIO) at shelf, (3) scan table of contents in PIO to locate a specific logical information object (LIO) at a table, and (4) look through parts of the LIO retrieved to locate specific information needed.

This pattern is typically not considered browsing because what is looked for, either an information object or information itself, is fully specified and predefined. The patron's intent to go after a specific item is evident in the statement "I was looking for a specific book" or "I couldn't find my book" or "to find exactly what I was looking for."

In the following excerpts and hereafter, I stands for the interviewer and U stands for user. Note that in some episodes the result of scanning the shelf may turn out to be "no item retrieved," as shown in L009#4 and L009#5, but the overall pattern remains the same.

*I:* I saw you go downstairs, that's the second floor, and you checked with the card catalog; what did you intend to accomplish at that stage and how successful were you? (#4)

*U:* Well, I was looking for a particular protein enzyme and I wanted to find out about the size of the protein, that's what I want to find out. How big that protein is. And there is a handbook called *Enzyme Handbook* that I was looking for.

*I:* Before you came here you knew the book?

*U:* Yeah. So I was looking for that book. I got the number and went down to look for it.

*I:* Okay, so after you went downstairs, scanning the shelves, did you find what you wanted? (#5)

*U:* No. I could not find my book.

Rather than to locate a specific piece of data within an information object, one variation in scanning the item retrieved is to confirm the correctness of the item (F005#1; F009#1<2>) by applying some objective criterion such as page number or title of an article needed. Scanning for confirmation is usually not considered a browsing activity, because the person appears to have a strong knowledge about the utility of the item or have experience with the item under consideration beforehand.

Consider example F005#1:

*I:* So after I met you coming in at the door, I observed you go to the bound periodicals section. You kind of scanned the shelves and then you selected a journal, took it over to the table and flipped through it a little bit. What was your intent with that activity?

*U:* To make sure I picked up the right journal and make sure the article I was looking for was in that particular one.

*I:* Okay, with that activity did you feel you were successful or unsuccessful?

*U:* Successful.

*I:* Successful, and why did you feel that way?

*U:* Because I found the article.

In other instances, scanning the item retrieved is to confirm whether the item has been read before (W037#2) or whether it has the piece of information needed (F007#3). From W037#2:

*I:* Then I saw you return the *Star Ledger* to the newspaper rack, do a little more [scanning] and select what looked like ...

*U:* *The Westfieldian.*

*I:* The local paper.

*U:* Yeah, I looked through there, I didn't, wasn't quite sure if I did see it the last time I was in here, but I believe I did see that issue. So I didn't spent too much time on that.

From F007#3:

*I:* Okay, after you spoke with [the librarian], then you both went back to the periodicals section and I saw you select a bound periodical volume and just do a real quick flip through that. What was your intent with that activity?

*U:* Okay, it was an old Treasury Bulletin that I was not looking for, I just looked at it to make sure that it had the tables that I needed.

*I:* Okay, um, and with that particular activity, did you feel successful or unsuccessful?

*U:* Successful.

*I:* Okay, and why did you feel that way?

*U:* Um, I was able to locate the table.

As with locating a specific item, scanning to confirm something can also occur at various levels of information resource: (1) scanning meta-information at a bookshelf to confirm nothing interesting or useful is missed (W079#4); (2) scanning an information object such as a journal to confirm that it has the article needed (W037#2; F005#1); or (3) scanning a part of an information object such as a journal article to confirm that it has the data that is needed (F007#3).

Thus, a nonbrowsing activity takes place when a patron intended to locate a specific item. Such item can be in any level of document/resource specificity, a piece of meta-information, an information object, or information (F004#1,#2, #3). It often involves making use of a secondary tool to find out the item's location in the library. The patron identifies and selects the item after scanning the bookshelf to locate the exact position of the intended item. If the item is located, it may then be scanned to confirm that it is indeed the item intended; otherwise the patron would leave the resource area without retrieving any item. This is a characteristic of a typical information-seeking task.

**Situational Browsing**

This pattern is characterized by examining other unknown items during the process of locating a specific item, once the general area containing the needed item is identified.

Case L049#3 is a good example. The patron, looking for geotechnical information for his projects, searched in the OPAC by author and found the specific author's work listed. He then went to the book stacks in order to retrieve it. While he was approaching the specific area of the book stacks identified in the OPAC, he was exposed to another related section of interest in the neighborhood and decided to find some books on a topic of interest—"ground water" (L049#2). He did so by examining several parts of two items selected off that shelf, "trying to look for some particular topics" he was interested in. He then proceeded to the specific section of the bookshelf where the previously identified item was located. During the latter process, he scanned the items nearby and selected a few items in sequence for examination in turn (L049#3).

The browsing type can be described as examining information objects to evaluate items with common characteristics, although L049#3 also involved scanning meta-information to locate a specific item when the patron tried to find the item identified in the computer.

The major characteristic of situational browsing is scanning near a known item or a known class. The activity may occur before a prespecified item is found (e.g., L049#2). In other instances, looking for a specific item and scanning for items potentially appropriate but not considered beforehand takes place at the same time in one single episode, as in L049#3. After going to a TD section (a general call number for a class of books) of the bookshelf to look for a specific book identified in the computerized catalog a moment earlier, the person was also observed to pull out several books and scan them.

*I:* When you were at the TD section you said you were looking for something that [was] from the catalog. But I also saw you pulling out several books.

*U:* Oh, sure.

*I:* Okay, what did you intend at that time?

*U:* Because that is my favorite aisle, it is related with my profession, so you see there is foundations, there is soil dynamics, there are a lot of subjects that are real interesting, the geology of technical engineering. But I was looking at some titles and then I decided to take the one that I found there. I found it no problem and I found by chance another one that I wanted to read.

The patron later commented: "[I was] looking for a specific book and browsing at the same time" (L049 #3).

However, scanning near a known item or class does not necessarily have to relate to books on the shelf. Looking through parts of an information object, such as a journal in which articles with a certain similarity are grouped by the scope and intended audience of that journal, can result in discovering additional information or useful items that were not intended to be found beforehand. Case L048 #4<8> is a good example. The patron, who tried to find some papers from the reference list that he brought with him, stated: "Well, first of all I just pick all of the papers that I want and I find out there is a very good paper . . . I just want to go through that." With the third volume of the same journal he went through, he explained: "First, I want to find some other paper [which] maybe has a relationship with my topic. Second, I want to find, maybe there is something general about my research. So doing the same thing, doing two things at the same time."

Another example follows (F021#1):

*I:* When I met you in the back of the library, you went directly to the loose periodicals area, went to where the *Fortune* magazines were, and you selected an issue, flipped through the pages and returned the issue; that happened about eight times. And during this flipping and selecting, it was the same activity, flipping through, you also had set aside two issues. What was the intent with that activity?
*U:* Um, well when I came here I knew exactly what I was looking for: an article on a company that had possible data to file on our reports that we do. The balance of payments. So I had remembered reading the article but I didn't remember what issue it was. So I was looking through the different issues, but I couldn't find it, but in the process I found other things.

Unlike the previous example, L049, where the patron was encouraged to scan the rest of the shelf, in this case the general location of what was looked for was known, but the patron had no knowledge of the exact location of the item in terms of issue number or publication date of the specific item and made no use of any aids such as a bibliographic tool. Thus, the patron was forced to "scan through" each issue of that magazine to locate what he wanted to find. The browsing activity involved is scanning an LIO to locate specific information. This example illustrates that scanning a series of logical items (articles) to locate a specific item in an information object (journals) involves evaluating items not known beforehand and thus may lead to discovering unexpected useful information.

On the other hand, situational browsing may also take place when the attempt to find a specific item fails and the patron then scans the shelf to see if there is anything else available for substitution. For example, in the public library, the patron in case W059#1 was observed going directly to the rental book area and scanning the shelf. The patron then selected a book, looked at the jacket, and decided to keep that book. When asked what was the intent of that activity, the patron stated,

*U:* I was looking for a specific book on the best seller list which they didn't have. I picked another which is very ... [inaudible] and I will attempt it.

*I:* Okay, at that point did you feel you were successful or unsuccessful?

*U:* Successful enough because I can always get what I was looking for another time.

*I:* And why did you feel that way?

*U:* Because I'm in a real hurry and the book I picked will probably suit my needs.

In episode L004#6, the person was observed moving from stack 27 to stack 30, scanning the book spines along the shelves. He explained, "Yeah, because I didn't find the book I was looking for, so I was just looking for other books, because it was the same material."

Scanning near a known item or class is a type of browsing called expansion by O'Connor (1993), which is characterized by "scanning a resource to look for potentially interesting or useful items not considered beforehand."

During this scanning and identification process, a second level of scanning (examining the item retrieved) is to evaluate some attributes of the item such as the subject (L049#3), informativeness (F006#2), value (F006#1<2>), usefulness (L004#5), or level of treatment (L004#6), in order to decide whether the item is appropriate to serve the patron's need. The following excerpts from F006 and L004 are two examples of what happened when the patron examined the item retrieved.

From F006#2:

*I:* Okay, then you selected another volume. You looked at the beginning and then you looked in the middle and read a little bit. What was the intent with that activity?

*U:* I was looking in the index to find the page that the company is listed on. Um, when I did find the page it wasn't all that informative.

The patron in L004#6 further explained how the judgment was made through scanning the selected item when he was asked how successful it was: "It wasn't successful; most of them weren't focused enough on the topic that I was looking for."

This is an instance when the level of treatment rather than topical relevance was used as a criterion for deciding whether a document was appropriate.

Instances involving scanning the content of the item to judge the helpfulness or to look for additional information (F007#5) rather than looking at some identifiers of the item such as the call number, page number, issue number, or title of a journal article to confirm the correctness of the item should be noted. Although the difference is not sharp, it lies in the fact that the patron in the latter situation is more assertive than the former in finding what is expected within the item retrieved.

*I:* Okay, then you went back to the journals area, by that point the librarian had located the journal you were looking for, and I saw you flip through it real quick and then go back to the front and flip through it again. What was your intent with that activity?
*U:* I was, I had located the table that I wanted, but I was looking at some additional tables to see if they might help and to see how much it was, to see if I could copy it or if I should take the journal back to the office with me.

Based on the preceding discussion, situational browsing is a browsing pattern encouraged by a structured display or information organization scheme through which items with some similarities are brought together in a single place. It may take place before or after a specific item is found, or during the process of locating a specific item in that resource area. The types of browsing involve examining information items not known beforehand to make a value judgment, thus to evaluate items, intending to support the original purpose.

**Opportunistic Browsing**

Opportunistic browsing is differentiated from situational browsing because it is characterized by scanning other items incidental to the original purpose during the process of locating a specific, intended item.

F009 is a good example. The person came with a specific item in mind to look for and then went directly to the resource area to find the location of the item on the shelf. With no success in finding the item needed, he moved around looking for a librarian's help to locate the specific item. He then picked up some other item that happened to be displayed on the way to the reference desk and scanned the contents of the item retrieved and found something of interest. Thus, display along a path leading toward another resource area in the library allows such opportunistic browsing to take place.

When the patron picks up and scans such an item, browsing is characterized by scanning for evaluation or scanning to see what is there. In the preceding instance (F009#2), such browsing activity is incidental to the activities conducted toward the original purpose. For example, right afterward, the F009 patron resumed pursuit of the item he intended to seek at the time he entered the library.

From F009#3:

*I:* Okay, then you went over to the reference librarian and you asked her a question, um, and then you both went over to the business reference area and she selected a book. What was the intent with that activity?

*U:* The intent was to find another book.

*I:* Would you say you were successful or unsuccessful?

*U:* Successful.

*I:* Okay, and why did you feel that way?

*U:* Because I found, or Kathy found the book for me.

Situational browsing differs from opportunistic browsing in that in situational browsing the entry point of browsing is near the location of a known item on a given path in the same resource area to support the original goal, whereas in opportunistic browsing scanning an information object to evaluate or learn something of potential interest occurs on some path taken toward finding a specified item. Thus, while the structure of information organization appears to be influential for situational browsing, movement between resource areas is another factor influencing opportunistic browsing.

## Looking for Some Things with Common Characteristics

Looking for things with common characteristics includes two sets of patterns in which the patron looks for items that share one or more characteristics, such as a topic, an author, a genre, an event, current things, a type of document format, or a writing style. The first pattern set involves scanning meta-information either using secondary tools such as OPACs or indexes and abstracts to identify items of interest (systematic browsing), or without such tools (evaluative browsing). In those episodes not involving secondary tools, scanning a series of items to identify and select an item for further examination, which is often conducted iteratively, is noted. The second pattern set, focus browsing, is a combination of systematic and evaluative browsing in which the items identified in the secondary tools serve as entry points to look for similar items not identified in the tools.

### Systematic Browsing

Systematic browsing is represented by cases L062#1 and L036, in which various aspects of the user's needs are explored systematically by looking through citations under various descriptors or subject headings, or citations under a specific heading in various issues of indexes and abstracts are examined in sequence. Thus, this pattern involves making use of bibliographic tools for identifying items that share some common characteristics. Secondary tools such as index journals or OPACs are used to identify items on a topic or in an area of interest. That is, scanning meta-information to locate or evaluate some things with common attributes to support the overall purpose of the visit characterizes this pattern. Browsing in this instance involves examining items without real knowledge of whether they will serve the patron's need because only the representations of items intended to locate are scanned for evaluation.

For example, in L062#1, the patron, conducting research on "helicopter rotors," typed various keywords (e.g., aerodynamics, helicopters, helicopter rotors) into the OPAC and scanned the list under each topic to "see if there is anything listed on the subject." He said, "I also didn't have any other authors or any particular books that I was looking for. Just to look for very general information on the subject."

While he was scanning the citations, he would select a few items to look at their further descriptions in order to make a judgment on their helpfulness. However, because of the lack of specificity in the "full" description of the item, the uncertainty about the utility of the item was high.

*I:* Then you typed "ful." What did you intend here? [The symbol "ful" is a system option to obtain full bibliographic information on a title.]
*U:* I was hoping it would give a more complete listing on what the book was about.

Similarly, while looking at one citation selected from a list that was brought up by another subject approach, the patron commented that "it seemed that airplane design would have something to help me" and then typed in the "ful" command. When asked his intention, he stated,

*U:* To know what aspect of the airplane design it was. I thought it would give me a full description. And it really didn't, you know that it didn't really help me at this step.
*I:* Why do you feel that way?
*U:* It didn't give any more information that I needed.

Thus, these examples of scanning meta-information to evaluate items on a topic demonstrate a kind of browsing activity that might also take place at the shelf, as discussed previously, except that the specificity of information provided is much higher with an actual information object itself than with such representations.

In L036, the bibliographic tool used was a specific index and abstract, which the patron had experience in using it before he came into the library. A topical keyword or subject descriptor (e.g., robotics sensors) was used to locate the appropriate section and then select potentially useful items (i.e., citations) from the title lists for further examination in the abstract of each selected item. In the following example, (L036#4) the patron was observed to scan the contents of an abstract called *Computer and Control Abstracts* across several years, looking through the index and main body from issue to issue. When asked his intent, he stated, "I was looking for articles relating directly to robotics sensors. . . . I knew . . . the information that I was looking for was under one specific title [he actually meant subject heading]. He repeated such scanning activities in each volume, looking under the part of the same heading."

In the next few episodes the patron scanned the library's Union List of Journal Holdings and the OPAC to see if specific items were held in the library, a pattern previously described as nonbrowsing. When asked what would be the next step afterwards, he stated that he would continue to obtain the real items (i.e., specific documents). When this happens, the process turns into focus browsing, discussed later.

**Evaluative Browsing**

This pattern is represented by W004 and W059 and deviates from systematic browsing in that the patron goes directly to a resource area. The browsing type involves examining information objects to evaluate items with common characteristics. Evaluative browsing, illustrated by the following episodes, demonstrates empirically the most salient characteristics of the traditional concept of direct shelf browsing as described in most library literature. The pattern involves the following processes: (1) coming with a general interest or topic in mind, (2) going directly to the resource area, (3) selecting intended information objects after scanning the shelf, (4) looking through parts of the whole item to see if the item is of interest or contains useful information, and (5) repeating steps 3–4 several times. In this pattern, the patron does not come with a specific predefined item to look for but knows or is aware of a topic or certain genres or types of publication he would like to look at. His knowledge about the structure of resources as arranged by the library is implied by the direct movement to the intended resource area and in statements such as, "I immediately have to check this spot" (W004#1).

From W004#1<1>:

*I:* The first thing that I saw you do was going right over to the new nonfiction area and browse. Looks like you selected a book from the shelf, looked at jacket in the front of the book, and you kept it at that point. Can you tell me what your intention was then?

*U:* Well, I guess as soon as I began looking at the book and after seeing the jacket and the subject, I decided that it might be a book that I would like to read.

*I:* Okay, do you think you were successful in that activity?

*U:* Yes, I do, I think so.

*I:* Why?

*U:* Why do I feel that way? Well, because I'm quite interested in current things and I do like nonfiction and this library continues to buy new nonfiction material and I immediately have to check this spot.

From W059#3:

*I:* Okay, after the fiction area you moved over to the new nonfiction area. I saw you pick up two books, look at them, replace them, and you picked up a third, looked at the jacket, the cover, and you kept that. What was your intention there?

*U:* There are some nonfiction books I would like to read. I don't have the list of what I was really looking for with me but I do always scan for my husband as he is a historical nonfiction history buff, and I found one, *A Portrait of Stonewall Jackson*, which he may enjoy.

*I:* Do you feel you were successful or unsuccessful?

*U:* Successful.

*I:* And why did you feel that way?

*U:* There was one book I liked, there were many books, some others have more interest to me, and I don't have the time right now, this is a hurry visit.

Nevertheless, the patron's knowledge about what is in the resource area is not adequate. Thus, the goal of the scanning process is to identify items with potential interest by examining the information on the book spine, cover, or other parts of the item under consideration. For example, the same patron conducted the following activities in the second episode (W004#1<2>):

*I:* Okay, you continued to browse there, you selected a book, looked at the cover, and put it back on the shelf, selected another, looked at the jacket and found a book, and you kept it. What was your intention at that time?

*U:* I guess I mostly lean toward biographies; the book I probably put back was not biographical. I'm trying to remember what it was. I think it may have been a book about oceans, questions and answers.

*I:* Okay, so the book you put back, do you feel you were successful?

*U:* Successful in what?

*I:* In regard to what you were intending to do?

*U:* Deciding what not to read. Yes, I think that was, I was successful in deciding that I didn't want that book and that it was really not worth my time spending on it, so I continued looking down the row.

Another good example is W079. The patron, moving from the new fiction area to new nonfiction area to rental book area during the visit, conducted the same activities repeatedly in each resource area: scanning the bookshelf and examining several items selected off the shelf (W079#3):

*I:* After that, you went over to the new nonfiction area. You did the same thing, browsing, looking at covers, jackets, flipping through the books, and then finally you found something that, I guess, looked of interest to you, so you kept it. What was your intention there?

*U:* Just to, something I didn't know whether I wanted to glance through here or take out.

*I:* Okay with your activity in the nonfiction area, did you feel successful or unsuccessful?

*U:* I guess successful if I can follow the same train of thought.

*I:* Okay, and why did you feel that way?

*U:* It was enough to, enough to feel successful, the fact that there was enough there to look for. Nothing struck my interest one way or another.

From W079#8:

*I:* Okay, then you kind of browsed the rental book area after you did a last browse in the new fiction area, and you did the same type of thing, you read the covers, the jacket, but you didn't select anything at that point. What was your intention there?

*U:* Just to browse. I wondered why they had a separate rental section as opposed to one you could take out on your card.

*I:* Did you feel you were successful or unsuccessful at that activity?

*U:* Successful.

*I:* And why did you feel that way?

*U:* Because I was able to dismiss, you know, getting involved in rent-a-book.

In this pattern, the patron was observed to do the same thing iteratively—an iterative process of scanning a resource in the field, identifying and selecting an item of potential interest, and then examining the item. The result of each examination may be positive or negative, depending on whether there is a good match of the attributes of the item and the attributes the patron seeks. Table 12.1 showed these attributes as criteria for evaluation.

As an illustration of some attributes used to evaluate the item scanned, notice that "biographies" were mentioned in W004#1<2>, cited previously, and "good" and "diversion reading" were applied in the following episode (W059#2):

*I:* After the rental books you started browsing in the new fiction area, selected a book, read the jacket, and kept the book. What was your intention at that point?

*U:* Just to find some diversion reading that sounded reasonably good.

*I:* Do you feel you were successful or unsuccessful?

*U:* Successful enough.

*I:* Why did you feel that way?

*U:* The story sounded like it might have some interest to me, as a diversion.

A reasonable question is how one selects a certain book but not others. When one subject was asked how he went about selecting the material on the shelf, he stated, "You look at the shelf and you see titles, and you see information is not enough, and so you take a look at the whole book, you know, like just the cover, you will get more information. Taking that information into account, you can decide whether or not you want to take that book out." (L049#2).

When he was observed to select a book and skim the back part and text of the book quickly and then keep the book, he further explained the intention of the scanning act and the process of how the decision was made: "I was trying to look for some specific topics, some particular topics, I mean, and I found what I wanted [by] looking at the index. Then, after knowing the page, going to the page and looking at the text" (L049#2).

In another instance, the patron explains what happened when he selected a book, just scanned the text, and did not look at the index part: "I do it all the time, because, I don't know, it is something you can't explain, you know the cover is old, and the title is, and the author is not well known, so you wouldn't go to see the index at all, you wouldn't waste your time" (L049#5).

These comments illustrate that scanning behavior for evaluation first used information at the first sight, such as cover and title, and may refer to looking at different parts of an item, to applying various criteria such as topic, currency, and authority, and to selecting a document as appropriate. In other instances, such a scanning process may be just a glimpse at the book jacket, as in the W004#1 episode cited previously.

Evaluative browsing in several instances appears to be a regular behavior, as indicated by statements such as, "I usually make a habit of going through the business section" (W037#1<2>) or "I do always scan for my husband [in the new nonfiction area]" (W059 #3) or "This library continues to buy new nonfiction material and I immediately have to check this spot" (W004 #1<1>).

This represents a typical browsing activity in which the browser's object is not specific and the browser's goal is essentially to evaluate, upon encounter, some unknown items that are of potential interest.

**Focus Browsing**

Focus browsing is a deviation from systematic browsing in that the patron goes to the actual resource area to look for items of interest after using the bibliographic tool. Under this circumstance, the items with location indicators (e.g., call numbers) identified in the tool serve as an entry point for patrons to the location where items with similar characteristics are grouped. For example, the fact that items with similar characteristics to the one identified in the catalog beforehand are arranged together on the shelf encourages browsing to take place at the shelf.

W014 is a good example. The patron did a few subject searches in the computerized catalog, including one on ships, and then he went over to the 623s shelf, "the general call number for anything on ships." This implied that the patron did not know what was available on the topic of interest in the specific library. Instead of going directly to a resource area, scanning citations in the computer using a subject search approach may first be adopted to identify the location of items of potential interest.

In the following episode, scanning the bookshelf is then adopted when the results of the search in the computer were not satisfactory (W014 #2):

*I:* And then you went over to the 623s shelf. What were you trying to accomplish at that point?
*U:* That is the general call number for anything on ships, so if I didn't find anything in the catalog, maybe the title on the shelf would point it out.

The patron went back and forth between 621s and 623s, scanning that section. His remark on what he was doing and the intent behind the activity points to a salient characteristic of browsing, that is, scanning to look for an unknown item that might be of interest *and* at the same time to locate a prespecified item. Although behaviorally the patron might not look as if he had something to look for or as if he were searching the call number of the desirable item, searching for a specific item and looking for some things of interest took place in one single scanning activity.

From W014 #6<1>:

*I:* Then you went back to the 621s and you seemed to browse in that section again. What did you intend to accomplish at that point?

*U:* I guess at that point I was just browsing in general.

*I:* How successful were you that time?

*U:* No different.

*I:* And why do you feel that way about it?

*U:* Well, I still wasn't able to find anything that either interested me or what I was looking for.

From W014#6<2>:

*I:* Then, finally you did pull out a book and you looked at it and you went through the pages. What were you trying to accomplish at that point?

*U:* The title interested me, it was something I didn't see in the, on the computer, but the title looked interesting, so I browsed through it.

*I:* And what did you intend to accomplish when you browsed through it?

*U:* Sort of a hit or miss to see if there was something worth looking into.

*I:* And how successful do you feel you were in that respect.

*U:* Well, for what I was looking for, not very successful.

*I:* Why do you feel that way about it?

*U:* Ah, well something that I thought was interesting didn't turn out to be interesting, I guess.

In episode W014#6<2>, we see that it was the title that attracted the patron's attention when the patron selected an item and scanned the contents. The goal of scanning is to evaluate the value of the item with respect to whether it is worth looking into, as indicated a bit later on (W014#8):

*I:* And then you found your way to the 378s, I think it was.

*U:* 387s.

*I:* Okay, and what were you looking for at that point?

*U:* Same reason I was looking at 623; it's a major call number for ships.

*I:* And were you successful at that point in finding books on ships?

*U:* Probably a little better, yes.

*I:* And why do you feel that way?

*U:* I found one or two books that I thought were interesting and if I wanted to look at something further I would use them.

Thus, systematic browsing is characterized by scanning citations to identify items on a topic of interest (steps 1, 2, 3 in the following list), whereas focus browsing proceeds from the tool to where the actual items are located by taking the additional steps, 4, 5, and 6:

1. Coming with a general interest or topic in mind
2. Going to secondary tools, e.g., OPAC
3. Searching a topic of interest
4. Going to the shelf, looking for a specific item and general information
5. Selecting an item and looking through parts of the whole item to assess the value or utility of the item
6. Holding or returning the item

A noteworthy statement was made by the patron in L049, among others, when he was observed to scan the shelf under this pattern. He was asked at that moment whether he was looking for a specific, preidentified item, as indicated earlier in the interview. He stated that he was "looking for a specific book and browsing at the same time" (L049#2). Thus, the patron, making use of a bibliographic tool to identify a potentially useful item, is led to engage in a scanning activity to sample other items at the shelf at the moment to locate a specific item, identified in the tool, in the same resource area in which documents with some similarity are grouped (as indicated by the call number in this example).

As in situational browsing, during the process of locating a specific item, other items located near the known item but not identified in the tool are also scanned and selected to examine the contents to support the purpose of the visit. However, focus browsing differs from situational browsing in that the patron is not pursuing a known item as prespecified beforehand, and his knowledge about the contents of the items identified in the tool is not adequate, and the value or utility of those items is undetermined. Thus, each item identified in the tool serves more as a reference point than as a target to be located. Hence, in focus browsing, we see browsing involve an iterative process of scanning, identifying, selecting, and examining items that share common characteristics to judge the utility of items selected.

## Keeping Up-to-Date

### Monitoring Browsing

Monitoring browsing can be viewed as a special case of learning in which something as an object often refers to items with a characteristic of novelty or with continuous development. The resource scanned often involves periodicals, such as newspapers and professional journals, whose articles (logical information objects) tend to provide information of new developments in the world or in certain intellectual areas. Depending on a patron's knowledge about the resource under consideration, the object may range from a specific location within a specified resource to some information items not known beforehand. The typical browsing under this situation involves scanning logical information objects to keep up with something sharing common characteristics, described as monitoring browsing.

F001 #1<4> is an example of keeping up with daily happenings in a specified routine column. The type of browsing involves scanning logical information objects to keep up with information in a location:

*I:* Okay, and then you picked up the next [section] and you read a little more in depth. I believe this was the final section of the paper. You read what looked like the beginning and then you kind of flipped through the last pages of the section.

*U:* Right.

*I:* What was your intent with that activity?

*U:* I just read the routine columns that appear in section 3 of the *Wall Street Journal* and I just wanted to follow up on the day-to-day news.

*I:* Okay, did you feel you were successful with that activity?

*U:* Yeah.

*I:* And why did you [feel that way about it]?

*U:* Those are pretty good summaries of what's happened, they're pretty quick to read, they give you an overview.

W037 #1<2> is an example of keeping up in an area of interest in the newspaper, such as market and investments in the business world. The type of browsing involves scanning logical information objects to keep up with information sharing a common characteristic.

*I:* Okay, and then you sat down and started to read. I think the first section you were reading was the business section? What was your intention at that point?

*U:* Well, I look at what's going on in the business world and I look at the market, investments.

*I:* Do you think you were successful?

*U:* Well, it brought me up to date, you know.

*I:* And why did you feel that way?

*U:* Well, I, well, I usually just make a habit of going through the business section, I look at the paper every other day and they have that in there.

W037 #2 is a good example of scanning information to keep up with a specific location of interest in the newspaper as a habitual activity:

*I:* Then I saw you return the *Star Ledger* to the newspaper rack, do a little more [scanning], and select what looked like the local paper.
*U:* The *Westfieldian.* Yeah, I looked through there, I didn't, wasn't quite sure if I did see it the last time I was in here, but I believe I did see that issue, so I didn't spent too much time on that. Then when I put that back the *New York Times* was there.
*I:* Going back a minute to the local paper, did you feel successful for that particular activity for your intent?
*U:* Yeah, I usually look at the obituary column.... Usually certain things in the paper you have to keep up on that you miss otherwise.

L001 #1 provides a good example of scanning journals of interest to keep up-to-date on the recent developments in a field. The patron went directly to a specific location in the library, looking for most recent material (i.e., journals) in an area of interest, nursing administration. Browsing in this instance involves identifying information objects to keep up with items sharing common characteristics (i.e., information dealing with recent developments and nursing administration):

*I:* You said you came to the library to look at some materials, especially journals to get some idea of what is going on in your field, the nursing field. The first thing you did [was] go to the shelves, the journal stacks, and I saw you take down some materials. What did you try to accomplish at that time?
*U:* I wanted to look for the most recent material I could find that was bound. I know the other section there was more, but I wanted to see what I could find just to see anything that was interesting to me that I had been looking for. I found something on administration that was interesting. And the other ones I just picked to see, you know, the professional information.

As a result, the patron considered it a success and commented: "I was looking for the administration, like I said, and I found one book [she meant a bound journal] that had a lot on administration. I didn't get to read it all today, but I know it's there now. And the research material, I wanted to see if any research was being done, and I found the *Nursing Research Journal.*"

Note that in the preceding examples, the information scanned is used in the sense that it adds to the patron's knowledge about current events. From these examples, monitoring browsing can be characterized by direct movement to a specific physical location of a resource area known to the person and by the type of browsing described as scanning logical items in some information objects to keep up with general information or information with common characteristics. The patron's previous experience or knowledge about the potential value of a location or an information object encourages the patron to engage in browsing activities, which may be conducted as a habit. This pattern involves glancing through logical information items not known beforehand in an area of interest, serving as an ongoing information acquisition activity or as a monitoring technique.

### Learning or Finding Out

Learning or finding out refers to situations in which the patron's intent to find out information appropriate for use or to know of something of interest motivates some sort of scanning activities. Two patterns under this theme are distinguished on the basis of whether the information of interest is specified beforehand or not.

#### Indicative Browsing

Indicative browsing is characterized by scanning parts of an information object to learn something specified as information sharing a common characteristic such as a named event or commodities.

In F023, the patron first went right over to the newspaper area where the old back issues hang in the folders. He looked through a few folders and selected a stack of issues to find back issues of the *Wall Street Journal* in the month of February on commodity prices. So he went specifically to those newspapers (F023#1<2>):

*I:* Okay, you sat down at the table and you picked up the first issue of the newspaper you were looking at and you pulled out what looked like the money section. And you opened up to the middle and you started to read and then you wrote down some information. What was your intent with that activity?

*U:* I was trying to find, again, the analysis for each of the specific commodities that I was interested in and reporting on. And I remembered what page it was on because it's consistent through all their newspapers. And once I figured out what section and what page it was on, I just went directly to that each time, that place in the newspaper.

*I:* Okay, with that activity, did you feel successful or unsuccessful?

*U:* Well, again, successful in finding it, but the information wasn't exactly what I was hoping for.

*I:* And why did you feel that way?

*U:* Again, just that there was a discrepancy between what I had wanted and what appeared in the paper. And I can't say that was true for all of it, some of it I did find was helpful.

The patron was observed conducting the same procedures about six or seven more times, looking at different commodities from issue to issue. In some issues he found the right commodity and the right analysis that he was looking for, and in some there were only a couple of commodities he was looking for and they didn't match up to what he wanted.

Indicative browsing involves identifying parts of an information object to learn specific information or information sharing common characteristics. It can be characterized by scanning unknown items in an information object with direct movement to a known resource or location.

**Preparatory Browsing**

Preparatry browsing is characterized by learning something not specified, where no specific information or logical information object is sought. Rather, an information object known to the patron as having potentially interesting articles is scanned to look at whatever appears of interest. Similar to evaluative browsing, thus may involve a process of identifying items of interest to read through examining a series of unknown (logical) items. It is preparatory in the sense that information gained in the process is often not for immediate use; rather, it simply adds to the stock of personal knowledge. W037#3<1> and <2> are two other examples.

From W037#3<1>:

*I:* Then,... I saw you pick that [*New York Times*] up and then sit down to read the first section. What was your intention at that point?

*U:* Just to see more news, [see] if I got anything different out of there. I mean you could read that paper all day long if you wanted to.

*I:* Right. Did you feel successful?

*U:* It served my purpose.

*I:* Okay.

*U:* I mean, I didn't read it that thoroughly, you know, maybe I picked up a few articles here and there, but, ah, in the summer time I probably spend more time reading that really closely because I have more time, you know.

*I:* Why did you feel that way with the first section?

*U:* Well, it had a couple of articles I read, you know.

From W037#3<2>:

*I:* Then, you went to the business section, business page. What was your intention at that point?

*U:* Well, usually the *New York Times* has a little more in-depth, better business section than the other paper. I guess the *Wall Street Journal* would be even better, but I didn't want to stay here that long.

*I:* Do you feel you were successful while you were reading that particular section?

*U:* Yeah, it was, um-huh.

*I:* And why do you feel that way?

*U:* And why I felt that way, I don't know, that's the way I always feel. (Laughter)

From W037#3<3>:

*I:* Okay. After that you flipped to the *Science Times*. What was your intention at that point?

*U:* Um-huh. Well, sometimes they have something different in the science section; usually whatever they have is interesting.

*I:* Did you feel successful?

*U:* Yeah, um-huh.

*I:* And why did you feel that way?

*U:* It is something that was interesting, it was different, you know. I mean usually they don't have the same things in every day, and a lot of times you read them, it might be interesting to you just while you read it, and you probably won't remember it unless it is something unusual, you know.

While scanning to learn something in general, for instance in newspapers, a patron may be prompted by the convenience of having the resource in hand or by being proximate to an area of interest to learn about other specific information, as illustrated by an episode in W037#1<4>:

*I:* Then I guess you continued on into the following section. What was your intention at that point?

*U:* Just to browse through the paper, see what ads were in the paper. Even in both papers I was curious to see what ads the airlines had in there. I heard over a radio show that they had some special in there, but I didn't find it in reference to what they were talking about. It was a talk show.

. . .

*I:* Did you feel successful in the second section of the continuation?

*U:* Not any more so, one section to the other, you know. I mean, I was just going through it seeing what I could pick up. There weren't any special articles or ads in the paper, you know, just browsing.

Indicative browsing and preparatory browsing start with scanning a resource area to select an intended information object to find out or learn about something of interest. Both involve scanning a series of unknown (logical) items to identify and read something of potential interest. Indicative browsing involves identifying logical information objects to learn or gather desirable information specified beforehand, thus indicative in nature, whereas preparatory browsing involves identifying logical information objects to learn whatever appears of interest but is not specified, thus preparatory in nature. Note that although information can be examined to make a value judgment on the item scanned for future reading, information is examined and used in these two patterns for the purpose of information acquisition.

## Goal-Free Browsing

### Invitational Browsing

This pattern is characterized by scanning information or information objects to satisfy intrinsic motivation with no stated goal in mind. Often a given path of a resource area is followed (e.g., scanning sections of a newspaper or bookshelf sequentially). Browsing is invitational in that there is no specified objective to look for or learn about; the goal is open-ended to the extent that it is determined almost completely by external objects such as the appearance of books. In this situation, the patron may not be fully aware of why a particular item is selected, an indication of the absence of an identifiable object in the patron's mind.

W037#3 is a good example. Note that the patron used the word *browsing* in this discourse to describe what he was doing.

From W037#1<5>:

*I:* Okay, then you went on to the accent section. What was your intention at that point?

*U:* More browsing.

*I:* Still browsing.

*U:* Yup. Yup.

*I:* Did you feel successful in this particular section of the paper?

*U:* Um-huh.

*I:* And why did you feel that way?

*U:* Well, there again, I didn't find anything really too interesting in anything I read, you know, still was browsing.

*I:* So, you felt successful in terms of your purpose in browsing?

*U:* Yeah, I was successful the time I spent there, I mean it's not wasted effort.

From W037#3<3>:

*I:* Okay, then the last section of the *Times* you took a look at was the Metropolitan News section. What was your intention at that point?

*U:* Just browsing.

*I:* Browsing?

*U:* Yeah.

*I:* Did you feel successful while you were browsing?

*U:* Sure.

*I:* And why did you feel that way?

*U:* Not for any special reason, you know.

It is useful to look at case W037 both as a whole and as a series of scanning activities cited in different sections of this analysis. It would be very difficult to tell, strictly from the behavior, whether the patron is looking up something, or learning something in general, or keeping up with something in particular. In fact, in this case, the patron conducted a number of similar scanning activities with differing goals in mind. Nevertheless, all activities involved scanning some unknown items. Thus, browsing appears to be more a cognitive concept than a behavioral one to the extent that it involves scanning and examining items not known beforehand.

## Summary

Table 13.1 summarizes the ten patterns of browsing and nonbrowsing. The result of this analysis may be compared with other frameworks of browsing, such as that by O'Connor (1993), who proposed four sorts of browsing: expansion, vague awareness search, monitoring information environment, and creativity. These four are reflected here by, respectively, situational browsing, focused browsing, monitoring browsing, and invitational browsing. On the other hand, what is generally taken as "direct search at shelf" (e.g., Hyman 1972) corresponds more closely to evaluative browsing. These browsing patterns provide some answers to the questions How does browsing occur? and What motivates people to browse?

With respect to goal, there are five general kinds of motivational contexts in which browsing occurs, or five browsing themes: (1) to look for a specific item, (2) to look for items sharing common characteristics, (3) to keep up-to-date with something, (4) to learn about something, and (5) as a goal-free activity. In an information setting such as a library, browsing as a goal-directed activity, including nonbrowsing and situational, opportunistic, and systematic browsing, is most notable. Further, browsing can be conducted to support the original purpose, or it can be conducted incidental to the original purpose. Thus, the belief held by many information service agents (e.g., librarians) that browsing is necessarily a "not-knowing-what-one-wants" behavior or an inferior search strategy is not warranted. Situationally speaking, browsing is performed to identify items of interest when the nonbrowsing search in a bibliographic tool fails to reveal a satisfactory result.

**Table 13.1**
Dimensional Taxonomy of Browsing Patterns

| | Process | | | Influences | | | |
|---|---|---|---|---|---|---|---|
| Pattern | Resource Form | Goal | Object | Movement | Resource Focus | Purpose | Knowledge: Location, Content |
| *Specific* | | | | | | | |
| Nonbrowsing | Meta/PIO | Locate | Specific | Directed | Structure | Support | Low, high |
| | LIO | Locate | Specific | | | | High, high |
| | Info | Confirm | Specific | | | | |
| Situational | Meta | Locate | Specific | Directed | Structure | | Low, high |
| | PIO | Evaluate | Common | Interrupted | Content | Support | Middle, low |
| Opportunistic | Meta | Locate | Specific | Directed | Structure | | Low, high |
| | PIO | Learn | Specific | Interrupted | Content | Incidental | |
| | PIO | Entertain | General | Undirected | Content | Incidental | Low, low |
| *Common* | | | | | | | |
| Systematic | Meta | Locate | Common | Directed | Content | Support | Low, low |
| Evaluative | PIO | Evaluate | Common | Directed | Content | Support | High, low |
| Focus | Meta | Locate | Common | Undirected | Structure | Support | |
| | PIO | Evaluate | Common | Directed | Content | Support | |
| | PIO | Evaluate | Common | Undirected | Content | Either | |
| *Up-to-Date* | | | | | | | |
| Monitoring | LIO | Keep up | Common | Directed | Content | | |
| | | Location | Common | Undirected | Content | Support | High, low |
| *Finding Out* | | | | | | | |
| Indicative | LIO | Learn | Specific | Directed | Content | Support | |
| Preparatory | LIO | Learn | General | Undirected | Content | Support | |
| *Goal-Free* | | | | | | | |
| Invitational | Info | Entertain | None | Undirected | Content | Either | Low, low |

Meta = meta-information; PIO = physical information object; LIO = logical information object; Info = information.

However, shelf browsing is also conducted to locate a specific item identified in the bibliographic tool, when searching in a bibliographic tool is perceived as successful. It is physical proximity to similar materials that induces browsing activity. Additionally, browsing is performed when one is familiar with the feature of a specific resource location, such as New Nonfiction area in a library or a column in a newspaper, and purposively sets out to browse that area to see what is there, to see if there is anything of interest, or to keep up with ongoing and new developments. Finally, browsing is also performed as a habitual activity with a specific information object such as a newspaper known to contain information of potential interest.

# 14

# Results: A Refined Framework of Browsing

## A Model of the Browsing Process

The initial proposed framework of browsing can now be modified based on the empirical findings. The initial framework originally included four dimensions: behavior, motivation, cognition, and resource, with two subdimensions associated with each individual dimension. These subdimensions, respectively, were scanning and movement, purpose and goal, knowledge and plan, form and focus of resource. These dimensions, as identified from the literature, are theoretically important to understand browsing. However, it is still not clear what constitutes browsing behavior and how one can adequately describe a browsing behavior using these dimensions.

The results of the empirical analyses suggest a model of the browsing process portrayed in table 14.1. In three of the dimensions, one of the original subdimensions appears to be more useful in understanding the process of browsing, the exception being the cognitive dimension. Instead of using "knowledge" or "plan" to describe a browsing process, "object" has been identified as a salient aspect of the cognitive dimension.

In the library and information science literature, "object" has often been subsumed under browsing "goal," which is presumably to search or locate information needed. Browsing has been typically described as "searching without a well-defined goal or search criteria." However, the results of this study suggest that there are different types of goals when people browse, such as evaluating the utility of an unknown item or learning something of interest by glancing through an item not known beforehand. One important finding in discovering people's intention during scanning a resource is that people often have subliminal interests that are not constantly actively sought after. Those information-related interests are pursued as a result of stimulated association with information items surrounding them. People use the local or current information need as the focal point that opens them up to

**Table 14.1**
Dimensions of Browsing Process

| Dimension | Subdimension |
|---|---|
| Behavior | Scanning |
| Motivation | Goal |
| Cognition | Object |
| Resource | Form |

other things. Thus, one characteristic of browsing is associativity—the linking of information stimuli (or making associations). The elements identified in the goal dimension allow us to understand the multiplicity or potentiality of browsing—the intrinsic, interest-driven as well as extrinsic, task-oriented motivations for browsing.

The vagueness of search goal or object sought, in essence, refers to not looking for a specific item. For example, after scanning the shelf, the patron in L049 flipped through two books retrieved from the shelf to see if particular topics were included in the contents (L049#2<2> and <3>). In this instance, no prespecified item was being looked for. Rather, unknown items were evaluated according to certain topics of interest; that is, items with some common characteristics were sought. The vagueness of search goal does not mean that people do not know what they want. They want something of interest or utility that is not specified beforehand. An object seems vague because no specific item is sought. Unknown information items are directly examined to determine their value or utility as they are made available to the patron. Such interactivity—the reduced cognitive load of specifying what is needed or intended because individuals may interact directly with informational stimuli that are potentially useful—is another characteristic of browsing. Ill-defined search criteria can be more explicitly described in terms of four types of browsing object—items with common characteristics, items in a known location, general knowledge, and no object—with differing degrees of search criterion specificity.

Thus, it is important to recognize that people have different kinds of goals or intentions associated with an observed scanning behavior. In addition, the notion of vagueness of object sought can be better construed as no prespecified, known item is looked for. It is in this sense that a browsing process can be characterized by the lack of specificity of goal and object.

The four distinct acts of browsing were derived from the observation of scanning as a nonverbal behavior. For example, the empirical data show the following behaviors:

1. "Looking" without identifying something needed or of interest (e.g., scanning the bookshelf and leaving without finding what one wants or is interested in; F007#1<1>)
2. "Identifying" without selecting any item of interest (e.g., scanning the pages of a newspaper and finding no articles concerning a specific area of interest; F031#1<1>)
3. "Selecting" without examining the item retrieved (e.g., retrieving the book located on the shelf and leaving; F019#2<1>)
4. "Examining" the item retrieved (e.g., looking through the book to see if it is helpful; L004#5<1>)

It is the idea of examining unknown items by scanning or moving through an information space that characterizes browsing as a nonverbal behavior. Thus, another characteristic of browsing is accessibility through scanning—the ability to expose oneself to and sample (not necessarily systematically) many information stimuli that might otherwise be unknown or inaccessible.

The four components in the resource dimension help us understand the browsing process in terms of examining a series of unknown items. For example, examining unknown items to locate something of interest can take place with various media, including physical information objects such as fiction books, or logical information items such as articles in a newspaper, and meta-information such as citations or subject headings in an OPAC. It is also observed that people may examine a series of information items themselves, such as numeric data or tables in a journal (F007#5<1>). Thus, central to our perspective, browsing does not have to be associated with specific media, even in a print-based library. Catalog browsing, shelf browsing, or journal browsing all share this characteristic: looking through a series of unknown items. These items are catalog cards (meta-information), books (physical information objects), and articles (logical information objects), respectively. However, they differ in providing the flexibility—the ability to sample as easily as one wishes—during browsing; this is a major difference between a representation (meta-information) and a real information object. As one patron stated with disappointment, while examining the citation list in the OPAC, "I was hoping it would give a more complete listing on what the book was about" (L062#1). Hence, the form of resource involved, whether it is meta-information or an information item itself, is a dimension of the browsing process.

Thus, in the new model for describing the browsing process, scanning is the salient component of the behavioral dimension. Goal is the central element of motivational dimension. Object is the major cognitive aspect. And form appears to be characteristic of the resource dimension. These four subdimensions in the preliminary model are hereafter referred to as the four dimensions of the refined model.

**Summary of Outcomes**

While browsing outcomes are generally mentioned in the various literatures, they are primarily covered in the library studies and information science literatures (see table 9.4), although part I showed that information-seeking outcomes, especially those related to access, are underemphasized in all the literatures. Browsing may have considerable negative outcomes (or intervening limitations): (1) high demands on attention, (2) low efficiency for specific retrieval, (3) exposure to distractions, (4) information overload, (5) vulnerable to personal biases and cognitive reinforcement, (6) subject to limitations on browsing by most current systems, and (7) diminishing returns (Marchionini 1995, 188, his table 6.3). Primary caregories of outcomes across the literatures include serendipitous finding, modification of information requirements, finding the target information, learning, disorientation, information overload, cost of time, enjoyment, information gathering, opinion leadership, impulse buying, and monitoring/surveillance. The literature on accessing information and communication provides much greater treatment of consequences, in the outcomes facet, as discussed in part I.

While the consequences of browsing are not the primary focus of part II, Chang (2000) has recently reanalyzed the data reported here to identify influences on the extent of browsing, general consequences, the nature of unsuccessful browsing outcomes, and influences on those consequences. Near the end of the interviews, she asked the library patrons, "How successful were you?" and "Why do you feel that way about it?"

Extent of browsing (indicated by total time and number of episodes) was influenced by the amount of time the browser was able to spend in the library, the user's scheme of information organization, proximity to desirable materials, the browser's goals, knowledge, experience, interests, and expectations, and feedback from the information resource. Four main categories of factors influencing the perceived outcomes of browsing include (1) the browser's intentions, (2) the amount or quality of information found, (3) the utility of what is found, and (4) whether what is found is helpful for solving problems or making judgments. General categories of outcomes include accidental findings, modifying the initial information need, finding the desired information, learning, feeling relaxation or recreation, gathering information, keeping updated, satisfying curiousity, partially successful browsing, and unsuccessful browsing. *Unsuccessful browsing* included not finding what one wanted, discovering an inadequate amount or quality of information, or not finding useful or interesting things. *Partially successful browsing* comprised interactions among some of these outcomes: finding some intended object but not being happy with the amount or quality, not finding what one wanted but discovering some novel or potentially useful information, and accomplishing some but not all multiple purposes.

Here are a few examples from the interviews for selected outcomes (Chang 2000). Phrases in italic type emphasize the category being discussed.

### Accidental Findings

From L072#5:

*I:* Okay, then in terms of this whole locating activity, how successful were you?

*U:* For the overall day?

*I:* No,... for while you were at the stacks.

*U:* Probably pretty good.

*I:* Why do you feel that way?

*U:* Well, for both the things which I came here with information about in terms of call numbers or EPA document numbers, I was able to go locate those and will be walking out with them. *I even went so far as to find some things I didn't expect to find.*

### Learning, Getting Informed

From W088#2<2>:

*I:* Okay, and then you actually sat down and you read the first magazine and you read it, then you flipped through the pages, continued reading. What was your intent with that activity?

*U:* Merely to scan to see if there was anything of strong interest that I might want to read. I actually only read two of the articles but most, both of these magazines were fairly, heavily pictures so, not a lot of reading material.

*I:* Okay, for this activity did you feel successful or unsuccessful?

*U:* Oh, successful. *It increased my knowledge of current events.*

*I:* And why did you feel that way?

*U:* *Because I read things that I had not read before.*

### Relaxation, Recreation

From L026#9<2>:

*I:* When you paged around, how successful were you, did you find something interesting? You said that for the last five minutes you just paged through.

*U:* Yeah, *I paged through just to see if I would find something that might be interesting* and not related to what I was doing, *just to give me a break*, and I did find something interesting, as I said, it was about the television stuff, and it was fun to read for a while, *it gave me a well-needed break.*

**Getting Updated**

From W004#3:

*I:* Was your intention at this point different from the first intention where you were looking for a health magazine?

*U:* Well, only in that I was looking for something on a different topic. A different type of magazine, that was my intention.

*I:* Okay, do you feel you were successful?

*U:* Yes.

*I:* Why do you feel that way?

*U:* Well, I guess it's that *Newsweek* sums up pretty well what takes place thoughout the world and *it has a lot of good concise articles that can keep me up-to-date.*

**Satisfying Curiosity**

From W079#5:

*I:* Okay, then you sat down in the little sitting area there, reading area, and you picked up one of your books and you kind of looked through the beginning, slowly paged through the rest of the book. What was your intention with that activity?

*U:* Curiosity, it happened to be, the book was *What Do People Do in Bed.*

*I:* Oh. That was the title, huh?

*U:* Yeah, it was the title. *It just struck my curiosity about why someone would write a book and whether it was worthwhile reading*, and it was, it wasn't worthwhile taking out. But it satisfied my curiosity, though. I mean, it wasn't a particularly interesting book, so I put it back.

*I:* Did you feel successful or unsuccessful with that?

*U:* Successful.

*I:* And why did you feel that way?

*U:* *Because it satisfied my curiosity.*

## The Refined Framework of Browsing

Figure 14.1 portrays a conceptual understanding of the browsing patterns identified in this chapter. This revised framework makes explicit the major components of each general dimension identified in the preliminary model with respect to the influences on the process of browsing and the process of browsing itself. That is,

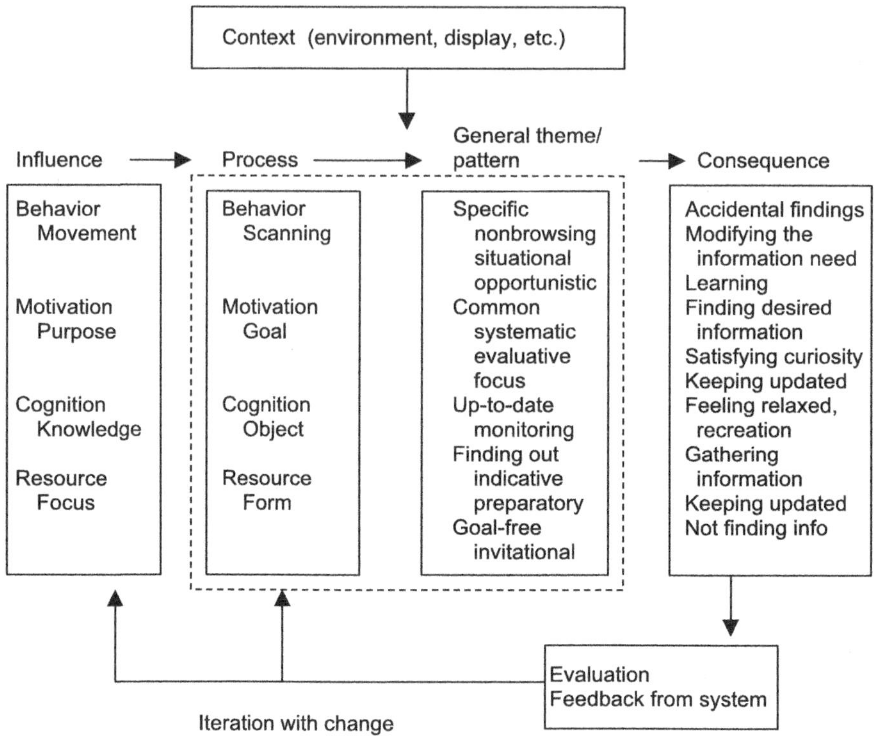


**Figure 14.1**
Refined Framework of Browsing

movement, purpose, knowledge, and focus in the behavioral, motivational, cognitive, and resource dimensions, respectively, influence the browsing process in which people engage. In turn, the browsing process (in behavioral, motivational, cognitive, and resource dimensions) helps to determine the general themes (specific, common, up-to-date, finding out, and goal-free) and specific patterns of browsing.

The initial browsing framework (see figure 10.1) identified from the literature analysis was, in fact, based on the influence factors of browsing rather than on the defining ones. Those factors are not capable of describing the browsing process itself, because the browsing process was unclear in the literature and has been typically treated as a one-dimensional concept. Such a simple concept of browsing is typically reflected in the literature as "searching without well-defined search criteria."

As the result of the analysis in this chapter, knowledge appears to be an influence factor instead of a process one. That is, people engage in different types of browsing or nonbrowsing behavior as described by the four general themes in the new model, depending on the kind of knowledge they bring with them. A patron may come to a library to look for something, with incomplete information about what is available in the whole spectrum of bibliographic tools. Thus, instead of specifying what she is looking for, she instead engages in scanning activity to locate the object sought. For example, in one case a patron remembered seeing a needed article in *Fortune* magazine but couldn't remember what issue it was in. So, he paged through each issue of that magazine to find what he wanted. Since his focus of resource is the contents, we see him engage in scanning an LIO (logical information object) to locate a specific item. In another case, the patron knew the name of the author of an article but did not know the complete title or where to start looking for it. In both of these instances, the patron's knowledge about what to look for was high but his knowledge of where to look for it was low. However, in the latter case, the patron first made use of an index to find out the source of the article needed. We see her scan meta-information to locate a specific item.

Similarly, if a patron knows from experience that a specific area in the library (e.g., New Fiction section) consistently provides new materials, and therefore goes directly to the location to see what is on display there, we can say that the patron's knowledge about location is high. However, since she does not know beforehand what she expects to find, her knowledge about what to look for is low. On the other hand, a patron may come to the library to look for materials to gain a background understanding about a topic but does not know exactly where to look for those materials. In this situation, the patron's knowledge about what to look for and where to look is low. If the focus is to find out about a resource structure, we see her scan meta-information to evaluate items sharing common characteristics. Thus, focus of a resource and knowledge about location, contents, and structure/path of a resource both influence the type of browsing activity people engage in.

The discussion of the notion of browsing in the previous literature has also focused on the planned/unplanned nature of browsing and the presence/absence of a meaningful purpose during browsing. The empirical findings of this study suggest that browsing is meaningful and purposeful but can be goal-free or have no object at the outset. Browsing can be both planned or unplanned. However, it is better understood by the fact that browsing can take place in support of an overall purpose, be incidental to the original purpose, or be the purpose itself. For instance, browsing can be situational, opportunistic, and invitational, respectively, in these situations.

Thus, the refined framework based on the empirical evidence makes explicit some concepts associated with browsing in the literature such as "vagueness" of goal or object, and clarifies the role of knowledge or lack of it. It provides an analytical language, through characterization of the browsing process, that allows us to systematically describe various types of browsing behavior or better articulate "the levels of browsing," as Herner (1970) puts it. Furthermore, this study makes another contribution to the literature by identifying the five general motivations (general themes) for browsing and the nine related patterns of browsing, and by systematically describing the situations in which various types of browsing take place.

# 15

# Future Research and Implications for the Frameworks of Accessing and Browsing Information and Communication

These studies were undertaken to explore the phenomena of accessing and browsing information and communication in various situations and with various resources. The initial conceptual frameworks were derived from analyses of previous research literatures, by refining and clarifying the dimensions and concepts through comparison of the unique and common aspects. These initial conceptual frameworks were then tested and refined based upon various case studies and multiple sources of data. The resulting refined frameworks provide a deeper and multidimensional understanding of the concept and nature of accessing and browsing information and communication.

## Accessing Information and Communication

Four major issues and concerns underlie the range of factors implied in conceptualizing, studying, and promoting access to information and communication: the conceptualizations of information, what is implied by the various conceptualizations of access to information, facets of the information-seeking process, and the potential interactions of mediation and technology with access.

*Information* may be conceptualized as a thing (commodity/resource), data in the environment, representation of knowledge, and part of the process of communicating. *Access* may be conceptualized as access to knowledge, technology, communication, control, goods/commodities, and knowledge of and ability to exercise rights. *Facets* of the accessing process include context, situation, strategies, and outcomes. Access is affected by a variety of *influences and constraints*, including physical, cognitive, affective, economic, social, political, and mediative. Conceptualizations and analysis of access across six research literatures involve common as well as unique assumptions and emphases. This implies that studying or attempting to affect access from any single research literature is likely to miss, as well as impose, certain dimensions and assumptions about access. Accessing information and communication is clearly a multidimensional, interactive, iterative, and dynamic process.

**Implications**

The framework for accessing information has the potential to serve as the basis for development of a diagnostic evaluation tool for systems designers, implementers and managers, and users. When designing or implementing a system, what are the factors that can create or intensify barriers to access? What considerations can contribute to ease of access? If the concern is security or privacy, what are the factors to consider? What are the tensions inherent in issues or implementations of access and information systems? When developing new systems, such as digital libraries, with greater potential for widespread access, what are the influences and constraints that can be understood in order to better meet the needs of users (Borgman 2000)? What are the likely facets of the information-seeking process, and what are users likely to do with the information they retrieve? How can such systems facilitate the production, use, and evaluation of information or constructing meaning through communication as interactivity and networking become more commonly available?

Consideration of access to information with sensitivity to non-elite users or non-users of information systems carries implications for theory and research as well as for policy and practice. If, indeed, hegemonic power constructs with regard to access to information lie primarily in the power to set and follow the terms of the dialectic rather than in intentional efforts to limit access, then it is essential that both those with privileged access and those without access be explicitly considered in design, development, implementation, purchase, or use of an information or communication resource or system. They must be considered, also, in policy development and implementation. To do otherwise risks the unintentional placement or reification of barriers to access where there need be none, and the unintentional oversight or misunderstanding of situations where barriers have been overcome. Given that the primary lobbying groups represent corporate interests, the interests of individuals in the process of seeking to gain access to information—even those dimensions that are commonly treated in the various literatures—can get lost. Such interests, however, are of primary import in policy issues affecting rights of participation in a democracy. Particularly as interactive forms of accessing information, such as the World Wide Web, become more widely available, the tensions inherent in issues of access grow more salient. The balance between privacy and monitoring, or between intellectual property and the ease with which information can be duplicated and redistributed, for example, carries important implications for policy debates. The framework can guide practice in future analyses, understandings, and applications of access to information and communication.

**Future Research**

Future research can seek to account more comprehensively for all the dimensions of access, especially as they affect non-elites. In particular, including in future research non-users and potential users of information resources and systems who have experienced barriers to access can inform both theoretical development and practice. Future research might work toward developing the framework as an evaluative or diagnostic tool, helpful in assessing whether a given information or communication resource or system provides the various forms of access as well as expected or whether access can be facilitated. Such an evaluative tool might also be used in assessing features of designs for potential systems or in selecting features of a system under consideration or in actual use. A further application could be to assess user satisfaction or to guide design that reduces obstacles to access.

In this regard, the current research provides highly valid and reliable, operationalized categories of the dimensions of access, which could relatively easily be converted into survey or interview items associated with the use and non-use of particular information and communication resources. These operationalizations can contribute to identifying the broad range of interdependent conceptualizations of, influences and constraints on, and facets involved in, access for improved design, development, implementation, and evaluation of information and communication systems.

For example, people in different facets could provide initial feedback (through online prompts or system-collected usage patterns) on which conceptualization of access is being emphasized, and on those influences and constraints most relevant to that facet. These responses could be used to help identify the user's context as well as to revise and redesign that stage of the access system. In particular, the categories identified and tested in this study move toward a comprehensive operational definition of access to information and its components that can be applied to participatory design or providing access through, for example, digital libraries (Borgman 2000). This comprehensive view of access to information can define concepts for designers and can contribute to human factors analysis.

The framework can serve to sensitize future research to issues of access, with implication for those with privileged access as well as for those struggling to gain access to information. Service providers, in particular, as well as researchers in particular literatures, could be challenged to consider which dimensions of access they are not considering, or for which they are holding implicit research area assumptions (such as are indicated in tables 3.6, 3.7, and 4.1), in their public roles or organizational training.

The research presented in part I, while based on a comprehensive review of the literature and a rigorous approach to operationalization and assessment, is of course preliminary. It only considers two of the primary dimensions—influences/constraints and facets—and only considers two samples (though chosen intentionally to maximize variance). Additional in-depth as well as multivariate studies are needed to fully explore the interactions among the dimensions. Further development of a framework for understanding access will have the potential to contribute to theory, design, policy, management, and application.

## Browsing Information and Communication

Browsing, in essence, is an examination of unknown items of potential interest by scanning or moving through an information space in order to judge the utility of the items, to learn about something of interest in the item, or to satisfy curiosity about something. Actual sampling is not essential to the browsing process, as it is not necessary that any specific item be identified as of potential interest. However, browsing is often associated with the vagueness of information objects sought; hence, it often involves sampling unknown items in order to make a value judgment. The nature of browsing is fundamentally evaluative and inclusive. Evaluation means comparison and contrast among alternatives and thus supposes the inclusion of many alternatives not known beforehand for further examination. Searching (or nonbrowsing—what has typically been seen as information seeking or analytical search), on the other hand, is indicative and exclusive. Indicative means seeking a definite target and thus the exclusing other choices.

At the microlevel, the nature of a browser's goal and specificity of object sought are the two most important factors influencing the way people browse. The proposed taxonomy of browsing, which reflects the insights gained both from integration of research literatures and from the empirical evidence, provides a better, more comprehensive, and more analytical language for describing variations in browsing behavior and allows us to discuss various processes of browsing. At the macrolevel, distinct patterns of browsing have been identified to suggest how browsing occurs and why people browse, by taking into account the user's overall purpose, movement between resource areas, knowledge about the resource under consideration, and the information organization scheme embedded in the display.

Part II shows that the concept of browsing is multifaceted. It serves as a search strategy when people are exposed to many alternatives while looking for useful or interesting documents, or in locating information items not considered beforehand or not found in the bibliographic tools. It also serves as a screening technique to help people decide what not to read, to filter out an unknown item of potential interest or use that is actually not interesting or useful after examination. Browsing also serves as a viewing pattern to the extent that the browser intends to identify something of potential interest to read by glancing through or "skimming" unknown items encountered in the process but stopping as soon as the item no longer holds the browser's interest. Such an evaluative viewing process can often result in a learning effect simply because of the opportunity of encountering the unknown. Finally, browsing is also a recreational activity that people engage in to satisfy an intrinsic need for enjoyment or diversion.

## Implications

**Theoretical Implications** If browsing behavior is characterized by examining unknown items by scanning or moving through an information space, this seems to explain why people constantly browse, because we are often surrounded with unknown items—all kinds of information objects and information, or even meta-information—in this complex and fast-changing world, physically, intellectually, and increasingly, virtually. Books are added to a location or reshelved in the library, new topics or fields are emerging in an area of interest, entire domains of multimedia information and communication become available through the Internet. Furthermore, if people constantly browse, and browsing is evaluative in nature, then understanding what sets of criteria or attributes that people use or look at during the evaluation process is important. It is often difficult to evaluate a single item; evaluation is made easy by comparison and contrast among items. Thus, providing good alternatives for consideration is important to browsing and is a good design principle.

The results of part II suggest that when people expose themselves to an information environment, they often bring with them several information needs or interests as well as more or less relevant prior knowledge at the same time. People consciously pursue some of the needs and may not be fully aware of other ones. Those latent needs may not be consciously pursued but are brought out upon encountering informational objects that correspond to those latent interests and prior knowledge. That is, those needs or interests are likely to emerge through stimulated association by the information encountered during the information-seeking or evaluation process (Allen 1996). Thus, browsing as a nonverbal behavior is a way to fulfill the information needs that are at the nonverbal stages (Taylor 1968) by allowing users direct interaction with information resources in order to recognize their value or utility.

Further, although some information-seeking behavior may start with looking for a specific item, during the process if the patron is allowed to be exposed to other information items without asking to do so, it would encourage the patron to examine the items encountered and thus increase the possibility of discovering items of potential use or interest—at some risk of overload or confusion. It would increase the possibility even more when information items are arranged according to some similarities. Thus, the specific item sought is often used as a reference point rather than as an object in itself; in this sense, content may serve as a locational and semantic representation of other content, depending on how the user approaches it. The specific item sought may well be a reflection of the patron's limited knowledge about what external resources are available. Indeed, information seeking is fundamentally problem-driven and interest-oriented. People generally are not pursuing highly specific items; rather, they look for alternatives in the context of an uncertain and complex information environment in which a large amount of information is presented. Thus, serendipity is not blind luck. It can be encouraged by, or as a result of, situational browsing or monitoring browsing in which information not considered beforehand can be articulated and used to support the overall purpose that initiated the visit of the information environment.

People engage in different patterns of browsing depending on the kind of knowledge they bring with them. It follows that people engage in browsing as an ongoing information acquisition strategy to keep up with the constantly changing world, or to take advantage of being near a resource area, because browsing allows patrons (users, audience members, consumers, organizational members, citizens, researchers) to expose themselves to unsought information items. Thus, they are able either to evaluate the item encountered without deliberately doing so or to enlarge their knowledge about an external information resource or the external world in general. Value judgment and personal knowledge are required in information seeking so that no further efforts will be put toward items not worth looking into, or further effort can be guided to another intellectual territory based on the knowledge gained through such a process. Thus, in order to systematically increase a patron's knowledge about a resource, a structured display of information items, which brings items with similar characteristics together, should be encouraged.

This study supports the proposition that browsing is a way of coping with "subject indeterminacy" (O'Connor 1993). Users may be uncertain about what search paths to follow and what contents are to be expected. People browse to evaluate a document's utility, which is not inherent in the text itself. People browse to find something "interesting" to read. What makes a document interesting to a person is subject to an individual's interpretation and is not a characteristic of the document itself. This discussion suggests that the nature of information retrieval is a situated action and interactive in nature (Suchman 1987). The goal of such situated action is to evaluate what is encountered in the course of browsing but unknown—but not necessarily dissimilar—beforehand. Further, people browse to take advantage of being near a resource area to learn about what alternatives are available and to discover what potential uses they have, with the least effort, through sampling the resources of an information environment. In this sense, browsing is a situated learning process, allowing people to acquire information and engage in communication of interest at their convenience, or to find out information that is not immediately needed but is of potential value. Browsing is indeed not only an important search strategy and an information acquisition strategy but also a highly valuable social behavior.

**Implications for System Design** Marchionini (1995, ch. 6) provides a variety of suggestions as to how systems can facilitate browsing. These include closer linkage between input and output (so the user can more quickly iterate the process based upon intermediate results), explicit tools for browsing such as scrolling, multiple windows, pop-up associations, alternative views, hypertext links (especially if they are sensitive to context or to prior link paths), highlighting the query terms in the retrieved text, conceptual boundary indicators, zooming in and out of the retrieval space, "thumbnail" representations of multiple images, portraying only significant visual aspects, presenting images or sounds rapidly to allow the user to identify the initial search space, varying color or changing sound frequencies, direct interface manipulation through graphical slider controls, relevance feedback, clustering of results to indicate conceptual or semantic proximity, and so on. He groups such suggestions into three main categories: (1) representations (conceptual displays and physical displays), (2) mechanisms (user control, query styles, manipulation, and system help), and (3) system features (quick response, excellent display, advanced retrieval algorithms, data structures, and input devices) (122, his table 6.4). Note that increased—not less or random—organization actually facilitates browsing by associating similar materials, providing neighborhood and boundary identifiers, and generating multiple relevant access points.

System designs need to solve conceptual problems (how to represent meaning, what cues are used to indicate salient aspects of information spaces, how users' mental models affect perceptions of systems and information) and technical problems (real-time interaction, high resolution, managing windows) to support the coordination of mental and physical activies involved in browsing (Marchionini 1995, 139). Central to this challenge, Marchionini argues, is the need to be able to represent and manage data easily, rapidly, and in multiple ways, as browsing is driven more by exposure, association, instant user choices, and access than is analytical searching. Such systems must facilitate parallel and continuously information subprocesses (141), while representing both primary (information) and secondary (physical and logical information objects, and meta-information) resources. Representations—both of individual objects and comparisons across objects—allow the user to decide whether to more closely inspect or select an object, through *descriptive* surrogates (which identify object attributes, such as author, institution, knowledge domain, medium, total amount of content) or *semantic* surrogates (which identify object meanings such as titles, abstracts, thumbnail image collections, the relevant information problems).

Marchionini suggests several mechanisms for managing representations. Complex systems designed to support browsing would allow user control of the relative detail of, proportion of, number of views into, or shifting domain-based versions of, descriptive and semantic representations. They would also provide annotation and evaluation of the objects, from other users or in reference to other resources, to aid in generating associations, creating semantic maps, weighting flows of associations across resources, and assessing the neighboring conceptual space. *Probes* allow users to develop and test hypotheses about the nature of the resource, such as through (1) assessing the initial results of full-text searches based on some central terms, (2) combining and synthesizing results from several databases, (3) using relevance feedback to suggest related concepts, (4) sending questions to topic-related listservs to see what kinds of responses result, (5) or activating agents or knowbots that conduct dynamic, personalized searches that help keep users up-to-date by providing regular links to or summaries of classes of topics (as is now commonly available through Internet portals). *Zooms and pans* provide more or less detailed or wider views into an information space, such as (1) providing browsing multiple images (or sounds, text, or online atlases and street guides) until the user wants to see the detail of a specific object, or (2) scanning within a document or activating links to broader topics in related materials. *Filters and templates* restrict what is browsed, based on some common or frequent pattern (in the simplest example, range of years), or even a highly unique view unknown to the user (such as some linguistic associations) that the system might suggest. One way to "bound" browsing activity is to set some kinds of filters or limits on what the user might be exposed to; sorting, ranking, categorizing, or selecting all help the browser know where to focus and how to evalute resources quickly. Recursively, a system might store examples of other users' successful browsing patterns as "templates" that one might try out. Context-sensitive pop-up menus or icons that change when the cursor is nearby are simple examples of display templates. Finally, Marchionini suggests alternative mathematical or geometric models for representing relations among objects (a form of meaning), such as extent of similiarity indicated by angles, distances, shapes, and other topological operations. Marchionini provides several more futuristic scenarios in the final chapter of his book (1995).

An information system that will respond helpfully to a user's (both individual and collective) difficulty in articulating an explicit informaton need should (1) accept minimal semantic expressions of need, (2) contain or refer to expert knowledge, (3) be able to define new ideas so as to lead to user understanding, (4) facilitate internal sharing of essential information between group members, and (5) facilitate activities of gatekeepers in performing an intermediary function to outside information sources, and (6) provide both browsability and classification (Allen 1996). Browsability is especially key in answering questions of failure of perception, as it allows novel experiences to be linked to something already known and understood. For example, browsing of classification structures helps to link users' mental maps with experts' mental maps and institutional structures.

The findings in part II also have some implications for system design. The object dimension suggests that people look for some things that share common characteristics. These characteristics may include topic, event, quality, and novelty. In other situations, people are led to examine items in a specific location identified as of high potential interest. Alternatively, they may want to learn what is there in general. This implies that it is useful to make explicit to potential users the characteristics of a physical location or an electronic site and apply users' common interests to organize materials sharing common characteristics within. This may be a dynamic process, depending on the social membership of various users and the life cycle of their information needs as well as the resource.

For example, World Wide Web interfaces can be set up first by introducing what is available in general to encourage invitational browsing. The first screen can serve as a tour map to the Internet resources. It can support situational browsing by grouping together sites with similar scope or intended users and then by common interests identified from various user groups within each site. For instance, by understanding "novelty" as a criterion used when people browse, "Something New!" or "What's New?" can be set up as a category of each site and subdivided by aspects of users' interests, such as new acquisitions (facilities, resources), new policies, and new events to support monitoring browsing. This approach is one reason why the Yahoo-type Web search engine, using human-developed categories, is preferred by the majority of users.

Similarly, suppose that we have 500 cable TV channels. The interface may designate channels 1–100 as sports channels, channels 101–200 as news channels, channels 201–300 as educational programs, 301–400 as music channels, and 401–500 as movie channels so that channels with the same focus or falling into the same general category can be easily identified as a group for systematic or situational browsing. (Note, however, this particular example assumes the linear, sequential indexing of channels by number, similar to book shelving in libraries by classification number and physical proximity. In a truly virtual domain, sequential numbering is an unnecessary constraint.) Within a given general category such as news, channels with similar focus, such as local news, can be grouped as a second-level cluster and differentiated from news channels with an international focus so that people can browse without remembering what channel number should be selected in order to do so. A third level of clusters may be set up by "quality" of broadcasting or "interestingness" ratings of programs provided by similar groups of users. In any cluster, the user could choose to have the system go through each channel (or sets of channels associated with various attributes) momentarily to support evaluation browsing and allow the user to make a selection for inclusion in a temporary selection pool for further examination.

On the other hand, the goal dimension suggests that a system interface may set up categories by the user's goal as an alternative rather than just by contents of a resource. This makes the system more user-focused and dynamic. For example, one motive is to keep up with the developments in an area of interest. "Keeping up" can be a category on the interface to support monitoring browsing, which leads the user to choose from a list of events or research topics for scanning periodically (which is why most Web sites have a "what's new" section, or "ticker" banners with recent information fitting the user's profile or recent searching choices). Further, one important finding in this research is that, in many instances, locating a specific item and browsing to learn what other items exist in the collection occur simultaneously in a single episode. This suggests that a system interface should be equipped with both searching *and* browsing capabilities such that, in response to a search query, finding the desired item should prompt the user to be exposed to similar items and the system to provide various layers of information specificity within each item for further examination. Since the patron in such a situation is ready to select items of interest and to examine their content to evaluate their utility based on certain characteristics of the document structure and contents, the interface can facilitate this process by making search capabilities available at all levels of specificity. That is to say, when a patron is browsing a document to judge its utility, the user should be allowed to specify some attributes of interest and be prompted with those sections of the text that include the specified attributes.

Of great research interest is the extent and kinds of impacts such systems might have on users, their needs, and their browsing patterns. "Humans know much more than they consciously realize they know" (Hayles 1999, 203), and embodied knowledge, developed through habitual action and familiar contexts, cannot be totally formalized, and formalization changes the nature of the knowledge. Thus, new technologies that alter habitual physical actions and behavioral patterns—such as new processes and patterns of browsing—may alter the nature of that habitual if tacit behavior as well as the kinds of knowledge and knowing that are possible.

**Practical Implications** Practically, some suggestions can be made for better organization and representations of information and better display of materials as well as for effective information seeking and retrieval.

With the understanding that people browse not only to seek and learn information but also as a recreational experience in an information environment, information providers and organizers such as librarians should arrange physical layout and displays in such a way that encourages both successful and enjoyable browsing. This entails a structured display and open access to all kinds of material. Since some browsing patterns are likely to be encouraged by knowing a specific location of interest, it is helpful to highlight parts of a collection with high potential to meet patrons' needs or interests. Classifying material by genre in a public library or grouping material by special topics in a stand-alone display with a salient sign on it are examples. It is also useful to make the signage system clear and well placed. One specific suggestion can be made about shelf labels: Since numeric labels to most people are only a location indicator (i.e., abstract metadata), they should be accompanied by topical headings to help make patrons aware of the potential value of the items displayed. This is already a common practice in bookstores, and of course Web sites, but not so common in the library.

By recognizing the notion of browsing as a nonverbal behavior with multiple motives, librarians can become more aware of the cognitive aspect of patrons' information-seeking behavior. It is not just a simple behavior of locating a document;

it is also an information-gathering activity, an information-evaluation behavior, a learning process, and intrinsically entertaining. Therefore, librarians should consider how to promote library materials through different patterns of browsing. For example, the layout or wayfinding system in the library can be designed to encourage opportunistic browsing by placing material displays along the paths to a related class of collection. It is also a good idea to consider the library as a showroom in which one can promote less well-known materials according to users' interests, by displaying the materials in a stand-alone rack with a salient sign on it to make users aware of it and to encourage evaluative browsing. Since people may browse simply to see what catches their eye or to keep up-to-date in a general way, librarians could change the displays from time to time to create a sense of novelty and thus encourage invitational browsing. Clearly virtual/digital libraries and other online resources have a considerable advantage in this regard—their materials are not limited to physicial, sequential location in information space.

**Future Research**

Once we are able to clearly and operationally describe various influences, dimensions, and patterns of browsing, and a way to discuss various situations that lead people to browse, several aspects of browsing warrant further research.

In the data set analyzed in part II, the evaluation and consequence of browsing were identified through the patron's response to the interviewer's questions: How successful were you with that activity? and Why do you feel that way about it? Chang's (2000) analysis of these browsing outcomes was summarized in chapter 14. Certainly, we could learn a lot more about the relationships among the browsing factors, processes, and outcomes.

Factors that appear to be influential in determining the extent or amount of browsing could also be analyzed. For example, three such factors suggested in the following examples are: (1) available time, (2) convenience (physical proximity), and (3) organization of information or display.

Example 1: Trying to find some items for recreational reading, a patron said, when she found one book she liked in each of two areas of interest, "I'm in a real hurry and the book I picked will probably suit my needs." "There was one book I liked. There were many books, some others have more interest to me and I don't have the time right now, this is a hurry visit." (W059)

Example 2: "I kind of looked through the ones I had listed first.... Then, while I was there, I just looked at all the rest." (L062)

Example 3: The patron started browsing at the shelf by discovering that its arrangement brought togetherin one place items that were similar to what he intended to find: "Ya, when I got there ... Well, I wrote down the call numbers and it seemed like a lot more were under the same number TL. I think, that was 570 or something. So, when I got there, all the titles looked good or looked like they might have something. So I pulled them out and looked in the table of contents. And some of them looked good, and some of them didn't. So I kept the good ones, and put the other ones back." (L062#2) Similarly, observed moving from stack 27 to stack 30 and scanning the book spines along the shelves, a patron stated, "Yeah, because I didn't find the book I was looking for, so I was just looking for other books, because it was the same material." (L004 #6)

Future research may also test the browsing framework in alternative settings. Interesting examples include shopping malls, tourist areas in large cities, and complex exploratory video games. The library and the shopping mall are suitable laboratories for both theoretical and practical reasons. For one, cultural assumptions about these two contexts are very different. A shopping mall is assumed to be more recreation-oriented, whereas the library is seen as more information-oriented. One may argue that the difference is a matter of a degree: one can go to the library for a recreational purpose and to the shopping mall for product information, but it is the difference in emphasis that matters. Second, the differing orientation of the two environments is also reflected in the literature reviewed. A good example is teleshopping. It was originally advertised as a time-saving, convenience-support, and task-oriented device. However, an empirical study of 500 teleshoppers found that most teleshoppers are recreational users: they teleshop for fun rather than for the sake of convenience or saving time (Shim and Mahoney 1991). Further, shopping malls may be good research sites to compare to the more traditional sites such as libraries because they vary in various theoretical dimensions identified in the literature, such as object sought (real-object/commodity versus representation/information), display (one is purposefully designed to attract people to browse while the other is less so), browser's motivation (one may be more intrinsic or recreation-oriented, the other may be more extrinsic or task-oriented), or implicit knowledge (the system of shopping mall behavior is commonly known to browsers, whereas libraries may be difficult to use because of the classification scheme and physical arrangement), and so on. The two environments represent distinct contexts and situations in which people engage in browsing behavior. Practically, the shopping mall is a common and important context of concern to many other disciplines, including business, marketing, and sociology. Therefore, additional sites such as shopping malls could be chosen for further testing the utility and generalizability of this framework.

## Conclusion

In the end, we return to the main assumptions and themes of this book. The information-seeking process is much broader and interdependent than much traditional research, especially in some literatures, have treated it. Crucial to understanding this process is identifying and analyzing the roles that access plays, especially in limiting participation by non-elites in all aspects of information provision and service. Access is a multidimensional concept with a wide variety of influences, aspects, and consequences. Browsing, too, is a much more extensive component of information seeking than is usually presented. Browsing is also a multidimensional and subtle concept, involving a wide variety of factors and outcomes. Furthermore, we expand the typical conceptualization of access and browsing to involve communication as well as information, which are inseparable. Perhaps the most general conclusion, however, is that accessing and browsing information and communication are fundamental and pervasive human and social activities, central to survival, learning, understanding, creating, enjoying, and interacting.

# References


Adams, W. C. 1986. Whose lives count? TV coverage of natural disasters. *Journal of Communication* 36: 123–133.

Agada, J. 1999. Inner-city gatekeepers: An exploratory survey of their information use environment. *Journal of the American Society for Information Science* 50 (1): 74–85.

Agosti, M., G. Gradenigo, and P. G. Marchetti. 1992. A hypertext environment for interacting with large textual databases. *Information Processing and Management* 28 (3): 371–387.

Aguilar, F. J. 1967. *Scanning the business environment*. New York: Macmillan.

Aigrain, P., and V. Longueville. 1992. Evaluation of navigational links between images. *Information Processing and Management* 28 (4): 517–528.

Akeroyd, J. 1990. Information seeking in online catalogs. *Journal of Documentation* 46: 33–52.

Albrecht, T. L., and M. B. Adelman. 1987. Communicating social support: A theoretical perspective. In *Communicating social support*, ed. T. L. Albrecht and M. B. Adelman, 18–39. Newbury Park, Calif.: Sage.

Allen, B. L. 1996. *Information tasks: Toward a user-centered approach to information systems*. San Diego: Academic Press.

Allen, K. B. 1988. Viewpoint: The right to access information in an information age. *Information Management Review* 3 (3): 57–64.

Allen, T. J. 1969. Information needs and uses. *Annual Review of Information Science and Technology* 4: 3–31.

Allinson, L., and N. Hammond. 1989. A learning support environment: The hitchhiker's guide. In *Hypertext: Theory into practice*, ed. R. McAleese, 62–74. Norwood, N.J.: Ablex.

American Library Association. Commission on Freedom and Equality of Access to Information. 1986. *Freedom and equality of access to information: A report to the American Library Association*. Chicago: American Library Association.

Antonoff, M. 1989. The PRODIGY promise. *Personal Computing* 13 (5): 66–78.

Apted, S. M. 1971. General purposive browsing. *Library Association Record* 73 (12): 228–230.

Archea, J. 1977. The place of architectural factors in behavioral theories of privacy. *Journal of Social Issues* 33: 116–137.

Armenikas, A., S. C. Harris, and K. W. Mossholder. 1993. Creating readiness for organizational change. *Human Relations* 46: 681–703.

Arrington, C. 1992. The zapper! All about the remote control. *TV Guide*, August 15, 8–13.

Arrow, K. J. 1962. Economic welfare and the allocation of resources for invention. In *The rate and direction of inventive activity: Economic and social factors*. Princeton, N.J.: Universities-National Bureau for Economic Research Conference.

———. 1979. The economics of information. In *The computer age: A twenty year view*, ed. M. L. Dertouzos and J. Moses, 306–317. Cambridge, Mass.: MIT Press.

Arthur, P., and R. Passini. 1992. *Wayfinding: People, signs and architecture*. New York: McGraw Hill.

Ashford, S. I., and A. Tsui. 1991. Self-regulation for managerial effectiveness: The role of active feedback seeking. *Academy of Management Journal* 34: 251–280.

Atwood, R., and B. Dervin. 1982. Challenges to sociocultural predictors of information seeking: A test of race vs. situation movement state. In *Communication Yearbook 5*, ed. M. Burgoon, 549–570. New Brunswick, N.J.: Transaction.

Auster, E., and C. W. Choo. 1991. Environmental scanning: A conceptual framework for studying the information-seeking behavior of executives. *Proceedings of the Annual Meeting of the American Society for Information Science* 28: 3–8.

Auster, E., and S. B. Lawton. 1984. Search interview techniques and information gain as antecedents of user satisfaction with online bibliographic retrieval. *Journal of the American Society for Information Science* 35: 90–103.

Ayris, P. 1986. The stimulation of creativity: A review of the literature concerning the concept of browsing, 1970–1985. Working Paper No. 5. Sheffield, U.K.: Center for Research on User Studies (CRUS), University of Sheffield.

Babbie, E. 1986. *The practice of social research*. 4th ed. Belmont, Calif.: Wadsworth.

Bagdikian, B. H. 1990. *The media monopoly*. 3d ed. Boston: Beacon Press.

Bailey, C. W., Jr. 1990. Intelligent multimedia computer systems: Emerging information resources in the network environment. *Library Hi Tech* 8 (1): 29–41.

Baker, S. L. 1986a. The display phenomenon: An exploration into factors causing the increased circulation of displayed books. *Library Quarterly* 56 (3): 237–257.

———. 1986b. Overload, browsers, and selections. *Library and Information Science Research* 8 (4): 315–329.

———. 1988. Will fiction classification schemes increase use? *RQ* 27 (3): 366–376.

Bamford, H. E., and C. N. Brownstein. 1986. National Science Foundation support for computer and information science and engineering. *Information Processing and Management* 22 (6): 449–452.

Bankapur, M. B. 1988. On browsing. *Library Science with a Slant to Documentation* 25 (3): 131–137.

Baroudi, J. J., M. H. Olson, and B. Ives. 1986. An empirical study of the impact of user involvement on system usage and information satisfaction. *Communications of the ACM* 29: 232–238.

Bates, B. J. 1988. Information as an economic good: Sources of individual and social value. In *The political economy of information*, ed. V. Mosco and J. Wasco, 76–94. Madison: University of Wisconsin Press.

———. 1993. The macro social impact of communication systems: Access, bias, control. Paper presented at the International Communication Association Annual Conference, May, Washington, D.C.

Bates, M. J. 1986a. An exploratory paradigm for online information retrieval. In *Intelligent information systems for the information society*, ed. B. C. Brookes, 91–99. New York: Elsevier.

———. 1986b. Subject access in online catalogs: A design model. *Journal of the American Society for Information Science* 37 (6): 357–376.

———. 1986c. What is a reference book? A theoretical and empirical analysis. *RQ* (fall): 37–57.

———. 1989. The design of browsing and berrypicking techniques for the online search interface. *Online Review* 13 (5): 407–424.

———. 1990. Where should the person stop and the information search interface start? *Information Processing and Management* 26 (5): 575–591.

Batley, S. 1989. Visual information retrieval: Browsing strategies in pictorial databases. Ph.D. diss., University of Aberdeen, 1988. Dissertation Abstracts International.

Bawden, D. 1986. Information systems and the stimulation of creativity. *Journal of Information Science* 12: 203–216.

Beauvoir, S. de. 1989. *The second sex*. Trans. H. M. Parshley. New York: Vintage Books. (Original work published 1949)

Beheshti, J. 1992. Browsing through public library catalogs. *Information Technology and Libraries* 11 (3): 220–228.

Behr, R. L., and S. Iyengar. 1984. Television news, real-world cues, and changes in the public agenda. *Public Opinion Quarterly* 49: 38–57.

Belenky, M. F., B. Clinchy, N. R. Goldberger, and J. M. Tarule. 1986. *Women's ways of knowing: The development of self, voice, and mind*. New York: Basic Books.

Belkin, N. J. 1978. Information concepts for information science. *Journal of Documentation* 34 (1): 55–85.

———. 1980. Anomalous states of knowledge as a basis for information retrieval. *Canadian Journal of Information Science* 5: 133–143.

———. 1981. Ineffable concepts in information retrieval. In *Information retrieval experiment*, ed. K. Sparck Jones, 44–58. London: Butterworths.

Belkin, N. J., C. L. Borgman, H. M. Brooks, T. Bylander, W. B. Croft, P. Daniels, S. Deerwester, E. A. Fox, P. Ingwersen, R. Rada, K. Sparck Jones, R. Thompson, and D. Walker. 1987. Distributed expert-based information systems: An interdisciplinary approach. *Information Processing and Management* 23: 395–409.

Belkin, N. J., S.-J. Chang, T. Downs, T. Saracevic, and S. Zhao. 1990. Taking account of user tasks, goals and behavior for the design of online public access catalogs. *Proceedings of the Annual Meeting of the American Society for Information Science* 27: 69–79.

Belkin, N. J., C. Cool, A. Stein, and U. Thiel. 1995. Cases, scripts, and information-seeking strategies: On the design of interactive information retrieval systems. *Expert Systems with Applications* 9 (3): 379–396.

Belkin, N. J., P. G. Marchetti, and C. Cool. 1993. BRAQUE: Design of an interface to support user interaction in information retrieval. *Information Processing and Management* 29 (3): 325–344.

Belkin, N. J., R. N. Oddy, and H. M. Brooks. 1982a. ASK for information retrieval. Part I. Background and theory. *Journal of Documentation* 38 (2): 61–71.

———. 1982b. ASK for information retrieval. Part II. Results of a design study. *Journal of Documentation* 38 (3): 145–164.

Belkin, N. J., and S. E. Robertson. 1976. Information science and the phenomenon of information. *Journal of the American Society for Information Science* 27: 197–204.

Belkin, N. J., and T. Saracevic. 1991. Design principles for third-generation online public access catalogs: Taking account of users and library use. In *Annual review of OCLC research: July 1991–June 1992*, ed. E. Jul and K. Sproat, 43–45. Dublin, Ohio: Online Center for Library Computing.

Belkin, N. J., and A. Vickery. 1985. *Interaction in information systems: A review of research from document retrieval to knowledge-based systems*. London: The British Library.

Bell, D. 1973. *The coming of post-industrial society: A venture in social forecasting*. New York: Basic Books.

Bell, W. J. 1991. *Searching behaviour: The behavioural ecology of finding resources*. London: Chapman and Hall.

Bellin, D. 1993. The economic value of information. *Knowledge: Creation, Diffusion, Utilization* 15: 233–240.

Beniger, J. R. 1986. *The control revolution: Technological and economic origins of the information society*. Cambridge, Mass.: Harvard University Press.

Bentham, J. 1969. *A Bentham Reader*. New York: Pegasus.

Berger, C. R. 1979. Beyond initial interactions: Uncertainty, understanding, and the development of interpersonal relationships. In *Language and social psychology*, ed. H. Giles and B. S. Clair. Oxford, U.K.: Basil Blackwell.

Berger, P. L., and T. Luckmann. 1966. *The social construction of reality: A treatise in the sociology of knowledge*. New York: Doubleday.

Berlo, D. K. 1960. *The process of communication: An introduction to theory and practice*. New York: Holt, Rinehart, and Winston.

Blair, D. C., and M. E. Maron. 1985. An evaluation of retrieval effectiveness for a full-text document-retrieval system. *Communications of the ACM* 28: 289–299.

Blau, P. M. 1954. Patterns of interaction among a group of officials in a government agency. *Human Relations* 7: 337–348.

Bloch, P. H., and M. L. Richins. 1983. Shopping without purchase: An investigation of consumer browsing behavior. *Advances in Consumer Research* 10: 543–548.

Bloch, P. H., N. M. Ridgway, and D. L. Sherrell. 1989. Extending the concept of shopping: An investigation of browsing activity. *Journal of the Academy of Marketing Science* 17 (1): 13–21.

Blumler, J. G., and E. Katz, eds. 1974. *The uses of mass communications: Current perspectives on gratifications research.* Beverly Hills, Calif.: Sage.

Bodker, S. 1989. A human activity approach to user interfaces. *Human-Computer Interaction* 4: 171–195.

Boisot, M. 1998. *Knowledge assets: Securing competitive advantage in the information economy.* Oxford, U.K.: Oxford University Press.

Boll, J. J. 1985. Shelf browsing, open access and storage capacity in research libraries. Occasional Paper No. 169. ERIC Document Reproduction Service ED 260–721.

Borgman, C. L. 1986a. Human-computer interaction with information retrieval systems: Understanding complex communication behavior. In *Progress in communication sciences*, ed. B. Dervin and M. J. Voigt. Vol. 7, 91–122. Norwood, N.J.: Ablex.

———. 1986b. Why are online catalogs so hard to use? Lessons learned from information-retrieval studies. *Journal of the American Society for Information Science* 37: 380–400.

———. 1989. All users of information retrieval systems are not created equal: An exploration into individual differences. *Information Processing and Management* 25: 237–251.

———. 2000. *From Gutenberg to the global information infrastructure: Access to information in the networked world.* Cambridge, Mass.: MIT Press.

Borgman, C. L., A. L. Gallagher, S. G. Hirsh, and V. A. Walter. 1995. Children's searching behavior on browsing and keyword online catalogs: The science library catalog project. *Journal of the American Society for Information Science* 46 (9): 663–684.

Borgman, C. L., D. Moghdam, and P. Corbett. 1984. *Effective online searching: A basic text.* New York: Marcel Dekker.

Borgman, C. L., and R. E. Rice. 1982. Computer-monitored communication data: Prospects and problems for communication research. *Proceedings of the Annual Meeting of the American Society for Information Science* 19: 37–40.

Borgman C. L., V. A. Walter, and J. Rosenberg. 1991. The science library catalog project: Comparison of children's searching behavior in hypertext and a keywork search system. *Proceedings of the Annual Meeting of the American Society for Information Science* 28: 162–169.

Borko, H. 1968. Information science: What is it? *American Documentation* 19: 3–5.

Botan, C., and M. McCreadie. 1993. Communication, information, and surveillance: Separation and control in organizations. In *Information and behavior.* Vol. 4: *Between communication and information*, ed. J. R. Schement and B. D. Ruben, 385–397. New Brunswick, N.J.: Transaction.

Boulding, K. E. 1961. *The image: Knowledge in life and society.* Ann Arbor: University of Michigan Press.

Bourque, S. C., and K. B. Warren. 1987. Technology, gender, and development. *Daedalus* 116 (4): 173–198.

Bradach, I. L., and R. C. Eccles. 1989. Price, authority, and trust: From ideal types to plural forms. *Annual Review of Sociology* 15: 97–118.

Braman, S. 1989. Information and socioeconomic class in U. S. constitutional law. *Journal of Communication* 39 (3): 163–179.

Braverman, H. 1974. *Labor and monopoly capital: The degradation of work in the twentieth century.* New York: Monthly Review Press.

Breivik, P. S., and E. G. Gee. 1989. *Information literacy: Revolution in the library.* New York: Macmillan.

Brown, J. S. 1986. From cognitive to social ergonomics and beyond. In *User-centered system design: New perspectives on human-computer interaction*, ed. D. A. Norman and S. W. Draper, 457–486. Hillsdale, N.J.: Erlbaum.

Brown, J. S., A. Collins, and P. Duguid. 1989. *Situated cognition and the culture of learning.* Technical Report No. 481. Urbana: Center for the Study of Reading, University of Illinois.

Buckland, M. K. 1990. Information retrieval and the knowledgeable society. *Proceedings of the Annual Meeting of the American Society for Information Science* 27: 239–244.

———. 1991a. Information as thing. *Journal of the American Society for Information Science* 42 (5): 351–360.

———. 1991b. *Information and information systems.* Westport, Conn.: Greenwood Press.

Buckley, P., and J. Long. 1990. Using videotex for shopping—a qualitative analysis. *Behaviour and Information Technology* 9 (1): 47–61.

Budd, R. W. 1974. Human communication: A framework for the behavioral sciences. Paper presented at a meeting of the American Society for Information Science, Washington, D.C.

———. 1987. Limiting access to information: A view from the leeward side. *The Information Society* 5: 41–44.

Budd, R. W., R. K. Thorp, and L. Donohew. 1967. *Content analysis of communications.* New York: Macmillan.

Burkert, H. 1997. Privacy-enhancing tehcnologies: Typology, critique, vision. In *Technology and privacy: The new landscape*, ed. P. Agre and M. Rotenberg, 125–142. Cambridge, Mass.: MIT Press.

Canter, D., R. Rivers, and G. Storrs. 1985. Characterizing user navigation through complex data structures. *Behaviour and Information Technology* 4 (2): 93–102.

Caplinger, M. 1986. Graphic database browsing. *ACM SIGOIS Bulletin* 7: 113–119.

Card, S. K., T. P. Moran, and A. Newell. 1983. The human information-processor. Chap. 2 in *The psychology of human-computer interaction*, 23–97. Hillsdale, N.J.: Erlbaum.

Carlson, J., and R. Zmud. 1999. Channel expansion theory and the experiential nature of media richness perceptions. *Academy of Management Journal* 42 (2): 153–170.

Carmel, E., S. Crawford, and H. Chen. 1992. Browsing in hypertext: A cognitive study. *IEEE Transactions on Systems, Man and Cybernetics* 22 (5): 865–883.

Carr, D. 1991. Minds in museums and libraries: The cognitive management of cultural institutions. *Teachers College Record* 93 (1): 6–27.

Case, D. 2001. *Finding information.* New York: Academic Press.

Celoria, F. 1968. The archaeology of serendip. *Library Association Record* (Oct.): 251–253.

Chang, S.-J. 1993. Relating information needs to information uses in specific contexts: What's in the literature and what's missing. Occasional Paper No. 2. Rutgers University, School of Communication, Information and Library Studies, New Brunswick, NJ 08903.

———. 1995. Toward a multidimensional framework for understanding browsing. Ph.D. diss., Rutgers University, School of Communication, Information and Library Studies, New Brunswick, NJ 08903.

———. 2000. Research on browsing behavior in the libraries: An empirical analysis of consequences, success and influences. *Journal of Library and Information Studies, National Taiwan University* (Fall), in press.

Chang, S.-J., and R. E. Rice. 1993. Browsing: A multidimensional framework. *Annual Review of Information Science and Technology* 28: 231–276.

Chatman, E. A. 1987. The information world of low-skilled workers. *Library and Information Science Research* 9: 265–283.

———. 1991. Life in a small world: Applicability of gratification theory to information-seeking behavior. *Journal of the American Society for Information Science* 42 (6): 438–449.

Chen, C., and P. Hernon. 1982. *Information seeking: Assessing and anticipating user needs.* New York: Neal-Schuman.

Cherry, C. 1985. *The age of access: Information technology and social revolution. Posthumous papers of Colin Cherry*, ed. W. Edmondson. London: Croom Helm.

Chiang, W. S., and N. E. Elkington, eds. 1993. *Electronic access to information: A new service paradigm. Proceedings of a symposium held July 23–24.* Mountain View, Calif.: Research Libraries Group.

Choo, C. W. 1995. *Information management for the intelligent organization: The art of scanning the environment.* Medford, N.J.: Information Today.

———. 1996. Towards an information model of organizations. In *Managing information for the competitive edge*, ed. E. Auster and C. Choo, 7–40. New York: Neal-Schuman.

———. 1998. *The knowing organization: How organizations use information to construct meaning, create knowledge, and make decisions.* New York: Oxford University Press.

Choo, C. W., and E. Auster. 1993. Environment scanning: Conceptual and empirical perspectives. *Annual Review of Information Science and Technology* 28: 279–314.

Christensen, E., and J. Bailey. 1997. A source accessibility effect on media selection. *Management Communication Quarterly* 10 (3): 373–387.

Cleveland, H. 1985. The twilight of hierarchy: Speculations on the global information society. In *Foundations of organizational communication*, ed. S. H. Corman, S. P. Banks, C. H. Bantz, and M. E. Mayer, 370–374. White Plains, N.Y.: Longman.

Cleverdon, C. 1974. User evaluation of information retrieval systems. *Journal of Documentation* 30: 170–179.

Coates, J. F. 1986. *Issues management: How you can plan, organize and manage for the future.* Mt. Airy, Md.: Lomond Publications.

Compaine, B. M. 1985. Players and stakes in the media industry. In *Electronic publishing plus*, ed. M. Greenberger, 71–93. White Plains, N.Y.: Knowledge Industry.

Conklin, J. 1987. Hypertext: An introduction and survey. *IEEE Computer* 20 (9): 17–41.

Conklin, J., and M. L. Begeman. 1989. gIBIS: A tool for all reasons. *Journal of the American Society for Information Science* 40 (3): 200–213.

Cooper, W. S. 1973a. On selecting a measure of retrieval effectiveness. Part I. The "subjective" philosophy of evaluation. *Journal of the American Society for Information Science* 24: 87–100.

———. 1973b. On selecting a measure of retrieval effectiveness. Part II. Implementation of the philosophy. *Journal of the American Society for Information Science* 24: 413–424.

Corner, P., A. Kinicki, and B. Keats. 1994. Integrating organizational and individual information processing perspectives on choice. *Organization Science* 5 (3): 294–308.

Coser, L. A., C. Kadushin, and W. W. Powell. 1982. *Books: The culture and commerce of publishing*. New York: Basic Books.

Cove, J. F., and B. C. Walsh. 1987. Browsing as a means of online text retrieval. *Information Services and Use* 7 (6): 183–188.

———. 1988. Online text retrieval via browsing. *Information Processing and Management* 24 (1): 31–37.

Cramton, C. D. 1997. Information problems in dispersed teams. In *Academy of management best papers proceedings*, ed. L. Dozier and J. B. Keys, 298–302. Statesboro: Georgia Southern College.

Crane, D. 1969. Social structure in a group of scientists: A test of the "invisible college" hypothesis. *American Sociological Review* 34 (3): 10–27.

Croft, W. B., and R. H. Thompson. 1987. I3R: A new approach to the design of document retrieval systems. *Journal of the American Society for Information Science* 38: 389–404.

Cuff, R. N. 1980. On casual users. *International Journal of Man-Machine Studies* 12: 163–187.

Culnan, M. J. 1983. Environmental scanning: The effects of task complexity and source accessibility on information-gathering behavior. *Decision Sciences* 14 (2): 194–206.

———. 1984. The dimensions of accessibility to online information: Implications for implementing office information systems. *ACM Transactions on Office Information Systems* 2 (2): 141–150.

——— 1985. The dimensions of perceived accessibility to information: Implications for the delivery of information systems and services. *Journal of the American Society for Information Science* 36 (5): 302–308.

Culnan, M. J., and M. L. Markus. 1987. Information technologies. In *Handbook of organizational communication: An interdisciplinary perspective*, ed. F. M. Jablin, L. Putnam, K. H. Roberts, and L. W. Porter, 420–443. Beverly Hills, Calif.: Sage.

Cutting, D. R., D. R. Karger, J. O. Perdersen, and J. W. Tukey. 1992. Scatter/Gather: A cluster-based approach to browsing large document collections. In *Proceedings of the 15th annual international ACMSIGIR conference on research and development in information retrieval*, ed. N. Belkin, P. Ingwersen, and A. M. Pejtersen, 318–329. Cambridge, Mass.: Association for Computing Machinery.

Daft, R. L., and R. H. Lengel. 1986. Organizational information requirements, media richness and structural design. *Management Science* 32 (5): 554–571.

Daft, R. L. and K. Weick. 1984. Toward a model of organizations as interpretation systems. *Academy of Management Review* 9 (2): 284–295

Daniels, P. J. 1986. Progress in documentation: Cognitive models in information retrieval. An evaluation review. *Journal of Documentation* 42: 272–304.

Davenport, T., and L. Prusak. 1998. *Working knowledge: How organizations manage what they know*. Boston: Harvard Business School Press.

Davies, R. 1989. The creation of new knowledge by information retrieval and classification. *Journal of Documentation* 45 (4): 273–301.

Davis, T. B. 1984. The influence of the physical environment in offices. *Academy of Management Review* 9: 271–283.

Day, H. I. 1979. Why people play. *Loisir et Societé (Society and Leisure)* 2 (1): 129–147.

De Fleur, M. L. 1982. Toward an integrated model of mass media effects. In *Theories of mass communication*, 233–255. New York: Longman.

Deci, E., and R. Ryan. 1985. *Intrinsic motivation and self-determination in human behavior.* New York: Plenum Press.

Deetz, S. 1989a. Communication technology policy and interest representation: Habermas' theory of communicative action. Paper presented at a meeting of the International Communication Association, May 30, San Francisco.

———. 1989b. Representation of interests and communication technologies: Issues in democracy and policy. In *Introduction to Communication*, ed. S. Deetz, 128–145. 2d ed. Needham Heights, Mass.: Ginn. (Reprinted from S. Deetz, *Communication and the culture of technology*. Pullman: Washington State University Press, 1980.)

———. 1990. Suppressed conflict, consent, and inequitable interest representation. Paper presented at the annual meeting of the International Communication Association, June, Dublin, Ireland.

———. 1992. *Democracy in an age of corporate colonization: Developments in communication and the politics of everyday life.* Albany: State University of New York Press.

Dempsey, L., and R. Heery. 1998. Metadata: A current review of practice and issues. *Journal of Documentation* 54 (2): 145–172.

Dervin, B. 1976. The everyday information needs of the average citizen: A taxonomy for analysis. In *Information for the community*, ed. M. Kochen and J. C. Donohue, 19–38. Chicago: American Library Association.

———. 1980. Communication gaps and inequities: Moving toward a reconceptualization. In *Progress in Communication sciences*, ed. B. Dervin and M. J. Voigt. Vol. 2, 73–112. Norwood, N.J.: Ablex.

———. 1983. An overview of sense-making research: Concepts, methods, and results to date. Paper presented at the annual meeting of the International Communication Association, May, Dallas, Texas.

———. 1989. Users as research inventions: How research categories perpetuate inequities. *Journal of Communication* 39 (3): 216–232.

———. 1992. From the mind's eye of the user: The sense-making qualitative-quantitative methodology. In *Qualitative research in information management*, ed. J. D. Glazier and R. R. Powell, 61–84. Englewood, Calif.: Libraries Unlimited.

Dervin, B., and K. D. Clark. 1987. *ASQ: Alternative tools for information need and accountability assessments by libraries.* Belmont, Calif.: Peninsula Library System.

Dervin, B., and P. Dewdney. 1986. Neutral questioning: A new approach to the reference interview. *RQ* 25 (4): 506–513.

Dervin, B., and M. Nilan. 1986. Information needs and uses. *Annual Review of Information Science and Technology* 21: 3–33.

Dervin, B., and P. Shields. 1990. Users: The missing link in technology research. Paper presented at the Communication Technology Section Meeting, International Association for Mass Communication Research, August, Lake Bled, Yugoslavia.

Dewhirst, H. 1971. Influence of perceived information-sharing norms on communication channel utilization. *Academy of Management Journal* 14: 305–315.

Doctor, R. D. 1991. Information technologies and social equity: Confronting the revolution. *Journal of the American Society for Information Science* 42 (3): 216–228.

———. 1992. Social equity and information technologies: Moving toward information democracy. *Annual Review of Information Science and Technology* 27: 43–96.

Dordick, H. S. 1987. The emerging information societies. In *Competing visions, complex realities: Social aspects of the information society*, ed. J. R. Schement and L. A. Lievrouw, 13–22. Norwood, N.J.: Ablex.

———. 1989. Telecommunications in an information society. In *Human communication as a field of study: Selected contemporary views*, ed. S. S. King, 203–209. Albany: State University of New York Press.

Dorr, A. 1980. When I was a child I thought as a child. In *Television and social behavior*, ed. S. Withey and R. Abeles, 191–230. Hillsdale, N.J.: Erlbaum.

Dorr, A., and D. Kunkel. 1990. Children and the media environment: Change and constancy amid change. *Communication Research* 17 (1): 5–25.

Doty, P., A. P. Bishop, and C. R. McClure. 1991. Scientific norms and the use of electronic research networks. *Proceedings of the American Society for Information Science* 28: 24–38.

Downing, J.D.H. 1989. Computers for political change: PeaceNet and public data access. *Journal of Communication* 39 (3): 154–162.

Downs, R. M. 1979. Mazes, minds, and maps. In *Sign systems for libraries: Solving the wayfinding problem*, ed. D. Pollet and P. C. Haskell, 17–32. New York: Bowker.

Dozier, D. M., and R. E. Rice. 1984. Rival theories of electronic newsreading. In *The new media*, ed. R. E. Rice, 103–127. Newbury Park, Calif.: Sage.

Drabenstott, K. M., A. N. Demeyer, J. Gerckens, and D. T. Poe. 1990. Analysis of a bibliographic database enhanced with a library classification. *Library Resources and Technical Services* 34 (2): 179–198.

Dreier, P., and S. Weinberg. 1979. Interlocking directorates. *Columbia Journalism Review* (Nov.–Dec.): 51+.

Drucker, M. 1990. On track with eye-trac research. *Target Marketing* 13 (9): 57–58.

Drucker, S. J., and G. Gumpert. 1991. Public space and communication: The zoning of public interaction. *Communication Theory* 1 (4): 294–310.

Durrance, J. C. 1984. *Armed for action: Library response to citizen information needs.* New York: Neal-Schuman.

———. 1989. Information needs: Old song, new tune. In *Rethinking of the library in the information age.* Vol. 2: *Issues in library research: Proposals for the 1990s*, 159–177. Washington, D.C.: U.S. Government Printing Office.

Egan, D. E., J. Remde, and L. Gomez. 1989. Formative design-evaluation of superbook. *ACM Transactions on Information Systems* 7 (1): 30–57.

Egan, D. E., M. E. Lesk, R. D. Ketchum, J. R. Lochbaum, M. Littman, and T. K. Landauer. 1991. Hypertext for the electronic library? CORE sample results. In *Hypertext '91 Proceedings*, 1–14.

Eisenberg, E. M. 1984. Ambiguity as strategy in organizational communication. *Communication Monographs* 51: 227–242.

Eisenhardt, K. M. 1989. Building theories from case study research. *Academy of Management Review* 14 (4): 532–550.

Ellis, D. 1989. A behavioural approach to information retrieval system design. *Journal of Documentation* 45 (3): 171–212.

Erdelez, S. 1996. Information encountering on the Internet. In *Proceedings of the 17th national online meeting*, 101–107.

Ettema J., and G. Kline. 1977. Deficits, differences and ceilings: Contingent conditions for understanding the knowledge gap. *Communication Research* 4: 179–202.

Evans, P. 1990. Browsing as an information seeking technique. Unpublished manuscript.

Feldman, M. S., and J. C. March. 1981. Information in organizations as signal and symbol. *Administrative Science Quarterly* 26: 171–186.

Fenn, P. S., and P. K. Buckley. 1990. Ordering goods with videotex: Or just fill in the details. *Behaviour and Information Technology* 9 (1): 63–80.

Fine, S. 1984. Research and the psychology of information use. *Library Trends* (spring): 441–460.

Fish, R. S., R. E. Kraut, R. W. Root, and R. E. Rice. 1993. Video as a technology for informal communication. *Communications of the ACM* 36 (1): 48–61.

Fortner, R. S. 1995. Excommunication in the information society. *Critical Studies in Mass Communication* 12: 133–154.

Foskett, D. J. 1983. *Pathways for communication*. London: Bingley.

Foss, C. L. 1989. Tools for reading and browsing hypertext. *Information Processing and Management* 25 (4): 407–418.

Foucault, M. 1977. *Discipline and punish: The birth of the prison*. Trans. A. Sheridan. New York: Vintage. (Original work published 1975)

Fox, C. J. 1983. *Information and misinformation: An investigation of the notions of information and misinformation, informing and misinforming*. Westport, Conn.: Greenwood Press.

Fox, M. S., and A. J. Palay. 1979. The BROWSE system: An introduction. *Proceedings of the Annual Meeting of the American Society for Information Science* 16: 183–193.

Freire, P. 1969. *Pedagogy of the oppressed*. New York: Continuum.

Frenkel, K. A. 1989. The next generation of interactive technologies. *Communications of the ACM* 32: 872–881.

Friedberg, A. 1991. Les Flaneurs du Mal(l): Cinema and the postmodern condition. *PMLA: Publications of the Modern Language Association of America* 106 (3): 419–431.

Froehlich, T. J. 1992. Ethical considerations of information professionals. *Annual Review of Information Science and Technology* 27: 291–324.

Fulk, J., C. W. Steinfield, J. Schmitz, and J. G. Power. 1987. A social information-processing model of media use in organizations. *Communication Research* 14: 529–552.

Furlong, M. S. 1989. An electronic community for older adults: The SeniorNet network. *Journal of Communication* 39 (3): 145–153.

Galbraith, J. R. 1973. *Designing complex organizations.* Reading, Mass.: Addison-Wesley.

———. 1974. Organizational design: An information processing view. *Interfaces* 4: 28–36.

Galvin, T. J. 1991. From document delivery to information access: Convergence at the national level. In *Access service: The convergence of reference and technical services*, ed. G. M. McCombs, 131–140. New York: Haworth.

Gandy, O. H., Jr. 1988. The political economy of communications competence. In *The political economy of information*, ed. V. Mosco and J. Wasco, 108–124. Madison: University of Wisconsin Press.

———. 1989. The surveillance society: Information technology and bureaucratic social control. *Journal of Communication* 39 (3): 61–76.

———. 1993. *The panoptic sort: A political economy of personal information.* Boulder, Colo.: Westview.

Gardner, H. 1983. *Frames of mind: The theory of multiple intelligences.* New York: Basic Books

Garson, B. 1988. *The electronic sweatshop: How computers are transforming the office of the future into the factory of the past.* New York: Simon and Schuster.

Gecsei, J., and D. Martin. 1989. Browsing access to visual information. *Optical Information Systems* 9 (5): 237–241.

Geertz, C. 1973. Deep play: Notes on the Balinese cockfight. In *The interpretation of cultures*, 413–453. New York: Basic Books.

Genova, B., and B. Greenberg. 1979. Interests in news and the knowledge gap. *Public Opinion Quarterly* 43: 79–91.

Gerstberger, P. G., and T. J. Allen. 1968. Criteria used by research and development engineers in the selection of an information source. *Journal of Applied Psychology* 52 (4): 272–279.

Gillespie, A., and K. Robins. 1989. Geographical inequalities: The spatial bias of the new communications technologies. *Journal of Communication* 39 (3): 7–19.

Gilligan, C. 1982. *In a different voice: Psychological theory and women's development.* Cambridge, Mass.: Harvard University Press.

Gitlin, T. 1980. Media routines and political crises. In *The whole world is watching*, 249–282. Berkeley: University of California Press.

Glauser, M. J. 1984. Upward information flow in organizations: Review and conceptual analysis. *Human Relations* 37: 613–643.

Grande, S. 1980. Aspects of pre-literature culture shared by on-line searching and videotex aspects. *Canadian Journal of Information Science* 5: 125–131.

Granovetter, M. S. 1973. The strength of weak ties. *American Journal of Sociology* 78: 1360–1380.

———. 1983. The strength of weak ties: A network theory revisited. *Sociological Theory* 1: 201–233.

Greenberg, B. S., and C. Heeter. 1987. VCRs and young people: The picture at 39% penetration. *American Behavioral Scientist* 30: 509–521.

Greenberger, M., and J. C. Puffer. 1989. Telemedecine: Toward better health care for the elderly. *Journal of Communication* 39 (3): 137–144.

Greene, R. J. 1977. The effectiveness of browsing. *College and Research Libraries* 38 (4): 313–316.

Grover, V., and R. Sabherwal. 1989. Poor performance of videotex systems. *Journal of Systems Management* 40 (6): 31–37.

Haeckel, S., and R. Nolan. 1993. Managing by wire. *Harvard Business Review* 71 (5): 122–133.

Hall, K. 1981. The economic nature of information. *The Information Society* 1 (2): 143–166.

Hall, S. 1982. The rediscovery of "ideology": Return of the repressed in media studies. In *Culture, society and the media*, ed. M. Gurevitch, T. Bennett, J. Curran, and J. Woollacott, 56–90. London: Routledge.

———. 1989. Ideology and communication theory. In *Rethinking communication.* Vol. 1: *Paradigm issues*, ed. B. Dervin, L. Grossberg, B. J. O'Keefe, and E. Wartella, 40–52. Newbury Park, Calif.: Sage.

Hammond, N., and L. Allinson. 1988. Development and evaluation of a CAL system for non-formal domains: The hitchhiker's guide to cognition. *Computing Education* 12: 215–220.

Hancock-Beaulieu, M. 1989. Subject searching behavior at the library catalogue and at the shelves: Evaluating the impact of an online public access catalogue. Ph.D. diss., City University, London.

———. 1990. Evaluating the impact of an online library catalogue in subject searching behavior at the catalogue and at the shelves. *Journal of Documentation* 46 (4): 318–338.

Hannabuss, S. 1989. Dialogue and the search for information. *ASLIB Proceedings* 41 (3): 85–98.

Harbison, R. 1988. *Eccentric spaces.* Boston: Godine.

Harding, S. 1987. Introduction: Is there a feminist method? In *Feminism and Methodology*, ed. S. Harding, 1–14. Bloomington: Indiana University Press.

———. 1991. *Whose science? Whose knowledge? Thinking from women's lives.* Ithaca, N.Y.: Cornell University Press.

Hardy, A. P. 1982. The selection of channels when seeking information: Cost/benefit vs. least-effort. *Information Processing and Management* 18 (6): 289–293.

Harris, R., and P. Dewdney. 1994. *Barriers to information: How formal help systems fail battered women.* Westport, Conn.: Greenwood Press.

Hart, P. J., and R. E. Rice. 1991. Using information from external databases: Contextual relationships of use, access method, task, database type, organizational differences, and outcomes. *Information Processing and Management* 27 (5): 461–479.

Harter, S. P. 1992. Psychological relevance and information science. *Journal of the American Society for Information Science* 43 (9): 602–615.

Hayes, R. M. 1993. Measurement of information and communication: A set of definitions. In *Information and behavior*. Vol. 4: *Between communication and information*, ed. J. R. Schement and B. D. Ruben, 2–33. New Brunswick, N.J.: Transaction.

Hayles, N. K. 1999. *How we became posthuman: Virtual bodies in cybernetics, literature, and informatics*. Chicago: University of Chicago Press.

Haythornthwaite, C., and B. Wellman. 1998. Work, friendship and media use for information exchange in a networked organization. *Journal of the American Society for Information Science* 49 (12): 1101–1114.

Hearn, G. 1989. Active and passive conceptions of the television audience: effects of a change in viewing routine. *Human Relations* 42 (10): 857–875.

Heeter, C., and B. S. Greenberg. 1985. Profiling the zappers. *Journal of Advertising Research* 25 (2): 15–19.

———. 1988. *Cable-viewing*. Norwood, N.J.: Ablex.

Herman, E. S., and N. Chomsky. 1988. *Manufacturing consent: The political economy of the mass media*. New York: Pantheon.

Herner, S. 1970. Browsing. In *Encyclopedia of Library and Information Science*. Vol. 3, 408–415. New York: Marcel Dekker.

Hewins, E. T. 1990. Information need and use studies. *Annual Review of Information Science and Technology* 25: 145–172.

Hickson, D. 1987. Decision-making at the top of organizations. *Annual Review of Sociology* 13: 165–192.

Hildreth, C. R. 1982a. Online browsing support capabilities. *Proceedings of the Annual Meeting of the American Society for Information Science* 19: 127–132.

———. 1982b. The concept and mechanics of browsing in an online library catalog. In *Proceedings of the 3d national online meeting*, 181–196.

———. 1987a. *Online library catalogs as information retrieval systems: What can we learn from research?* London: Read.

———. 1987b. Beyond Boolean: Designing the next generation of online catalogs. *Library Trends* 35 (4): 647–667.

Hildreth, C. R., ed. 1989. *The online catalogue: Development and directions*. London: Library Association.

Hill, D. B. 1984. Viewer characteristics and agenda setting by television news. *Public Opinion Quarterly* 49: 340–350.

Hiltz, S. R. 1986. The "virtual classroom": Using computer-mediated communication for university teaching. *Journal of Communication* 36 (2): 95–104.

Hiltz, S. R., and K. Johnson. 1989. Measuring acceptance of computer-mediated communication systems. *Journal of the American Society for Information Science* 40 (6): 386–397.

Hiltz, S. R., and M. Turoff. 1985. Structuring computer-mediated communication systems to avoid information overload. *Communications of the ACM* 28 (7): 680–689.

Hirscheim, R., and H. K. Klein. 1989. Four paradigms of information system development. *Communications of the ACM* 32: 1199–1216.

Hochschild, A. R. 1983. *The managed heart: Commercialization of human feeling*. Berkeley: University of California Press.

Howard, D. L. 1991. What the eye sees while predicting a document's pertinence from its citation. In *Proceedings of the American Society for Information Technology*, 87–97.

Hudson, H. E. 1988. Ending the tyranny of distance: The impact of new communications technologies in rural North America. In *Competing visions, complex realities: Social aspects of the information society*, ed. J. R. Schement and L. A. Lievrouw, 91–104. Norwood, N.J.: Ablex.

Huestis, J. C. 1988. Clustering LC classification numbers in an online catalog for improved browsability. *Information Technology and Libraries* 7: 381–393.

Hulley, A. J. 1990. Navigation, browsing and understanding in an anatomical "hypermedia" environment. *Current Psychology: Research & Reviews* 9 (2): 162–180.

Hyman, R. J. 1971. Access to library collections: summary of a documentary and opinion survey on the direct shelf approach and browsing. *Library Resources and Technical Services*, 15 (4): 479–491.

———. 1972. *Access to library collections: An inquiry into the validity of the direct shelf approach, with special reference to browsing*. Metuchen, N.J.: Scarecrow Press.

Innis, H. A. 1951. *The bias of communication*. Toronto: University of Toronto Press.

Intner, S. S. 1991. Education for the dual role responsibilities of an access services librarian. In *Access services: The convergence of reference and technical services*, ed. G. M. McCombs, 107–126. New York: Haworth.

Iselin, E. 1989. The impact of information diversity on information overload effects in unstructured managerial decision making. *Journal of Information Science* 15: 163–173.

Jablin, F. M. 1985. Task/work relationships: A life-span perspective. In *Handbook of interpersonal communication*, ed. C. Miller and M. L. Knapp, 615–654. Beverly Hills, Calif.: Sage.

Janes, J. W. 1989. The application of search theory to information science. *Proceedings of the Annual Meeting of the American Society for Information Science* 26: 9–12.

Janis, I. L. 1971. Groupthink. *Psychology Today* (November): 43–76.

Jansen, S. C. 1989. Gender and the Information Society: A socially structured silence. *Journal of Communication* 39 (3): 196–215.

Jarboe, G. R., and C. D. McDaniel. 1987. A profile of browsers in regional shopping malls. *Journal of the Academy of Marketing Science* 15 (spring): 45–52.

Jeon, J.-O. 1990. An empirical investigation of the relationship between affective states, in-store browsing and impulse buying. Ph.D. diss., Department of Management and Marketing, University of Alabama. Dissertation Abstracts International.

Johnson, B. M., and R. E. Rice. 1983. Redesigning word processing for productivity. *Proceedings of the American Society for Information Science* 20: 187–190.

———. 1987. *Managing organizational innovation: The evolution from word processing to office information systems*. New York: Columbia University Press.

Johnson, J. D. 1987. A model of international communication media appraisal: Phase IV, generalizing the model to film. *International Journal of Intercultural Relations* 11: 129–142.

———. 1996. *Information seeking: An organizational dilemma.* Wesport, Conn.: Quorum Books.

Johnson, J. D., W. A. Donohue, C. K. Atkin, and S. H. Johnson. 1995. A comprehensive model of information seeking: Tests focusing on a technical organization. *Science Communication* 16: 274–303.

Johnson, J. D., and H. Meischke. 1993. A comprehensive model of cancer-related information seeking applied to magazines. *Human Communication Research* 19: 343–367.

Joseph, B., E. R. Steinberg, and A. R. Jones. 1989. User perceptions and expectations of an information retrieval system. *Behaviour and Information Technology* 8 (2): 77–88.

Julien, H. 1999. Barriers to adolescents' information seeking for career decision making. *Journal of the American Society for Information Science* 50 (1): 38–48.

Kanter, R. M. 1977. *Men and women of the corporation.* New York: Basic Books.

———. 1983. *The change masters: Innovation and entrepreneurship in the American corporation.* New York: Simon and Schuster.

Katzer, J. 1987. User studies, information science, and communication. *Canadian Journal of Information Science* 12 (3/4): 15–30.

Katzer, J., and P. T. Fletcher. 1992. The information environment of managers. *Annual Review of Information Science and Technology* 27: 227–263.

Kedzie, C. R. 1997. The third waves. In *Borders in cyberspace: Information policy and the global information infrastructure*, ed. B. Kahin and C. Nesson, 106–128. Cambridge, Mass.: MIT Press.

Keller, J. 1995. Public access issues: An introduction. In *Public access to the Internet*, ed. B. Kahin and J. Keller, 34–45. Cambridge, Mass.: MIT Press.

Kellerman, K., and B. Reynolds. 1990. When ignorance is bliss: The role of motivation to reduce uncertainty in uncertainty reduction theory. *Human Communication Research* 17: 5–75.

Kerlinger, F. N. 1986. *Foundations of behavioral research.* 3d ed. New York: Holt, Rinehart, and Winston.

Kerwin, A. 1993. None too solid: Medical ignorance. *Knowledge: Creation, Diffusion, Utilization* 15: 166–185.

Kiesler, S., J. Siegel, and T. W. McGuire. 1984. Social psychological aspects of computer-mediated communication. *American Psychologist* 39: 1123–1134.

Kirsch, I. S., A. Jungeblut, L. Jenkins, and A. Kolstad. 1993. *Adult literacy in America: A first look at the results of the National Adult Literacy Survey.* Princeton, N.J.: Educational Testing Service.

Kling, R. 1980. Social analyses of computing: Theoretical perspectives in recent empirical research. *Computing Surveys* 12: 61–109.

Kohlberg, L. 1981. *Essays on moral development.* Vol. 1: *The philosophy of moral development: Moral stages and the idea of Justice.* San Francisco: Harper and Row.

———. 1984. *Essays on moral development.* Vol. 2: *The psychology of moral development.* San Francisco: Harper and Row.

Kolb, D. A. 1984. *Experiential learning: Experience as the source of learning and development.* Englewood Cliffs, N.J.: Prentice Hall.

Korzybski, A. 1958. *Science and sanity: An introduction to non-Aristotelian systems and general semantics.* 4th ed. Lakeville, Conn.: International Non-Artistotelian Library.

Kramarae, C. 1988a. Gotta go Myrtle, technology's at the door. In *Technology and women's voices: Keeping in touch*, ed. C. Kramarae, 1–14. New York: Routledge and Kegan Paul.

Kramarae, C., ed. 1988b. *Technology and women's voices: Keeping in touch.* New York: Routledge and Kegan Paul.

Kraut, R. E. 1989. Telecommuting: The trade-offs of home work. *Journal of Communication*, 39 (3): 19–47.

Kraut, R. E., R. S. Fish, R. W. Root, and B. L. Chalfonte. 1990. Informal communications: Form, function, and technology. In *People's reactions to technology: In factories, offices, and aerospace*, ed. S. Oskamp and S. Spacapan, 145–199. Newbury Park, Calif.: Sage.

Kraut, R. E., and J. Galegher. 1990. Patterns of contact and communication in scientific research collaboration. In *Intellectual teamwork: Social and technological foundations of cooperative work*, ed. R. E. Kraut, J. Galegher, and C. Egido, 149–171. Hillsdale, N.J.: Erlbaum.

Krendl, K. A., M. C. Broihier, and C. Fleetwood. 1989. Children and computers: Do sex-related differences persist? *Journal of Communication* 39 (3): 85–93.

Kubey, R., and M. Csikszentmihalyi. 1990. *Television and the quality of life: How viewing shapes everyday experience.* Hillsdale, N.J.: Erlbaum.

Kuhlthau, C. C. 1985. *Teaching the library research process: A step-by-step program for secondary school students.* West Nyack, N.Y.: Center for Applied Research in Education.

———. 1991. Inside the search process: Information seeking from the user's perspective. *Journal of the American Society for Information Science* 42 (5): 361–371.

———. 1993. *Seeking meaning: A process approach to library and information services.* Norwood, N.J.: Ablex.

Kwasnik, B. 1992. A descriptive study of the functional components of browsing. In *Proceedings of the IFIP TC2nd G2.7 working conference on engineering for human-computer interaction*, 191–202. Finland: Ellivuori.

Lancaster, F. W. 1978. *Toward paperless information systems.* New York : Academic Press.

Larose, R., and J. Mettler. 1989. Who uses information technologies in rural America? *Journal of Communication* 39 (3): 48–60.

Larsen, S. 1988. The idea of an electronic library: A critical essay. *Libri* 38 (3): 159–177.

Lawrence, G. S., and A. R. Oja. 1980. *The use of general collections at the University of California: A study of unrecorded use, at-the-shelf discovery, and immediacy of need for materials at the Davis and Santa Cruz Campus Libraries. Final Report.* Research Report RR-80-1. ERIC Document Reproduction Service ED 191-490.

Lelu, A. 1991. From data analysis to neural networks: New prospects for efficient browsing through databases. *Journal of Information Science* 17: 1–12.

Levine, M. M. 1969. An essay on browsing. *RQ* (fall): 35–36, 93.

Levitan, K. 1980. Applying a holistic framework to synthesize information science research. In *Progress in communication sciences*, ed. B. Dervin and M. Voigt. Vol. 2, 421–273.

Lewis, L. H. 1987. Females and computers: Fostering involvement. In *Women, work, and technology: Transformations*, ed. B. D. Wright, M. M. Ferree, G. O. Mellow, L. H. Lewis, M.-L. D. Samper, R. Asher, and K. Claspell, 268–280. Ann Arbor: University of Michigan Press.

Licklider, J.C.R. 1965. Appendix I: Proposed experiments in browsing. In *INTREX: Report of a planning conference on information transfer experiments*, ed. C.F.J. Overhage and R. J. Harman, 187–197. Cambridge, Mass.: MIT Press.

Liebscher, P., and G. Marchionini. 1988. Browse and analytical search strategies in a full-text CD-ROM encyclopedia. *School Library Media Quarterly* 16 (4): 223–233.

Lievrouw, L. A. 1988. Four programs of research in scientific communication. *Knowledge in Society* 1 (2): 6–22.

———. 1994. Information resources and democracy: Understanding the paradox. *Journal of the American Society for Information Science* 45 (6): 350–357.

Linowes, D. F. 1989. *Privacy in America: Is your private life in the public eye?* Urbana: University of Illinois Press.

Littlejohn, S. 1989. *Theories of human communication, third ed.* Belmont, Calif.: Wadsworth.

Longman. 1978. *Dictionary of Contemporary English.* White Plains, N.Y.: Longman.

Losee, R. M., Jr. 1992. A Gray code based ordering for documents on shelves: Classification for browsing and retrieval. *Journal of the American Society for Information Science* 43 (4): 312–322.

———. 1995. Determining information retrieval and filtering performance without experimentation. *Information Processing & Management* 31 (4): 555–572.

Lunin, L. F., and R. Rada. 1989. Perspective on hypertext: Introduction and overview. *Journal of the American Society for Information Science* 40 (3): 159–163.

Luria, A. R. 1976. *Cognitive development: Its cultural and social foundations.* Trans. M. Lopez-Morillas and L. Solotaroff. Cambridge, Mass.: Harvard University Press. (Original work published 1974)

Machlup, F., and U. Mansfield. 1983. *The study of information: Interdisciplinary messages.* New York: Wiley.

MacMullin, S., and R. Taylor. 1984. Problem dimensions and information traits. *Information Society* 3 (1): 91–111.

Maheswaran, D., and B. Sternthal. 1990. The effects of knowledge, motivation, and type of message on ad processing and product judgments. *Journal of Consumer Research* 17: 66–73.

Majchrzak, A., R. E. Rice, N. King, A. Malhotra, and S. Ba. 1999. Computer-mediated interorganizational knowledge-sharing: Insights from a virtual team innovating using a collaborative tool. *Information Resources Management Journal* 13 (1): 44–53.

Malone, T. W. 1983. How do people organize their desks? Implications for the design of office information systems. *ACM Transactions on Office Information Systems* 1 (1): 99–102.

Malone, T. W., K. R. Grant, F. A. Turbak, S. A. Brobst, and M. D. Cohen. 1987. Intelligent information-sharing systems. *Communications of the ACM* 30 (5): 390–402.

March, J. C. 1994. *A primer on decision making: How decisions happen.* New York: Free Press.

———. 1999. *The pursuit of organizational intelligence.* Malden, Mass.: Blackwell.

Marchand, D. A., and J.F.W. Horton. 1986. *Infotrends: Profiting from your information resources.* New York: Wiley.

Marchionini, G. 1987. An invitation to browse: Designing full-text systems for novice users. *Canadian Journal of Information Science* 12 (3/4): 69–79.

———. 1989. Information-seeking strategies of novices using a full-text electronic encyclopedia. *Journal of the American Society for Information Science* 40 (1): 54–66.

———. 1995. *Information seeking in electronic environments.* New York: Cambridge University Press.

Marchionini, G., S. Dwiggins, A. Katz, and X. Lin. 1993. Information seeking in full-text end-user-oriented search systems: The roles of domain and search expertise. *Library and Information Science Research* 15 (1): 35–69.

Marchionini, G., and A. Komlodi. 1998. Design of interfaces for information seeking. *Annual Review of Information Science and Technology* 33: 89–130.

Marchionini, G., and P. Liebscher. 1991. Performance in electronic encyclopedias: Implications for adaptive systems. *Proceedings of the Annual Meeting of the American Society for Information Science* 28: 39–48.

Marchionini, G., and B. Shneiderman. 1988. Finding facts vs. browsing knowledge in hypertext systems. *IEEE Computer* 21: 70–80.

Markey, K. 1987. Searching and browsing the Dewey Decimal Classification in an online catalog. *Cataloging and Classification Quarterly* 7 (3): 37–68.

Markey, K., and P. Atherton. 1979. Part III: Online searching test. In *Online searching of ERIC: Executive summary of a five part report with a collection of recommendations and suggestions for redesign of the ERIC record and online data base.* ERIC Document Reproduction Service ED 180–432.

Marx, G. T., and S. Sherizen. 1986. Monitoring on the job: How to protect privacy as well as property. *Technology Review* 89 (Nov.–Dec.): 62–72.

Massicotte, M. 1988. Improved browsable displays for online subject access. *Information Technology and Libraries* 7 (4): 373–380.

McAleese, R. 1989. Navigation and browsing in hypertext. In *Hypertext: Theory into practice*, ed. R. McAleese, 6–44. Norwood, N.J.: Ablex.

McCain, R. A. 1988. Information as property and as a public good: Perspectives from the economic theory of property rights. *Library Quarterly* 58: 265–282.

McCombs, G. M., ed. 1991. *Access services: The convergence of reference and technical services.* New York: Haworth.

McCreadie, M. 1997. A framework for understanding access to information. Ph.D. diss., Rutgers University, School of Communication, Information and Library Studies, New Brunswick, NJ 08903.

McCreadie, M., and R. E. Rice. 1999a. Trends in analyzing access to information. Part I: Cross-disciplinary conceptualizations. *Information Processing and Management* 35 (1): 45–76.

———. 1999b. Trends in analyzing access to information. Part II: Unique and integrating conceptualizations. *Information Processing and Management* 35 (1): 77–99.

McGee, J. V., and L. Prusak. 1993. *Managing information strategically.* New York: Wiley.

McGuire, W. J. 1974. Psychological motives and communication gratification. In *The uses of mass communications: Current perspectives on gratifications research*, ed. J. G. Blumler and E. Katz, 167–196. Beverly Hills, Calif.: Sage.

McKinnon, S. M., and W. J. Bruns, Jr. 1992. *The information mosaic.* Boston: Harvard Business School Press.

McLuhan, M. 1964. *Understanding media.* New York: Signet.

McLuhan, M., and Q. Fiore. 1967. *The medium is the massage: An inventory of effects.* New York: Bantam.

Menzel, H. 1966. Information needs and uses in science and technology. *Annual Review of Information Science and Technology* 1: 41–70.

Merriam-Webster. 1986. *Webster's third new international dictionary of the English language, unbridged ed.* Springfield, Mass.: Merriam-Webster.

———. 1993. *Merriam-Webster's collegiate dictionary, tenth ed.* Springfield, Mass.: Merriam-Webster.

Meyrowitz, J. 1985. *No sense of place: The impact of electronic media on social behavior.* New York: Oxford University Press.

Michel, D. A. 1992. A file structure model of library search behavior. Ph.D. diss., University of California, Graduate School of Library and Information Science, Los Angeles.

Mick, C. K., G. N. Lindsey, and D. Callahan. 1980. Toward usable user studies. *Journal of the American Society for Information Science* 5: 347–356.

Miller, V. D., and F. M. Jablin. 1991. Information seeking during organizational entry: Influences, tactics, and a model of the process. *Academy of Management Review* 16: 92–120.

Mooers, C. 1951. Information retrieval viewed as temporal signalling. In *Proceedings of the international congress of mathematicians, Cambridge, Mass., 1950.* Vol. 1, 572–573. Providence, R.I.: American Mathematical Society.

Morley, D. 1993. Active audience theory: Pendulums and pitfalls. *Journal of Communication* 43: 13–19.

Morrison, E. W. 1993a. Longitudinal study of the effects of information seeking on newcomer socialization. *Journal of Applied Psychology* 78: 173–183.

———. 1993b. Newcomer information seeking: Exploring types, modes, sources, and outcomes. *Academy of Management Journal* 36: 557–589.

Morse, P. M. 1970. Search theory and browsing. *Library Quarterly* HO: 391–408.

———. 1973. Browsing and search theory. In *Toward a theory of librarianship: Papers in honor of Jesse Jauk Shera*, ed. C. H. Rawski. Metuchen, N.J.: Scarecrow Press.

Mulgan, G. J. 1991. *Communication and control: Networks and the new economies of communication.* New York: Guilford Press.

Murdock, G., and P. Golding. 1989. Information poverty and political inequality: Citizenship in the age of privatized communications. *Journal of Communication* 39 (3): 180–195.

Muter, P., and P. Maurutto. 1991. Reading and skimming from computer screens and books: The paperless office revisited? *Behaviour and Information Technology* 10 (4): 257–266.

Newby, G. 1993. Virtual reality. *Annual Review of Information Science and Technology* 28: 187–230.

Nielsen, J. 1990. Miniatures versus icons as a visual cache for videotex browsing. *Behaviour and Information Technology* 9 (6): 441–449.

Noble, G. 1987. Discriminating between the intrinsic and instrumental domestic telephone user. *Australian Journal of Communication* 11: 63–85.

Noerr, P. L., and K.T.B. Noerr. 1985. Browse and navigate: An advance in database access methods. *Information Processing and Management* 21 (3): 205–213.

Nohria, N., and B. Eccles. 1992. Face-to-face: Making network organizations work. In *Networks and organizations: Structure, form, and action*, ed. N. Nohria and H. Eccles, 288–308. Boston: Harvard Business School Press.

Nutt, P. C. 1984. Types of organizational decision processes. *Administrative Science Quarterly* 29: 414–450.

O'Connor, B. 1985. Access to moving image documents: Background concepts and proposals for surrogates for film and video works. *Journal of Documentation* 41 (4): 209–220.

———. 1988. Fostering creativity: Enhancing the browsing environment. *International Journal of Information Management* 8: 203–210.

———. 1993. Browsing: A framework for seeking functional information. *Knowledge: Creation, Diffusion, Utilization* 15 (2): 211–232.

Oddy, R. N. 1977. Information retrieval through man-machine dialog. *Journal of Documentation* 33 (1): 1–14.

Oddy, R. N., and B. Balakrishnan. 1991. PTHOMAS: An adaptive information retrieval system on the connection machine. *Information Processing and Management* 27 (4): 317–335.

Olney, T. J. 1989. Viewing time, attitude toward the ad, emotional response, and related content as aspects of advertising effectiveness: Antecedents of zipping and zapping. Ph.D. diss., Columbia University. Dissertation Abstracts International.

O'Neill, M. J., and C. R. Jasper. 1992. An evaluation of models of consumer spatial behavior using the environment-behavior paradigm. *Environment and Behavior* 24 (4): 411–440.

O'Reilly, C. A., III. 1978. The intentional distortion of information in organizational communication: A laboratory and field investigation. *Human Relations* 31 (2): 173–193.

———. 1980. Individuals and information overload in organizations: Is more necessarily better? *Academy of Management Journal* 25: 756–771.

———. 1982. Variations in decision makers' use of information sources: The impact of quality and accessibility of information. *Academy of Management Journal* 25: 756–771.

O'Reilly, C. A., III, J. A. Chatham, and J. C. Anderson. 1987. Message flow and decision making. In *Handbook of organizational communication: An interdisciplinary perspective*, ed. F. M. Jablin, L. L. Putnam, K. H. Roberts, and L. W. Porter, 600–623. Newbury Park, Calif.: Sage.

Overhage, C.F.J., and R. J. Harman, eds. 1965. *INTREX: Report of a planning conference on information transfer experiments.* Cambridge, Mass.: MIT Press.

Paisley, W. 1980. Information and work. In *Progress in communication sciences*, ed. B. Dervin and M. J. Voigt. Vol. 2, 113–165. Norwood, N.J.: Ablex.

Paisley, W., and E. B. Parker. 1965. Information retrieval as a receiver-controlled communication system. In *Education for information science*, 25–31. London: Macmillan.

Palmquist, R. 1992. The impact of information technology on the individual. *Annual Review of Information Science and Technology* 27: 3–42.

Paris, C. L. 1988. Tailoring object descriptions to a user's level of expertise. *Computational Linguistics* 14 (3): 64–78.

Pejtersen, A. M. 1989. A library system for information retrieval based on a cognitive task analysis and supported by an icon-based interface. In *Proceedings of the 12th annual international ACMSIGIR conference on research and development in information retrieval*, ed. N. J. Belkin and C. J. van Rijsbergen. Cambridge, Mass.: Association for Computing Machinery.

Pemberton, J. M. 1998. Knowledge management (KM) and the epistemic tradition. *ARMA Records Management Quarterly* 32 (3): 58–62.

Perin, C. 1991. Electronic social fields in bureaucracies. *Communications of the ACM* 34: 75–82.

Perry, W. G., Jr. 1970. *Forms of intellectual and ethical development in the college years: A scheme*. New York: Holt, Rinehart, and Winston.

———. 1981. Cognitive and ethical growth: The making of meaning. In *The modern American college*, ed. A. Chickering, 76–116. San Francisco: Jossey-Bass.

Perse, E. 1990. Audience selectivity and involvement in the newer media environment. *Communication Research* 17 (5): 675 ff.

Peters, T., and R. Waterman, Jr. 1984. *In search of excellence: Lessons from America's best-run companies*. New York: Warner Books.

Pfaffenberger, B. 1990. *Democratizing information: Online databases and the rise of end-user searching*. Boston: G. K. Hall.

Poland, J. 1991. Informal communication among scientists and engineers: A review of the literature. *Science and Technology Libraries* 11 (3): 61–73.

Polanyi, M. 1997. The tacit dimension. In *Knowledge in organizations*, ed. L. Prusak, 135–146. Boston: Butterworth-Heinemann.

Pollet, D., and P. C. Haskell, eds. 1979. *Sign systems for libraries: Solving the wayfinding problem*. New York: Bowker.

Pool, I. de S. 1983. *Technologies of freedom*. Cambridge, Mass.: Harvard University Press.

Porat, M. U. 1977. *Information economy: Definition and measurement*. OT Special Publication 77–12(1). Washington, D.C.: Department of Commerce/Office of Telecommunications.

Powell, W. W. 1990. Neither market nor hierarchy: Network forms of organization. In *Research in organizational behavior*, ed. S. B. Bacharach, 295–336. Greenwich, Conn.: JAI Press.

Protess, D., and M. McCombs, eds. 1991. *Agenda setting: Readings on media, public opinion, and policymaking*. Hillsdale, N.J.: Erlbaum.

Pryluck, C. 1976. *Sources of meaning in motion pictures and television.* New York: Arno Press. (Originally presented as Ph.D. diss., University of Iowa, 1973)

Rada, R., and C. Murphy. 1992. Searching versus browsing in hypertext. *Hypermedia* 4 (1): 1–30.

Radway, J. A. 1983. Women read the romance: The interaction of text and context. *Feminist Studies* 9 (1): 53–78.

———. 1984. *Reading the romance: Women, patriarchy, and popular literature.* Chapel Hill: University of North Carolina Press.

Rakow, L. F. 1988. Women and the telephone: The gendering of a communications technology. In *Technology and women's voices: Keeping in touch*, ed. C. Kramarae, 207–228. New York: Routledge and Kegan Paul.

Randhawa, B. S., and W. E. Coffman, eds. 1978. *Visual learning, thinking, and communication.* New York: Academic Press.

Randolph, W. A. 1978. Organizational technology and the media and purpose dimension of organization communications. *Journal of Business Research* 6: 237–259.

Random House. 1987. *The Random House Dictionary of the English Language, second ed.* New York: Random House.

Reinsch, N.L.J., and B. W. Beswick. 1990. Voice mail versus conventional channels: A cost minimization analysis of individual's preferences. *Academy of Management Journal* 33: 801–816.

Rice, R. E. 1984. Mediated group communication. In *The new media: Communication, research, and technology*, ed. R. E. Rice, 129–154. Beverly Hills, Calif.: Sage.

———. 1987. Computer-mediated communication and organizational innovation. *Journal of Communication* 37 (4): 65–94.

———. 1988. Issues and concepts in research on computer-mediated communication systems. In *Communication Yearbook*, ed. J. A. Anderson. Vol. 12, 436–476. Newbury Park, Calif.: Sage.

Rice, R. E., and C. Aydin. 1991. Attitudes toward new organizational technology: Network proximity as a mechanism for social information processing. *Administrative Science Quarterly* 36: 219–244.

Rice, R. E., and C. L. Borgman. 1983. The use of computer-monitored data in information science and communication research. *Journal of the American Society for Information Science* 34: 247–256.

Rice, R. E., and D. Case. 1983. Electronic message systems in the university: A description of use and utility. *Journal of Communication* 33 (1): 131–152.

Rice, R. E., S. Chang, and J. Torobin. 1992. Communicator style, media use, organizational level, and use and evaluation of electronic messaging. *Management Communication Quarterly* 6 (1): 3–33.

Rice, R. E., and U. Gattiker. 2000. New media and organizational structuring of meanings and relations. In *New handbook of organizational communication*, ed. F. Jablin and L. Putnam, 544–581. Newbury Park, Calif.: Sage.

Rice, R. E., and G. Love, 1987. Electronic emotion! Socioemotional content in a computer-mediated communication network. *Communication Research* 14: 85–108.

Rice, R. E., and E. M. Rogers. 1980. Reinvention in the innovation process. *Knowledge: Creation, Diffusion, Utilization* 1: 499–514.

Rice, R. E., and D. E. Shook. 1986. End-user computing: Access, usage and benefits. *Proceedings of the Annual Meeting of the American Society for Information Science* 23: 265–270.

———. 1988. Access to, usage of, and outcomes from an electronic messaging system. *ACM Transactions on Office Information Systems* 6 (3): 255–276.

Roberts, N. 1982. A search for information man. *Social Science Information Studies* 2, 93–104.

Robertson, S. E. 1981. The methodology of information retrieval experiment. In *Information retrieval experiment*, ed. K Sparck Jones, 9–31. London Butterworths.

Robinson, M. J. 1979. Prime time chic: Between newsbreaks and commercials, the values are L.A. liberal. *Public Opinion* (Mar.–May): 42–48.

Rogers, E. M. 1983. *Diffusion of innovations.* 3d ed. New York: Free Press.

———. 1986. *Communication technology: The new media in society.* New York: Free Press.

Rogers, E. M., L. Collins-Jarvis, and J. Schmitz. 1994. The PEN Project in Santa Monica. *Journal of the American Society for Information Science* 45 (6): 401–410.

Root, R. W. 1988. Design of a multimedia vehicle for social browsing. In *Proceedings of the 1988 conference on computer-supported cooperative work*, 25–38.

Ross, J. 1983. Observations of browsing behaviour in an academic library. *College & Research Libraries* 44 (4): 269–276.

Ruben, B. D. 1985. The coming of the information age: Information, technology, and the study of behavior. In *Information and behavior*, ed. B. D. Ruben. Vol. 1, 3–26. New Brunswick, N.J.: Transaction.

———. 1993. Integrating concepts for the Information Age: Communication, information, mediation, and institutions. In *Information and behavior.* Vol. 4: *Between communication and information*, ed. J. R. Schement and B. D. Ruben, 219–236. New Brunswick, N.J.: Transaction.

Rubinyi, R. M. 1989. Computers and community: The organizational impact. *Journal of Communication* 39 (3): 110–123.

Rule, J. B. 1974. *Private lives and public surveillance: Social control in the computer age.* New York: Schocken.

Salomon, I., and F. S. Koppelman. 1992. Teleshopping or going shopping? An information acquisition perspective. *Behaviour and Information Technology* 11 (4): 189–198.

Sanchez, R. 1997. Managing articulated knowledge in competence-based competition. In *Strategic learning and knowledge management*, ed. R. Sanchez and A. Heene, 163–187. Chichester, U.K.: Wiley.

Sanoff, H. 1991. *Visual research methods in design.* New York: Van Nostrand Reinhold.

Saracevic, T. 1971. Selected results from an inquiry into testing of information retrieval systems. *Journal of the American Society for Information Science* 22: 126–139.

———. 1975. Relevance: A review of and a framework for the thinking on the notion in information science. *Journal of the American Society for Information Science* 27: 321–343.

———. 1990. Information science revisited: Contemporary reflection on its origin, evolution, and relations. Rutgers University, School of Communication, Information and Library Studies, New Brunswick, NJ 08903.

Saunders, C., and I. W. Jones. 1990. Temporal sequences in information acquisition for decision making: A focus on source and medium. *Academy of Management Review* 15 (1): 29–46.

Savolainen, R. 1995. Everyday life information seeking: Approaching information seeking in the context of "way of life." *Library and Information Science Research* 17: 259–294.

Savoy, J. 1992. Bayesian inference networks and spreading activation in hypertext systems. *Information Processing and Management* 28 (3): 389–406.

Schamber, L. 1994. Relevance and information behavior. *Annual Review of Information Science and Technology* 29: 3–48.

Schank, R. C. 1982. *Dynamic memory: A theory of reminding and learning in computers and people.* New York: Cambridge University Press.

Schement, J. R. 1989. The origins of the Information Society in the United States: Competing visions. In *The Information Society*, ed. G. Salvaggio, 29–50. Hillsdale, N.J.: Erlbaum.

———. 1993. Communication and information. In *Information and behavior.* Vol. 4: *Between communication and information*, ed. J. R. Schement and B. D. Ruben, 2–33. New Brunswick, N.J.: Transaction.

Schement, J. R., and T. Curtis. 1995. *Tendencies and tensions of the information age: The production and distribution of information in the United States.* New Brunswick, N.J.: Transaction.

Schement, J. R., and L. A. Lievrouw. 1987. A third vision: Capitalism and the industrial origins of the Information Society. In *Competing visions, complex realities: Social aspects of the information society*, ed. J. R. Schement and L. A. Lievrouw, 33–46. Norwood, N.J.: Ablex.

Schement, J. R., and H. B. Mokros. 1989. The social and historical construction of the idea of information as thing. Paper presented at the Annual Conference of the American Society for Information Science, November, Washington, D.C.

Schiefer, G., M. Harkin, L.-N. Netter, Q. Scally, and M. Wilkinson. 1990. Farm-related information use and users: A discussion of some European videotex experiences. *Knowledge in Society: The International Journal of Knowledge Transfer* 3 (3): 58–66.

Schiller, D. 1989. Informational bypass: Research library access to U. S. telecommunications periodicals. *Journal of Communication* 39 (3): 104–109.

Schiller, H. I. 1981. *Who knows? Information in the age of the Fortune 500.* Norwood, N.J.: Ablex.

———. 1983. Critical research in the information age. *Journal of Communication* 33 (3): 249–257.

———. 1987. Old foundations for a new (information) age. In *Competing visions, complex realities: Social aspects of the information society*, ed. J. R. Schement and L. A. Lievrouw, 23–32. Norwood, N.J.: Ablex.

———. 1988. Corporate speech, power politics, and the First Amendment. *The Independent* 11 (6): 10–13.

———. 1989. *Culture Inc.: The corporate takeover of public expression.* New York: Oxford University Press.

Schiller, H. I., and A. R. Schiller. 1988. Libraries, public access to information, and commerce. In *The political economy of information*, ed. V. Mosco and J. Wasko, 146–166. Madison: University of Wisconsin Press.

Schutz, A. 1967. *The phenomenology of the social world.* Evanston, Ill: Northwestern University Press.

Schutz, A., and T. Luckmann. 1973. *The structures of the life-world.* Evanston, Ill.: Northwestern University Press.

Scrivener, S. 1983. Perceptual factors in the design of information displays. In *Computer graphics '83: International conference proceedings.* London.

Shaffer, C. A. 1992. Data representations for geographic information systems. *Annual Review of Information Science and Technology* 27: 135–172.

Shelton, R. 1982. The lure of the browsing room. *Library Journal* 107 (4): 410–413.

Shenouda, W. 1990. Online bibliographic searching: how end users modify their search strategies. *Proceedings of the Annual Meeting of the American Society for Information Science* 27: 117–128.

Shim, S., and M. Y. Mahoney. 1991. Electronic shoppers and nonshoppers among videotex users: shopping orientations, videotex usages, and demographics. *Journal of Direct Marketing* 5 (3): 29–38.

Shneiderman, B., D. Brethauer, C. Plaisant, and R. Potter. 1989. Evaluating three museum installations of a hypertext system. *Journal of the American Society for Information Science* 40 (3): 172–182.

Siefert, M., C. Gerbner, and J. Fisher, eds. 1989. *The information gap: How computers and other new communication technologies affect the social distribution of power.* New York: Oxford University Press.

Simon, H. A. 1976. *Administrative behavior: A study of decision-making processes in administrative organization.* 3d ed. New York: Free Press.

Singer, B. D. 1980. Crazy systems and Kafka circuits. *Social Policy* 11 (2): 46–54.

Slack, J. D. 1984. Surveying the impacts of communication technologies. In *Progress in communication sciences*, ed. B. Dervin and M. J. Voigt. Vol. 5, 73–109. Norwood, N.J.: Ablex.

Smead, R. J., J. B. Wilcox, and R. E. Wilkes. 1981. How valid are product description and protocols in choice experiments? *Journal of Consumer Research* 8: 37–42.

Smith, K. C., S. J. Carroll, and S. J. Ashford. 1995. Intra- and interorganizational cooperation: Toward a research agenda. *Academy of Management Journal* 38: 7–23.

Smithson, M. 1989. *Ignorance and uncertainty: Emerging paradigms.* New York: Springer-Verlag.

———. 1993. Ignorance and science: Dilemmas, perspectives, and prospects. *Knowledge: Creation, Diffusion, Utilization* 15: 133–156.

Soderston, C. 1986. A study of spatial models and human navigation within complex computer interfaces. Ph.D. diss., Department of Communication and Rhetoric, Rensselaer Polytechnic Institute. Dissertation Abstracts International.

Solomon, P. 1997a. Discovering information behavior in sense-making. I: Time and timing. *Journal of the American Society for Information Science* 48 (12): 1097–1108.

———. 1997b. Discovering information behavior in sense-making. II: The social. *Journal of the American Society for Information Science* 48 (12): 1109–1126.

———. 1997c. Discovering information behavior in sense-making. III: The person. *Journal of the American Society for Information Science* 48 (12): 2217–1138.

Sonnenwald, D. H. 1995. Contested collaboration: A descriptive model of intergroup communication in information system design. *Information Processing and Management* 31 (6): 859–878.

Sparck Jones, K. 1981. *Information retrieval experiment.* London: Butterworths.

———. 1988. Fashionable trends and feasible strategies in information management. *Information Processing and Management* 24: 703–711.

Spender, J.-C. 1998. Pluralist epistemology and the knowledge-based theory of the firm. *Organization* 5 (2): 233–256.

Spring, M. B. 1991. Informating with virtual reality. In *Virtual reality: Theory, practice, and promise*, ed. S. K. Helsel and J. P. Roth, 3–17. Westport, Conn.: Meckler Publishing.

Sproull, L. S. and S. Kiesler. 1991. *Connections: New ways of work in the networked organization.* Cambridge, Mass.: MIT Press.

Sproull, L. S., S. Kiesler, and D. Zubrow, 1984. Encountering an alien culture. *Journal of Social Issues* 41 (3): 31–48.

Star, S. L., and K. Ruhleder. 1996. Steps toward an ecology of infrastructure: Design and access for large information spaces. *Information Systems Research* 7 (1): 111–134.

Staw, B. M., L. E. Sandelands, and J. E. Dutton. 1981. Threat-rigidity effects in organizational behavior: A multilevel analysis. *Administrative Science Quarterly* 26: 501–524.

Stephenson, W. 1986. Play theory of communication. *Operant Subjectivity* 9 (4): 109–122. (Originally presented in 1965)

Stone, S. 1982. Humanities scholars: Information needs and uses. *Journal of Documentation* 38 (4): 292–313.

Story, G. A., L. O'Gorman, D. Fox, L. L. Schaper, and H. V. Jagadish. 1992. The RightPages image-based electronic library for alerting and browsing. *Computer* 25 (9): 17–26.

Su, L. 1987. Performance measures for evaluating information retrieval systems: A literature review. Unpublished manuscript, Rutgers University, School of Communication, Information and Library Studies, New Brunswick, NJ 08903.

Suchman, L. A. 1987. *Plans and situated actions: The problem of human-machine communication.* New York: Cambridge University Press.

Swanson, D. R. 1965. The evidence underlying the Cranfield results. *Library Quarterly* 35: 1–20.

———. 1977. Information retrieval as a trial-and-error process. *Library Quarterly* 47: 128–148.

———. 1987. Two medical literatures that are logically but not bibliographically connected. *Journal of the American Society for Information Science* 38 (4): 228–233.

———. 1989. Online search for logically-related noninteractive medical literatures: A systematic trial-and-error strategy. *Journal of the American Society for Information Science* 40 (5): 356–358.

Swinehart, J. W. 1968. Voluntary exposure to health communications. *American Journal of Public Health* 58: 1265–1275.

Tague, J., and R. Schultz. 1989. Evaluation of the user interface in an information retrieval system: A model. *Information Processing and Management* 25 (4): 377–389.

Taylor, R. S. 1962. The process of asking questions. *American Documentation* (October): 391–397.

———. 1968. Question negotiation and information seeking in libraries. *College & Research Libraries* 29: 178–189.

———. 1986. *Value-added processes in information systems*. Norwood, N.J.: Ablex.

———. 1991. Information use environments. In *Progress in communication sciences*, ed. B. Dervin and M. J. Voigt. Vol. 10, 217–255. Norwood, N.J.: Ablex.

Tessier, J. A., W. W. Crouch, and P. Atherton. 1977. New measures of user satisfaction with computer-based literature searches. *Special Libraries* 68: 383–389.

Thomas, J. B., S. M. Clark, and D. A. Gioia. 1993. Strategic sensemaking and organizational performance: Linkages among scanning, interpretation, action, and outcomes. *Academy of Management Journal* 36: 239–270.

Thompson, R. H., and W. B. Croft. 1989. Support for browsing in an intelligent text retrieval system. *International Journal of Man-Machine Studies* 30: 639–668.

Treichler, P. A., and E. Wartella. 1986. Interventions: Feminist theory and communication studies. *Communication* 9: 1–18.

Trevino, L. K., R. H. Lengel, and R. L. Daft. 1987. Media symbolism, media richness, and media choice in organizations: A symbolic interactionist perspective. *Communication Research* 14 (5): 553–575.

Trevino, L. K., R. H. Lengel, E. A. Gerloff, and N. K. Muir. 1990. The richness imperative and cognitive styles: The role of individual differences in media choice behavior. *Management Communication Quarterly* 4 (2): 176–197.

Trevino, L. K., and J. Webster. 1992. Flow in computer-mediated communication: Electronic mail and voice mail evaluation and impacts. *Communication Research* 19: 539–573.

Tuori, M. I. 1987. A framework for browsing in the relational data model. Ph.D. diss., University of Toronto, 1986. Dissertation Abstracts International.

Turkle, S. 1988. Computational reticence: Why women fear the intimate machine. In *Technology and women's voices: Keeping in touch*, ed. C. Kramarae, 41–61. New York: Routledge and Kegan Paul.

Tyckoson, D. 1991. Access vs. ownership: Changing roles for librarians. In *Access services: The convergence of reference and technical services*, ed. G. M. McCombs, 37–45. New York: Haworth.

U.S. Congress. Office of Technology Assessment. 1987. *The electronic supervisor: New technology, new tensions*. Publication OTA-CIT-333. Washington, D.C.: U.S. Government Printing Office.

———. 1990. *Critical connections: Communication for the future.* Publication OTA-CIT-407. Washington, D.C.: U.S. Government Printing Office.

U.S. National Commission on Libraries and Information Science. 1991. *Information literacy and education for the 21st century: Toward an agenda for action. A symposium.* Washington, D.C.: The Commission.

———. 1992. *Open forum on recommendations of the White House Conference on Library and Information Services.* Washington, D.C.: The Commission.

Vallas, S. P. 1988. New technology, job content, and worker alienation: A test of two rival perspectives. *Work and Occupations* 15: 148–178.

van House, N. 1983. Time allocation theory of public library use. *Library and Information Science Research* 5: 365–384.

Varlejs, J. 1986. Information seeking: Changing perspectives. In *Information seeking: Basing services on users' behaviors*, ed. J. Varlejs, 67–82. London: McFarland.

Via, B. J. 1991. RLIN research access project: An education in user expectations. In *Access services: The convergence of reference and technical services*, ed. G. M. McCombs, 15–25. New York: Haworth.

von Keitz, B. 1988. Eye movement research: Do consumers use the information they are offered? *European Research* 16 (4): 217–223.

von Krogh, G, and J. Roos, eds. 1996. *Managing knowledge: Perspectives on cooperation and competition.* Newbury Park, Calif.: Sage.

Vygotsky, L. S. 1978. *Mind in society: The development of higher psychological processes*, ed. M. Cole, V. John-Steiner, S. Scribner, and E. Souberman. Cambridge, Mass.: Harvard University Press.

Wade, S. J., and P. Willett. 1988. INSTRUCT: A teaching package for experimental methods in information retrieval. Part III. Browsing, clustering and query expansion. *Program* 22 (1): 44–61.

Walsh, J., and G. Ungson. 1991. Organizational memory. *Academy of Management Review* 16 (1): 57–91.

Webster, F., and K. Robins. 1986. *Information technology: A Luddite analysis.* Norwood, N.J.: Ablex.

Weedman, J. 1999. Conversation and community: The potential of electronic conferences for creating intellectual proximity in distributed learning environments. *Journal of the American Society for Information Science* 50 (1): 907–928.

Weick, K. E. 1979. *The social psychology of organizing, second ed.* Reading, Mass.: Addison-Wesley.

———. 1983. Organizational communication: Toward a research agenda. In *Communication and organizations: An interpretive approach*, ed. L. Putnam and M. Pacanowsky, 13–29. Beverly Hills, Calif.: Sage.

Weinberg, S. 1987. Expanding access to technology: Computer equity for women. In *Women, work, and technology: Transformations*, ed. B. D. Wright, M. M. Ferree, G. O. Mellow, L. H. Lewis, M.L.D. Samper, R. Asher, and K. Claspell, 281–290. Ann Arbor: University of Michigan Press.

Wellisch, H. 1972. From information science to informatics: A terminological investigation. *Journal of Librarianship* 4: 157–187.

Wersig, G. 1979. The problematic situation as a basic concept of information science in the framework of social sciences: A reply to N. Belkin. In *Theoretical problems of informatics: New trends in informatics and its terminology*, 48–57. Moscow.

Wersig, G., and U. Neveling. 1975. The phenomena of interest to information science. *The Information Scientist* 9 (4): 127–140.

Wersig, G., and G. Windel. 1985. Information science needs a theory of "information actions." *Social Science Information Studies* 5: 11–23.

Wilensky, H. 1968. Organizational intelligence. In *The international encyclopedia of the social sciences*, ed. D. Sills, 319–334. New York: Free Press.

Williams, F., R. E. Rice, and E. M. Rogers. 1989. *Research methods and the new media.* New York: Macmillan.

Williamson, K. 1998. Discovered by chance: The role of incidental information acquisition in an ecological model of information use. *Library and Information Science Research* 20 (1): 23–40.

Wilson, T. D. 1981. On user studies and information needs. *Journal of Documentation* 37 (1): 3–15.

———. 1997. Information behaviour: An interdisciplinary perspective. *Information Processing and Management* 33 (4): 551–572.

Wilson, T. D., and D. R. Streatfield. 1977. Information needs in local authority social services departments: An interim report on project INISS. *Journal of Documentation* 33: 277–293.

Wimmer, R., and J. Dominick, eds. 1991. *Mass media research: An introduction, third ed.* Belmont, Calif.: Wadsworth.

Wright, C. 1974. Functional analysis and mass communication revisited. In *The user of mass communications*, ed. J. G. Blumler and E. Katz, 197–212. Newbury Park, Calif.: Sage.

Wyer, R. S., Jr., and T. K. Srull. 1989. *Memory and cognition in its social context.* Hillsdale, N.J.: Erlbaum.

Yin, R. K. 1989. *Case study research: Design and methods.* Rev. ed. Newbury Park, Calif.: Sage.

Young, E. 1976. Eye movement recorder blows the lid off past tests of print ads, packages, and other marketing materials. *Marketing News* 10 (5): 3–4.

Zerbinos, E. 1990. Information seeking and information processing: Newspapers versus videotext. *Journalism Quarterly* 67 (4): 920–929.

Zmud, R. 1990. Opportunities for strategic manipulation through new information technology. In *Organizations and communication technology*, ed. J. Fulk and C. Steinfield, 95–116. Newbury Park, Calif.: Sage.

Zoellick, B. 1986. Selecting an approach to document retrieval. In *CD ROM*. Vol. 2: *Optical publishing: A practical approach to developing CD ROM applications*, ed. S. Ropiequet, J. Einberger, and B. Zoellick. Redmond, Wash.: Microsoft Press.

Zuboff, S. 1988. *In the age of the smart machine: The future of work and power.* New York: Basic Books.

# Index

Made in the USA
Middletown, DE
05 November 2026

36562493R00210

# Fundamentos de Cálculo I

Análisis Univariable con Python